Tell Them We Were Rising

Tell Them We Were Rising

Individuals of Color Through Slavery and
Jim Crow, in Nashville and Beyond

Paul Clements

ISBN: 978-0-578-33077-8

Library of Congress Control Number: 2021923581

Clearview Press

Franklin, Tennessee

Contents

Preface

Five years after the close of the Civil War, some 1500 members of the local Negro community marched through the streets of Nashville. They were celebrating the passage of the 15th Amendment to the Constitution of the United States, which protected a citizen's right to vote regardless "of race, color, or previous condition of servitude." Among the banners and signs, one read, "Tell Them We Are Rising." That source inspired the title of this book.

The first black person I ever knew was Emma. She was born only a couple of decades after the march took place, and may well have known a few of those who were there on that hope-filled celebration in 1870. Emma was probably around sixty when she took care of me. When I was two or three, she would walk me from my house on Clearview Drive over to Estes Road, and up past Woodmont School to the corner of Estes and Woodmont Boulevard. We would sit on a big flat rock at the southeast corner of the intersection, watching the cars and trucks going by. The rock was gone by the time I found out that it had been put there over a century earlier to mark a corner of the old Compton farm. I ended up knowing a lot about Henry W. Compton, and a good bit about the slaves he owned.

Back then I didn't recognize that Emma and I weren't the same color. I don't know when I noticed that she was darker than I was, and I'm not sure when I started learning about race. But an early lesson came because of a yardman who worked for one of our neighbors. He was up in years and when he came down the street in his old truck, I wondered why he never drove faster than fifteen or twenty miles an hour. And I wondered why black grownups were usually nicer to me than white grownups were, and why I almost never saw any colored children.

But one summer night when I was ten or eleven, I was playing outside with a few of my friends. That's when a black kid just walked up into Tom's backyard. He was about the same age as we were. His name was James, and his mother was employed by a family that lived across the road. He must have heard us running around. He was outgoing and funny, and he rode a bike like a madman. We were in awe of James, and although we kept hoping he'd show up again, that was the only time we ever saw him.

A lot happened before the next time I was around a black person my age. Along with a couple of racist cousins and an ultra-right-wing teacher I had in high school, it seemed like somebody was always around bad-mouthing black people. But I saw a lot when I watched the news on TV. I learned about the Nashville sit-ins and the Freedom Riders, and about the church bombing in Birmingham in 1963 and the murder of the Civil Rights workers the next year in Mississippi. And then there was the killing of Dr. King. It was pretty easy to see the moral difference between those fighting to preserve segregation and those who were trying to end it.

I was sympathetic to the black journey unfolding in America, but I didn't think I could do any more about the way black people were treated than I could about the treatment of native people or Jewish people, so I just went on living my life. But my interest in local history eventually led me to know John Egerton, who had dedicated much of his life to racial justice. One day he was telling me about a decorated black veteran who was on his way home after serving in World War Two. The man had been horribly beaten – basically for being black in the wrong place and at the wrong time. After a few seconds, John looked over at me and said, "Some things are just wrong."

I mostly stayed on the sidelines and did my work, but I kept running across old newspaper articles about people of color who had once lived in Nashville. I finally started putting the information into a separate file, and in 2020, after George Floyd and others died in race-related killings, it occurred to me that I should try to write about some of the compelling black individuals who had lived in and around Nashville – during both slavery and reconstruction.

I thought that black students might find additional inspiration if they knew more about what had taken place in their own backyards. Then I started thinking about how profoundly uninformed most white people are about the racial history of Nashville and of America. It seemed to me that some of them might benefit as much as I have from learning how things were – and how race relations got to be the way they are.

The people I've written about lived inspirational lives. This book is dedicated to them, and to the old black man who was so afraid of being stopped by a white policeman that he wouldn't drive through our neighborhood faster than twenty miles an hour. It is dedicated to Alonzo Napier, whose story broke my heart. It is dedicated to my friend, John Egerton, who once told me – in his simple and eloquent way – "Some things are just *wrong*." It is also dedicated to James, who I still talk about sometimes with my friend, Tom. And this book is dedicated to Emma, who was in my prayers every night when I was a child.

1

Slaves on the Cumberland Frontier

An eighteen-year-old slave named Jamie may have been the first individual of color to visit the future site of Nashville. Traveling down the Cumberland with his owner and three other white men in 1767, Jamie was present when Stones River was named for Uriah

Stone, who was a member of the party. Continuing downriver, the explorers apparently reached what was then called the French Lick – a small area of sulphur springs that would eventually become part of Nashville – before making their way to the Ohio. Jamie was loaned to a member of the group who chose to return to the east, and he saved the life of his white companion on their way back to Virginia.

Other slaves or free blacks may have come to the area in the years leading up to the Revolutionary War, but the next person known to have arrived in the Cumberland wilderness was Cornelius, a slave of the noted frontiersman, James Robertson. In March, 1779, Cornelius accompanied Robertson and nine others on a month-long journey that began on the Holston River in what later became East Tennessee, and led hundreds of miles to the French Lick – which was located about a mile north of where the State Capitol would stand many years later. The trek continued and Cornelius went north with Robertson to the Illinois country before they returned to the Holston settlements.

It is all but certain that Cornelius was with Robertson when he came back to the French Lick later in 1779. It would be about ten weeks before Cornelius was joined by a considerable number of other slaves, as well as by a few free Negroes, when the contingent of boats led by Colonel John Donelson arrived after having traveled some one thousand miles by river. But not all the blacks who left with Donelson had survived the journey. The first casualty occurred after only a week, when an unnamed "negro man" of Captain Hutchings died of exposure, "being much frosted in his feet and legs."

Two days later a number of slaves were among the 28 passengers on the boat of Mr. Stewart. They were all either killed or taken prisoner by a band of Cherokee Indians living in the vicinity of what would become Chattanooga. A little farther downriver, a young male slave drowned trying to escape from a boat that ran aground while it was being fired on from shore, but most of the party were uninjured and made their way on to the Ohio River. During the last 200 exhausting miles of the journey, "Hagar, an African woman, worked the side oars" of the boat that carried the family of James Robertson up the Cumberland to the French Lick.

Among the slaves who were members of the Donelson Party were a pair of girls who would live well into the next century. Many years after their deaths, they were remembered by an individual who had heard their stories when he was a child. "Two of the Negroes who were brought to the Cumberland country, Aunt Aliph and Aunt Sue, lived to a ripe old age – Aliph dying in 1860 and Sue in 1865. The events of the trip were indelibly impressed on their minds. They delighted to tell of the attacks by Indians, of the whirlpools and rapids at Muscle Shoals, and of the welcome when they finally arrived after the long voyage."

The Donelson Party reached its destination in April, 1780. Indian attacks had begun to ravage the fledgling settlements by then, and the slaves, along with a handful of free Negroes, were facing a perilous future. In mid-June a group of families fleeing their settlement on the Red River, about 40 miles northwest of French Lick, were attacked by Chickasaw warriors. About 15 settlers were killed, including a male slave owned by the Turpin family. The unnamed black man was later described as having "fought with distinguished bravery, encouraging his master and the others never to yield while life lasted. From his conspicuous bravery he was doubtless a mark, and he fell among the slain."

Around the same time, "a negro fellow and woman were taken" by Indians on Stones River, and a number of weeks later an attack on a few boats moving down the same river led to the loss of other slaves.

The soon-to-be-notorious Jack Civil, described as "a bright (light-skinned) mulatto – free, keen, and smart – brought in by Richard Henderson as a hired waiter" was captured during the assault, and ultimately chose to live with his captors. A single boat floated into the Cumberland and then drifted all the way down to the French Lick Station. A settler later recalled that, "there was a dead Negro in the boat," and a dog on the boat "had eaten his nose some."

A handful of whites, having survived the attack, tried to cross the Cumberland to safety, but the current was too strong. Finally, "Colonel Donelson's servant, Somerset, volunteered to swim the river with the aid of a horse. He succeeded in crossing, and hastened to the station. A few men returned with Somerset, taking axes to cut a float for the relief of their friends, who were suffering cold and hunger. They all passed over, and safely arrived at the station."

Cornelius survived those first brutal months on the Cumberland frontier, but he only lived two weeks into 1781. In the middle of January a large force of Chickasaw warriors attacked Freeland's Station, where the Robertson family was living. When the firing began, Cornelius was sleeping in front of a fire inside an unfinished cabin. When he went to the door he was shot in the thigh, and received three or four additional wounds before he died.

Warfare on the frontier raged on, and both slaves and free blacks would continue to endure danger and death for the next fourteen years. David Goin, a free mulatto, was killed at Mansker's Station a few weeks after the death of Cornelius, and Peter Barnett, a mulatto member of a surveying party, was killed in 1787 near where Clarksville was recently founded. Prior to the massacre at Ziegler's Station in 1792, a woman of color named Molly Jones "was scalped in the field, but was not dead," and two years later an unnamed black cook was killed near Holly Tree Gap in what would soon become Williamson County.

Along with those, there were probably many other victims of color, but there were also a number of survivors. Robert Renfroe, who had lived through the massacre of the party trying to escape from the Red River settlement in 1780, was a trusted frontier figure. In 1787, after the launch of what became known as the Coldwater Campaign, he was dispatched to meet the returning soldiers with crucial provisions. But perhaps the most noted slave on the frontier was Abraham Bledsoe, who was owned by Anthony Bledsoe, a frontier leader who settled in Sumner County.

William Hall, who had a highly distinguished military career and ultimately served as Governor of Tennessee, was well-acquainted with Abraham, who he described as "a mulatto fellow" and "a very intelligent servant of Colonel Anthony Bledsoe's family." Hall, whose own bravery was legendary, said that Abraham was "very brave and... a good soldier and marksman." In giving his account of the 1793 attack on Greenfield Station, near where Gallatin would stand, Hall told of how Abraham had killed a well known Indian before escaping into the fort.

And it was not long before Abraham Bledsoe faced another moment of intense danger, one that was described in some detail by William Hall. "Abraham... was passing one evening from Bledsoe's Lick fort up to Greenfield. When right in the thick cane-break, he met two Cherokee chiefs, Mad Dog and John Thomas... on their way to steal horses and murder any settlers who might fall in their way. Abraham met them at about ten paces off, and instantly drawing up his gun, he shot the Mad Dog dead in his tracks."

Abraham Bledsoe was remembered generations after his passing. A newspaper article written over a century after the close of the Indian

Wars contained information about Bledsoe that had been passed along by an elderly man. "On one occasion Abraham accompanied Miss Mollie Bledsoe, his young mistress, to a fort a few miles from Bledsoe's Station. After going about half the distance, they were attacked ay Indians. Abraham told Miss Bledsoe to run for the station while he kept back the Indians. She reached the station, as did Abraham. He lived to be very old, and died in the first decade of the 1800s. A braver man never lived."

2

The Amos Dresser Affair

Amos Dresser, a descendant of a Mayflower settler, was born in Massachusetts in 1812. His father died young, and his mother died when Amos was thirteen. He worked in a store and then, while he was still in his teens, he became a teacher. He went to New York, where he enrolled in the Oneida Institute, which was associated with the abolitionist movement. After leaving Oneida he travelled to Cincinnati and became a student at Lane Theological Seminary, and when student discussions of slavery were prohibited, he made plans to attend Oberlin College, another school noted for its opposition to slavery. At the age of twenty-two he went south in hopes of making enough money to pay tuition for the upcoming term. He spent eight days in Nashville, and shortly after he left to go back north, he wrote an account of his visit.

"I left Cincinnati for the purpose of selling the "Cottage Bible" to raise funds to complete my education. I took several copies of the Bible with me, and a number of pamphlets. Among the pamphlets were Sunday school periodicals, anti-slavery publications, and temperance almanacs. I arrived at Nashville on Saturday, the 8th of August, 1835, and took lodgings at the Nashville Inn. The young man who accompanied me, in bringing my books from the box in the barouche, omitted the anti-slavery tracts and other pamphlets. On Monday morning the barouche was taken to the shop of Mr. S.V.D. Stout to be repaired.

"In the course of the day, one of his workmen commenced rummaging through my carriage. In the box he found a February issue of the Anti-Slavery Record, with a cut representing a drove of chained slaves. In a short time it was noised around that I had been "circulating incendiary periodicals among the free colored people, and trying to excite the slaves to insurrection." I went to Mr. Stout and explained how it was that the pamphlets had been left in the barouche, and took the remainder of them and locked them in my trunk.

"The excitement continued to increase, and soon the report was that I had been posting handbills around the city, inviting an insurrection of the slaves. Knowing the charges to be false and unconscious of danger, I continued the sale of my Bibles until Saturday, the 15th of the month. As I was preparing to leave town to attend a camp meeting some eight or ten miles distant, a Mr. Estell, formerly an auctioneer and vendor of slaves, met me at the door and demanded 'those abolition documents.' He was highly excited – indicating agitation, even to trembling. On presenting the pamphlets, I requested him to read before he condemned them, and this seemed to inflame his rage.

"I proceeded to the campground, where I was taken in charge by Mr. Broughton, the principal city officer, who exhibited the kindest deportment. On arriving at my boarding house, I found the Mayor, John P. Erwin, waiting for us. He wished me to appear before the Committee of Vigilance. I replied that it would give me pleasure to do so, as I wished it understood just what I had and had not done, and I wished it to take place immediately.

"We repaired to the courtroom, which was at once crowded to overflowing. The roll of the Vigilance Committee was called, and the meeting called to order. The mayor stated that in consequence of the excitement produced by the periodicals in my possession, he had caused me to be arrested and brought before the committee. He also stated that he had taken charge of my trunk, which he delayed opening until my return. The trunk was produced, and on being interrogated, I replied that I preferred that they should examine it for themselves.

"The officer first laid a pile of clothing before the Committee, followed by my books, among which was found Rankin's *Letters on Slavery* and Bourne's *Picture of Slavery in the United States*. I informed the Committee that these were for my perusal, as I wished to compare my own observation, while in the slave states, with what had been written. Then my private letters were read with eagerness.

"One letter – from a very aged lady – ran, 'Preached a stream of abolition 250 miles long,' in travelling from Cincinnati to Cleveland. Great importance was attached to this. Another spoke of the 'inconsistency of celebrating the Fourth of July, while so many among us were in bondage.' Another, from a gentleman known to entertain unfavorable sentiments for abolitionism, jestingly concluded, 'Now don't spend more than half your time among the niggers.' This was cheered by the crowd. Great stress was laid on these extracts, and I was questioned very minutely about the authors of the letters. They labored much to prove that I was sent by some society as an insurrectionary agent.

"The trial continued from between four and five o'clock in the afternoon until eleven at night, when I was called upon for my defense. Whilst I told them I believed slaveholding to be inconsistent with God's law, I said that in bringing about emancipation, the interests of the master were to be consulted as well as those of the slave. And I said that the whole scheme of emancipation contemplated that the slave should be put in possession of rights which we have declared as inalienable from him as a man; that he should be considered as an immortal fellow being… that he should be treated as our neighbor and our brother.

"After my remarks ended, the crowd was requested to withdraw whilst the Committee deliberated on the case. I was directed to a private room to await their decision. Up to this period my spirits were calm. I did not entertain an apprehension that there would be so flagrant a violation of my rights as an American citizen. This confidence was strengthened by the circumstances of the case. What I had done, I did openly. There was no law forbidding what I had done. And among my triers, there was a great portion of the respectability of Nashville. Nearly half of the Committee were professors of Christianity.

"My expectations were soon shaken. On entering the room where I was, Mr. Broughton said that he feared it would go hard with me. Some of the Committee were in favor of thirty-nine lashes and some were for inflicting one hundred lashes, while others thought me worthy of death. I was summoned to hear the decision, which was prefaced by a few remarks – 'That they had acted with great caution and deliberation, and had acted conscientiously, with a full recognition of their duty to their God.'

"They found me guilty of being a member of an Anti-Slavery Society in Ohio, of having in my possession periodicals published by the American Anti-Slavery, and they *believed* I had circulated these periodicals, and advocated the principles they advocated in the community. They then pronounced that I was condemned to receive twenty lashes on my bare back, and ordered to leave in twenty-four hours. The doors were then thrown open, and the crowd was admitted. The sentence, being repeated, was received with great applause, accompanied by the stamping of feet. Then the crowd was ordered to proceed to the Public Square, and to form a ring.

"By no one was there so much exasperated feeling shown as by Mr. Hunt, editor of the National Banner & Nashville Whig. He set himself to work, securing my journal, sketch book, and letters. It was displayed in his pale, death-like countenance and in his agitated frame, and in the furious air with which he seized the papers and tied them up in his handkerchief, at the same time eyeing me with rage.

"I entered the ring that had been formed. The chairman, accompanied by the Committee, expressed his gratification at the order by which the whole proceeding had been characterized. While some of the company was engaged in stripping me of my garments, a motion was made that I be exonerated. This brought furious imprecations on the head of the man who made the motion, and the commotion was only appeased by the sound of the whip upon my naked body.

"I knelt to receive the punishment, which was inflicted by Mr. Broughton with a heavy cowhide. When the infliction ceased, a feeling of thanksgiving to God arose in my soul, to which I began to give utterance. A death-like silence prevailed for a moment, then was broken with, 'God damn him, stop his praying.' I was raised to my feet by Mr. Broughton, and conducted by him to my lodging, where it was thought safe for me to remain.

"The next morning, owing to the great excitement that still prevailed, it was necessary for me to leave the place in disguise, with only what clothing I had about my person. I left property to the amount of nearly $300, sacrificing at least $200 on my barouche and horse, which I was obliged to sell."

Amos Dresser

Despite his financial setback, Amos Dresser soon enrolled at Oberlin College, and was able to make money as a lecturer for the American Anti-Slavery Society. Following his graduation he married, and after serving as a missionary in Jamaica, he was a pastor and later a teacher. He ultimately wrote a book, lectured on abolition and temperance in

Europe, and served various church congregations from Ohio and Indiana to Nebraska and Kansas.

Dresser's ordeal illustrates the vehemence with which the majority of Nashvillians, including those of the upper-caste, would defend slavery against even the slightest challenge. And it defined the threat that loomed over all people of color during slave times – that if they did not submit to slavery, there would be hell to pay.

3

Frank Parrish

Frank Parrish was born in 1804 in Williamson County, on the northern outskirts of Franklin, to a slave woman named Clara, who was called Clary. He was fathered by Colonel Joel Parrish, who owned his mother, and although the circumstances of Frank's birth made him a slave, he was raised in the Parrish home and treated as a member of the family. His father died when Frank was seven or eight years old, and as he grew up he formed an especially close bond with Colonel Parrish's widow, Susannah Parrish. Many years later James Thomas, a mixed-race

BATHING HOUSE.

"This is the purest exercise of health,
The kind refresher of summer heats."

THE undersigned, respectfully informs the citizens of Nashville and its vicinity, that, as the season for the pleasant and healthful exercise of Bathing is fast approaching, he has at considerable expense prepared and fitted up an establishment, at which may be enjoyed "the luxury of the falling spray," or the "lucid coolness of the flood"—THE SHOWER, COLD OR TEPID BATH. He has prepared every convenience to give pleasure to those who partake of this useful and agreeable recreation at his rooms; and assures the public that order and regularity shall be kept, so as to merit and he hopes ensure the approbation of his customers.

The Bath-House is situated next door to the Barber's Shop on Deaderick street, opposite the Office of the Banner and Whig, and will be opened on the 1st day of May, for the reception of visiters from 6 in the morning until 10 at night.

Ladies are respectfully informed that convenient apartments have been prepared, with every accommodation for their comfort, for their exclusive use ; and that female servants will always be in readiness to attend them.

The subscriber requests and hopes to receive the liberal encouragement of the community, in this effort to accommodate them with a luxury which is universally acknowledged to be most beneficial in its effects.

FRANK PARRISH.

Also at his Barber's Shop, next door, he keeps on hand for sale STOCKS, COLLARS, SUSPENDERS, best FANCY SOAPS, PERFUMERY of all descriptions, CURLS, PUFFS, &c. ; also the best SEGARS and TOBACCO.   F. P.

april20—R&U

Nashville barber who had been fathered by future U.S. Supreme Court Justice, John Catron, wrote about Parrish.

"Frank's father and master died when Frank was a mere boy, which left Frank the property of the widow Parrish. His devotion to Mrs. Parrish was as great as any child's could be to its parent. When Frank thought anything would please the old lady, he sent it to her."

In 1829 Parrish married Fanny Dismukes, a young slave owned by Ephraim P. Shall of Davidson County. But unlike the vast majority of slave marriages, their union was listed in the records of the county court. Frank may have already moved away from Williamson County by the time of the marriage, and almost forty years later a newspaper account described him as he was when he first arrived in Nashville.

"Frank Parrish entered a printing office in the capacity of pressman. This was before the application of steam to the printing press, when a vigorous constitution, strong arms, and tough sinews were necessary. These he had in an unusual degree. Few men were endowed with more strength and elasticity, and he was regarded as one of the best pressmen of the time."

Another description of Parrish, who was over six feet tall, referred to him as being of a "yellow complexion" – which meant being light-skinned – and having "woolly" hair. Despite being so well regarded as a pressman, he left his position with the newspaper, and in the early 1830s, after opening a barber shop in Nashville, he worked as a barber in New Orleans.

Parrish had taken on Alphonso M. Sumner, a mixed-race Negro, as his partner, and in 1833, while Parrish was in Louisiana, Sumner ran the barber shop in Nashville. Alphonso Sumner was also a teacher, and he managed to open a school for the children of free black parents – probably the first of its kind in the city. A few slave children were allowed to attend as well, but in a few months the school was shut down. Sumner was accused of writing letters to a pair of local slaves who had taken refuge in Detroit. The letters supposedly contained "important information," and after nearly being whipped to death by vigilantes, Sumner was forced to leave town and was warned to never return.

The loss of his partner may well have been what brought Frank Parrish back to Nashville later the same year. He quickly established himself as a successful barber in his shop on Deaderick Street. The next year, as Frank was gaining more and more customers through a combination of charm and his abilities as a barber, a decision by the Tennessee Supreme Court revealed the way free Negroes were viewed in Nashville, and well as across the South. Chief Justice John Catron, the father of Frank's future friend and protégé, James Thomas, wrote the court's unanimous decision that Tennessee slaves who were emancipated would be transported to Africa.

"A will emancipating slaves, or a deed of manumission, is binding and communicates a right to the slave. But until the State – the community of which the emancipated person is to become a member – assents to the contract between the master and the slave, it is an imperfect right. Adopting a new member into the body politic is vastly important in every community, and especially in ours... where the free negroes' vote is of high a value as that of any man.

"Degraded by their color and condition in life, the freed negroes are a very dangerous and most objectionable population where slaves are numerous. Therefore, no slave can be safely freed but with the assent of the government where the manumission takes place. Manumission is an act of sovereignty, just as much as naturalizing a foreign subject. The highest act of sovereignty a government can perform is to adopt a new member, with all the privileges and duties of citizenship.

"We think it is clearly inconsistent with the policy of the state, and the interest of its citizens, to give the assent of the government to the manumission of slaves, upon any terms short of their immediate removal, not only beyond our jurisdiction, but beyond the limits of the United States of America.

John Catron

"The injustice of forcing our freed negroes on our sister states without their consent, when we are wholly unwilling to be afflicted with them ourselves, is a plain and direct violation of moral duty. To treat our neighbors unjustly and cruelly, and thereby make them our enemies, is bad policy and contrary to our interest. We are ejecting this description of population, fearing it will excite rebellion among the slaves, or that the slaves will be rendered immoral to a degree of depravity inconsistent with the safety and interest of the white population. These are fearful evils.

"But are they not more threatening to Virginia (just recovering from the fright of a negro rebellion) and to the Carolinas – and to Georgia, Alabama, Mississippi, and Louisiana than they are to us? Compared with the whites, most of them have two slaves to our one. Some of them have almost ten to our one. How can we, as honest men, thrust our freed negroes on our neighbors of the South?

"Suppose the non-slave holding states northwest of the Ohio River were willing to receive our freed negroes. Would it be good policy to locate them beside our great rivers, forming wretched free negro colonies in constant intercourse with our slaves? Such a population inhabiting a country near us would become a most dangerous receptacle to our runaway slaves. The time would soon come when the attempt to seize harbored slaves would produce war with such people, and serious collisions with the State within which whose jurisdictions they resided.

"All the slave holding States, it is believed, as well as many non-slave holding States, have adopted the policy of exclusion. The consequence is the free negro cannot find a home in the United States that even promises safety, and assuredly none that promise comfort.

"The Colonization Society has formed a colony of free blacks at Liberia, on the coast of Africa. The people residing there are all from the United States, speak our language, pursue our habits, profess the Christian religion, are sober, industrious, moral, and contented. They are enjoying a life of comfort and equality, which is impossible to enjoy in this country, where the black man is degraded by his color and sinks into vice and worthlessness from want of virtuous and elevated conduct. The black man in these states may go and come when it pleaseth him – without a domestic master to control the actions of his person. To be politically free – the equal of the white man.

"The slave here – who receives the protection and care of a tolerable master – holds a condition superior to the negro who is freed from domestic slavery. The slave taunts his fellow slave by telling him, 'he is as worthless as a free negro!' The free black man lives amongst us without hope. He seeks no avocation, and is sunk in degradation. The free negro is a degraded outcast, and his fancied freedom is a delusion.

"Generally, and almost universally, society suffers, and the negro suffers, by emancipation. These are some of the reasons why we assent to the emancipation of slaves only upon the condition that they be transported to the coast of Africa."

The perception expressed by Chief Justice Catron on behalf of his fellow justices was shared by many, if not most, local white citizens. Within a few months – later in 1834 – a Constitutional Convention was held in Nashville. The constitution that had been written in 1796 was replaced by a new document – one that stripped free black men who owned land of their right to vote. But despite the treacherous racial environment that surrounded him, Frank Parrish, who enjoyed the protection of his mistress and a number of friendly whites, was able to prosper.

His extroverted nature was evident in an advertisement he placed in a local newspaper in 1837, after he opened a bath house at his Deaderick Street location. And a few months later when he took out another poetic ad in the National Banner and Nashville Whig, he displayed his continuing fondness for rhymes.

NASHVILLE BATH HOUSE.

THE undersigned respectfully informs the public that his BATH HOUSE situated on Deaderick street will in future be kept open from early in the morning until 10 o'clock at night, for the reception and accommodation of visiters. The great expense he has been at fitting up this establishment—and the convenience of its arrangement, together with the many advantages to be derived from the use of the bath, he hopes will secure for him a liberal patronage from a generous public.

If you wish for long life, contentment and health
More va'uable far than the tinsel of wealth,
For its kindly promotion the Bath is the thing,
Whether in winter or autumn, or summer or spring.

FRANK PARISH.

February 28, 1837—tf.

In addition to the services he provided in his barber shop and bath house, he sold a wide assortment of combs and wigs, as well as unrelated items such as live partridges. Years later his friend James Thomas wrote about Frank's outgoing spirit.

23

National Banner and Nashville Whig,
June 7, 1837

BATHING.

TO THE LADIES,

THE Grecian fiction of Venus being of Ocean born, is typical of the aid of which beauty is expected to derive from frequent ablution and bathing. But we fear the Ladies are not adequately impressed with the full importance of the practice to which the above beautiful thought refers. They spend much time and labor at the toilette; but neglect the means which are best calculated to insure the very objects for which they toil so assiduously. They are certainly not aware of the great benefits which result from the constant use of the warm bath, or they would not neglect it on any account. After fatigue or exertion it has a most soothing and exhilirating effect. On the score of vanity alone, a lady should rigidly and regularly follow the practice of daily ablution. In order to preserve health as well as beauty, the warm bath is a most important auxiliary. It throws off every thing that effects unpleasantly the operations of a healthy system;—it gives *softness* to the skin, *brilliancy* to the complexion, *lustre* to the eyes, *buoyancy* to the *spirits*, and *elasticity* and *grace* to every *movement* of the lady. Our variable climate which either freezes or melts, requires the warm bath more than a regularly tempered uniform region. A warm bath to a lady is worth all the etceteras of the toilette. Bathing does not consist merely in washing the hands or rubbing a wet towel over the face and sometimes the neck, the ablution ought to extend over the whole surface. We would most sincerely recommend the use of the warm bath to the better and fairer portion of the inhabitants of Nashville.

Haste to the bath ye fair and bright,
That fairer ye may be.
And brighter far than starry night;
And sweet as Araby.

FRANK PARISH.

"The most conspicuous character in Nashville was Frank Parrish. Frank was as free to do as he pleased as a man could be. Everybody thought he was free. He was a fine looking man, six feet one inch in height. He was a barber and an elegant dresser – by nature polite and gentlemanly in manner. Anything Frank wanted in the community, he could get. Any protection he needed would be furnished. The worst they could say of Frank was that he was foolishly extravagant. Frank would borrow twenty-five or fifty dollars from his white friends, and promise to return it the next day, which – if somebody worse off than himself didn't call on him for help – he would."

In 1840, after over ten years of marriage, Frank's family included his wife Fanny, their ten-year-old daughter, Ann, and an unnamed older female who was almost certainly his mother, Clara. While Fanny and Ann were both listed as "free colored," Frank was listed as a slave, as was Clara, if the older female was indeed his mother. Because he was a slave, Frank's status was precarious. His mistress, Susannah Parrish, was in her mid-seventies by then, and she was well aware of what could happen to Frank following her death. At some

24

point, perhaps when her will was about to be prepared, some or all of her children and grandchildren apparently had a meeting. James Thomas described some of what followed.

"When they about got through, one of the heirs inquired, 'What about Frank?' All except one said, 'Well Frank has been good to the old lady, and I am willing to let Frank go.' But that one said, 'I want all that is coming to me.' There was but one way to settle that part of the estate – to sell Frank on the block at the Market House to the highest bidder. When Frank heard what they were going to do with him, he almost made a blue streak through the house with his choicest profanity."

That meeting may have led Susannah Parrish to submit, with the help of an attorney, a petition to the Williamson County Chancery Court in 1840.

"Joel Parrish of Williamson County departed this life leaving certain negroes, among which is a mulatto man slave named Frank – commonly called Frank Parrish – by profession a barber, and now living in Nashville. I do not consider it desirable to keep Frank in his present situation. I believe Frank should be sold and the proceeds divided among my children and their children. My object would have been, if the law had permitted, that Frank should be emancipated, but as that cannot be done, I wish a home secured to him, and such protection given him, against the possibility of bad treatment, as the law will permit. He was raised in the family, and is of good character and habits. My object is for the benefit of Frank. It will not be for the interest of my children or their children that Frank should be kept in the family as a slave, and given to anyone at my death, nor do I believe it practicable to do so. Now I, Susannah Parrish, the widow of Joel Parrish, for one dollar, have given all my interest in Frank to have Frank sold and the proceeds divided among my children and their children."

But when Susannah's will was written the following year, Frank's status was still uncertain and she was clearly determined to have the matter resolved.

"I desire that my faithful servant Frank be free at my death. He has been to me, ever since the death of my husband, a faithful, obedient, and valuable servant. My last desire is that neither my daughter, nor any of my grandchildren interfere with Frank, nor endeavor to continue him in slavery."

Although her will was straightforward, Susannah was still concerned about Frank and the codicil she added was meant to further insure his safety.

"My will directed that my mulatto slave Frank be emancipated. If he is not emancipated, I hereby give Frank to my friends Hinchey Petway, Thomas Washington, Francis B. Fogg, Edwin H. Ewing, and Richard Fletcher. I hope they will take care of and protect Frank Parrish."

Susannah Parrish chose Frank's protectors well. Petway was her son-in-law, and Washington, Fogg, Ewing, and Fletcher were four of Nashville's most prominent lawyers. In order for Frank to be protected, he was purchased by Edwin H. Ewing – who would soon serve a term in the United States House of Representatives. According to James Thomas, who became an apprentice barber under Parrish around the same time, "Mr. Ewing and Frank had always been friends, and from the time of that transaction they became firmer friends."

Frank Parrish retained the degree of freedom he had enjoyed before the death of Susannah Parrish. His advertisements – which continued to exhibit his effusive personality – frequently appeared in

Nashville newspapers. Another one of his submissions came during the summer of 1838.

In addition to operating his barber shop and bath house, he served for a time as a barkeeper on the steamboat *Nashville*. His wife Fanny died in 1846, and in 1850 Frank was the head of a household that included only his mother and his twenty-year-old daughter, Ann. His relationship with Edwin H. Ewing remained strong, and in 1851 Frank accompanied Ewing and a number of other wealthy young Nashville men on a trip abroad. James Thomas wrote of one part of the journey that he found especially amusing.

> WARM BATHS.
>
> During this hot, suffocating, broiling weather, the warm bath taken three times a week, is of essential service to the whole system. It cleanses the skin, promotes digestion, clears the head, and cools and invigorates the whole man. The inestimable benefits derived from the warm or tepid bath, are not easily enumerated, and but little known, in comparison to their great influence in restoring exhausted nature, over-wrought by excessive fatigue, or indeed, excess of any kind. To merchants, professional men and mechanics, who are compelled to labor all day long either mentally or physically, the warm bath is a great restorative. Its effects in tranquilizing the nerves and giving a healthy action to all the functions of the human system have been sufficiently tested, both by experience and the universal practice of all civilized and polished nations, from the days of the Pharoahs down to the present hour. It is the only real panacea, save exercise, wholesome food, fresh air, temperance and cleanliness, in the known world.
>
> FRANK PARRISH.
>
> Frank Parrish is the boy,
> His baths are so nice;
> So cool and refreshing,
> Here's one in a trice.
>
> The hot or the cold bath—
> Whichever you please,
> We're waiting and ready,
> Walk in if you please.

Republican Banner, August 6, 1838

"In 1851 Mr. Ewing and a party of gentlemen went to make a tour of Europe, Palestine, and Egypt, and they took Frank. Frank was taken for the principal man of the party. Wherever they went, Frank brought up the rear, but the attendants pulled him to the front. It kept Frank busy trying to explain, 'I am not the one,' but people thought him only modest and heaped more attention on him."

During the course of the tour, Parrish distinguished himself in an incident that took place in Egypt. As the party was travelling by boat on the Nile, the crew got into a pitched battle with a large band of local men. When Ewing intervened in an attempt to make peace, he was knocked down and beaten. Frank rushed to Ewing's aid and was shot in the neck, and the wound was serious enough that it was some time before he fully recovered. The story of his bravery made Frank even more of a celebrity when the party returned to Nashville, and he received additional acclaim for the mementos he brought home from the Holy Land – a rock from Mount Sinai, and vials of water from the Jordan River and the Dead Sea.

Not long after his return to Nashville, a relationship developed between Frank and twenty-one-year-old Sarah Jane Harding – the all-but-white daughter of David Morris Harding, a wealthy landowner, and his mixed-race slave, Priscilla. Their impending marriage led Edwin H. Ewing to engineer the emancipation of both Frank and Sarah Jane from slavery, and to obtain permission for them to legally remain in the state. Ewing's approach not only relied on the reputation of Frank and Sarah Jane in the community, it also required Ewing's knowledge of the law, and his influence with the eleven magistrates of the Davidson County Court who had to give their approval.

"A petition of Edwin H. Ewing for the emancipation of his Negro man Frank, commonly called Frank Parrish – about forty-eight years of age, and of yellow complexion and with wooly hair – was presented this fourth day of October, 1853. The court, after hearing the petition and proof of the good character of Frank Parrish, finds that he should be emancipated and set free, and forever entitled to the privileges of a free man of color upon giving his bond of $1000 – being his value – that he shall forthwith remove from the State of Tennessee. With Edwin H. Ewing as his security, Parrish entered his bond, conditional on his immediate removal from the State."

The emancipation accomplished the first part of Edwin Ewing's strategy to help Frank Parrish. Then in the same court and on the same day, he presented a second petition to the magistrates, all of whom would have been very familiar with Frank. With Ewing underwriting another bond, the cooperation of the court was essentially assured.

"Frank Parrish came to be heard this day before County Court, to remain in Tennessee. The court being satisfied from testimony that Frank Parrish is a person of good character and ought to be permitted to remain in Davidson County, it is decreed that Parrish, on giving bond with good security in the sum of $500 that he will keep the peace, be of good behavior to all white citizens of this State, and not become chargeable to the county, be permitted to remain as a free man of color in the County of Davidson."

Ewing prepared similar petitions on behalf of Sarah Jane. Both of her petitions won unanimous court approval as well, and after their marriage, Frank and Jane were able to live together as free people of color. Frank continued to operate his barber shop beside the Nashville Inn, and in April, 1856, he was preparing to open another shop in the St. Cloud Hotel. A newspaper article contained a light-hearted article about his latest venture.

"In connection with his profession, Frank Parrish – a barber and a gentleman to boot – has, in the shaving saloons of Paris, seen and learned everything worth seeing and learning. But as for any monsieur telling him anything about shaving which he didn't know before – the idea is preposterous. Now settled down at the St. Cloud, he is proceeding to set up for the reception of his friends, as well as for guests of the hotel. He will have a bathing room connected with his shaving room, and having been in the far distant Eastern lands, where the luxuries of a good bath are appreciated, we may be sure Frank will have all the appointments of his bath complete."

Less than two weeks later, one of the most destructive fires in the city's history not only consumed the Nashville Inn and the Davidson County Courthouse and five large business houses, it claimed Frank's shop on the Public Square. The next month, in early May, his mother Clara died at the age of sixty-nine, and in June Frank was attacked by a vicious dog. His leg was so badly injured that he was unable to walk for several months, and amputation was a continuing possibility. He was still recovering when Sarah Jane died in September. But an indication that Frank still had his sense of humor appeared three months later in a newspaper item.

"Frank Parrish, the most celebrated knight of the razor in this region, requests us to say that having nearly recovered from an unfortunate wound in the leg from the bite of a dog – Frank says the hair of the dog *won't* cure the bite, so that question is settled – he is prepared to entertain his old friends at his shop in the St. Cloud."

Frank moved forward with his life after the events of 1856, and a portion of his energy was devoted to music. At some point he had taken up the clarinet, and following the death of his wife, and perhaps earlier, he performed in the band led by Jordan McGowan, Nashville's most noted musician. In the spring of 1859 a newspaper took note of Frank when the group played at the Memphis racetrack.

"Yesterday was a fine day for the races. One feature at the race course is the music. The leader of the band is Jordan McGowan, well known in Middle Tennessee as an excellent player on the violin, but the band contains a more remarkable man than Jordan. Frank Parrish – a large, fine-looking specimen of African who plays the clarinet with much skill – formerly belonged to the Honorable Edwin Ewing, and was his body servant for a number of years. In that capacity Frank visited Europe and Egypt with his master, and while in Cairo they were attacked by Bedouin Arabs, and Mr. Ewing would have been killed had his servant not received the ball aimed at his master."

But issues of race and slavery were festering in the background, and an eruption took place at the close of 1859. A young state legislator from Sumner County, Richard H. Barksdale, was trying to make a name for himself, and he introduced a bill that threatened to turn the life of Frank Parrish – and the lives of free persons of color across the state – upside down. And a most unlikely figure spoke out against the proposed law, for which – because of the Virginia uprising led by the abolitionist, John Brown, at Harpers Ferry – there was broad support in the legislature.

The individual who opposed the bill was none other than John Catron, who had castigated free Negroes twenty-five years earlier, and who by then had become an associate justice of the United States Supreme Court. Although Catron consistently supported slavery, over the course of his career there had been times when he displayed an independent streak, and fighting against Barksdale's "Free Negro Bill" was one of those times. A letter from Catron appeared in a Nashville newspaper at the close of 1859.

"The bill before our Legislature proposes to enslave, or drive from the State, the free colored population now amongst us. It provides that these persons, if they are adults, shall be seized and sold if found here after the first day of next May, and that the children shall be bound out. The adults are allowed to emigrate to Africa, or they may seek a master and go into slavery.

"Who are these people? Not one in a hundred has ever been a slave. Usually their mothers, grandmothers, or great-grandmothers were slaves who were emancipated by masters for meritorious services, or by the courts according to law. They all have a vested right to freedom. My objection to this bill is that it proposes to commit an outrage, to perpetuate oppression and cruelty. This depressed and helpless portion of our population is designed to be driven out, or enslaved for life, and as no slave can hold property, have their property forfeited. Mothers are to be sold and driven away from their children – many of them infants. The children are to be bound out until they are twenty-one years of age, and then leave the State or be sold.

"Of these women and children there is hardly one in ten of unmixed Negro blood. Some are half-white and many have half-white mothers and white fathers, and in many Negro blood is almost extinct. In what nook or corner of the State are the principles of humanity so deplorably deficient that a majority of the white inhabitants would commit an outrage not committed in a Christian country of which history gives any account?"

Another opponent to the Barksdale bill was Representative William B. Ewing, a nephew of Edwin H. Ewing. During a debate on the floor of the House in early December, Ewing addressed a false claim that was made on behalf of the bill.

"Mr. Barksdale says that Negroes have no rights. He says emphatically that they have no rights to property, no rights to person, and no rights to liberty. I believe the supreme judicial authority of this State understands differently. The Supreme Court has decided that a free man of color might sue for false imprisonment, and was entitled to recover damages. In the case of David and Moses it was decided that although they were in a state of servitude, these men could sue for freedom and property under our laws. In the case of the freed servants of Harding, the court decided that the slave has a right to freedom under the provisions of the will of his master, and is entitled to inherit both real and personal estate. It is a new idea to me that Negroes have no rights."

Because his uncle was Edwin H. Ewing, William Ewing was well aware of the case regarding "Harding's servants," which had come about, in part, to resolve the question of whether Frank could inherit what his wife, Sarah Jane, who died in 1856, had left him in her will.

But in providing examples of Negroes who owned property, Ewing failed to mention that Frank Parrish not only owned local real estate, he also owned five slaves. The five individuals – a black woman in her late thirties and four children – may have merely been kept as slaves by Parrish in order to protect them, but the nature of their servitude is unclear.

Although one version of the "Free Negro Bill" was passed in the State House of Representatives and another won approval in the State Senate, the bill was never enacted into law. Public sentiment had turned against the idea of forced removal, and the House and Senate versions were never reconciled, but free blacks remained highly vulnerable.

By 1860 fifty-six-year-old Frank Parrish, who was an amateur ornithologist, had married his third wife, an eighteen-year-old woman named Priscilla, and they were living in their home on Franklin Pike. Although the war soon brought an end to the world he had known, Frank Parrish navigated through the various changes, and by the time the fighting ended, he had become one of the leaders of the Negro community in Nashville. Along with such notable local figures as Nelson Walker, Peter Lowery, and Henry Harding, he came to the forefront on one particular occasion when racial tensions in Nashville reached a boiling point.

In 1866, when it was rumored that an insurrection was being planned by Nashville Negroes, the credibility Parrish had with the most powerful whites in the city came into play. He was one of those appointed to investigate the unrest, and after he reported that no insurrection was underway, tensions quickly cooled. Frank Parrish's health began to fail, and he died in June, 1867. The notice of his death contained a brief biography and mentioned that he was survived by his wife and three children, and it included the following observation.

"By his correct conduct, integrity, and skill, Frank Parrish built up a good business and made many friends. He was a general favorite with all the old citizens of Nashville, and of the distinguished men of the State. Considering his want of education and the difficulties which environ the path of the colored race in this country, he must be regarded as having been a good businessman. Properly educated and disciplined, he might have accumulated a fortune."

His impact on the community continued after his death. Just before Parrish died, a movement was launched to desegregate the railways of the South Nashville Street Railroad Company, which provided separate cars for whites and blacks. Along with the white people who wanted to attend his funeral, a large crowd of blacks was waiting to ride south of town to the City Cemetery and witness Frank's burial. A newspaper account described what took place among one group of Negro mourners.

"Some of them, not choosing to wait for the car assigned them, determined upon forcibly taking possession of the street cars. Into the cars they pushed – as one by one the rattling conveyances rolled up – the drivers loudly remonstrating. In several cases white people left the cars, but the colored intruders were obstinate, and declared that their ten cents amounted to as much as anybody's. A superintendent was compelled to place himself in the door of one of the cars in order to keep them out. Of the others, however, they gained full possession. The colored car coming up, served to relieve the pressure and the excitement finally died away without serious results."

As the decades passed fewer and fewer people remembered Frank Parrish. Edwin H. Ewing, his friend and liberator, survived until 1902, and James Thomas lived until 1913, but the time eventually came when no one had any recollection of the man who had been, for a time, "the most conspicuous character in Nashville."

4

Priscilla and Fanny Harding

On a late September day in 1856, an expensive iron coffin with a metal-covered glass faceplate was lowered into a grave in a small cemetery out in the country, ten miles from Nashville. The coffin contained the body of twenty-three-year-old Sarah Jane Parrish. The mourners included her husband, Frank Parrish, and her mother, Priscilla Harding, as well as Fanny Harding, who had once been Sarah Jane's mistress. They were only a few feet away from where, two years earlier, they had stood with Sarah Jane at the burial of her father, David Morris Harding. It is unlikely that her uncle, John Harding, or her first cousin, William Giles Harding, owner of nearby Belle Meade plantation, were among the mourners. Sarah Jane's casket was covered with earth, and her gravestone was put in place a short time later. Her resting place would remain undisturbed for the next 147 years.

Early Harding family residence

In 1798, nearly sixty years before the death of Sarah Jane Parrish, her grandfather, Giles Harding, had settled on that land with his family. It was just north of the confluence of the Little Harpeth and Big Harpeth Rivers, and some ten miles southwest of what was then the small town of Nashville. Brush and trees were cleared and fields were planted, and a modest brick home was built on a rise overlooking a creek and an old frontier trail. Giles Harding had conventional attitudes when it came to slavery. Those views were reflected in a petition he signed soon after his arrival.

"Considerable inconvenience arises from diverse Negroes in Nashville keeping houses of entertainment, as well as by trading with other Negroes in the county. It is a disgrace to the town. We therefore pray that a law may be passed to prohibit any Negro or

Negroes from keeping a house in town, and we think it will be advisable to pass a law to prevent masters of slaves from allowing their slaves any such liberties."

By the time Giles Harding died in 1810, most of the older Harding children had left home. When his son, David Morris Harding, turned twenty-one in 1816, he inherited the farm on which he was raised. He seems to have been called Morris, and a few months later he married fourteen-year-old Fanny Davis, who had grown up some three miles to the northwest. She was the daughter of the noted frontiersman, John Davis, and apparently displayed the same independent spirit for which he was noted.

The same year that Morris Harding and Fanny married, Priscilla, a light-skinned, sixteen-year-old slave girl, came to the Harding farm. Priscilla had been born in 1800 in Goochland County, Virginia, where the Harding family lived before moving to Tennessee. She was probably accompanied by her sister, Mary, a light-skinned girl close to the same age. A description written many years later described Priscilla. "In appearance, she was a very small woman with a French cast of features – jet black hair and eyes."

Given her physical characteristics and that she was from Goochland County, and considering the unusual relationship she would have with both Morris and Fanny Harding, it is conceivable that Priscilla was a blood relation of Morris Harding. She may have been the offspring of a cousin, or even of his older brother, George, the oldest of Giles Harding's children, who had stayed in Virginia when the rest of the family moved to Tennessee. And considering that she arrived the year of the marriage, she may have been a wedding present.

The union between Morris and Fanny Harding yielded no children, but within a few years he began fathering children by Priscilla. She eventually gave birth to ten children – all of whom, like Priscilla, were slaves. Decades later, James Thomas, a former Nashville slave with close ties to the family, wrote about Morris Harding, but due to the tenor of the times, he did not use Harding's name.

"One gentleman lived about ten miles out of the city, whose wife had no children. But… his servant woman had about six children, all his. The madam attended them as carefully when sick or in need, as she would her own."

It seems clear – from what Thomas wrote, as well as from what subsequent evidence suggests – that Fanny, unable to have children of her own, was especially close to the children that were sired by her husband and born to Priscilla. And judging from what would come to pass years later, Priscilla and Fanny, who were nearly the same age, maintained a close relationship. The slave children fathered by Morris Harding must have been treated comparatively well, but other individuals who came into Harding's possession had a far different experience.

Harding had begun buying slaves soon after he turned twenty-one, and in the early 1820s he became heavily engaged in the slave trade. In 1821 he traveled to Virginia and bought 17 people, and the following year he journeyed to Maryland and purchased another 30 individuals there and in Virginia. On July 22, 1822, when he was in the upper part

$50 REWARD

RUNAWAY on the 4th of the present month, from the subscriber living ten miles south-west from Nashville, two negro men, SAM and JOHN ; Sam is about 27 years of age, five feet 10 or 11 inches high, stout made, and has a double lip, and is very fond of playing the fiddle.

John is a very black smooth skin fellow, 22 years of age, 5 feet 10 or 11 inches high, he stutters very bad when spoken to. I purchased John in Maryland, and Sam high up in Virginia, there is no doubt but what they are aiming to get back again. The above reward will be paid to any one who will deliver said negroes to me, or secure them in any jail so that I get them, or twenty five dollars for either.

DAVID M. HARDING.
August 28, 1822.———3t

Nashville Whig

of Virginia, he bought a slave named Sam, and not long after they reached the Harding farm, Sam and another slave named John ran off. Harding's advertisement appeared in a local newspaper at the end of August.

It is not known if Sam and John were recaptured, and the fate of the other individuals Harding purchased and brought to Tennessee is also uncertain. Some might have been sold in Nashville, but they were likely transported further south by river and sold in places like Louisiana or Mississippi. But few if any of those who were bought in Virginia and Maryland remained on the Harding farm. While Harding bought nearly 50 people in 1821 and 1822, the census of 1830 recorded only eight slaves living on the Harding place. That number grew to 19 by 1840, but eight of those individuals were under ten-years-old, and some must have been the children born to Priscilla.

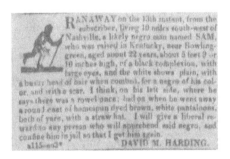

National Banner and Nashville Whig, April 26, 1828

As Morris Harding's children became more numerous, his farm grew larger. Adjoining tracts were purchased, and his property eventually included 1500 acres. A second and more substantial brick house had been built at some point, perhaps around the time when Morris and Fanny married. Located only a few yards to the northeast of the original dwelling, it would be expanded over the years. It may well be that all of Priscilla's children – from her eldest, Jefferson, born in the mid-1820s, to her youngest, tellingly-named Fanny Priscilla, born in the mid-1840s – made their home in the older structure.

Along with Priscilla and her children, Priscilla's sister Mary Ball, who ultimately became the Harding family cook, also lived on the farm. And there was a small group of people living on the place in 1820 who are surrounded by mystery. In that year the census recorded six free persons of color living on the Harding farm. No free Negroes were indicated in subsequent censuses, and who they were and what became of them is not known.

Although they were legally slaves, judging from the freedom enjoyed by Priscilla's oldest child, Jefferson, the mixed-race Harding children had considerable freedom. A legal document mentioned that in 1844, when Jefferson was around sixteen, he was allowed to travel north.

"In 1844, with the consent of David Morris Harding, he went to Ohio, and Harding intending to confer freedom upon him, he remained there as a free man for some months. Another time, and with the like intent, he went to Illinois and remained four months."

That Jefferson returned to Tennessee on each occasion might indicate that he did not like where he was, or perhaps that he merely missed home. His brothers and sisters must have also been well treated, and several years later, one of them was emancipated. In 1853, soon after Sarah Jane Harding reached her twenty-first birthday, Morris Harding petitioned the County Court, not only requesting that his daughter be emancipated, but that she be allowed to remain in Tennessee.

A wedding was at hand, and rather than have an unrecognized slave marriage, Sarah Jane, and probably both Priscilla and Fanny, must have wanted the union to be legally sanctioned. Sarah Jane was described in the petition as being, "of bright mulatto complexion, and with straight hair and high features," and having "good moral character."

Edwin H. Ewing, a family confidant who owned her prospective husband, forty-eight-year-old Frank Parrish, was one of the region's most talented attorneys. Ewing, Parrish's friend as well as his owner, not only secured both emancipations, he was able to obtain permission for them to remain in Tennessee. When their marriage was recorded, they were not even designated as persons of color. And Ewing would soon play another role in the lives of both Priscilla and Fanny Harding.

The previous year another leading lawyer, Return J. Meigs, had been retained by Morris Harding to draw up his will. Its provisions regarding his children were included at Fanny's insistence, and the document written in 1852 was almost certainly prepared under her direct supervision. Edwin H. Ewing was made Harding's executor.

"I do hereby emancipate and set free from bondage forever my former slaves Priscilla, or Sylla, and her children Jefferson, Caroline, Sarah Jane, Spotswood, William, Cornelia, and George, and all other children of the said Priscilla, born or that may be born within nine months after my decease, and all the children of her daughters, born in my lifetime or afterwards. And I give and bequeath for the use and benefit of Priscilla and her children… one half of my estate.

"It is my earnest desire that the slaves, emancipated aforesaid, may be permitted to remain in Tennessee, and I request my executor to obtain for them, if possible, the privilege of living in this state as free persons of color. But if it becomes necessary for all or any of them to remove, then I desire my executor to cause them to be carried to such place as he may deem most consistent with their interest, and see that they are established in their new abode as favorably as possible."

When the will was written, the name of the youngest child, eight year old Fanny Priscilla – named for both her mother and her mistress – was accidentally omitted. Her mother must have noticed the omission, but she had a larger concern. As the political controversy over slavery became more intense, the position of free Negroes was

41

increasingly precarious. There were calls for all free persons of color to be enslaved or sent out of the state, or even shipped to Liberia. A codicil to her husband's will, written the month before his death in 1854, contained provisions meant to further protect Priscilla and her children.

"I authorize my executor to sell the residue of my land not given to my wife, and also the slaves, except those assigned to her and those to be emancipated. In regard to Priscilla and her children, it is my will as to the children who are not yet 21 years of age, that they take their freedom from my will, and that no application be made to emancipate them in any court whereby they shall be compelled to leave Tennessee. But as to those who are now 21 years of age, including Priscilla, and to all as they arrive at the age of 21, they are to have the liberty of applying for their freedom, and immediately have their shares of my estate."

Priscilla would have almost certainly traded her other blessings for better health for her sons and daughters. Two children had died before her husband, and death was a constant presence for much of the 1850s. Cornelia had died around 1853, Caroline was in her mid-twenties when she died in 1855, and her daughter Sarah Jane died the following year – only three years after her marriage to Frank Parrish. And her sons William and Spotswood were dead by the end of 1858, leaving Jefferson, George, and Fanny Priscilla as her only surviving children.

As required by the codicil to the will of Morris Harding, his 33 slaves were divided into two groups. They were all brought together and examined by two men who were there to determine the monetary value of the group. But a slave named Peter had become "unruly before the crop was made," and he was sold to one of the appraisers. Fanny Harding must have already decided who would

42

remain with her, and it is clear that she meant for families to stay together.

Along with Priscilla's sister, Mary Ball, Fanny kept Mary's daughter, Sarah, as well as Wesley and Samuel, who were probably Sarah's children. She also kept four men who were likely the most indispensable workers on the place, along with Mary Anda and her three children, and three apparently motherless brothers aged ten, twelve, and fourteen. The remaining sixteen individuals, Sally and her four children, Lucy and her three daughters, and Maria and her five children, along with a thirty-one-year-old man named Henry, were all sold by Edwin H. Ewing, the executor of the will, to his older brother, John O. Ewing, for their legally-established value. The proceeds, just under $7000, would be paid to Priscilla and her children when and if the terms of the will were determined to be legal.

And John O. Ewing also purchased of the southern section of the farm – a 715 acre tract across the Little Harpeth River – for $25 per acre. That money was also held for Priscilla and her children, and the land was soon bought back by Fanny. But the will raised a number of legal questions about whether the intended heirs were legally entitled to inherit property, and until the courts decided the matter, the inheritance was not fully distributed. It took until 1859 for the case to reach the Tennessee Supreme Court, which finally ruled that the heirs should receive their share of the estate. They ultimately divided over $38,000 – the equivalent of more than one million dollars a century-and-a-half later.

There was more and more political pressure to banish free persons of color from Tennessee, and that possibility likely caused Priscilla to leave the place where she had lived for over 40 years. In the summer of 1858, she and her three children moved to a farm she bought adjoining the campus of Wilberforce University, near Xenia, Ohio. It was an area that had been a safe haven for blacks from the South, and especially for individuals from Nashville, for a number of years.

Wilberforce University

Following the death of his white father in 1846, Carroll Napier, an emancipated slave who would become a resident of Nashville, had gone to Ohio along with his brothers. Many years later the community would be mentioned by James C. Napier, one of Carroll's sons. "We traveled to Ohio, where we joined a colony of free families, which my father and his brothers had formed some years before near Xenia. At this place a school, Wilberforce, had been organized for Negroes."

Details of her arrival in Xenia eventually appeared in an early history of the area. "Mrs. Priscilla Harding came from Tennessee. A large two-story frame house, a barn, and several other farm buildings were erected, and all bespoke prosperity and wealth. All the land bordering the creek – and a saw mill and a grist mill – were included in the Harding farm. Mrs. Harding was the first person in the community to own a fine carriage. It was drawn by two spirited black horses, bedecked with a silver mounted harness. These horses came from the Belle Meade stock farm of Nashville, Tennessee. When Mother Harding came to Wilberforce, she brought a good-sized pillow slip, half filled with gold coins, and had to her credit a large bank account."

After she had been in Ohio for over a year, with most of the estate still to be distributed and needing a financial representative, Priscilla named Fanny Harding to act on her behalf. Despite her comfortable circumstances, an account written some years later disclosed the darkness in her life. "Mrs. Priscilla Harding moved to Greene County after raising a family of ten children and burying seven of them. But after taking up her abode here, her eldest son was taken sick and died, and a year later the youngest one was claimed by death, leaving her but one child."

Jefferson Harding had married Cornelia Austin early in 1859, only seven months after coming to Xenia, and along with his brother and sister, he attended Wilberforce University in 1860. His classmates included James C. and Elias Napier as well as several other young free Negroes from Nashville. But his health was apparently declining, and at the end of September, 1860, after returning to Davidson County, he wrote a will that affirmed the close relationship he had with Fanny Harding. In addition to providing for his widow, Cornelia, Jefferson left $1500 to Fanny, and at Cornelia's death the balance of his inheritance from his father's estate would also go to Fanny, "for purposes understood by her." Whether the money was intended to take care of a family member is unknown, but the trust he placed in Fanny is clear.

And Jefferson's will contained a second mystery. In his codicil he mentioned, "my negro woman slave, Emma, who is now in Mrs. Harding's possession." It seems likely that Emma was Emma Seay, the widow of his brother, Spotswood, who had died soon after his marriage in 1856. The fact that they received a marriage license suggests that she was free, but if Emma the widow and Emma the slave were the same individual, the continuing uncertainty faced by free blacks in Tennessee may explain why she might have become Jefferson's nominal slave.

Fanny Priscilla, like her brothers Jefferson and George, attended Wilberforce, and she was still a student when she died of tuberculosis

45

in 1862 at the age of seventeen. Her will stipulated that she should be buried in Tennessee, "with the remains of my brothers and sisters," and she appointed Fanny Harding and Edwin H. Ewing as co-executors.

Fanny Harding stayed on her Davidson County farm during the Civil War, and several slaves remained with her. Her will was written in 1864, and although the Confederacy seemed to be collapsing, the status of her slaves was still unclear. She must have felt that they might be vulnerable following her death, and that may have been what led her to direct that "my mulatto boy Henry" and "my two Negroes Sam and West" should only be set free after her passing. Fanny Harding died the next year – along with slavery.

Priscilla remained in Xenia with her son, George, the last of her ten children, but she was soon joined by her sister, Mary Ball, as well as by Sam and Henry, who were probably Mary's grandchildren. When Priscilla Harding died in 1877, her eulogy, written by a member of her church, appeared in the *Xenia Gazette*.

"Her life has caused all who knew her to love her. In 1872, there being a desire to build a church near her, and offer was made to purchase an acre of her land. She rejected the offer and gave the land, and she assisted in building a house for the worship of Him she loved so well. She was a friend to the poor, fed the hungry, clothed the naked, and gave eyes to the blind. When a call for assistance was made, she was always ready to respond. She never lost an opportunity of doing good. She had been a Christian for fifty-six years. The last time I visited her she said, 'Behold my witness – it is in the heavens. My record is on high. Goodbye, Elder! Meet in heaven.'"

Her only surviving child, George, prospered and ultimately fathered at least eight children. Most of his children had children of their own, and the number of Priscilla and Morris Harding's descendants would continue to expand over the following decades. Mary Ball remained in Ohio for a number of years, but she kept in touch with the nephew of Fanny Harding, Edward D. Hicks, a former Confederate officer who had inherited the old home place. Many years later his daughter, Emma Hicks McDonald, wrote a reminiscence of the people she had known growing up on the old Harding farm.

"Among Aunt Fanny's Negroes who had been slaves, there were several half-white children of Morris Harding, to whom Aunt Fanny had made him give half of his property. They moved to Xenia, Ohio. After her death, Negroes who needed help came home. A request of Aunt Fanny's was that no Negro who came home and needed help should be refused. Many of them are buried in the lower part of the graveyard.

"Aunt Mary Ball had been a cook. She lived for years after Aunt Fanny's death. She and my mother did not get along, but she was very fond of my father, who sent her money to live on. When Mary was in Ohio she would send us boxes of food – fruit cakes, preserves, and things she thought she made better than anyone else. One box was so heavy that the express charge was twelve dollars.

"After a year or so, without any notice, she walked into my father's office and said, 'Marse Ed, I've come home to die.' He brought her out that afternoon, and a room was made comfortable for her. She was not well, and I was the one who took her a tray of food from our table three times a day. She often went to the graveyard. She told us she talked to Aunt Fanny, and to her husband Andy, who had been dead for years. One day she was found unconscious in the garden. We took her to her room and got Dr. Hill, but she never regained consciousness.

"She had brought all of her burial clothes with her – linen

underclothes and a silk dress. Her funeral was just what she would've wanted. She was taken to a place under the walnut and elm trees, and buried as close to Aunt Fanny as could be arranged."

Over a century after the burial of Mary Ball, much of the place where Priscilla and Fanny and Morris Harding had lived for most of their lives was sold out of the Hicks family. It became the site of Ensworth High School, and along with the springhouse and a few outbuildings, it was announced that both brick dwellings would remain intact. But it was felt that the old cemetery – rather than providing a compelling connection to the past for future generations of students – would detract from the appearance of the quadrangle that was to occupy the same area, and school officials decided that the graveyard should be relocated to another part of the campus.

Those same officials were notified that because of the close connections between Fanny Harding and Priscilla and her children, one or more iron coffins might be encountered when the graves were moved. Iron coffins had been popular prior to, during, and for several years following the Civil War. They were far more expensive than wooden caskets, and provided considerable protection to the remains inside. When the grave of a Confederate officer, killed at the Battle of Nashville in 1864, was robbed in 1977, his decapitated corpse, having been carefully embalmed and interred in an iron coffin, still had pink flesh and hairy legs.

The exhumation of the Harding cemetery took place in 2003. Although most of the graves, including the graves of Fanny and Morris Harding, were not marked, the grave of his daughter, Sarah Jane Parrish, had a headstone. When her grave was opened, an iron coffin with a broken glass face plate was pulled out of the ground. Of the eight iron coffins that were ultimately unearthed, four had been breached by roots or by rocks, but the other four were essentially intact, and of those, two appeared to be pristine.

Iron coffins were no longer in use by the time Mary Ball was buried in the 1880s. What was presumed to be her grave was opened, but any remains had long since decomposed. But there were nails from a wooden casket that had rotted away, and mixed in with the earth were a large number of well-preserved pieces of bright blue silk – very likely the remnants of a burial dress. When the lid was raised from the coffin of Sarah Jane Parrish, the broken face plate had brought about the decomposition of nearly everything but her skeleton, but near her skull was a tortoise shell comb that must have been in her hair when she was buried. In an age when slavery is typically presented without nuance, the story of Priscilla and Fanny Harding, like what lay beneath the surface of the old cemetery, can serve as a reminder of how complex the past can be.

5

John McCline

In 1934 a former Territorial Governor of New Mexico, Herbert Hagerman, prepared an introduction for a manuscript written by a man he had known for more than a half century.

"This history is printed just as Mac handed it to me, except for a few changes in punctuation and arrangement. He first showed me the manuscript, which is all in his own writing, some four years ago, but I was then so busy that I failed to appreciate this rather unusual document. Since then, however, I have read it a number of times, and it holds my attention in a rather strange manner. That he is here in 1934 – a man in full possession of his memory, who was a slave on a southern plantation – is intriguing in the extreme. Mac is an unusual character – cheerful and optimistic, curious and interested in what is going on around him, and not overly affected by rank and position. He has always found life worth living, and is, on the whole, quite a philosopher, as well as a keen observer."

The individual referred to as "Mac" was John McCline, and the account he wrote of his early life indicates the depth of his intelligence and the nature of his spirit.

"I was about ten years old at the beginning of this history. My mother died when I was two, leaving a daughter and four boys, I being the youngest of the family. I do not remember our sister, who died at an early age. My father, John McCline, for whom I was named, belonged to James Smith, who owned a grocery store in Silver Springs, in Wilson County. Father hired his time from his master. He was a huckster, owning his own horse and a covered wagon. He made two trips a week into Nashville, and made a fairly good living. I used to see him quite often when I was on my way after the cows. He always had a present for me – sometimes it was a silver dime, or a bit of candy, or a pocket knife. He was so kind."

The hamlet of Silver Springs was about twelve miles east of the plantation on which young John McCline lived. The turnpike from Nashville to Lebanon, the county seat of Wilson County, connected the two places.

"The four boys – Richard, Jefferson, Armstead, and I – were brought up by Grandmother Hanna. As early as I can remember, Grandmother lived in a two-story frame house on the north side of the pike, about a mile from Stones River. Buck, the shoemaker – the only one on the place who could read – and his wife Betsy and their son Frank, lived on the top floor. Frank and I were chums, spending most of our time about the house, carrying wood and water and doing work of various kinds between milking times, when we had to keep the calves away from the cows.

"Grandmother was doubtless a very handsome woman in her youth. She was very light in complexion, and had dark brown hair. She was the mother of three children – two sons, Stephen and Richard, and my mother. Uncle Stephen and Uncle Richard were the two most useful men on the place. Both were married. Richard had two children and Stephen had four, but Stephen's wife and children belonged to the Ridleys, and we saw very little of them."

Many years later, John McCline, who was born around 1852 and was a child when he lived at Clover Bottom, was able to describe his master and mistress in considerable detail.

"Dr. James Hoggatt was one of the richest men in Davidson County. He had three splendid plantations – his farm at Murfreesboro, devoted chiefly to raising cotton, and a plantation in Mississippi, and his 2000 acre estate, Clover Bottom, eight miles east of Nashville. His three-story residence was situated on a slight knoll about a quarter of a mile from the pike. Dr. Hoggatt was a typical southern gentleman. Faultlessly dressed in a suit of black broadcloth, he might have been mistaken for a minister of the gospel. Strolling leisurely about the grounds of his estate, he seemed happy and contented. The Doctor's family consisted of himself, his wife, and two nieces."

Clover Bottom mansion

James Hoggatt was the second of three sons of John Hoggatt, a Revolutionary War officer who came to Davidson County after the Indian wars came to a close in 1795. The elder Hoggatt bought an expanse of fertile land in a large bend in Stones River, not far from where it flowed into the Cumberland. James was born in 1798, the year after his family settled in the bend. He was trained to be a physician, but chose not to practice medicine. He married in 1820 and a daughter was born the next year, but his wife died in 1826. He remarried in 1831 – no children were born to his second wife – and his daughter later died without children, By 1850 his two nieces, the teenage daughters of Colonel Meredith P. Gentry, who had served six terms in the United States Congress, were the only children in the family. McCline had a very clear recollection of his mistress.

"Mrs. Hoggatt was a stout, handsome woman, about forty years old. While her interest was chiefly confined to her garden and a dairy with 40 cows, nothing on the place escaped her attention. She was an early riser and saw to it that the eight women who milked the cows, along with their boy assistants, were on the job. A rawhide whip, three feet long with a wrist band attached, was used unsparingly. When she struck there was a stinging and lasting impression."

Mary Ann Sanders had married thirty-three-year-old Dr. James Hoggatt soon after she turned eighteen. A member of a highly-prominent Sumner County family, she was not only a granddaughter of General Daniel Smith, one of the founding fathers of Tennessee, she was the half-sister of Andrew Jackson Donelson, who had been President Jackson's private secretary. Donelson later served as the American minister to both Texas and Prussia, before becoming Millard Fillmore's running mate in the 1856 presidential campaign. Doctor Hoggatt was nearly sixty and Mrs. Hoggatt was in her mid-forties when they were described by John McCline.

"The Doctor's chief hobby was raising mules. He owned the finest jack in the county and had 50 brood mares. Every two years 100 mules were sent to the Nashville market, and he realized a large profit. There were three mills on the place – a grist mill, a saw mill, and a gin mill – and there was a carpenter shop and a blacksmith shop, so that any ordinary building could be put up or repaired by

Mary Ann Hoggatt

the slaves on the place. The overseer, James Anderson, was kind, considerate, and well-educated, and did no whipping. The colored people were happy, and there seemed to be no appearance of slavery.

"There were many superstitions at Clover Bottom. The herb doctor, the hoodoo, and the conjurer were all to be found, and Wyatt bore all those distinctions. He was of medium height, and had light brown skin and short, white stubby whiskers. He lived alone in an old two-story house a half mile from the other cabins."

Wyatt was about nineteen when Dr. Hoggatt bought him from Anthony Clopton, Hoggatt's brother-in-law, in 1825, but he was in his early fifties when McCline knew him.

"The children stood in vital fear of Wyatt. None dared to even go near his house. It was said that his concoctions, made up of deadly poisons, were put up in bottles and sold with instructions of how to use them on enemies. When it was necessary to remove an enemy by charm, the purchaser was to bury the bottle under his enemy's doorstep early in the morning, and when he walked out the door, something would happen to him.

"Wyatt's duties were to look after the jack, and he also had charge of feeding the hogs being fattened for winter killing. Every man and woman on the place had special work laid out. Stephen was the head carpenter and miller, with Austin as his assistant. Abe was the blacksmith, Uncle Jordan was the head gardener, and Daniel was the painter. And the general work of the farm – planting, cultivating, and looking after the stock – was attended by 15 men, with David at the head. Just south of the Hoggatt's house was Mistress's garden, containing about 50 acres. All the women, and the children large enough to handle a hoe or pull weeds, were used exclusively in the garden.

"Five hundred hogs and many cattle were fattened and killed every year. The cold, frosty days of December, generally before Christmas, was hog killing season. Three huge kettles were set on a rock foundation and filled with water, and fires were built under them. Great fat hogs were killed in a pen nearby and dragged to the kettles. They were dipped to soften the bristles and quickly taken out, and several men with sharp knives would scrape them until they were white.

"Then fifteen women – Grandmother Hanna, the oldest, at their head – would be on hand with tubs and sharp knives to scrape the lard from the guts. Some of the lard was given to them, and also the chitterlings, which they cleaned and put away in jars. Hundreds of pounds of leftover scraps were also given to the women, out of which sausages were made. Wagon loads of hogs, dressed whole, were sent to market, and the smoke house, a substantial brick building 40 feet long by 30 feet wide, was always well-filled with curing meat.

"During the summer months, milking began at five o'clock in the morning. Each woman used a piggin to milk. It was a cedar pail and would hold a about a gallon. Four large cedar tubs with bright brass hoops around them were placed on a wide board table, and into these the women strained the milk. Many times Mistress Hoggatt, not fully dressed, would appear with her rawhide whip.

"The first thing she would do was look into the tubs to see if the amount of milk was above or below the average. Then she would go to Hanna, the head woman in the pen, and complain that the cows were doing poorly for that time of year. The cows were not fed in the morning before going out to pasture. Mrs. Hoggatt did not know that there was a lot less milk at the morning milking. Every woman and boy was in fear of her. No one knew when he or she would get a whack from the rawhide. She never struck without leaving a mark, and everyone kept out of her way as much as possible.

"There was a large two-story frame building with a long covered porch on the north side. A room on the first floor was used as a spinning room. Here the women who had babies to nurse were engaged with their spinning wheels, turning cotton – and sometimes wool – into thread for knitting and other purposes. Another room upstairs was occasionally used as a sort of jail where runaways might be contained.

"In those days the method of cutting the corn was commonly called pulling fodder – going through and pulling the leaves off the stalks and tying them in bundles. The corn was left to season and dry on the stalks, and later, in September, it was pulled off the stalks. Then it was hauled and piled up in front of an immense crib, where it was husked and thrown in. The greatest event on the Hoggatt place, and the one most enjoyed by the colored people, was corn husking on beautiful nights.

"On the night when the shucking was to begin, 50 men or more, along with women and visitors from neighboring places, would join in. Someone would start a familiar song, and the work would go on until twelve o'clock, when all would adjourn to one of the largest cabins, where supper would be served. Supper was eaten and, as a rule, the merriment wound up with a dance. Vann, who was also a good singer, played the fiddle, assisted by Abe, the blacksmith, with the banjo.

"In the spring of 1858, Mr. Anderson, the overseer, resigned and married Miss Ridley, of an adjoining plantation. He was succeeded by Richard Phillips, who was brutal and ignorant – an example of the poor white trash of that time. He brought one of the largest and most vicious bloodhounds I had ever seen with him. Among his instruments of torture was a ball and chain to fit around an ankle, and a black snake whip seven feet in length with a pound of lead in the butt for the purpose of knocking a man down."

Richard Swepton Phillips had been born to nineteen-year-old parents in Rutherford County, Tennessee, in 1826, less than ten months after their marriage. His father eventually became an overseer on a farm in an area of Davidson County bordering Rutherford County, and that likely led the younger Phillips to follow the same vocation. The younger Phillips was twenty-six when he married in 1852, and he and his slightly older wife, Margaret, were still childless when he became the new overseer at Clover Bottom.

Slave cabins at Clover Bottom

"Until the coming of Phillips, the colored people lived in cabins and houses scattered about the place, but he said there was too much liberty among the slaves, which would lead to a spirit of unrest. In the fall, after the crops had been gathered and put away, two rows of cabins, ten in each row, were built. They were good frame houses of one room each, the lumber having been taken from the forests on the place. Each house had one big door which closed with a hook. The houses were whitewashed inside and out, and each twenty-foot front yard was kept clean by sweeping. A large pot hung in each fireplace so that cooking could be done with some convenience, and all had a Dutch oven for baking. The beds were all made by carpenters on the place.

"When Phillips came, I had to report to his house every night for a week or so and take lessons in counting from Mrs. Phillips, who taught me to count from one to a hundred. When I qualified for my new job, I was given a fine black mule named Nell to ride, and early every morning I would drive the 40 cows into two separate pens where they would be milked. After the milking I would get breakfast, and then drive them to a large pasture two or three miles away, where I left them to graze."

John McCline was probably no more than seven years old when he took on his new responsibilities, which included much more than driving the cows to pasture.

"Returning to the house, I would hitch Nell to a cart with a barrel, and haul water from a spring about a quarter of a mile from the house.

It took many barrels to fill the big tank that stood near the kitchen door, and it usually took me until noon. Then I would unhitch and feed Nell, and go to my grandmother's and get my dinner. My next duty was, if the men were working a good ways from the house, to take dinner to them in the field. I was proud of my new job.

"Along in August, Grandmother's bill of fare generally consisted of boiled potatoes, bacon, greens of some kind, cornbread, and buttermilk. She would put the greens, potatoes, and bacon into a large piggin, and lay a big pone of hot cornbread on top, and the buttermilk was put into a tin pail. I set the piggin on my head, and with the pail of milk in one hand, I would start for the fields. It seemed to me that I was doing a man's work, and I was glad to get away from my grandmother, who was always calling for a bucket of water, or wanting me to do some sweeping.

"I had been on the job about a month without a complaint from Mistress or from the overseer. For about ten days I had been taking the cows across the pike to the north woods pasture, but when I went for them one afternoon, a cow was missing. After searching for more than an hour, I drove the others home and reported the missing cow. The next morning, after I had driven them out to the pasture, I met the overseer.

"Phillips walked up to me and grabbed the back of my collar, and told me to stick my head between his legs. After he had my head clasped between his knees, he unbuttoned my trousers, pulled up my shirt, and with a rawhide three feet long he gave me a whipping on my bare back. That night when I went home and told Grandmother, she took me in her arms and cried for a long time. Then she bathed my back and soothed it with some kind of liniment, and put me to bed.

"The entire week was given to us at Christmas time. Every man on the place was given a suit of clothes, consisting of a coat, a shirt, a pair of trousers, and a pair of shoes. The cloth from which the suits were made was from cotton grown on the Murfreesboro farm and spun on the looms there. The women, and boys big enough to work, were also given shoes and enough cloth to make dresses for themselves and the children. On Christmas morning each family would receive ten pounds of flour and two pounds of white sugar called sugar loaf, which was considered a luxury. Grandmother usually broke it up in small pieces and issued it out in the form of candy."

The Hoggatt mansion was destroyed in a fire in February, 1859, and the event was described by McCline many years later.

BURNING OF DR. HOGGATT'S RESIDENCE ON THE LEBANON TURNPIKE.—The fine residence of Dr. Hoggatt, situated on the Lebanon turnpike, about six miles from the city, was entirely destroyed by fire on Monday last. The roof took fire from a defect or crevice in the chimney flue, which was being burned out at the time, through which the sparks were communicated to the dry frame work, and the whole roof was in a blaze before the fire was discovered. Though the greater part of the furniture was saved through the timely assistance of neighbors, the Doctor's loss can scarcely be estimated at less than $30,000.

Republican Banner, February 9, 1859

"Fire was discovered on the roof, and the alarm was given. Everyone grabbed a pail, or anything that would hold water, and ran to the big cistern near the kitchen, but the cistern was soon dipped dry. As there was no possibility of checking the flames, the men were told to go in and bring out such things of value as could be saved without danger to themselves. The great house was completely gutted. Nothing but the walls and the chimney were left standing. About two inches of snow lay on the ground, and it was a strange sight to see household furniture scattered about on the snowy lawn. Master and Mistress made their home with the Phillips until April, when they went north while the house was being rebuilt.

"News of John Brown was being whispered about at this time, and secret meetings were called by plantation owners like Donelson,

Dodson, Ridley, and others. To prevent any outbreak among the slaves, the masters decided to organize a company of patrollers to scout the country and the pike at night, and apprehend any Negroes they found. If they could not give a good account of themselves, the Negroes were to be held until a further inquiry would be made. There were many poor whites living in the neighborhood, and those who were too poor were provided with a horse, a gun, and a bullwhip.

"The overseers were notified by the masters to search all the cabins and quarters for arms. We were informed by Phillips that there would be no more night visiting from one plantation to another without a pass from him or from the Master. The appeal for a pass was made to his wife, and was readily granted. Passes were secured for attending a Saturday night frolic at some neighboring plantation, and the patrollers often went and looked around. Young men would be asked their names and their owners' names, and then a demand was made to see their passes. The patrollers were also required to visit the cabins – the purpose being to catch people off their guard."

It was probably in the spring of 1859 when the home where John McCline lived became a refuge. He and his brothers lived on the bottom floor with their grandmother – below where Buck, the shoemaker, lived with his family.

"Early in May a slave ran away from the Dodson place, five miles north, and came to our house. He was a friend of Buck's, and he was concealed for about ten days. One Sunday six men, preceded by several bloodhounds, rode up to the house and dismounted. They asked Frank and I to hold their horses, and drew their pistols. Buck had seen them from his window, and hid his friend downstairs in the fireplace. When the men passed through and went up the stairs, he came out and made his escape.

"Late the same day, Master sent for Buck to explain why he had harbored a runaway slave. Buck, who had never been whipped, knew the reason he was sent for. Rather than suffer the disgrace and the whipping he was sure to get, he ran away. A large reward was offered for his capture, and although the poor whites scoured the country for miles around, they were unable to apprehend him."

Regardless of what else was taking place, work on the Hoggatt plantation continued day after day, week after week, and month after month.

"The churning was done on the porch of the laundry, a two-story brick building just across from the smoke house. The churns were as big as a barrel, requiring a good deal of strength to move them, and twice a week Frank, my brother Jeff, and I would report at nine in the morning and proceed with churning. Mistress was always nosing around.

"One morning while I was working in the garden, she had given me a grubbing hoe, and told me to dig up a hotbed. I did not know how to go about it. She took the hoe and dug with ease, and then handed it back to me. It seemed dreadfully heavy, and I could not do it as she did. She became furious. She had a stick about three feet long and the size of a broom handle. She snapped out, 'You impertinent rascal!' and she struck me on the back. I fell as flat as if I had been shot. She left and I got up, and began digging the best I knew how.

"Late one rainy night, two men came to our house. The roof leaked a little, and Grandmother was up moving things about. The first one to enter was a dark-complexioned, thick-set man with a black beard. His long black whip was wrapped about his shoulders. On each side of the door was a cedar chest, in which she kept things like clean linen and dresses. He plunged in, turning everything over from top to bottom, and found a bottle of whiskey. He took a big drink and passed it to his partner, and then went out.

"Many changes were made at this time. The chief one was the retiring of old Richard as the market man. He had served faithfully for many years, and grown old and rheumatic in the service. He was succeeded by Zuccarello, who was white and spoke good English, and could read and write. He appealed to Mistress Hoggatt as being better suited than old Richard for driving bargains in market products. He took charge of the market wagon on the first day of 1860, and he and Phillips soon became fast friends."

Sydnor Zuccarello was about twenty-seven years old, and had worked in Nashville before coming to the Hoggatt place. Along with his wife and three children, he moved into an old brick house that stood on the edge of Mrs. Hoggatt's garden. John McCline would remember

Zuccarello Residence

that only a few months later, in April, Jordan, the head gardener, was killed by a young slave named Cynthia. Despite his age, McCline was fully aware of what had taken place.

"At the time of his death, Jordan was about fifty years of age, and his wife had been dead many years. It was the talk about the place that he was very much in love with Cynthia, but that she did not encourage his attentions. There was no doubt that she struck the fatal blow. She was a queer girl – seldom seen in company with the girls and boys of her age.

"On the day following the murder, Master went to the laundry, where Cynthia was confined. He questioned her closely, and she denied everything. He had her stripped to the waist, and having taken off his coat and rolled up his sleeves, he began whipping her. After each blow he would ask, 'Why did you kill Jordan?' She denied it to the last, and he whipped her until the blood ran in streams down her back. She finally fainted, and he left her there. The laundry girls, who were sewing upstairs, came down and revived her. She was confined to her bed for two weeks, recovering from the beating she had received.

"During the time Phillips had been on the place, he had beaten many men, women, and boys, but there was one man he had never struck, and of whom he was afraid. Austin was a tall and powerful mulatto. He carried a knife, and he was often heard to say, 'This is for Phillips the day he strikes me with that whip, unless Master is there and says so.' There can be no doubt that Phillips heard of this.

"Dr. Hoggatt intended to remove the ugly rail fence, and have a board fence built on both sides of Lebanon Pike. One day in October five of the men, Austin being one, were about a mile from the house building the fence, and I was coming out of the stable with Nell to go for the cows. Phillips and Zuccarello passed the door with their shotguns on their shoulders, and went down on the pike where the men were at work on the fence.

"On reaching the men, Phillips took his whip off his shoulders and laid it on the ground. Then he took a piece of rope from his coat pocket, and called to Austin to come over and cross his hands. Austin was using a long-handled shovel to dig a post hole. He stopped and said, 'I ain't done nothing to be whipped for, and I ain't going to be whipped unless Master says so.' Phillips said, 'Then you won't come over here and cross your hands?' Austin said, 'No sir.' Phillips dropped the rope, and with an oath he picked up his shotgun, then aimed and fired. Austin threw up his left hand when he saw that Phillips was determined to shoot, and it was shot off at the wrist and only hung by a little flesh. Buckshot entering his face and throat, Austin died instantly.

"Just after the shooting the stage was coming up the pike, and Phillips had the men move the body where it could not be seen. Then he and Zuccarello shouldered their guns and walked away. The remains of Austin were placed in a wagon and hauled to his cabin. When his wife, Dilsey, began to scream and cry, Mistress sent word that if she didn't stop, she would come down with a rawhide and wear her out. When Phillips reported the killing, we learned that Master told him it was a bad time to kill a nigger because it was only a few days before the election.

"In January, 1861, they caught Buck thirty miles away in Wilson County. Getting his trail with bloodhounds, they followed him for ten days. He had to wade streams to keep the dogs from tracing him, and his feet were badly frozen. Near a creek, with the hounds in close pursuit, he climbed a tree to escape being torn to pieces. Buck was delivered to Phillips, and the slave hunters were paid their reward – $150. With a ball and chain attached to one leg, he was locked up until his feet were well, and then he was sent south to the sugar plantation. His wife and Frank never heard of him after that."

Nashville was taken by Union forces in February, 1862, and ten months later young John McCline made a decision that changed his life.

"One clear cold day in the last part of December, I went for the cows that were feeding along the pike. A regiment or two of Union infantry were going to Nashville, and I directed Nell to the board fence along the pike. They were followed by a large covered ambulance, and when it got opposite of where I stood, a soldier walked up to me and said, 'Come on, Johnny. Go with us up north and we will set you free.' I wondered how he knew my name, and I slid from Nell's back, climbed over the fence near where Austin had been killed, and was off with the Yankees. Nell, realizing her freedom, turned and ran out of sight.

"As I reached the lane leading up to the house, I could see Mistress Hoggatt, her two nieces, the Doctor, and the house girls, standing on the lawn looking at the soldiers pass. As we marched past the toll gate, the two Blankenship boys jumped from their seats and walked up beside me. They taunted me by saying, 'You are running away, and we are going to tell your master.' The sun had set, and as we trod along the thought occurred to me, 'What am I doing? What have I done?' I began to think of my grandmother and my home, and tears came into my eyes."

John McCline was around ten years old when he ran away. He accompanied the 13th Michigan Infantry, and was soon serving as a teamster – caring for and driving a team of mules. Less than a month after leaving Clover Bottom, the regiment saw action at the Battle of Stones River, and after the unit was engaged in the Chickamauga Campaign the following year, it participated in General Sherman's march from Atlanta to the sea in 1864. McCline, who was around thirteen when the war ended, remained with the 13th Michigan until the regiment mustered out in June, 1865.

The young former slave travelled to Michigan with a colonel in the regiment, and his intelligence and personality helped him find work. By 1870 he was employed as a hotel porter. In 1874, possibly in the wake of a very brief and unhappy marriage, he left Michigan for Chicago, where he worked as a waiter in a popular hotel, the Palmer House, for a couple of years, but he was increasingly anxious to contact his family.

"I felt a desire to get in touch with my brother, so I got a friend to write to my former mistress, Mrs. Hoggatt, asking her to let me know about my family and my former companions on the plantation. She wrote me that I would find my brother, Jeff, working at the Grand Hotel in Indianapolis. I wrote Jeff and when he replied, I went to Indianapolis. In the fall I proposed that we go south, so we returned to Nashville where we visited quite a number of our kin folks."

John McCline's grandmother, Hanna, may have been dead by the time of his visit in the mid-1870s, but she had been alive in 1870.

When the census was taken that July, she was staying in the Hoggatt mansion with Mary Ann Hoggatt, who had been a widow since the death of Dr. Hoggatt seven years earlier. McCline's uncles, Richard and Stephen, still lived nearby with their families, and a number of others were living on the place as well. His friend, Frank, along with Wyatt, were among over sixty other black people living at Clover Bottom. All of them had taken Hoggatt as their surname.

Richard Phillips

And the adults were still working under the supervision of Richard Phillips, who had remained in his position as the overseer. McCline did not describe the details of whatever reunions there were, and there is no record that he ever went back again.

John McCline

"During the years he had been looking for me, Jeff attended school. He had taught in colored schools, and he wanted me to go to school. The Nashville Institute was a school for the education of colored people. The fee was nine dollars a month for room and board, and I furnished myself with books. They taught reading, writing, spelling, and arithmetic from about September to the first of May, and I made enough progress that they considered that I knew enough to teach in a common school. Hearing that a teacher was needed in the little town of Hartsville, about 45 miles from Nashville, I walked all the way there. I was paid $25 a month, and I taught the rudiments of spelling and reading to about 35 children, but the funds ran out and I was forced to give up the school."

After going back to The Nashville Normal and Theological Institute for another term, McCline moved to St. Louis, where he worked in an upscale hotel and gradually became an ardent reader. He later relocated to Colorado, and went to work for Herbert Hagerman, a member of a prominent family in Colorado Springs.

When Hagerman was appointed Territorial Governor of New Mexico by Theodore Roosevelt in 1906, McCline was put in charge of caring for the executive residence.

John McCline remained in New Mexico for the rest of his long life. He worked for a time as a janitor in a church, and became an avid baseball fan and was known as a meticulous gardener. The years passed, and it may have been in the 1920s – when he was in his seventies – that he wrote the account of his life before and during the Civil War. His narrative did not touch on what became of the people he remembered from his childhood. He probably knew that Mary Ann Hoggatt had been dead since 1887, but may not have known what became of Richard S. Phillips, the long-time overseer on the Hoggatt place, who died in 1914 at the age of 87. It is unlikely that John McCline ever read the brief newspaper article announcing the death of the man who had once killed a slave on the side of a turnpike.

"The death last week of Mr. R. S. Phillips caused much regret. He was a devout member of the Methodist Church, a man of high integrity, and most generous in his dealings with his fellow man. He was known as a man who never turned away empty handed anyone who asked him for aid. For a large part of his life he held the position of manager of the Hoggatt Farm, and in this position he was highly successful."

When McCline was in his mid-eighties he married a woman around half his age, and they were occasionally mentioned in the local newspaper, the *Santa Fe New Mexican*. In 1944 an article mentioned that he was "the oldest Republican in New Mexico." And when he died in 1948 – nine months after Jackie Robinson made his first appearance in the Major Leagues, and six months before the integration of the United States Armed Forces – a last article noted his passing.

"A fine human being died here Monday after 95 years of a useful life. John McCline was a Negro born in slavery, but dignified in freedom. Those who knew him agree that he was a splendid gentleman, a person of devoted loyalty, and a credit to the human race."

6

Peter and Samuel Lowery

Peter Lowery was born in 1810 in North Carolina – very likely in Anson County on the border of South Carolina. His mother was a slave woman named Jane Lowery, who appears to have been owned by William Hicks Hamer, a longtime resident of Anson County. The Hamer family had lived in Anson County since before the Revolutionary War, as had a white family named Lowery. There were two white residents of Anson County named Peter Lowery – a father and son – and sharing a less-than-common name with a

Petition to Emancipate Peter Lowery, 1837

slave child in such a sparsely populated county may well have been more than a coincidence. But both Jane and her son Peter had dark skin, as did the son Peter eventually fathered. If there was a connection between Jane and the white Lowery family, it may not have been biological.

Soon after Peter was born, the Hamer family left North Carolina and moved to Tennessee, and the few slaves they brought probably included Jane and her infant son, Peter. Aside from a single mention that he had lived twelve miles from Nashville in Davidson County, little is known of Peter Lowery's early life in Tennessee. When he was around twenty he married a young Cherokee woman, Ruth Mitchell, and their son, Samuel, was born in 1832 – the same year that William Hicks Hamer died.

By then Peter may have already bought himself from his owner, but buying himself did not guarantee his freedom. State law exposed him to the possibility of being forced to leave Tennessee, and further steps were taken to protect him. In 1835 a bill of sale was recorded in the office of the register of deeds, but instead of the Hamer heirs merely selling Peter to Samuel Seay, a prominent resident of Nashville, there was apparently an unwritten agreement behind the document. Although Seay was listed as his buyer, Peter Lowery was actually being placed under Seay's protection.

In 1837 Seay submitted a legislative petition asking that Peter be emancipated by an official act of the Tennessee Legislature. It was signed by many of the leading citizens in the city, including former Governor William Carroll and two ex-mayors of Nashville.

"To the Honorable Senate and House of Representatives of Tennessee. The petition of Samuel Seay, a citizen of Davidson County, would respectfully represent to your honorable body that he is the owner of a negro man by the name of Peter, commonly called Peter Lowry, about twenty-seven years of age, whom he is desirous that the legislature should emancipate. Your petitioner would state that said negro was raised in the county of Davidson, that from his youth upwards he has been distinguished for his fidelity and industry, that he has always demeaned himself submissively and humbly towards white persons and has endeavored to obey the laws of the community in which he lived, and that by his attention to business he has not only accumulated money enough to pay for himself, but has also purchased a hack and horses with which he can earn a sufficient support to prevent his ever becoming a charge to the community in which he lives."

The petition was granted, but Lowery's vulnerability was reflected in a second petition that was submitted by Samuel Seay in 1839.

"Peter Lowery, a man of color, has gained the confidence, friendship, and esteem of those citizens with whom he has become acquainted. He has purchased his freedom from his original owner, but because he could not, under the existing laws of this state, remain here and be entitled to citizenship, the right to him has been vested in Samuel Seay. He has no

Samuel Seay

guarantee for the continuance of his freedom in case of the death of Seay – in whom he has placed such confidence. He holds his freedom only by Seay's will and permission. Under the existing laws he must continue to be liable to be sold into bondage. He is unwilling to leave the state in which he has lived for so many years, and for whose citizens he manifests so strong an attachment. The undersigned petitioners pray you to pass a law to perpetuate his liberty and allow him to remain as a citizen within this state."

The second petition was apparently rejected, but with the continuing support of so many leading members of the white community, Peter Lowery was able to raise his family and maintain his business in relative peace. Because his wife Ruth was not a slave, neither was their son Samuel, but Peter was said to have eventually bought the freedom of his mother, Jane, and of several of his brothers and sisters. Peter Lowery was a man of deep theological conviction, and by the time he was emancipated, he was actively engaged in spreading the Gospel among members of the local black community. Years later he wrote about his early religious activities.

"I joined the white Christian church in 1832, and remained with them over fifteen years. During my connection I was treated with the utmost courtesy and respect. The white brethren called on us to organize and exercise supervision over our colored brethren, and they often gave the church to us to hold our meetings. Sometimes they would give way on Sunday nights for our meetings, until the church became so full that there was not enough room for the white and the colored.

"Then we concluded to establish a church separately for the colored people. Having no lot or house, I made a gift of a lot to the brethren of color. Then we built a house that was worth about $1600, of which I paid $1000. After we were in the house, the white brethren organized the congregation, and I was chosen teacher. I continued as pastor for over fifteen years, until after the war."

During the 1840s both he and Samuel received instruction from Reverend Tolbert Fanning, founder of Franklin College, where Peter may have been employed as a janitor. Ruth Lowery died in 1841, and the next year he married Lucinda Dotson, a light-skinned woman with at least two children.

Tolbert Fanning

Along with his religious piety, Lowery was known for his business acumen. In the 1840s, presumably after buying the freedom of his family members, he regularly purchased property. By 1850 he had bought four lots in Nashville, and he was living on a tract of land near Franklin College – a few miles east of Nashville. Along with his wife and one of her children, the household included his mother Jane, who would die the following year at the age of sixty-six, as well as his son Samuel, and Peter's younger brother, Shadrack.

Although Peter Lowery continued to lead his church and was listed in the 1850 census as a farmer, he still drove his hack and was engaged in

ICE! ICE!

I WILL keep during the present season, first rate I C E at my Depot on Lower College Street, second door below the Second Presbyterian Church. My terms will be as low as others.
M.-y 23—1m.   PETER LOWERY.

Republican Banner, June 7, 1856

selling ice during the summer. Authorities shut down his church late in 1856 when rumors of a slave rebellion swept Nashville and the surrounding region, and the following spring he petitioned the City Council to allow night services to resume. The opposition of Godfrey Fogg, a local alderman born in Connecticut, was reported in a local newspaper.

"Fogg said he did not believe any good resulted from negro preaching. If negroes desired religious instructions, the churches in the city were all open to them. Negro preachers could not explain the fundamental principles of Christianity; they were not competent. There were many things connected with the night meetings which were objectionable and demoralizing. He moved for its rejection. The motion prevailed unanimously."

Samuel Lowery had the same work ethic as his father. After working at Franklin College and being tutored by Tolbert Fanning, he became a school teacher at the age of sixteen, and then taught for four years. Samuel joined the Christian Church in 1849 and became a minister, almost certainly at his father's church, and in 1858, the year he married, he left Nashville to become the pastor of a Christian Church in Cincinnati.

Samuel Lowery

Samuel and his wife soon left Cincinnati. They moved to Canada where they lived for three years, and where he established a church and brought a number of converts to the Christian Church. They moved back with their children to Ohio, and in 1863 – following the issuance of the Emancipation Proclamation – Samuel left his family in Ohio and returned to Tennessee, where the Civil War was much more in evidence. He preached to black soldiers and to former slaves who had taken refuge in

Nashville, and then became chaplain of the 9th U. S. Colored Heavy Artillery.

Peter Lowery's church had reopened back in the late 1850s. He continued to preach, and although he owned real estate worth some $15,000 and was still driving his hack on the eve of the Civil War, his financial position was not confined to the money he earned or to the land he owned. It is unclear who the individuals were and why he owned them, but in 1860 he had five slaves that were collectively worth $3000.

Even though the city had been taken by Federal forces earlier in 1862, slavery had not yet come to an end in Nashville. On November 1, 1862, Peter Lowery's thirty-year-old stepdaughter, Caroline Dotson, was sold to a slave trader and taken to Atlanta, where she was kept in a pen by a second slave trader until she was finally purchased. It would be three years later – six months after the end of the war – before his wife, Lucinda, placed an advertisement in a local newspaper seeking the whereabouts of her daughter. By 1870 Caroline would be back in Nashville, living with her mother and Peter, and working as a seamstress.

Samuel Lowery's family returned to Nashville after the end of the war, and he went back to teaching school and preaching. In 1865 he wrote a newspaper notice about his father's church.

"The Christian Congregation informs the public that divine services will be held every Sunday in Lowery's Chapel. This commodious building was raised by Elder Peter Lowery, the veteran teacher of the Christian reformation in this vicinity, the first founder of a Christian church among people of color, and for sixteen years the pastor of the Second Christian Church. Having spent over thirty years as an advocate of the Gospel, he will unfurl the banner of the Cross, and labor to build up the cause of Christ. Good men and women will be welcomed, but all persons who sustain falsehood, ambition, and vice, and will not acknowledge the truth, will be called upon to repent."

A decade after a largely-false rumor of a slave rebellion swept the city, both Peter and Samuel Lowery, along with a number of others, became involved in defusing a similar situation. In October, 1866, Nashville was exposed to an unsubstantiated rumor concerning its black population. A letter from Tennessee's Secretary of State to the mayor of Nashville, Matt Brown, ignited the crisis.

"I have just learned that the freedmen, or many of them at least, are in a high state of excitement. Some of them, I am informed, contemplate violence. There seem to be two causes of irritation. First, the arrest of so large a number of them as vagrants, when they allege to have been only temporarily out of employment. Secondly, it seems that a number of young negroes, whose parents are here, have been taken to Mississippi and sold, and are being enslaved."

The origin of the rumor had been reported several days earlier in a local newspaper.

"Nashville has for a long time been infested by a large number of negroes who have no visible means of support. Many of the poor wretches live in filth and poverty, with scarcely enough clothing to cover their nakedness, and nothing to eat except what they beg or steal. In vain have planters and others importuned them, offering good homes and good wages, but they spurned every offer. Their filthy habits breed disease, and something must be done to remedy the evil. Captain Cavitt, of the police, informs us that yesterday his force arrested about forty idle negroes under the vagrant act. This morning they will have a hearing before the Recorder."

A number of days went by before fears of impending violence began to spread. Articles in opposing newspapers described the situation in dramatically different ways. The Union & Dispatch, which reflected the political views of both moderate and partisan Republicans, reported its version of events.

"About a week ago the city police arrested a large number of Negroes on the charge of vagrancy. Some were boys from ten to fifteen years of age, arrested while going to or from school, or playing marbles. They were tried by Recorder Wilkinson and nearly all were fined. Some of them paid, and about fifty colored persons were sent to the workhouse to work out fines and costs ranging from five to fifty dollars.

"Last Friday, Foster Cheatham and Lafayette Beach stated to Wilkinson that they had made contracts with these persons to work on their plantation in Northern Mississippi, and that they would pay the fines and costs in each case and furnish the necessary transportation. Upon this, Wilkinson ordered the release of fifty-one persons from the workhouse, and they were marched to the depot, placed on the cars, and taken south. The only justification we have heard is that they went voluntarily. This could hardly be the case. The young boys were not even allowed to see their own mothers before leaving."

The conservative view shared by partisan Democrats appeared in the Union & American.

"Considerable excitement prevailed in the city yesterday afternoon and last night, by rumors of a contemplated outbreak by the negroes. Well-founded rumors had, it appears, reached officials at the Capitol that the negroes were in a state of intense excitement in consequence of the recent arrest of colored vagrants. Letters were also read in the colored churches on Sunday that the negroes confined in the workhouse had been sent to Mississippi and sold into slavery.

"Of the gang of laborers taken by Cheatham, not one went against his will. They were under sentence to serve terms in the city prison, and almost every negro accepted the offer by Cheatham to pay them out and give them employment picking cotton. They had their free choice to go or stay. The scoundrels who would attempt by foul libel to invite the negro to deeds of violence and bloodshed – that would result in his certain annihilation – deserve a more severe punishment than is known to the law."

Two days after the letter from the Secretary of State, both Peter and Samuel Lowery were among several leaders of the black community who helped to quell the rumor of a violent uprising. Samuel wrote the resolution that the group endorsed.

"The so-reported outbreak of the colored citizens of Nashville has been thoroughly examined by us, as the old citizens of this place, and we find there is no foundation for such a report, and we denounce the exaggeration as a wicked attempt to enthrall us with bloodshed and suffering. We feel that we have been injured by a report gaining circulation that letters of an incendiary character have been read in our churches – which is also untrue. We commend the integrity and interest of the colored citizens of Nashville as allied with the white citizens to advance their general welfare and prosperity."

The following day the plantation owners, apparently after being prompted by an official of the Freedmen's Bureau, met with black leaders. They offered transportation back home to anyone wishing to leave, or to pay a good wage to those who were willing to stay and work. Most of the adults soon left the plantation, and shortly before Thanksgiving a representative of the Freedmen's Bureau brought all of the minors back to Nashville.

Nashville had not only become home to thousands of former adult slaves, there was also a large number of black children, including many orphans. Both Peter and Samuel Lowery would dedicate many of their remaining years to establishing a way for individuals to escape poverty. Some years later, the elder Lowery described the situation he faced to a newspaper reporter.

"In 1866 the chaotic condition of the South made it difficult to provide for the education of children of any class. There were many colored children, as there are still, for whom public schools offered little opportunity. Being the children of widows, or of very poor fathers, these boys and girls could not be maintained at home while attending school. If bread and meat were to be provided, their labor in the fields was necessary. An attempt was made in Tennessee to save this helpless class of colored boys and girls from lives of want – or worse."

The article went on to explain the way Lowery, with the help of his son, chose to attack the problem. The school he wanted to build was partly inspired by Franklin College.

"In order that such children might have the education necessary to enable them to become self-supporting men and women, and to become worthy members of the community, the Tennessee Manual Labor University was established. A farm of three hundred acres was purchased, shops and other necessary buildings were erected, and tools were provided.

"The institution was not only free, but self-supporting, and it fed and clothed its pupils during the period of their attendance. The school sought to give its pupils a plain education that people who work with their hands actually need, and at the same time teach them to work. While learning to read, write, and cipher, the boys were taught to be farmers, wheelwrights, blacksmiths, and carpenters, while the girls were trained in all branches of women's work."

In March, 1867, Lowery's campaign to raise money was noted in a newspaper article.

"Reverend Peter Lowery, an old and highly respected colored citizen of this place, has been canvassing the city for some days to obtain aid for the Tennessee Manual Labor University. Over 283,000 freedmen, lately advanced to citizenship, are dwelling with us under the same laws and government. By the oracles of God and the laws of Tennessee, this once enslaved people are our fellow citizens. Let every path of improvement be opened to them. Skillful mechanics and artisans will go out from this school to become the teachers of others. Instead of an army of mere farmhands, a strong force of ingenious workmen will go forth into all portions of the State to exert a wholesome influence in every county."

Peter Lowery went to some of the city's wealthiest citizens and received donations to fund the school, which was located in Rutherford County, twenty-seven miles east of Nashville and three miles north of Murfreesboro. Financial support for the school was dependent on the quality of Lowery's reputation, and when a report appeared that he was aligned with the radical wing of the Republican Party, he quickly responded.

"I see my name published as a delegate to the convention to nominate a candidate for Congress. My name was used in that connection without my knowledge or consent. I am not engaged in politics, but as the Lord helps me, I am trying to build up a school for the elevation of my race, and endeavoring to lead them into the ways of peace and righteousness."

Peter Lowery was president of the Tennessee Manual Labor University, Lucinda's son Frederick Dodson was one of several trustees, and Samuel Lowery, who served as Secretary, wrote an appeal for the money that was required to sustain the institution.

"We desire to put into immediate operation our manufacturing department – a grist mill and a saw mill, and cotton and woolen mills, and to manufacture agricultural and other useful implements. It will require one hundred thousand dollars to put this institution in successful operation. While it is for the development of colored citizens, it proscribes neither race nor sex, nor age or condition. All those of good moral character will be admitted. Colored orphans, now uncared for, will find a home and be prepared for the duties of life."

Tennessee Manual Labor University.
Rev Peter. Lowry, President of the Tennessee Manual Labor University, leaves for Memphis to-day, to solicit aid for that institution. *En route,* he will stop at Springfield, Clarksville, Paris and Brownsville. We commend him to the favorable consideration of all who appreciate the objects of his mission.

Republican Banner, October 8, 1868

Peter Lowery continued to receive donations as he travelled across the state, but there was little support from the white Christian Church. Early in 1868 one hundred students were already being educated at the school, and more money was needed for necessary improvements. In May, 1868, Daniel Wadkins, a local Negro minister and a noted educator, was hired to help raise money for the school. Samuel Lowery was also working on behalf of the school, and his travels took him from Cincinnati to Cleveland, and on to New York, where he received a contribution from noted former-abolitionist Horace Greeley, and then to Washington, where President Andrew Johnson made a sizeable donation.

But charges of financial impropriety were soon leveled against both the younger Lowery and Reverend Wadkins. The Lowerys and Daniel Wadkins were staunch Republicans, and given the political environment in Tennessee in the late 1860s – with old-line Democrats in fierce opposition to progressive Republicans – suspicions arose that conservative leaders within the white Christian Church, along with their political allies, might be trying to undermine the school.

The white Christian Church conducted a public investigation. Both Samuel Lowery and Wadkins would be exonerated, but the relationship between Wadkins and the senior Lowery had become acrimonious, and the controversy crippled the institution's credibility. In 1871 the school was operating and the farm was in cultivation, but the land was still unpaid for. The Tennessee Manual Labor University lacked the resources to maintain the institution envisioned by Peter and Samuel Lowery, and in 1879 Peter Lowry made another appeal.

"On account of indebtedness, for the last few years we have been compelled to suspend holding school at our institution. Except for the timely aid extended by Judge William F. Cooper, the land and building would have reverted to vendors. May the Lord bless Judge Cooper. I especially ask the white people to extend aid to this university, and aid in diffusing knowledge among the colored youths of this state.

"I believe that fostering colored institutions of learning will be the strongest argument against the folly of colored emigration that now prevails among the colored people of the South. This is the only institution in the United States where colored youth can obtain an education without money. Colored people ought to come up to this good work as one man, but I regret to say that the proper zeal and liberality has never been manifested on their part for the welfare of this university."

Following Peter Lowery's final unsuccessful fundraising trip to New York City in 1881, the institution for which he had worked so hard ceased operation. Samuel Lowery had been deeply involved during the first years of the school, but he had also studied law while he was living near Murfreesboro.

When the 1870 census was taken, Samuel and his wife, Adora,

resided near the school with their seven children, and at the end of the year he was admitted to the Nashville bar. Four months later, presumably after moving to Nashville, he became the first man of color licensed to practice in the federal courts in Tennessee, and in 1880 he would become the first Negro lawyer in the nation admitted to practice law before the United States Supreme Court.

Samuel Lowery Admitted to U.S. Supreme Court (1880)

Samuel Lowery was an impressive orator, and he was not reluctant to share his political views. In the spring of 1875 he had spoken to a largely black audience at a colored convention on emigration.

"Coming forward, Lowery said unless there was a decided change in political feeling, he was in favor of depopulating Tennessee of every Negro residing in it. The vagrant act was confining many Negroes in county workhouses, but not a single white person had been confined there. A Negro would be sent to the Penitentiary for stealing a gingercake, but a white man who would kill a hundred Negroes would not be harmed. He was in favor of putting the whites of Tennessee on probation, and if the condition of blacks was not bettered after ten years, he was for emigrating."

When he made his speech, Lowery had already decided to leave the city. Three days later, shortly before he moved his family to Huntsville, Alabama, Lowery took two of his daughters to see a small exhibition on raising silk. It was given by James W. Theobald, an Englishman who lived in Nashville. Lowery's fifteen-year-old daughter, Ruth, named for her deceased Cherokee grandmother, convinced Samuel to buy some silkworm eggs, which hatched soon after the family arrived in Huntsville.

Ruth was fascinated by the prospect of making silk. In 1876 she and her father won premiums for the silk-related items they exhibited at the county fair in Huntsville. Ruth died the following year, and around the time of her death, Samuel spoke at a political rally on the grounds of the Huntsville courthouse. His speech, delivered in front of an audience that included both blacks and whites, received notice in a local newspaper.

"Samuel Lowery made one of the most incendiary speeches we have heard. He assailed Judge Wyeth for not having Negroes on juries, and charged that Negroes cannot get justice from white juries. Lowery said he wanted all of his civil rights. He could not go into some of the churches in Huntsville and sit where he pleased. He said he did not feel like a free man in the South. He said he walked with his head down, and bent like a hoop on a barrel."

Samuel, likely acting to honor his daughter, continued to learn as much as he could about making silk, and he kept pursuing the vision he shared with his father about helping uneducated blacks in the South escape poverty. Despite his widely-known political views, Lowry managed to secure the help of Reuben Chapman, who had served as Governor of Alabama in the 1840s. Chapman provided twenty-five acres of land, and what was referred to as Lowery's Industrial Academy was planned. When he travelled north in 1878 to solicit the money he needed to move forward, the New York Times took notice.

"Samuel Lowery, a colored lawyer of Huntsville, Alabama, is the secretary and treasurer of an institution for the educational and industrial training of colored youth. He thinks that the cost per acre of silk culture would be the same as that of cotton, and estimates production at from 150 to 200 pounds of silk per acre – worth $4 to $6 per pound in New York. Mr. Lowery has come north to establish the necessary market, and also to procure the improved labor-saving devices employed in the preparation of silk for market."

He continued to be an outspoken proponent of black advancement, and in May, 1879, the year after his trip to New York, Lowery returned to Nashville as a delegate to the National Conference of Colored Men. Several newspaper reporters covered the event.

"Cedar Street and the avenues leading to the capitol were alive with people of all classes, condition, and color. By noon the galleries of the hall of the House of Representatives were packed with people of both sexes and races. Not a seat was vacant."

There were other speakers and then Samuel Lowery was recognized and he presented his resolution.

"The Democratic party of the South has proclaimed to the world that this is a white man's government, made expressly for them, and that they will not suffer – at the peril of their lives – the choice of colored men to positions of honor and emoluments where they are in the majority. They will resort to the disruption of this government rather than permit the civil and political equality of our race in the South.

"We have trusted in vain the hope to enjoy liberty in this land of our ancestry, from whose unpaid labors its wealth and prosperity have sprung. The pledge given us by Republicans for freedom and human rights has been stealthily snatched from us, and our posterity, without any redress. We are denied the right of a trial by a jury of our countrymen, and as a consequence, misdemeanors are executed as felonies, and the courts are crowding the prisons, coal mines, and penitentiaries where our race, under the pretense of law, is sold into slavery as in days of yore.

"They deny school privileges to improve the minds of our youths equally. We toil day and night to make more cotton for the landlord than we did in slavery, and we enjoy no more than a peck of meat with the labor of our women and children. The Lord has provided a land where we can enjoy all the rights of humanity. Resolved that we pledge our efforts to aid this cause for our freedom."

A year later Samuel Lowery returned to New York to solicit funds for his industrial academy, and while he was there he spoke to an audience in Brooklyn. The following day, news of his speech – "The Colored Exodus" – was reported in a local newspaper.

"Mr. Lowery opened his address by saying that the exodus by the colored people of the South was a fixed fact. The colored people had been made free men, yet they by no means enjoyed the privileges of free men. For years they had been living on the hope of having the promises held out to them carried into effect, but the white people having the power had not used it wisely.

"Colored people did not want to leave the South. It was their home. But repeated tramplings on their rights compelled them to do so. The colored men were the laborers of the South – they gathered the cotton, and were so active in other enterprises that without their labor and assistance, commerce in the South would dwindle into insignificance.

"Colored people were not given education, were not permitted to enjoy their political rights, were not recognized in the jury system, were not paid a fair price for their labor, and no respect whatsoever was shown to colored women. Regarding the political system, intimidation was the rule. White men were not punished for intimidation, and ballots were not counted. In order to stop the exodus, it was necessary that all these wrongs should be righted."

Lowery returned to Alabama and did what he could to make his school a success, but his efforts were in vain. He ran for a seat in the state legislature, but ultimately withdrew. Rather than continue to oppose the restrictions of Jim Crow through legislation, Lowery turned his back on politics and stopped practicing law. Instead he focused his energy on establishing silk manufacturing in Alabama, and extending it across the South.

In 1884 he attended the World Exposition in New Orleans. Competing against silk manufacturers from China, France, Japan, Italy, Mexico and other exhibitors in the United States, Lowery received the grand prize for the silk he

1884 New Orleans Exposition

produced. In 1885, following his triumph in New Orleans, Lowery expressed his intentions.

"My plans are to secure a suitable tract of land, and with the building of a good cocoonery, to raise a million silkworms. I propose to give employment to a class of boys and girls that are now idle, and teach them a skilled business, which will make them valuable citizens. With an apprenticeship of three months, the labor will be worth $1.50 to $3 per day. I will manufacture two dozen silk handkerchiefs and 200 yards of ribbon daily. I raised 200,000 cocoons this year and now have 250,000 eggs for next year's crop, and I have 500 mulberry trees."

His success in New Orleans led him to found a company with a group of prominent white investors, but the time and expense of mastering silk production had left him under more and more financial pressure. In 1886 he conveyed his circumstances to a longtime acquaintance.

"I am very poor. I have not yet struck a bonanza, but I still hope for a competency yet ahead. I have tried to abandon hope and become indifferent to its inviting fields, but when I do, I am really not myself. I know that I do not hope vainly or recklessly."

But as was the case with other goals he had pursued, his dreams related to silk would not come to pass. In the end, like his father, the harvest he reaped was largely one of disappointment. Peter Lowery slowly drifted into obscurity, and when his obituary appeared in February, 1888, no mention was made of how hard he had worked to elevate his race. But his eulogy captured the nature of his spirit.

"Brother Lowery obeyed the gospel in his young days and had been a proclaimer of the gospel for 40 years. He lived as a devoted member of the church until the day of his death. I never saw anyone who seemed to be more devoted to the Christian life than he. I do not remember ever meeting him that he did not ask me how I was getting along spiritually, and express his hopes of a brighter and better world than this."

Samuel Lowery slowly faded from prominence as well. Of the thirteen children born to his wife, Adora, seven were alive at the close of the century, but in 1900 the aging couple only had their youngest child living at home. By then he was supporting his family by selling the vegetables he raised in his truck garden. He was nearly seventy when he died near Huntsville, and when his funeral took place in June, 1902, much of what he had planted – much of what was growing in his garden at the time of his death – was still not ready for harvest.

By the time Thomas Lowery – the son of Samuel Lowery and

grandson of Peter Lowery – died in 1947, twenty-one-year-old
Medgar Evers, who had fought in the invasion of Normandy in
1944, was poised to enroll at Alcorn College, Martin Luther King
was an eighteen-year-old student at Morehouse College, nineteen-
year-old James Lawson was a student who would soon be imprisoned
for refusing to serve in the military, nine-year-old Diane Nash was
attending a Catholic school in Chicago, seven-year-old Jim Zwerg
was growing up in Appleton, Wisconsin, seven-year-old John Lewis
was living in poverty with his family in Pike County, Alabama,
Jackie Robinson had just finished his rookie season with the Brooklyn
Dodgers, and the age of Jim Crow was starting to unravel.

7

Daniel Wadkins

Nashville Union, March 21, 1865

Although he was a prominent teacher, minister, and political figure in Nashville, there is a degree of mystery surrounding the origins of Daniel Wadkins. He consistently claimed to have been born in Tennessee, but on one occasion he indicated that he had come to the state around 1835 – when he was a young man. And while the year of his birth appears in census records as having been as early as 1814 and as late as 1826, he was likely born in 1818. The identities of his parents, who were listed in the 1880 Census as natives of Virginia, are unknown, but during a speech he made in 1865, he related that his father, "a colored man," had fought under Andrew Jackson at

92

Horseshoe Bend, in the noted 1814 battle against a faction of the Creek nation.

In that same speech he mentioned that his father had sent him to school, but Wadkins failed to say if that was when he learned to read and speak Greek, as well as to speak some Latin and Hebrew. Aside from being tutored by Rev. Tolbert Fanning of Franklin College, it is unclear how much education Daniel Wadkins received, but he would spend a significant part of his life as a teacher, and he ultimately wrote an essay about early black education in Nashville. His account began with a period nearly thirty years before the outbreak of the Civil War.

H. R. W. Hill

"In March, 1833, Alphonso M. Sumner opened a small school for colored children on Church Street, there being an understanding that none but free children should attend. But H. R. W. Hill, a high-toned Christian gentleman, and a few others permitted their slaves to attend. Sumner was a barber as well as a teacher, and being obliged to spend most of his time in the shop, he employed me to assist him in teaching.

"The school consisted of twenty scholars and was satisfactorily conducted, but Sumner was accused of writing and sending letters containing important information to two fugitive slaves then living in Detroit. In consequence of these letters being discovered, Sumner was nearly whipped to death and compelled to leave the state, never to return. This occurrence occasioned so much feeling against colored schools that the free colored people, then numbering about 200 and being intimidated, thought it best to wait 'until the storm blew over.'"

Following his beating by the mob of vigilantes, Alphonso Sumner fled the city, perhaps to Cincinnati. The school for free black children was closed for a time, and then the progressive mayor, Henry Hollingsworth, was unsuccessful in his push for the establishment of such a school. The account by Daniel Wadkins described the continuing struggle to educate children of color in Nashville.

"There were no more schools until January, 1838, when the most energetic free colored citizens got up a petition to have a school for free children, which would be taught by a white man. John Yandle of Wilson County was employed and taught for two years. During this time there was an average of about thirty students who learned to read and write, and learn something of arithmetic and geography. But he could not teach them grammar, and I assisted him during the last year he taught. He was a Christian-hearted gentleman, and though threatened with violence more than once, he was not further troubled. Finding other business that paid better, he finally quit teaching.

"In 1841 Mrs. Sarah Porter, later Widow Sarah Player, opened a school in her house on Broad Street, and during that year she had about 25 scholars. I assisted her the next year, and she had a much larger school. The school gave general satisfaction, and the following year it was moved to a house south of Church Street. In 1845 she moved her school to Crawford Street, where she taught until 1856."

A number of years later James C. Napier recalled some of what he remembered about Sallie Player, who had been his teacher in the 1850s.

"Mrs. Sallie Player was a most delightful teacher. She was a woman of some education. Her husband, although a slave, also had some education. He belonged to a very excellent family of white people, whose slaves enjoyed every privilege that free people enjoyed."

Her husband, James Player, was owned by Thompson Player,

who was identified as a planter. His wife, Emma, was the daughter of Thomas Yeatman, who had been one of Nashville's wealthiest citizens before his death in 1833. Napier also noted that Daniel Wadkins received a measure of religious instruction at Franklin College, which was located a few miles east of Nashville. Franklin College was founded on strict religious principles by Tolbert Fanning, who prepared Wadkins, along with a handful of other Negroes, to be a minister in the Christian Church.

In his essay Wadkins also mentioned three other early black educators – Mrs. A. L. Tate, who taught for two or three years on College Street, Mrs. S. Thomas, who opened a school in 1846 and taught for one year, and Rufus Conrad, who would also have a school.

It must have been early in his career when Daniel Wadkins married his wife, Eliza, a slightly older, light-skinned, free woman who was born in North Carolina. They had two children by 1850, and that year, despite the widespread opposition to black education, Daniel was listed in the census as a "school teacher," the only Negro in the city to be classified in that manner.

"During 1841 I opened a school in a house on Front Street, near where the jail stood. There was an average of 35 scholars, and although it was understood that these schools were for free children, not a session was taught without slave children being admitted, and they were treated precisely as the nominally free.

"In 1844 I moved my school to a building near Lick Branch, between College and Cherry Streets, where I taught a large day school, and a night school, assisted by Joseph Manly and George Barber. Many young people acquired the rudiments of an English education during those six years. During this time the school numbered about 50 pupils. In 1850 the school was moved to the corner of Vine and Crawford Streets, where it was well attended. It was moved again in 1853, and the following year it was taught in the Second Colored Baptist Church, south of Demonbruen, near Summer Street."

Many years later James C. Napier described one of the buildings in which Wadkins conducted his school. "He taught school in an old church right over a branch. It was up on stilts, and was built for the slaves by their owners." He was able to teach in some places longer than in others.

"In 1855 I opened my school on the corner of Line and McLemore, continuing about two months and having about 60 scholars. One night a number of citizens, about a dozen in all, called at my residence. I was told, 'not to teach that Negro school another day. If Negro schools are taught, it must be done in Illinois, Indiana, or in some other free state – not here among the slaves.' I told them that 'able lawyers had been consulted, who said it was not against the law.' They replied that, 'the neighborhood objected, and if it is opened, you must look out for the consequences.'

"The next year it reopened for seven months on College Street, a little north of the Louisville Depot. Then the Captain of the Police came and said, 'he was ordered by the City Council to close the Negro School, and it must not be taught another day – that they were in possession of a great many facts that convinced them that the Negroes contemplated a general insurrection, and there was great excitement not only in Nashville, but throughout the South.'

The deepening political chasm surrounding slavery had turned more toxic during the 1856 presidential campaign. James Buchanan, the Democratic nominee, favored maintaining slavery, but his opponent, John C. Fremont, the first candidate nominated by the newly-formed Republican Party, ran in opposition to slavery. One of the campaign tactics employed by pro-slavery partisans was spreading the rumor that Fremont would foment insurrections among the nation's slaves, and many of those being held in slavery believed that freedom might come in the wake of a victory by Fremont.

By the fall of 1856 the pro-slavery campaign strategy was having an impact across the slave states. Whites, and particularly slave owners, focused their attention on the possibility of a slave uprising, while an unknown number of slaves, having been exposed to the rhetoric surrounding the issue, must have at least considered using violence to gain their freedom. Planned slave uprisings were reported from Texas to Maryland, and although many of those reports were only based on rumor, they gained considerable traction. At the end of November the Republican Banner contained information from the area around Clarksville.

"Considerable excitement exists throughout the adjacent country on account of the discovery of preparations of an insurrection among the slave population, to come off on the 24th of December. In the neighborhood of Louisa Furnace, a plan to blow up a church was discovered and thwarted. A keg of gunpowder had been placed under the building ready for the fatal match. A large collection of arms and ammunition had also been discovered and seized. Among the Negroes arrested and confined are the supposed ringleaders. The general opinion that prevails is that the plot is deep laid, and embraces the slaves throughout a wide extent of territory."

In counties across the region, groups of white vigilantes quickly formed. Only six days after the first newspaper report, there was an account of a shooting just a few miles north of Nashville.

"A Negro man belonging to Mrs. Connell, living in the neighborhood of Goodlettsville, was shot and died from the effects of the wound. The boy was at his wife's house, and the patrol called to ascertain if he had a pass. The Negro refused to allow the patrol to enter, and the door having been forced, he attacked the patrol with a hickory stick. The patrol shot the boy in self-defense."

On the same day of the killing in Goodlettsville, the City Council in Nashville took action against the supposed insurrection. Godfrey Fogg, a prominent local attorney and alderman, presented a comprehensive bill that was immediately passed. Five provisions were described in a local newspaper article.

As the City Council was passing its far-reaching ordinance, Nashville was increasingly apprehensive about reports that were being received.

"Yesterday our city was rife with rumors in relation to the insurrection at different points along the river. We understand that six Negroes who had been found guilty at the iron works were killed a few days since, and that two white men, known accessories in the matter, had nearly been whipped to death. It is also reported that four Negroes were hung today in Dover. We believe these outbreaks have been instigated

CITY COUNCIL.

Called meeting—Dec. 4.—The Board of Mayor and Aldermen met yesterday pursuant to a call for the purpose of adopting additional police regulations, and adopting such measures, in view of the rumored intentions of the slave population, as circumstances might require.

Ald. Fogg presented a memorial from a meeting of the citizens suggesting the adoption of such measures as in their judgment might be deemed necessary.

Ald. Fogg presented a bill in accordance with the memorial, providing in substance:

1st. There shall be no schools for negroes, free or slave, taught either by white persons or black.

2d. Any white man found teaching blacks shall be fined $50.

3d. There shall be no assemblage of negroes after sun down for the purpose of attending preaching; and no colored man shall be allowed to preach to colored people, and no white man after night.

4th. The Mayor of the city be authorized to employ such additional Police force, for day and night, for the next thirty days, as he may deem necessary, not exceeding fifty; and for thirty days the Police shall go on duty at 7 P. M., and their pay be increased to $2 per night.

5th. Prohibits free persons of color, removing from other counties, residing in this city, and provides for the arrest and imprisonment of all such. Also provides for the arrest of all free resident blacks under suspicious circumstances.

The bill passed three readings, became a law, and was ordered to be published. And the Board adjourned.

Republican Banner, December 5, 1856

98

by white men from the North – missionaries of Northern Abolitionism."

Two days later a rumor about an insurrection reached Springfield, 25 miles north of Nashville. The local vigilance committee issued a report that was signed by each of its members.

"A young man came to Springfield and told us that on the previous night, he and five others came on about 100 Negroes at an abolition speech. Some of the Negroes fired on the patrol. The patrol shot one Negro in the arm, and captured ten. However we have recently learned from various reliable sources in the neighborhood that the whole story is a fabrication."

A report from Murfreesboro also cast doubt on the rumors that were swirling across the region.

"Thursday evening there was some excitement in town, which increased after dark and continued throughout the succeeding day. It was not caused by an insurrection of the slaves, but by a sort of Vigilance Committee, or mob, that whipped, as we have been told, nearly every free Negro to be found in town, and ordered each one to leave and to return no more."

Reports continued to be received from outlying areas to the north and east of Nashville. Of some 35 slaves who were arrested and interrogated in Gallatin, four were hanged five days before Christmas. Given the lack of surviving records, the extent of a planned slave uprising in Tennessee is unclear, and the number of slaves who were killed is unclear as well.

With his school shut down, Daniel Wadkins was not able to teach during the years leading up to the Civil War. In 1860, when he may have also been serving as a preacher, he was supporting Eliza and their five children by working as a farm laborer, and their sixth and last child would soon be on the way. A few months after Nashville was captured by Federal troops, Wadkins received permission from Reverend Nelson Merry to open a school in the First Colored Baptist Church, and he resumed his teaching career.

"In the fall of 1862 I opened a school in the First Colored Baptist Church, assisted by J. M. Shelton and his wife. This school remained in operation for eighteen months, and in 1864 I commenced a school on High Street, near Line. From time to time I was assisted by Mrs. Lethe Elliot, Mrs. Sarah Ledwell, Mrs. H. G. Barber, Miss Ode Barber, Mrs. Mariah Patterson, and Miss Selena Walker. There were about 150 pupils in attendance, and the tuition was from $1 to $1.50 a month."

In his essay Daniel Wadkins did not describe some of the struggles he had faced. After he moved his school to High Street, a white missionary named Joseph McKee arrived from out of state and opened a school for Negro students – free of charge – in Reverend Merry's church. Competition for students soon brought Wadkins into conflict with both McKee and Merry, but he had other troubles with which to contend. His oldest child, eighteen-year-old Daniel, had already worked to build the imposing fortification that would become known as Fort Negley, just south of Nashville, and then – only a month after the opening of McKee's school – he enlisted in the 13th Colored Infantry. Young Daniel Wadkins would survive the Battle of Nashville, but his father's school would soon close its doors.

Despite all the times Daniel Wadkins had moved his school over the years, his commanding presence must have provided a degree of continuity. Decades later one of his former students, Fisk Jubilee Singer Ella Sheppard, described his teaching style.

"He gave out each word with such an explosive jerk of the head and spring around the body, that it commanded our profound respect. His eyes seemed to see everyone in the room, and woe be to the one who giggled or was inattentive, whether pupil or visitor, for such a one constantly felt a whack from his long rattan. He used the old Webster blue back spelling book. Each class stood up against the wall, head erect, hands down, toes straight. They spelled in unison in a musical intonation, swaying their bodies from side to side, with perfect rhythmical precision on each syllable, which we thought grand."

With the war winding down and the winter of 1865 giving way to spring, the elder Wadkins received a notable honor. He was the principal figure at a massive observance that took place after the Tennessee legislature ratified the Thirteenth Amendment – which would prohibit slavery in the United States. An article describing the event appeared in a local newspaper.

"Yesterday the colored people of Nashville held a high festival in celebration of their deliverance from slavery through the ratification, by the people of Tennessee, of the amendment of the Constitution abolishing slavery. The streets were thronged with dark and eager faces, and at half past ten the procession entered the public square.

"Preceded by marshals on horseback and a military band, on it passed, rank after rank – the United States flag, a carriage with the orator of the day, Reverend Daniel Wadkins, citizens, Sunday school boys and girls, women, school boys, fifes and drums, and lastly a long line of carriages, generally filled with well-dressed females. The appearance of the children was admirable – their bright faces were gleaming with enjoyment.

"There were among the banners the following mottoes. 'We aspire to elevation through industry, economy, and Christianity.' 'We can forget and forgive the wrongs of the past.' 'We ask not for social, but for political equality.' 'Will Tennessee be amongst the first or the last to allow her sable sons the elective franchise?'

"After passing through the principal streets, the procession continued to Watkins Grove where, amid music and waving flags, Reverend Wadkins was called to preside over the assembly. The exercises commenced with the singing of "Praise God from whom all blessings flow," and a touching silence came. Heads were uncovered and there was a prayer that heaven would bless the occasion, and deliver 'all our race' from bondage."

Then after he acknowledged the honor of being asked to speak, Daniel Wadkins addressed the audience.

"Thirty years ago I was told that my father had fought as soldier in the last war with England, at Horseshoe Bend and other places, under General Jackson. I was sent by my father to school, and received a fair English education. When I grew up I asked why, if my father and other colored men fought for their country, their sons were held in bondage? I asked intelligent white people, 'What did they fight for?' The reply was, 'For liberty.' But I asked, 'Where is the liberty they won? I have seen my father go to the ballot box and vote. Why am I not permitted to do the same thing?' I was told it was because I lived in a slave state.

"On the 1st of January, 1863, President Lincoln issued his proclamation, declaring the colored people in several parts of the country free. We were told that was merely a military measure – that when the war was over, old master and old mistress would come back and call upon us all to beg their pardon for going away from them. We were told that after some had been hanged as a warning to the rest, we should have to go to work for them again.

"What have we met for today? Not to celebrate that proclamation, but the occasion that took place in that capitol a few weeks ago when we, every man, were declared free. Years ago I heard of "free soil," and I often wondered how it felt to be on free soil. A few miles from

Cincinnati I stepped on free soil at last, and I thought it felt better. Little did I think that I should ever have the pleasure of addressing free colored men and women on free soil in Tennessee.

"In this state, in 1834, the Constitution was 'amended,' and the vote, formerly enjoyed, was taken away from all colored men in Tennessee. Let those who made Tennessee free remember that we now want them to take another step. It is said that we have not the necessary intelligence to vote, but have we enough intelligence to fight? Some time ago it was said that a white man with a stick in his hand could rout a whole regiment of colored folks. It does not look so now."

The Civil War ended less than a month later, but difficult times lay ahead for Daniel Wadkins. He ended his essay on education with a single sentence. "The school operated until the Fisk School was

Former Union Barracks, first site of Fisk School

opened as a free school in 1865, it and eight other schools taught by colored teachers closed." However painful it was to see his career as an educator come to an end, he was resilient. In the progressive political climate of the late 1860s, Wadkins sought to advance his position and serve his people through gaining political office. He was elected to the City Council in 1867, but was removed by A. E. Alden, the radical mayor, and the next year he ran for County Register and was defeated.

But by then Wadkins had agreed to play a key role in the establishment of the Tennessee Manual Labor School, an institution for Negroes that was led by Rev. Peter Lowery. He corresponded with Frederick Douglass, and after receiving his written endorsement, Wadkins embarked on a fundraising campaign that required extensive travel and took him to a number of states. He was later accused of misappropriating funds, but after a prolonged and public investigation, he was exonerated of any wrongdoing.

Benevolent Enterprise.

Elder Daniel Wadkins, an intelligent colored gentleman, duly accredited agent of the Tennessee Manual Labor School—distant from Nashville some twenty-five miles—is now in this city soliciting aid to complete the payment for three hundred acres of land, and for the necessary school buildings, the whole sum required being $20,000.

This institution is incorporated by the Legislature of Tennessee, is located in a populous district where it is greatly needed, and its benefits are restricted to no class, creed or color. The project has the countenance of all classes, and we hope our own citizens, notwithstanding the many demands made from day to day upon their charity, will make room for this appeal in behalf of a people not able to help themselves. Help the poor and the needy, the Lord will repay.

Pittsburgh Weekly Gazette May 5,1869

Because of his moderate approach to racial matters, Wadkins was recognized as a conservative. At one public meeting in 1869 he opposed Negro emigration from Tennessee, and in another he argued that white people were not inclined to oppress blacks and that the State Legislature would not pass any laws restricting their rights. More controversy followed in 1871 when his former mentor at Franklin College, Tolbert Fanning, made a number of racially insulting remarks that were reported in a local newspaper.

"Reverend Tolbert Fanning said Negroes were opposed to the white race, and most of them were under the control of men hostile to the best interests of the South. He said Negroes had no moral conception of right and wrong. He believed they had a soul, but that God intended them only for a certain place. Mr. Fanning said the Negro was physically, mentally, and morally below the condition that we want people in, and that he was made a useful laborer by putting him in slavery."

Wadkins was already regarded as being too compliant by many in the local black community, and because of his earlier relationship with Fanning, he must have felt especially compelled to make a public response.

"As a moral and religious teacher, and in view of my former confidence in Elder Tolbert Fanning, I have been asked why I ever spoke highly of a man who would say that we were the enemies of the white people, and many other hard things. He was more friendly to us when we were in slavery, and our value in dollars and cents might have had something to do with it.

"His most objectionable statements are that Negroes are the enemies of the white people,

Tolbert Fanning

that it is impossible to educate Negroes, and that Negroes are irrecoverably lost. In view of the conduct of Negroes since their introduction into this country, it is not easy to see how an intelligent Christian gentleman logically reaches such a conclusion.

"We cannot afford to be the enemies of any portion of our fellow citizens. Is it true that we cannot be educated? Who has patiently and honestly tried and found it a failure? If Elder Fanning will condescend to meet me at the Preacher's Union Association next Tuesday at 2:30 PM, he will have the opportunity of seeing a colored man, and not only hearing a little Latin and Greek, but also Hebrew. And Mr. Fanning says that we are irrecoverably lost. I rejoice that we are irrecoverably lost to slavery. I trust that our destiny is fixed on the side of perpetual freedom.

"I may be asked why I object so seriously to the specified utterances. If none of us deny that we are the enemies of the white people, those who are guilty of perpetuating unlawful acts will be encouraged to persist in them."

In his response to Tolbert, Wadkins had referred to himself as "a moral and religious teacher." Acting in that capacity a few months later, he released a 32 page pamphlet – "An Original Essay Containing Recommendations, Suggestions, Advice, and Instruction for the Colored People." A local review identified the historical significance of the work.

"In this little work – the first on any subject ever published by a colored man in Tennessee – is given a vast amount of sound, practical advice peculiarly suited to the condition of a recently emancipated people. We commend the rules of thought and conduct which the author lays down in a clear, concise style."

A subsequent article contained a selection from what Wadkins had written.

"It is very hard to throw off old habits, however costly or injurious. But we must consult our judgment and sense of duty more, and old habits and our feeling less, or we will miss our aim. Let us not forget that one of the great sources of knowledge is hearing. Delight more in hearing good books read, than in hearing cursing or swearing or obscene language. It is disgraceful and hurtful to try to live without work. He who tries hardest to live by shirking work is the worst man among us, and should be shunned as a deadly poison."

Despite all his efforts, Daniel Wadkins watched as the hope that had blossomed in the early days after emancipation fell under a deepening shadow. Those who had sustained slavery and who sought to restore as much as possible of the world they had known before the war, were returning to power. In order to utilize his gifts, Wadkins turned more and more to preaching, but he soon encountered additional roadblocks.

He received economic support from several congregations for his work as an evangelist, and by the time his pamphlet was published, Wadkins was living in Memphis. He not only established a church in Memphis, he would also bring together congregations in Mississippi and Kentucky. As a traveling evangelist, Wadkins was dependent on local white churches for the use of their facilities during off-hours, but because he preached to racially mixed audiences, his requests were often refused by the churches he approached.

Death of Elder Daniel Wadkins.

The death of Rev. Daniel Wadkins, a prominent colored divine of this city, will be a great loss to the colored people of this community, and the absence of his moral influence will be generally felt. He was a man of considerable information, educated above the average of his race. He enjoyed the confidence of the white people, and commanded the respect and reverence of his own race. He was one of the old citizens of the place. He was chaplain to the penitentiary under Gov. Hawkins' administration. His funeral will take place from the first (colored) Baptist church this evening at 3 o'clock.

Nashville American, May 11, 1883

Daniel Wadkins, who had been a member of the First Christian Church in Nashville since 1840, was present in 1874 when church leaders from across the region convened and introduced a proposition that gave a further indication of the depth of the shadow that covered the issue of race.

"Resolved, that we recommend to our colored brethren who have membership with whites, whenever practicable to withdraw themselves and form congregations of their own, believing that by so doing they will advance the cause of Christ among themselves."

Wadkins was nearing the age of sixty, but he continued to be active. By 1880 he was publishing a journal called the *Educator and Reformer*, in which he encouraged the same sort of moral behavior that had been recommended in his pamphlet. In 1881 the governor appointed him to be chaplain of the State Penitentiary, but he slowly slipped from prominence.

In the spring of 1883, the month before he died of heart disease, Daniel Wadkins was referred to as already deceased, but when he died that May, his funeral was well attended and his accomplishments and contributions were remembered. And for the decades that followed his passing, he was remembered by students he had educated, and by those to whom he had given guidance.

8

Randall Bartholomew Vandavell

"Yesterday morning the funeral of Rev. Randall B. Vandavell, colored, was one of the largest ever seen in Nashville. The crowds began to gather early at the Tabernacle, and 5000 were present by 10:30. The white Baptist pastors came in a body and occupied seats on the platform with the colored pastors of the city. The funeral procession arrived, and the audience arose and received the cortege in profound silence, broken only by the notes of the funeral dirge.

"Now and then, amidst the lamentation of friends of the dead pastor, members of his church, under the stress of religious feeling, began to shout. That weird, piercing note of grief, with the deep voices of the speakers and the music, lifted the audience. The services continued four hours, and all that time there was this awesome solemnity. Such a sight was never seen here before, and those who witnessed it can never forget it. A good, grand man has gone to glory and to God, and thousands, of both races, mourn his loss."

The funeral at the Tabernacle, which would later become known as Ryman Auditorium, took place at the beginning of 1899. More than a decade earlier, in the mid-1880s, Rev. William J. Simmons, President of the State University, Louisville Kentucky, compiled a book on notable American men of color, and he included an account of the life of Randall Bartholomew Vandavell.

"This good man has become an honored citizen, a useful preacher, and a man distinguished among the race and his brethren in the ministry. His success has been wrung from the severest circumstances."

The details Simmons provided were either drawn from notes he took in an interview, from a written account supplied by Reverend Vandavell, or from both. Simmons wrote in the third person, but the information clearly came directly from Vandavell, who would have written, or spoken, in the first person. What follows is presented in its original form – as it would have been related by Vandavell.

"I was born at Neely's Bend, on the Cumberland River, ten miles above Nashville. My mother's name was Sylvonia. She was the property of a Major Hall, who had brought her from Virginia when she was a baby in her mother's arms. My father's name was Lewis. He was the property of a man named Foster and served as a coachman. He was allowed to visit his wife only once a year. There were eleven children in the family."

In the account published by Rev. Simmons, the year Vandavell was born is given as 1832, but he might have been born as early as 1823 – the year that is carved on his tombstone. The 1870 Census

9

Ella Sheppard and the Fisk Jubilee Singers

In 1865 Ella Sheppard came back to Nashville, where she had been born fourteen years earlier. She was coming to visit her mother, Sarah

Hannah Sheppard. They had been separated for over a decade, and Ella could no longer picture the woman from whom she had been taken. Over the course of their three-month reunion, Sarah conveyed a good bit of family history to her daughter.

At least three generations of Sarah's family had been owned by the Donelsons – one of the founding families of the region. Ella's great-grandmother was a full-blooded Cherokee named Rosa, and her great-grandfather, Rosa's husband, had been born in Africa. But Rosa was not a slave. In order to stay with her husband, she apparently chose to live as though she was owned by the Donelson family. One of Rosa's fourteen children, Rebecca, was Ella's grandmother, and Rebecca's father was a Donelson slave named Jimmie.

Rebecca and Jimmie's daughter, Sarah, was born in 1827, and the information she passed along to Ella about her forbearers appears to have been especially accurate. In 1840, when the estate of Lemuel Donelson was being settled, the names of his slaves were recorded. Sarah was listed as the daughter of Rebecca, and along with Rosa – who was listed as Rose – there was a man named George. Many years later, when she was an old woman, Emily Donelson Walton, Lemuel Donelson's neice, would write about Guinea George, a Donelson slave who had been born in Africa.

Ella did not give the name of her African great-grandfather, but if Rosa's husband was Guinea George – as he likely was – she would have been told about his forceful character and his independent nature. Emily Walton, who was born in 1837, had a clear recollection of Guinea George.

"Every spring he would leave the plantation and go over on an island in the Cumberland River. He would come home in the fall, having camped out all summer, bringing sacks of dried fruits and nuts. He seemed to be a law unto himself. Most of the darkies were afraid of him. So were we children. He would tell the boys in the family about being a cannibal in Africa, and sing weird songs in his own language when at work in the field at cotton picking time. When the sun began to go down he would bring in his bag of cotton. He would put it down and go home, leaving the other slaves at work."

Ella also heard about her great-grandmother. After warning that there would be consequences for anyone who harmed her children while she was away, Rosa would leave the Donelson plantation from time to time and go back to visit her Cherokee homeland.

And Ella learned about her father, Simon Sheppard – the son of an unnamed slave woman and James Glasgow Sheppard, a prominent white North Carolinian who had settled in Mississippi. In 1838 Simon must have accompanied his white, twenty-two-year-old half-brother, Benjamin Harper Sheppard, to Nashville, where Benjamin married Lemuel Donelson's fifteen-year-old daughter, Phereby. By the time the slaves that had been owned by her father were divided in 1840, Phereby and her husband were living two miles southeast of Franklin, on the Williamson County farm where Lemuel had lived and died.

Phereby had been orphaned in 1832, and she was seventeen when she inherited twenty-seven of her father's slaves – including thirteen-year-old Sarah. Ella Sheppard was in her early twenties when some biographical details of her life were published, and as she was approaching old age she wrote more extensively about her life and her family. Taken together, those accounts paint an unusually clear picture of the acutely intelligent and compelling woman who had experienced slavery when she was a girl.

"The last years of my mother's life were lived largely in the past. She often told me incidents of the horrors of slavery, but it is not proper to tell some of the facts I have heard from my mother's lips. At the age of seventeen she was married in the parlor of the mansion. As a slave she was head nurse and housekeeper, and for a while my father was the coachman. Their first child died, and I, the second child, was born six years later.

"My earliest recollection is of my mother's tears over the cruelties of slavery. One day she discovered that the mistress had already begun to train me to spy upon her. I had made my first report, which the mistress magnified, and she threatened mother. Stung by this revelation, mother realized that it would teach me to lie and deceive, and eventually lead to the alienation of our affection. In agony of soul and despair, she caught me up in her arms. While rushing to the river to end it all, she was overtaken by Mammy Viney, who cried out, 'Don't you do it, Honey. Don't you take what you cannot give back.' She raised her eyes to Heaven and said, 'Look Honey, don't you see the clouds of the Lord as they pass by? The Lord has got need of this child.'"

A year earlier, in January of 1853, a slave woman belonging to Dempsey Weaver of Nashville had taken her two children, each under six years old, to the Cumberland River. She had tied their hands and drowned them both, and then drowned herself. Many years later Ella remembered when a slave woman in Nashville had slit the throats of her three daughters before cutting her own throat. That act took place during the first year of the Civil War, and the slave who took her life and the lives of her children was owned by the widow of President James K. Polk.

Sarah's mistress, Phereby Sheppard, had her first child at the age of sixteen and two more children were born before she was twenty. But in 1848, when Phereby was twenty-five, two of her children died of measles only fourteen days apart. The behavior Phereby would soon display may have been distorted by the darkness that had come into her life, or perhaps the darkness was there all along.

Simon Sheppard, Ella's father, was permitted to work for himself, and with another local man of color, Carroll Napier, he established what would become one of the most successful livery stables in Nashville. It was located on Cherry Street, and along with operating a facility that took care of horses, the business specialized in transporting passengers – for twenty-fives cents each – from the railroad depot to various destinations within the city. Ella would have been well aware of how hard he worked.

"My father kept a livery stable. He was doing quite a good business, owning four carriages and eight horses, and he bought himself from his young master, who was his half-brother, for $1800. He had been repeatedly promised by the

CARROLL NAPIER ....SIMON SHEPHERD.
NAPIER & SHEPHERD.

ARE now prepared to keep horses at their LIVERY STABLE, on Cherry Street, below the Verandah, by the day, week or year on favorable terms.

HACKS.

THEY are prepared to accommodate travellers, and transient customers with good hacks.

Passengers to and from the Railroad Depot 25 cents each. A share of custom is respectfully solicited. NAPIER & SHEPHERD.

Jan. 12th, 1854—1y.

Republican Banner, April 17, 1856

mistress, to whom mother belonged, that when he should accumulate $1300 more, he could have my mother. One night when I was three years old, my mother overheard the master pleading with the mistress to keep her promise. He had bought a plantation in Mississippi and they were going there.

"But she angrily cried out, 'Sarah shall *never* belong to Simon. She is *mine* and she shall *die* mine. Let Simon get another wife.' The next morning my broken hearted mother found the mistress alone, and poured out her soul. She finished by declaring, 'If you will immediately sell Ella to her father, I will remain your slave. If you do not, you lose both of us. My baby shall never be a slave.' Mother expected to be whipped to death for her boldness, but the mistress never told the master. The next day I was sold to my father for $350. I remained with my father in Nashville, and my mother was taken to Mississippi."

Late in her life Ella wrote an account of what her mother experienced when she reached Mississippi.

"With the new plantation the master had bought many slaves. On the day of the family's arrival, the slaves were lined up on either side of the avenue leading to the big house, along which passed the master and family, and the Tennessee house slaves. Arriving at her room, the mistress threw herself on the bed weeping. She said, 'Oh Sarah, how can I stand it?' My mother was also weeping for the poor slaves they had just seen.

"Every slave woman wore some sort of long trousers and a long hobble skirt and boots, and either a man's hat or a rag on her head. The girls looked like old women, and the old women looked like dried up animals. They had been so abused that even little girls of ten were misshapen. For a time my mother's grief was secondary to this suffering.

"Not one of the slave women even knew the garments that a woman should wear, nor the rudiments of domestic work. They only knew the severest form of farm life. The master and the mistress, with the aid of the Tennessee slaves, set about to relieve many of these conditions. The few Christians among the house slaves began to pray. My grandfather was the leader of the Christians, and often strengthened my mother's faith by telling her that she should yet join her daughter.

"Slaves often communicated with one another through their songs. When they sang, 'Steal away to Jesus,' it meant that there would be a secret meeting that night to worship the Lord and pray for a better day. My mother was at a prayer meeting in grandfather's cabin when a man from another plantation was present. He was in such agony of soul for the pardon of his sins that he forgot to get a pass. As they knelt in prayer for this soul, they were startled by a loud rap upon the bolted door from the butt of an overseer's whip. The poor penitent was dragged out, tied to a log, and severely whipped, and then he was held until he was claimed by his master."

In 1856 or 1857, after she had been separated from Ella for two or three years, Sarah accompanied Benjamin and Phereby Sheppard back to Nashville for a time.

"Once, when I was five or six years old, I saw my mother. My old master's family was on a visit, and just the day before they were to return, they gave my mother permission to see me for a little while. But when she came to leave me, she found it so hard and screamed so loud, that they said she never should see me again.

"My father had married again, and my stepmother did for me all that a mother could. She was a slave when they married, but my father soon purchased her, paying $1300. Her free papers had not been made out, and it had not been convenient to make the journey to Ohio, the nearest free state. Some six months before the war, my father failed in business – he could not meet certain debts. One night he was secretly warned by a white gentleman that his creditors intended to claim my stepmother. If a man bought his wife, she was considered his slave until free papers were made out, and could be taken for debt the same as any other property."

Simon Sheppard's principal creditor was Jacob McGavock, one of Nashville's wealthiest citizens. McGavock would subsequently win a court case, and take control of Simon's property north of the Capitol.

"My father quickly returned to his house, and hastened my stepmother off for Cincinnati that very night. They went a long distance to a station where they would not be recognized, to take the twelve o'clock train. Soon after, he took me and followed, leaving everything to his creditors. Here he began life over again. We had literally nothing to start with, but collected household furniture piece by piece. My stepmother took in washing and ironing, and when able to do so, she kept a private boarding-house. I attended the Seventh Street colored school, but when I was twelve years old I was obliged to leave my studies on account of ill health.

"When I was nearly fourteen, my mother wrote me that she was in Nashville, and wished me to come and see her. This was after the proclamation, and I remained with her three months, returning then to Cincinnati. I had commenced taking lessons in music. My teacher was a German lady, and she gave me lessons on the piano for a year and a half.

"Then came the sad event that threw my mother and myself upon our own resources, at the same time overwhelming us with grief. My father died of the cholera. We were at the Tawawa Springs, in Xenia, Ohio, where we went every summer, my father coming to see us whenever he had an opportunity. On this sad day mother expected him on the afternoon train, and had started to meet him. I had gone over to Wilberforce School to practice my music when the telegram came, telling of his death. When his affairs were finally settled, on account of a troublesome lawsuit, there was not a cent left for us. Everything went – even my piano.

"Then I had to work for myself till Mr. J. P. Ball, of Cincinnati, adopted me. He offered to give me a thorough musical education, with the understanding that I was to repay him at some future day. I took twelve lessons in vocal music from Madame Rivi. I was the only colored pupil, and I was not allowed to tell who my teacher was. And more than all that, I went in the back way and received my lessons, upstairs in a back room, from nine to quarter of ten at night.

In the middle of the first quarter, circumstances were such Mr. Ball was unable to carry out this purpose.

"A subscription school at Gallatin, Tennessee, then offered me a position. There were thirty-five scholars, but they did not all pay, and from the whole term's work I was able to save but six dollars. With this money I went to Fisk University, with the understanding that I should try to obtain work."

George White

Ella Sheppard likely came into contact with George Leonard White as soon as she got to Fisk. He was a member of the all-Caucasian Fisk faculty, and would become a major figure in Ella's life. White was the son of a blacksmith in rural western New York, and he had left home at fourteen and later become a schoolteacher. He was a devout Christian with a deep sense of social justice, and before the Civil War he ignored local opposition and established a Sunday school in Ohio for black children. Later, driven by his fervent opposition to slavery, he joined the Union and was a veteran of Gettysburg and Lookout Mountain when he arrived in Nashville during the final months of the war.

While working at the local Freedmen's Bureau, White volunteered his services and ended up teaching penmanship and establishing a choir at the Fisk Free Colored School. Although he was not formally trained in music, he had long been enthralled by choruses, and his involvement in music at Fisk would ultimately allow him to address the school's deteriorating financial position. But in 1865, when Ella Sheppard was struggling to make ends meet, that time was still a few years away.

"The first week a friend sent me one music scholar, and in a few weeks I had two others. At the end of the term I was sick, and spent the vacation with my stepmother. I entered school again in the fall and studied till Christmas, and then gave myself entirely to preparing for a concert that was shortly to be given. After the concert I was thrown upon my bed, and not able to do anything. Permission was granted for me to remain at the school, and to help, or pay, as I was able. I would have been forty-four dollars in debt at the end of the year, had it not been for the sewing I did at odd moments, or when confined to my bed. During that vacation I was offered the situation of assistant music teacher in the University."

A year or two after Ella Sheppard became Fisk's first faculty member of color, George White was appointed as Fisk's treasurer, and he became her mentor. The school was chartered as Fisk University in 1867, and the institution soon received praise for the education it was providing. It was expected to become a leading teachers college, but the old Federal army barracks occupied by the school was falling apart. Years later Ella described the suffering that students endured when winter came.

"The school was very poor and food was scarce. Many of us shivered through the winter with not an inch of flannel upon our bodies. The wind whistled around and groaned so fearfully that we trembled in horror in our beds, thinking the sounds were the cries of lost spirits of soldiers who had died in them. Our privations and the limited food began to tell on the vitality of the students. There was no money even for food, much less for repairs. Many a time a special prayer was said for the next meal."

With payments to vendors having to be delayed, and with White sometimes paying bills out of his own pocket, Fisk University limped along until White took action. Ella briefly wrote about the beginning of the Jubilee Singers.

"George L. White asked for volunteers to go north to sing money out of the hearts and pockets of people for our school. I retained my position as an assistant music teacher during the year, and at the close I was requested to remain and help drill the singers during the summer, before we started for the North."

The students who responded to White's call – the members of the first group of Fisk singers – had no idea what lay ahead. Isaac Dickerson, who sang bass, was from Virginia. He remembered seeing his father sold to a slave trader in Richmond. His mother died when he was five years old, and at the age of ten he accompanied his master who fought for the Confederacy. Following the war he was

Isaac Dickerson

taught to read by the son of a Jewish merchant in Chattanooga, and later, while working as a cook for a missionary, he attended school. After becoming a teacher and enduring unrelenting racial hostility from whites, Dickerson came to Fisk, where his affinity for music was soon recognized.

Greene Evans

Greene Evans, who was also a bass, was one of twenty-three children from a slave family in West Tennessee. He was twelve when the war began, and he fled south with his master and the other slaves. When he was separated from his family, he became the servant of a Union officer. Following the war he was a waiter and then a porter, and after hiring a teacher who taught him to read and write, he came to Fisk. Evans worked while taking classes, and between terms he built a schoolhouse and taught before returning to Fisk, where he became noted for his vocal gifts, and for his oratorical ability.

Thomas Rutling, a tenor, was born in Wilson County, some thirty miles east of Nashville. His earliest memory was seeing his mother crying as she was being led away after being sold. He never saw her again. He was around seven years old at the beginning of the Civil War. He was a trusted house servant, but what he overheard in the house would soon be reported to the

Thomas Rutling

rest of the slaves, who were aware that freedom was becoming more and more of a possibility. He was eleven years old when he came to Nashville in 1865, and the wife of a surgeon in the Union army taught him the alphabet and how to spell a few simple words. He entered the Fisk Free Colored School, and in the five years that followed, as he studied and worked to support himself, his vocal ability become more and more apparent.

Benjamin Holmes

Benjamin Holmes was the other tenor. He was a native of South Carolina, and had been taught the alphabet by his father. At the age of six or seven he became the apprentice of a Negro shoemaker, and gradually taught himself to read. He was around fifteen when the war began, and after being sold to a slave trader, he was confined in the slave mart in Charleston. Holmes was distinguished by his ability to read, and he was bought by a merchant who eventually placed him in a store in Nashville. Following the war and after a financial setback, he taught school in the outskirts of Nashville. It was a time of intense racial conflict, and not long after a bullet was fired into his schoolhouse while he was teaching, he enrolled at Fisk, where music awaited him.

Minnie Tate, the youngest of the first group of singers from Fisk, was a contralto, and she was born to free parents in Nashville in 1857. Her mother had been educated with white children and after teaching in the colored community, she had educated Minnie, whose low and resonant voice seemed to be at odds with her diminutive body.

Eliza Walker, another contralto who was short of stature, was born just south of Nashville in Flatrock. Her parents had different owners, and she was the next-to-the-youngest of eight children. The war was underway when Eliza, along with her mother and two of her other children, were liberated. Her father kept an ice house and was able to buy a small home, and although the property was soon lost, Eliza

Minnie Tate

was sent to Fisk at the age of nine. After four years her voice developed and her vocal gift was revealed.

Jennie Jackson was the granddaughter of George Jackson, Andrew Jackson's body servant. She was a soprano, and with her relatively dark complexion, she stood out from the other singers. Her mother was emancipated before Jennie was born, making Jennie free as well. She was brought to Nashville at the age of three, and when she was thirteen she got a job as a nurse, and later took in laundry and worked as a maid. By 1866 she had saved enough money to enter Fisk School, which she was able to attend off and on, depending on her ability to pay a few dollars for tuition. She began singing at Fisk, and George White not only took note of her powerful voice, he gave her a job working for his family.

Eliza Walker

Maggie Porter was also a soprano. She was born in 1853, and like Thomas Rutling, she was born in Wilson County, east of Nashville. When she was seven, with the war becoming more and more imminent, Maggie and her family were brought to Nashville. Her mother and father were separated for a time, but they were reunited before the Emancipation Proclamation was announced. After receiving some education in schools conducted by Daniel Wadkins and Rev. Joseph McKee, Maggie entered the Fisk School when it opened in 1866.

After two years, at the age of fifteen, Porter became a teacher in a school near Bellevue. A few months later, after the schoolhouse burned down under suspicious circumstances, suspicion centered on the Ku Klux Klan. She taught in two other schools, and then George White, who had taken note of her clear, strong voice while she attended Fisk, recruited her to be the lead voice in a concert that would lead to the formation of the Jubilee Singers.

Ella Sheppard, still the only teacher of color at Fisk, was asked by George White to serve as the pianist of the ensemble, and also to join in with her soprano voice. During that summer, before they went on tour, the Fisk students had no intention of performing any songs from slave times. Ella would remember, "learning from each other the songs of our fathers." And she added, "We did not dream of ever using them in public." But she was likely the quiet force behind bringing some old slave songs to George White. Some years later she would explain her understanding of the music that had been born out of the pain and suffering of slavery.

Jennie Jackson

"Shut out from religious culture and instruction – the Bible and the spelling book being chained – slaves were shut into their interpretation of God's word. Their religion was crude, but it had the true essence of Christianity. It gave them a childlike trust in God, as illustrated in the slave songs. Master musicians say that every phase of the human experience, save those of hatred and revenge, are expressed in the slave songs, which they call 'crystalized tears' and 'passion flowers of the slave cabin.' The slave songs were never used by us in public then. They were associated with slavery and the dark past, and represented things to be forgotten. They were sacred to our parents."

George White was enthralled by the first slave songs he heard, and with help from Ella Sheppard, he gathered as many additional songs as could be found. Ella introduced him to "Swing Low, Sweet Chariot," which she had learned from her mother, and over the next decade Ella would transcribe a number of other slave hymns – contributing to a collection that would eventually include over one hundred separate works. But the singers continued to only prepare for classical performances, and the slave songs remained in the background.

With very little money to sustain them and with many wearing borrowed clothes, the troupe left Nashville by train on October 6, 1871. An account written in 1904 described the difficulties the singers initially encountered.

Maggie Porter

"The trip appeared ill-timed. The first stop was at Cincinnati, and that Sunday and Monday the great Chicago fire occurred. People contributed to fire sufferers, not to the Negro singers. The trip was discouraging for weeks. They were denied admittance to hotels and dining rooms, driven from railroad waiting rooms, and shut out from churches which they wished to attend on Sundays. They were frequently believed to be white minstrels giving black-face performances, and on finding that the band was composed of genuine Negroes who sang classical music, the audience frequently exhibited disgust and disappointment.

"They sang operatic arias, oratorios, and cantatas, but nearly every city had organizations that could render the selections equally well. People did not tumble over one another in their haste to hear nine Negroes sing. They would announce that those who cared to remain after the performance could hear old plantation religious melodies, but as northerners did not know the beauties of the quaint folk songs of the plantation, there were frequently none from the audience who remained.

"The singers lived from hand to mouth, and the first of the new year opened dark for them. They reached New York City penniless. Arrangements were made for them to attend a praise meeting at a church, and to sing a few plantation songs at the close. When their time came to sing, they poured out the soul music of the slave cabins in a manner that aroused unbounded enthusiasm. A collection was taken up which was wonderful in comparison with the former ones, and newspapers began to feature other meetings. The tide had turned, and henceforth the singers were the Jubilee Singers. No more did they sing the classical music on which they had labored in countless rehearsals. Their concerts were devoted to singing their own songs."

A number of years later Ella Sheppard wrote a chronicle of the Jubilee tour that included an account of when the Fisk ensemble received its name, and she went on to detail the enormous success their tour achieved.

"The spiritual life of our little company was sustained by prayer. There came a time that we must have a name. A special prayer was offered. Toward morning our leader, Mr. White, opened his Bible to the scripture about the Jewish year of Jubilee. He came in with a beaming face and said, 'Children, you shall be called Jubilee singers.' Six months later we returned to Nashville with twenty thousand dollars, with which we bought the present site of Fisk University.

"We sang at the great World's Peace Jubilee in Boston in 1872. Worship always preceded the work of the day, and God's blessing was asked upon each concert. There was an audience of forty thousand people, and we sang the Battle Hymn of the Republic. The audience went wild with rejoicing. Women cried out, men shouted, and the great composer, Strauss, waved his bow in admiration.

"Five of the next six years were spent abroad. We crossed the Atlantic four times and traveled throughout the British Isles and most of the Continental Empire, not only to raise funds for our school, but in the higher service of Christian evangelism, and on behalf of the poor and the outcasts of the cities and towns. We sang in hospitals, jails, and asylums, and everywhere our soul music carried its message of comfort and hope.

"Nine of the crowned heads of Europe heard us with delight. Queen Victoria wrote to her daughter, the crown princess of Germany, that we had comforted her more than anything since the death of Prince Albert. We often assisted in evangelistic work, and thousands were converted during the meetings. Our journeying for the university lasted seven years. We traveled singing the simple slave songs of our people. When we returned home in 1878, we had not only raised $165,000 for Fisk, we had made thousands of friends who sent books, and furniture for Jubilee Hall."

The years of touring by the Jubilee Singers financed the acquisition of the property where the Fisk University campus would be located and the construction of Jubilee Hall. By the close of the third tour, Ella had enough money of her own to build a modest residence near the Fisk campus. She would live there for a time with her mother and with her half-sister, Rosa, who had been sired by a white man and born to Sarah during the war, while she was in Mississippi.

In 1882, in the parlor of George White's Nashville home, thirty-one-year-old Ella Sheppard married George Washington Moore, a graduate of Fisk who was committed to becoming a minister. Moore was the son of a white mother who had been kidnapped when she was a child and sold as a slave, and his father was a light-skinned relation of General Winfield Scott of Virginia.

Jubilee Hall

Nine months after the wedding, Ella Sheppard Moore gave birth to a son at Oberlin College, where her husband was pursuing a degree in theology. When Ella gave birth to a daughter in 1884, the Moore family, including Ella's mother Sarah, was living in Washington DC, where George was serving as a minister and teaching at Howard University, and where the couple had become friends of Frederick Douglass. They came back to Nashville in 1892 when Reverend Moore took a position with the American Missionary Association. Soon after moving back into her house near Fisk, Ella had her third child, a son.

Along with raising her children, Ella worked to promote Negro folk music, and she helped train student choirs at Fisk. In 1912 her mother was nearing death. Just before she passed away, while Ella soothed her by singing *Swing Low, Sweet Chariot*, Sarah briefly joined her daughter in song.

Ella Sheppard and daughter Sarah

A gifted writer, Ella wrote about her early life and about the Jubilee Singers, and she composed an especially thoughtful essay on slavery. In early January, 1914, Ella Sheppard Moore addressed students at Tennessee Agricultural and Industrial State Normal School, which later became Tennessee State University. A newspaper article mentioned her tours in Europe, and reported what she said about the music she had done so much to rescue.

"She declared that from the very fact that these jubilee songs have been appreciated by audiences that knew not a word of English, proves that they are really and truly soul music. At the close of her lecture she led the students in singing Swing Low, Sweet Chariot."

Three months later, on June 9, 1914, Ella Sheppard Moore – a brilliant, humble, and devout Christian woman who was universally admired – died at the age of sixty-three following an attack of appendicitis. Her funeral was held at Fisk, on the campus that she, along with the other Jubilee Singers and George White, had done so much to bring about. Beyond the music she brought to the world, her legacy included her writings about slavery – the institution that had cast such a dark shadow over her life.

Ella Sheppard Moore

"If you would know our past you must listen. The veil of Christian charity must be lifted high enough to catch a glimpse of American slavery – the so-called "Divine Institution" which led human hearts to forget the God of Abraham, Isaac, and Jacob. You must listen to horrible facts which were not considered too indecent for Negro women to experience for 250 years. We learned from our mothers, who witnessed and experienced every incident referred to. The worst facts cannot yet be told openly, but they are written on earth as in heaven.

"The Negro was stolen and introduced to American civilization and Christianity, which sanctioned a more vile and cruel form of human bondage than existed in Africa. American slave laws gave the master absolute control of the body and destiny of the slave. The cruelest results fell upon the defenseless head of the Negro woman, who was required to fill every vocation and relation to the white race – from the most sacred to the most brutal.

"Thank God there were some masters who respected and protected their slave women. Those who were house slaves – under honorable masters and kind mistresses – were greatly blessed above their less favored kin people serving in the yard and on the farm. They were able to sustain their honor and self-respect. They were the repositories of the confidences of both mistress and master, and had the abiding love of the children.

"Of such was my mother, upon whose heart hung the secrets of the white family. To this day letters of deepest affection pass between her and her former young mistress. But slavery broke my mother's heart. She often says, 'My back was never struck, but my heart is like a checkerboard, with its stripes of sorrow.' Slavery separated my father and mother, and I was taken from her when I was three years of age. When I found her again, I did not even know her face.

Sarah Hannah Sheppard

"The bitterest blow to the Negro was given to his social side. The sanctity of the home was neither respected nor protected, and was broken as the wishes of the master dictated. This condition permeated every class of master and slave. The Negro woman lived in constant dread. No matter how favorably situated she was with kind and affectionate owners, there was no assurance that she would not be torn away from her children and loved ones and sold to a coarse and illiterate master.

"The position and moral status of the Negro woman was largely controlled by the degree of morality possessed by the master. If the master desired to share the wife of a slave, the husband was powerless to interfere, and sometimes had to behold two sets of children in the little cabin. Friends of mine have looked into the faces of colored children whose white father was also their grandfather. Swayed – body, mind, and spirit – by a master class who found it necessary to close every avenue of intelligence and escape, was it strange that her body was subjected to the foulest demands of sensuality?

"As they witnessed that religion did not restrain the desires and actions of the white man, was it strange that poor ignorant Negroes failed to understand that true religion cleanseth? Was it strange that, to many, their religion was to be put off or on according to circumstances? A returned missionary stood upon the rostrum at a school commencement, and tears streamed down his face as he thanked God for what he beheld. And a mother sitting nearby softly said, "You old hypocrite. You sold me and my children to get the money to go to China.'

"Such were some of the conditions which rested upon Negro womanhood in America before the war, producing a motherless race of orphans – untutored, unloved, and standing mute in their suffering, and in their helpless poverty."

10

Dr. Robert Fulton Boyd

How was it that a ten-or-eleven-year-old boy, born into slavery on a Giles County farm, came to Nashville and managed to get work in the household of the most prominent physician in Tennessee?

When he was sixteen and had not yet learned to write, how was he able to seek out one of Nashville's wealthiest real estate investors, and come away with an agreement that not only allowed him to work part-time in exchange for meals, but permitted him to go to school? And how did that same young man eventually become one of America's leading black surgeons?

Robert Fulton Boyd, the son of Edward Boyd and Maria Coffee, was born near Pulaski on July 8, 1855. Aside from being listed on a pair of death certificates and on a bank record, there appears to be no other information about Edward, who was deceased by 1872. But more is known about Maria. She was owned by the family of William Meredith Rose, and she was sixteen years old when she gave birth to Robert. Maria had been born in Alabama in 1839 – probably in Franklin County, which was located in the northern part of the state.

Two of the largest slave owners in North Alabama were former Tennesseans, John Cockrill of Franklin County and John Coffee of Lauderdale County – located on opposite sides the Tennessee River from each other. Cockrill was named for his father, an early frontiersman who married a sister of James Robertson, long recognized as the founder of Nashville. Given that Maria's surname was Coffee, it seems likely that she, or possibly her mother, had once been a Coffee family slave, but when her death certificate was filled out many years later, a grandson gave only the last name of her father – "Cockrill."

Before she became the property of the Rose family, Maria was owned by John Cockrill. When he died in 1840, one-year-old Maria was inherited by the youngest Cockrill son, John Pike Cockrill, who was called Pike by the family. She was nearly ten when Pike Cockrill died in 1849, and then she was passed to his sister, Valeria Cockrill, who was married to William M. Rose of Giles County.

Maria would be described as a mulatto, and given the doors that would eventually be opened for her son, Robert Fulton Boyd, it seems likely that her father, "Cockrill," was not only white, but a highly-affluent and influential white. When Maria was born in 1839, John Cockrill, Valeria's father, was almost sixty and in the final two years of his life. But when his will was written not long before his death, he anticipated the possibility that a son or a daughter could be born after he died – indicating that he could still sire a child.

But Maria could have also been fathered by one his sons. She was born on March 19, 1839, and must have been conceived around June, 1838. The three living Cockrill sons were Sterling, who was around thirty-four at the time, Granville, who was almost thirty, and Pike, who was just past twenty. Pike was in Texas by October, 1838, but he could have left Alabama soon after Maria's conception. He apparently made the trip in advance of moving west, and likely returned to gather his possessions and escort his slaves – including Maria – to Texas.

Whether Maria was sired by old John Cockrill, by his son Pike, or by one of the other sons, there is another reason to suspect that her father was a member of that family. Along with the strong traits her son Robert must have inherited from Maria, he would grow up to exhibit several characteristics prevalent among the Cockrills – high intelligence, a notable degree of ambition, and exceptional leadership ability.

Of those who went west with Pike Cockrill, the only female slave old enough to have been Maria's mother was named Milly, but it is possible that her mother stayed behind, or that she was dead by the time the group departed. Maria spent the first part of her childhood in Texas, and in the spring of 1850, a year after the death of Pike Cockrill, his oldest brother, Sterling, had a group of nine slaves sent back to Franklin County. Maria remained in Alabama until she was almost fourteen, and in early 1853 she and most of the others were brought about fifty miles northeast to live in Giles County, just outside of Pulaski.

A little more than a year-and-a-half after she was brought to Giles County, fifteen-year-old Maria became pregnant by Edward Boyd, who may have been a slave on a nearby farm. She gave birth to Robert, and around two years later Edward and Maria would have a second child – Sally.

Robert Boyd was not yet weaned when he was separated from his mother, and they stayed apart for most of the period leading up to the Civil War. When Maria was taken south early in the war, Robert apparently stayed behind in Giles County. He likely did a variety of farm chores as he was growing up, and Maria finally came back in 1866. Another daughter had been born, and she took her son, and probably both of her girls, north to Nashville.

Robert would eventually be placed in the home of Dr. Paul F. Eve. Eve had been a neighbor of Sterling Cockrill after Cockrill moved to Nashville from Alabama prior to the war, and young Boyd would later have a close association with another prominent white man, James Hickman.

Paul F. Eve

Both Hickman and Sterling Cockrill had served in the Mexican War when they lived in North Alabama, and both had been deeply involved in slavery and in cotton. Hickman had been a cotton speculator as well as a Negro trader, and Cockrill not only owned cotton plantations in Alabama and Arkansas – on the eve of the Civil War he was the owner of 250 slaves. If Robert Boyd was indeed the half-brother, the nephew, or the son of Sterling R. Cockrill, that would explain how he ended up being associated with both Dr. Eve and James Hickman.

Young Boyd became a servant in the home of Dr. Eve, a highly-noted physician with an international reputation, who had been president of the American Medical Association in the late 1850s. At the beginning of the war, Dr. Eve had offered his services to the Confederacy, and after being appointed Surgeon General of Tennessee, he went on to serve as Chief Surgeon for Gen. Joseph E. Johnston. During his time with Dr. Eve, Robert took at least one remedial night school course at Fisk School, the forerunner to Fisk University, and learned to read. He watched Dr. Eve closely, and later maintained that his determination to become a surgeon originated with his observations of Dr. Eve.

Central Tennessee College

He went back to Giles County in 1868 and supported himself by doing farm work. Then returning to Nashville around 1870, he worked in a brickyard and hauled trash before approaching James Hickman, who despite his previous involvement as a slave trader, had been a Unionist during the Civil War. Robert Boyd worked half-days for Hickman and then attended Central Tennessee College before

147

cleaning buildings at night, and after three years he had not only become an accomplished reader and writer, he was keeping the books of Hickman's real estate company.

Boyd left his position in 1875 and taught school in Williamson County for a time, and then he went back to Giles County where he became a teacher, a principal, and a respected educator. But he still wanted to practice medicine, and in 1880 he came back to Nashville and enrolled in Meharry Medical College, where he graduated with

MEHARRY MEDICAL COLLEGE.

honors in 1882. He moved to Mississippi and briefly taught and opened a medical office, becoming the first black licensed physician to practice in the state, but then he came back to Meharry to become a chemistry professor.

Despite his successes, the overhanging threat of racism was always in the background. In late February of 1883 he was near Vanderbilt University and a bullet passed through his hat, narrowly missing his head. There were subsequent court appearances – on one occasion he was acquitted of assault and on another he was found not guilty of performing an abortion – but such distractions barely slowed him down.

Despite his early separation from his mother, Boyd was devoted to Maria. He provided for her, and at times for his sisters as well. Maria, who had been widowed when Edward Boyd died some years before, remarried in 1875. But it was an unfortunate marriage and she would be alone through many of the coming years. Robert Boyd either lacked the time or the inclination to marry and have a family, and he would be a lifelong bachelor.

Although he continued to serve as a faculty member at Meharry, Boyd was able to pursue his degree from Central Tennessee College, and he finally graduated, with honors, in 1886. And while serving on the medical school faculty, he enrolled in Meharry's Dental College and graduated as a Doctor of Dentistry in 1887. He would ultimately chair four separate departments at Meharry, and continue to expand his knowledge of medicine, taking post-graduate courses and working in several major hospitals in Chicago. Dr. Boyd opened his practice as soon as he received his degree in dentistry, and a decade later details of his life were described in a letter written by Laps D. McCord, a former newspaper editor in Pulaski who had known Boyd for a number of years.

"I have watched this man from his youth. I especially admire his devotion to his mother. His first earnings were spent for her comfort. When Boyd was a boy, struggling against prejudice and poverty and privation, he found the means to buy a home in Pulaski for his mother. He taught school at intervals to make money to attend Central Tennessee College, and then taught in the college while he was a student. By hook or crook, and with indomitable perseverance, he worked his way to a diploma. He entered Meharry Medical College in 1880 and, battling with poverty all the while, graduated with honor in 1882. When he hung out his shingle in Nashville in 1887 – the first Negro doctor to open and maintain an office – he had just $3.20."

Boyd usually avoided politics, but in 1888 he wrote a public response to what he regarded as a highly offensive editorial in a local newspaper.

"I have always advised friendly relationships between whites and blacks. Imagine my chagrin and surprise when I read in your Sunday issue that, "The solid South is solid white against solid black, solid intelligence and property against solid ignorance and pauperism. The whites of the South, if for no other reason, would be Democrats because Negroes are Republican, and self-preservation demands that they should unite against the Negro.' Why send out such poisonous and inflammatory editorials, which are calculated to raise the passions, fire the prejudices, and blind the judgments of whites?

"Two hundred and forty years of slavery left the Negro ignorant, degraded, and in the depths of poverty. During the first decade of his freedom, wonderful progress in intelligence and the acquisition of property have been made, but the masses are still ignorant. The masses of our people are poor and ignorant, but the desire to rise is very great. Instead of sending out inflammatory editorials, send out editorials advising the education of these ignorant people. Advocate for the erection of a large school in South Nashville for the education of the hundreds of colored children that are denied school advantages."

Dr. Boyd's practice soon became among the largest in the city. And even though he treated a large number of indigent patients, he built up a lucrative practice. Boyd was respected by physicians of both races, and within a few years he was recognized as one of the leading Negro doctors in the nation. He was also active in the Republican Party and became a noted local political figure, running unsuccessfully for both the state legislature and Mayor of Nashville.

In addition to everything else he did, Dr. Boyd was highly active in a benevolent association, The Independent Order of Immaculates. Like similar societies across the nation, the organization created a sense of community and gave its members other advantages, including what amounted to low-cost insurance that paid benefits for injury, illness, and death. But he devoted most of his energy to medicine and trying to improve the quality of the local black community. In 1895 he addressed the Tennessee State Convention of Colored Teachers – an event held in Nashville.

"A great deal has been said and written about the mortality of colored people in the South, especially in large cities. We die three and four times as fast as we are born in the large cities of the south. What is the cause and how can it be diminished? The dwellings of our people must be improved. Old dilapidated stables in narrow filthy alleys are not fit for human habitation. Damp, dark cellars with insufficiency of both light and air are occupied by our people.

"Homes in the dirty neglected parts of cities, where heaps of rubbish and animal matter are allowed to decay and send their poisonous odors from house to house – homes built back-to-back so as to prevent free ventilation, with only one entrance and a privy in the center – are the habitations of colored people. And these uninhabitable quarters are over-crowded. While one-third of the colored people in Southern cities live in such dwellings as I have described, most of the white population live in well-built houses in healthy portions of the cities. Is there any surprise that there should be a great disproportion in the mortality of the two races?

"In most Southern cities a colored man cannot rent a first class uptown building, or even a respectable building, no matter how much money he has. The low, dark, damp, confined, ill-ventilated cellars, basements, and alley houses are rented to colored people for as much as good quarters ought to bring."

Dr. Boyd held that stringent regulations were needed to break the cycle of high mortality. He suggested that it should be illegal for people to occupy cellars and stables and alley houses, and that landlords be fined for renting such places. He went on to stipulate that laws should prevent certain social practices.

"Break up church meetings in poorly ventilated houses, and prohibit the collection of large numbers of people in the dens where dancing and whiskey drinking are indulged in till the wee hours of the morning." He went on to address the sale of tainted food to poor people and the mortality of infants.

"The meats and vegetables which are not sold in the market and grocery houses – the spoiled meats and vegetables on which flies have preyed all day – are put in wagons and driven to the colored settlements where they are sold cheap. *Of course* the circumstances and condition of the parents affect the children.

"The death rate of colored infants is alarming. More than half the colored children born in Southern cities die before the third year, and about half of the remainder die before the twelfth year. Infant mortality will be reduced by at least one-half when our people learn that the care of a good physician is necessary. Ignorant grannies and meddling old women are largely responsible for the death rate of colored children. None but trained nurses and educated midwives under the direction of a physician should handle mothers and their infants."

By the time he delivered his speech, he had already resolved a separate problem. He understood the benefits that came from collaborating with other physicians, but black doctors were barred from the American Medical Association, and he became the driving force in establishing the American Medical Association of Colored Physicians and Surgeons. In a speech he gave before the convention around 1898, Dr. Boyd, the organization's first president, had some advice for his fellow doctors of color. "It will take a little time, but if we organize and study as we practice and investigate the ways of science, presently our white brethren will let the bars down."

Along with J.C. Napier, Dr. Boyd was a principal leader of the colored community, and he was deeply involved in seeing that local Negroes had a role in Tennessee's Centennial celebration. He wrote an open letter that appeared in a local newspaper.

"For the great parade I have appointed more than fifty aides – among them every colored preacher in charge of a congregation. I want 2000 horsemen. I respectfully ask the white people who have colored men working for them to lend their servants horses for this parade. This is an occasion upon which I wish the colored people to show that they have the same patriotism and loyalty to the state of our nativity that the white people have."

On May 1, 1896, despite a steady rain, Dr. Boyd led the black contingent – the final contingent in the parade – from downtown

Nashville to the Centennial grounds just west of the city. But the focus of his energy was on his work as a doctor. Even though he continued to spend the majority of his time on indigent patients, those who could pay provided him with a more than a comfortable living. Dr. Boyd had several real estate investments, and in 1899 he was the subject of an article in a black-owned Washington DC newspaper.

"Dr. R. F. Boyd has a singular hobby – buying property and farms, and building office buildings right in the midst of the white folks. He has just finished a brick structure with something like fifty rooms – sandwiched between a fine cathedral (St. Mary's) and the finest hotel in the city (the Duncan). Then he had the nerve to hire a Negro stone mason to chisel his black name, "Boyd" on a big piece of marble and put it way up high so everybody could see it."

In his 1895 address to the colored teachers, Dr. Boyd had also mentioned the need to have local hospitals for black people. Several years later, he would explain the necessity for hospitals controlled by Negroes.

"Only through a hospital managed by our own people can the Negro physician perfect himself in his profession. Only through them can the Negro-trained nurse practice her profession with satisfaction. White physicians do not, as a rule, care to consult with their colored brothers, and the colored patient thrives best amid surroundings that are congenial – in environments that suggest sympathy and beget confidence."

Dr. Boyd owned a building on Cedar Street, and he had been operating a clinic there since 1892. But the need for a larger facility led him to purchase a house on South Cherry Street in 1899. Mercy Hospital – initially a twelve-bed facility with an operating room and a nursing staff – opened there the following year. In 1902 Boyd proudly described the facility he had founded.

"The hospital is located in one of the most quiet, beautiful and healthful localities of the city. The site is high and well drained; the building large and commodious and up-to-date in all its apartments. There are two large wards – one for males and one for females – and private rooms.

"Great care is given to surgical work of all kinds, and especially to abdominal surgery and gynecology. Colored physicians all over the South may send or bring their surgical cases here and get every advantage that can be provided  by the best first-class hospitals and infirmaries. We have graduate-trained nurses in constant attendance, and the resident physicians are men of the race who have made marvelous progress for two decades in all branches of their work.

"Since the establishment of the hospital we have had a record of which few similar institutions can boast. During the first year we have had more than 140 surgical cases, including abdominal and other major operations, and yet the death rate was less than 3 per cent from all causes.

"Our operating room is well appointed, with an abundance of sunlight by day and gas light at night. Many of the physicians of the South – from Alabama, Arkansas, Mississippi, Texas, Kentucky, Missouri, Florida, and Georgia – have sent us cases. Until the other cities of the South are able to afford the facilities and accommodations – and the skill and experience of the Mercy Hospital – we feel that it is the duty of every colored physician to send his surgical cases to this hospital."

But the financial challenges were significant, and in 1904 Dr. Boyd appealed for help from the community.

Dr. Boyd and first class of nurses (Meharry Medical College Library and Archives)

"A large number of the indigent are cared for here with the same medical attention and nursing as those who can pay. We receive no public funds, and therefore appeal to your charity and benevolence. We have the first practical nurse training school in the South for young colored women. The hospital is greatly in need of money, provisions, fuel, bedding, cooking utensils, dishes, towels, and napkins, and clothing, for many who come are without a change of garments. Anything you give will be thankfully received."

Challenges were overcome and the hospital continued to evolve, and in 1909 a newspaper article described an efficient, well-run facility.

"Here young women of the Negro race are instructed in nurse training, and graduate nurses are sent out and largely employed by white physicians. The physicians from Meharry get their surgical training here, and its cases have been singularly successful. The hospital is well equipped, being able to accommodate fifty patients at a time, with thirty-five or forty rooms and a nurses' home. Mercy Hospital – the largest hospital in the South under Negro control – is perfectly clean, neat, and aseptic, and is a credit to the Negro race."

Mercy Hospital was partially destroyed by a fire in 1911, and after being rebuilt it was called Boyd's Clinic. Dr. Boyd continued to be heavily involved in business. In 1903 he had taken the lead in helping found a black-owned enterprise, the People's Cash Drug Store, located on Cedar Street, and in 1909 he helped found Nashville's second black-operated financial institution, the People's Savings Bank and Trust Company. In 1910, seeing an opportunity for the Negro community to gain ownership in an industry where most workers were black, he helped organize and became president of the People's Steam Laundry Company. And his leadership was further demonstrated two years later when he helped organize and became president of The Nashville Negro Board of Trade.

On the night of July 19, 1912, four months after the Negro Board of Trade was established, Dr. Boyd presided over one of the organization's initial meetings. The agenda included expressions of gratitude for Hadley Park. It had been dedicated two weeks earlier, and would quickly become a center of activity for the black community living in North Nashville. There was also a recommendation for where the Negro Branch of the public library should be built, and a report was given on a campaign to plant potatoes in vacant lots in black sections of the city.

Then, suddenly the next morning, Dr. Boyd died of an acute stomach ailment. In its next issue the Nashville Globe, the city's black newspaper, described how the news was received.

"The death of Dr. Boyd cast a gloom over the entire city such as has never been seen before. People stood on the streets staring at each other. Men, women, and children who have known Dr. Boyd all their lives wept. One of the most pathetic scenes was in and around the Boyd Infirmary, where the aged and infirm mother of the deceased has been a constant sufferer with paralysis for the past twelve months. Every practicing physician in the city went with bowed heads to render whatever assistance they could to the bereaved mother."

Sixteen years after leading a procession of black citizens in the Centennial parade of 1896, and after lying in state at his infirmary, Dr. Boyd's remains were taken in a horse-drawn hearse through crowd-lined streets of the city. His funeral procession was a half-mile in length, and some 6000 mourners packed the Ryman Auditorium, leaving thousands more to stand outside. A number of whites attended, including members of the Rose family – likely his cousins – who had once owned Boyd and his mother. Thousands were there to hear the eulogies that flowed from the stage, one of which must have struck a particular chord with the mourners.

"I remember Dr. Boyd rushing in, and I noticed a cloud over his face. He said, 'Mother is paralyzed.' Then he broke down and wept like a baby. No mother has had a better boy. My family was stricken down with measles, and Dr. Boyd – a perfect stranger – came and rapped on my door. He did not leave until he restored health to our house. Dr. Boyd was broad-hearted, liberal, polite, and he never tired in his kindness. A night never got too dark, the weather never got too cold or too hot for him for him to go on an errand of mercy. He gave his time in a way that made his life full – in the church, in his profession, in society – everywhere."

His mother, Maria, who would survive until 1917, was too feeble to attend and hear about his long time membership in the AME Church and the Christian principles that had guided him, and all of the additional praise for her son. Although Robert Boyd had left no survivors, his younger sister, Sally, had given Maria six grandchildren, and her descendants would include two Meharry-educated physicians.

During the final years of his life, there must have been times when Dr. Robert Fulton Boyd thought back to the grand parade that had commemorated Tennessee's one hundredth year. When he was riding through the rain that day in 1896, leading so many black Nashvillians out to what would become Centennial Park, did he know he was on his way to the place where old John Cockrill had settled back in the 1780s? And did he know that the noted frontiersman – a man who had once walked for five miles with a deer carcass across his shoulders to share with the inhabitants of a besieged fort – might have been one of his ancestors?

11

Henry Harding

HARDING HOUSE.

THE Proprietor of this new and comfortable establishment takes pleasure in informing the public
that having fitted it up in

GOOD STYLE,

He is prepared to furnish the traveling community with
such accommodations as may be desired by those traveling for pleasure or on business. His table will always
be furnished with the

BEST WHICH THE MARKET AFFORDS

He respectfully solicits the patronage of the traveling
public.   HENRY HARDING, Prop'r,
    11-14-1   116 North Cherry street, Nashville, Tenn.

On January 12, 1860, at a little after 10 o'clock in the morning,
a thirty-four-year-old slave named Henry Harding was taken out
into the yard of the Nashville jail. Two days earlier several slaves

had been arrested for stealing goods from local businesses. The goods included clothing, hats, shawls, bolts of cloth, and some fine tobacco. A newspaper article contained an extensive account of the crime.

"As the investigation progressed, the police proceeded to the residence of Gen. William Giles Harding, five miles from the city, where they found a large amount of stolen goods in the cabin of one of his women servants. These goods were taken there by Henry, a smart yellow (light-skinned) man who belongs to Mr. David McGavock, and is the husband of the woman occupying the cabin. Henry appears to be quite a speculator. He professes to have purchased these goods from Alf, a slave of Mr. Hamner on Front Street. Henry has been very successful as a trader. In addition to two or three hundred dollars found in his cabin, he has promissory notes of white men and negroes to the amount of $1500, upon which he has loaned money. He says he has been engaged in this business for many years. Henry was arrested and brought to town."

Along with his wife, Minta, the cabin was home to their daughter, Catherine, who was around eleven years old. Henry and the other defendants were quickly tried and convicted, and he was sentenced to receive 49 lashes from a leather strap. A subsequent newspaper story about the incident described Henry as "the capitalist of the party."

Belle Meade

David H. McGavock was the son of Francis and Amanda McGavock. His mother Amanda was the daughter of John Harding, who established the noted Harding plantation, Belle Meade. There is a reasonable explanation of how a slave with the surname,

Harding, ended up owned by a man named McGavock. Henry's mother may have been a gift from John Harding when his sixteen-year-old daughter, Amanda married Francis McGavock in 1823.

At some point after their marriage, probably when the home in which they would live was completed, Francis and Amanda McGavock moved onto part of her father's property. The tract they called *Clifflawn* was just down Richland Creek from the place where she had grown up.

Henry Harding was born around 1825, probably at Belle Meade, but possibly at *Clifflawn*. He was born close to the time when Amanda gave birth to Henry's future master, David McGavock. The details of Henry's parentage were not recorded, but his light

Clifflawn

complexion pointed to very recent white ancestry. Some years later Henry Harding was described as, "an intelligent man, nearly white, who was related to a good family and trusted to go about." And his affluence at an early age suggested that Henry had a wealthy father.

In 1917 J.C. Napier, a noted leader of the local black community, wrote briefly about Harding, with whom he had been especially familiar. "Henry Harding, a slave with some education, was a thorough business man from beginning to end. Everything he touched turned to money. He was allowed every liberty by his owners that a free person enjoyed. He was a carpenter and contractor. He did all the construction work on three plantations, (including) that of General Harding… and of David McGavock. One of the Hardings was his father. He was held as a slave until Emancipation

162

in 1863. He immediately came to Nashville and went into business building houses."

John Harding, who likely owned Henry's unnamed mother and who may well have been his father, was in his late forties when Henry was born. There are indications that when he was a bachelor in his early twenties, John Harding had fathered a mulatto girl named Rachel. But John's younger brother, David Morris Harding, might also have been Henry's father. He lived only five miles south of Belle Meade. He was about thirty at the time of Henry's birth, and ultimately sired a number of children by his slave woman, Priscilla.

Henry Harding spent his childhood on Richland Creek, and one detail from that period – well before he was a contractor – appeared in a newspaper article many years later. "He began to practice economy when a slave, and even when a boy he employed leisure hours in making wooden combs and other trinkets which he sold to other slaves."

A second source not only reveals the trade he learned and how he used the money he was able to accumulate, it also suggests that there was an unusual relationship between Henry and the McGavock family. "Harding was a wheelwright (wheel maker), in which trade he excelled. He acquired some little money as a slave, and used to lend to his master… when the old gentleman was hard up." Because David McGavock, Henry's owner, was nearly the same age as Henry, the "old gentleman" referred to was probably David's father, Francis McGavock.

After Henry received his 49 lashes in the jail yard, he likely went back home to recover. Given his subsequent economic involvement, the punishment he received did not deter him from his entrepreneurial activities. And after the Civil War began – before

Nashville was taken by Union forces in February, 1862 – he was still going where he pleased.

"I had a wife at General Harding's, whom I used to visit every week. That was about three miles from Henry Compton's. I occasionally visited the plantation of Compton for the purpose of seeing his wife, a concubine, a colored woman, and other black people."

By fall the McGavocks had abandoned *Clifflawn*, and a mocking newspaper account appeared in October.

"Mr. David McGavock went south some time since to get his rights. His negroes were impressed (seized) some weeks ago, and put to work on our fortifications, and fearing lest the remainder of his chattels, consisting of some forty women and children, should also be taken away, he was preparing to ship them south. One woman, who was suspected of harboring the *unscriptural* notion of

David Harding McGavock

running off, was chained to a tree near the house for ten days. The rest of the servants got wind of the plot and stampeded to the city, where they are disposed to think they are safe forever from the *humane* chains of their rebel master."

It appears that Henry stayed behind when the McGavocks went

south, and a newspaper account suggests that he might have taken refuge in the city.

"When the Emancipation Proclamation was issued he possessed the snug sum of $3500. As soon as he was made free he embarked in the hotel business, building in time the hotel adjoining the old post office on Cedar Street."

Henry and Minta, who ultimately gave her maiden name as White on their marriage certificate, had likely become husband and wife at Belle Meade in the middle 1840s, but they were not legally married until the spring of 1866. John Harding had died six months earlier, and David Morris Harding had been dead for over a decade by then.

In May of 1866, just after his marriage, Henry paid over $2000 for a lot in an expensive subdivision a few hundred yards north of the State Capitol, and he continued to invest in real estate over the years that followed. Harding's energy was extraordinary. In 1867, as the local labor market was still recovering from the war, he established a business which recruited and found employment for "nurses, cooks and farm hands."

In the autumn of 1866 a false rumor was spread that a violent uprising of Nashville blacks was being secretly planned. Henry Harding was one of the local leaders who convened in order to protect their community from whatever repercussions the propaganda was intended to produce. The meeting resulted in the following resolution.

"Whereas the so-reported outbreak of the colored citizens of Nashville has been thoroughly examined by us, as the old citizens of this place, and we find that there is no foundation for such a report in our actions, we denounce the report as a wicked attempt to enthrall us with bloodshed and suffering.... We feel that we have been injured by the report gaining circulation that letters have been read in our churches of an incendiary nature, which is also untrue. We hereby express our unreserved thanks to the city authorities for informing us of these rumors…"

During Reconstruction, while most whites who had been sympathetic to the Confederacy were determined to resurrect as much of the old racial order as they could, blacks, progressive local whites, and newly-arrived northerners – branded as carpetbaggers – attempted to institute a system in which blacks would no longer be subservient. In May, 1867, a petition was circulated throughout the city. It was signed by a number of prominent white citizens.

"To the South Nashville Street Railroad Company – The undersigned citizens of Nashville, having learned that colored citizens are excluded from seats in cars on your railroad… and that many worthy people are thereby subjected to much trouble and inconvenience… therefore respectfully petition that if there are any rules or regulations of your company which make distinctions between white and colored citizens, such rules may be abolished, and all persons, without distinction of color, who demean themselves properly, may be admitted to seats in your cars."

Early the next month a collision took place between the old order and those who were more progressive. Frank Parrish, one of Nashville's most noted mixed-race citizens, had died and a large number of individuals were waiting to ride the mule-drawn streetcars out to the cemetery. The cars reserved for whites were largely empty, and blacks, ignoring the orders of operators, finally started climbing aboard. There were threats and some pushing, but no injuries were reported.

Former Confederate soldiers and others who had given material support to the southern cause were disenfranchised, and on August 1, 1867, an historic election was held. An article appeared the next day in the *Union and American,* a conservative newspaper, ridiculing the election, which featured races for congress and for governor.

"Yesterday the first general negro ballot ever cast in this country was polled over the State of Tennessee... The farce is, as was expected, sufficiently complete, yet it does not lessen the exceptional significance and interest of the occasion. The day, whatever may be its consequence, is historic... The negroes voted in most cases like sheep, following the tinkle of the radical bell."

Conservatives charged the opposing faction with widespread voting fraud, and Henry Harding was accused of being at the center of the irregularities. In addition to his other endeavors, Harding operated a saloon on Cherry Street where voting certificates had been distributed – mostly to voters who supported candidates backed by the Radical mayor, A. E. Alden. An investigation was conducted, and when Harding was interrogated, he gave a clear and thorough denial.

He was questioned about his relationship with the mayor, but he was not asked about the crucial role he played in enabling Alden to take office. A Chancery Court lawsuit later claimed that Alden, who had no money and was legally required to own city property worth at least $500 in order to serve, was only able to take office after Henry Harding pretended to sell him enough property to allow Alden to become mayor. A few weeks after the election, the *Union and American* ran the following dismissive item.

"Henry Harding, the negro who peddled in voters certificates the day of the election, is building a fine, three-story brick house on Cherry Street, above the theater."

As a result of his intellect, his relative wealth, and his energetic nature, Henry Harding had quickly become a leader of the community being formed by those who had formerly been free blacks and slaves, and he joined with a number of others in trying advance the race to which he was assigned. In an 1868 news article listing a number of affluent local blacks, Henry was mentioned. "Henry Harding... recently built a commodious three-story brick *Hotel d'Afrique* (a disdainful term referring to a hotel for blacks) on Cherry Street above the old theater. He is worth about $15,000." Harding advertised his hotel, *the Harding House*, in newspapers as far away as Memphis.

When the 1870 federal census was compiled, Harding's real estate was valued at $30,000 and his personal property was worth $5,000. Living with him was his wife, Minta, their daughter, Catherine, and her husband, John B. Bosley, Jr. – the unacknowledged grandson of Charles Bosley – a former slave trader and perhaps the wealthiest man in the county.

Henry Harding was prosperous, but he was no a stranger to conflict. In 1867 he had been arraigned and fined for illegally reselling what he had bought at the Nashville market. In 1868 he was involved in a political disagreement with Randall Brown, a black leader of a rival political faction, and the encounter resulted in Brown's shirt being torn. In 1872 he would be tried for assault with intent to kill another man, but the case was weak and he was only required to pay a small fine. And in an incident reminiscent of his activities back when he was a slave, he was charged with receiving stolen goods for resale.

Minta Harding died late in 1870 or sometime in 1871, and in 1872, when he was close to forty-seven, Henry married Margaret Pickett. She was around seventeen years old and was the daughter of Rev. Calvin Pickett, a highly respected local Methodist preacher. Death returned to the Harding household again in 1873 when Henry's daughter, Catherine Bosley, died in August, possibly as a result of giving birth to her first child, who was named Minta.

Despite his occasional conflicts, Harding continued to be a respected local figure. He was one of the driving forces behind the establishment of a local branch of the Freedman's Savings Bank, which opened in 1871. Few freed slaves had been responsible for their own finances, and they not only needed a place to keep the money they earned, they needed an institution where they could receive economic advice. Frederick Douglas explained that the purpose of the bank was to help ex-slaves learn "lessons of sobriety, wisdom, and economy, and to show them how to rise in the world."

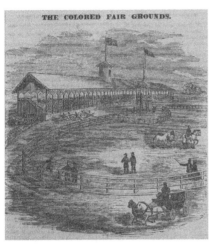

THE COLORED FAIR GROUNDS.

Republican Banner, August 20, 1871

In 1872 John M. Langston, a nationally-known black leader, made a political speech in Nashville and praised Harding. "In business tact and energy, Henry Harding would compare favorably with the white men of the country who have had no better opportunities than he."

As Harding continued to buy and sell real estate, he did what he could to improve the prospects of the black community. Harding was one of those who had organized Tennessee Manual Labor University in 1867, and in 1870 he took the lead in founding the Tennessee Colored Agricultural and Mechanical Association. Many years later a newspaper article described his commitment to advancing his race. "He, as one of thirteen, purchased the old Major Turner place for a colored fairgrounds. All of the others failed to meet their payments, and Harding had to pay the entire amount, about $15,000."

In 1874 Harding was one of the principal leaders who brought about a large meeting of politically active local blacks. He explained that by working together and voting together, separate factions of black voters could gain more political power. A newspaper article quoted him as saying, "The main point to be discussed by that body is the urgent necessity of the colored voters throughout the state sticking together and forming what might be called 'a balance of power' between the two parties, and stand ready to vote for the party that will award them their fullest rights…" At the meeting he was named as a delegate to what was called the Colored State Convention.

One of the resolutions that was adopted in May at the state convention read, in part, as follows. "Whereas there is now a bill before the Congress of the United States conferring on our colored citizens civil rights, and as it is our duty as men to arrange for the perfect development of posterity by means of instruction, we call the attention of the Congress to the fact that the public institutions of Tennessee are defective in point of principle and practice… and that their tendency is to breed discord and the spirit of caste and hate between citizens. And whereas the common or public schools of the country are the medium through which an education will reach the masses of citizens, we, as American citizens, demand that we shall enjoy them impartially, that we may encourage patriotism in a public where all are equal before the law…"

Henry Harding may have come away from the convention with a sense of optimism, but a financial disaster was only a few weeks away. In June, 1874, the Freedman's Bank collapsed due to corruption and mismanagement in the bank's main office in Washington. Harding was among the largest depositors at the branch he had helped found, and he lost most of his money in the collapse. Many of the 2000 individuals who had opened accounts there, most of them black and most of them small depositors, lost all their money as well.

With his hotel, the *Harding House,* in danger of being lost to creditors, the following year he opened a used furniture business and a real estate company, and was able to maintain his role as a respected local leader.

By 1876 Henry's twenty-one-year-old second wife had given birth to a daughter and a son. In July of that year his wife Margaret, who was called Maggie, became involved in a local altercation that was described in a newspaper article.

"Mrs. Henry Harding was arraigned on the charge of carrying concealed weapons, and with assault upon and the intent to murder Elias Napier… She is a fine-looking woman with a warm, rich olive complexion and dazzling black eyes which sparkled with unusual brilliancy at different stages of the trial. She is said to have been well-educated, is a good talker, and is held in great esteem by the colored people."

John B. Bosley Jr., who had married Harding's by-then-deceased daughter, Catherine, testified that Napier had said that Mrs. Harding "had been running around talking about him, and that she was no lady, as no lady would do so. And if she did so again, he would kick her out of town. Harding said, 'you may curse me, but you shall not abuse my wife.' At that juncture I got Harding to go into the house."

"Napier testified that he and Harding had quarreled, and Napier had told Harding that if he had such a wife as Harding had, he would kick her until she should know how to behave herself, and if Harding could not do it, he would do it for him. When Mrs. Harding came to Napier's house and called him out, she said that 'if he did not swallow what he had said against her, she would shoot the top of his head off.' Napier caught her hand as she was about to raise a pistol, and it was discharged in the air."

Maggie tried to shoot her pistol again, and Napier threw her down while he was getting the weapon out of her hands. Then she went to her carriage and got a whip, but Napier threatened her and the two were eventually separated. She was charged and bound over to Criminal Court, but the matter was ultimately put to rest.

Five years later, on the first day of October, 1881, Maggie Harding was in the news again. "The wife of Henry Harding, colored, and her little girl (eight-year-old Mabel) walked up to the rear door of the rear coach (reserved for white ladies) of the train for Chattanooga and tried to get in. The door was locked, and they went to the front door of the same car, which was also locked. The woman demanded that the door be opened. This was refused and she was told to take a seat in the middle car, but she had come to ride in the ladies car or on the platform.

"When the train was ready to start, the depot policeman endeavored to carry out the rule of the railroad, which does not permit persons to ride on the platforms. He had a scuffle with Harding's wife, in which he evidently came out second best. Superintendent (John W.) Thomas appeared and was invited by her to put her off. This he declined to do.

"He offered a special car – something not usually tendered except to railroad magnates and the President of the United States. This she rejected with scorn. She gave up the trip... and was seen no more. Subsequently Henry Harding had a warrant issued for the arrest of the depot policeman on a charge of assault and battery, and brought suit against the railroad company for $25,000 damages."

That incident in 1881 sparked other attempts by females of color to ride on train cars prohibited to blacks, but after a few days, the challenges to segregation ceased. Henry Harding continued to be a leader of his race. In 1884 Harding, along with J.C. Napier, John B. Bosley Jr., and six other local black leaders, attended the Republican convention in Chicago. By delivering as many black votes as they could, they hoped to advance the cause of their constituents by increasing their political influence, and their presence in Chicago was part of that process.

The next year Harding was one of several leaders who expressed how he felt about social equality. "We don't want any of this social equality... All we want is protection for us in life, liberty, and happiness... We are citizens and we want to be good citizens." A few days after his brief remarks, Harding experienced a small indication of racial progress when he was listed as being eligible to serve as a United States Circuit Court juror. He was the only black included in the long list of jurors.

Henry Harding was in his early sixties when he died in 1888 at his home on West Church Street. There was an article announcing his death. "He was one of the foremost men of his race and has always been popular, not only with his people, but with all who knew him. He accumulated a large independence in... business, the most of which he lost as a depositor in the Freedman's Bank. In 1875 he embarked in the second-hand furniture business. He continued in this line until about eighteen months ago, when he sold out and opened a real estate and brokerage office. At the time of his death Mr. Harding had by hard work accumulated a fortune of about $80,000."

His wife Maggie and their two children, Henry and Mabel, received a comfortable inheritance and continued to live just west of downtown Nashville. Maggie was involved in another altercation less than three years after Henry's death. In 1890 she and her son got into a gunfight with a neighbor, but no one was injured.

In the 25 years following Henry Harding's marriage to Maggie, her father, Rev. Calvin Pickett, worked quietly to advance the local black community. He was active in raising funds for black higher education, and on one trip to New York City he was able to raise $150,000. In 1898, when he was 75, he died as a result of a hotel fire while he was in New York on behalf of Meharry Medical College.

Maggie's daughter, Mabel, an accomplished musician, graduated from Meigs High School and attended Fisk University, and went on to become a school teacher. She died, apparently unmarried, in 1904, and Maggie died of tuberculosis around 1906. The eventual fate of Maggie's son, Henry, is unclear. But Henry Harding had at least one descendant. His granddaughter, Minta Bosley, would move north after her husband's death in 1903 and settle in Brooklyn. Although he would never see his three great-grandchildren, one of them, Catherine Bosley Allen went on to graduate from Howard University and became the first black librarian at the New York Public Library, where she would play a role in the black intellectual movement known as the Harlem Renaissance.

Henry Harding was one of many Nashville leaders who rose out of slavery and tried to help their race in its long journey to attain authentic citizenship, but the possibilities of the late 1860s and early 1870s were gradually choked off by the resurgence of the old order. In 1960 the Jim Crow era was finally beginning to fade. After the long years of lynchings and poll taxes and the suppression of constitutional and human rights, the example of Henry Harding would be emulated when local college students began a series of lunch counter sit-ins near the place where, a century earlier, he had endured 49 lashes from a leather strap.

12

John B. Bosley

Riding With a Prostitute.

One of the aristocratic darkies of the town, Coon Bosley [by name, was jerked up by the police about ten o'clock last night, in a beastly state of intoxication, while riding with Melinda Thompson, a saddle colored [*nymph du pave* of Gay Street. His case will be attended to by the Police Commissioner to-morrow.

Republican Banner, January 17, 1869

In Davidson County, in the spring of 1847, John B. Bosley, Jr. was born into a way of life that was dominated by the institution of slavery and attitudes about race. His father, John B. Bosley Sr., was the disinherited son of Charles Bosley, a slave trader who became a wealthy land owner. His mother was a mulatto woman named Alsey, who was very likely the daughter of a white man named William Cloud. Cloud was a man of property. He was born in South Carolina around 1775, and moved to Madison County, Alabama, before coming to Davidson County to live out his final years.

When William Cloud drew up his will in 1845 – the year before his death – he named John B. Bosley, Jr. as his executor. The first item of the will focused on "Siller" (Priscilla) and her four children, along with three others. Most of those who had been named were listed five years later in the 1850 Census as mulattos. Priscilla was probably the daughter of William Cloud and an unnamed slave woman who had accompanied him when he came to Alabama. Her children, along with the three who were named separately, were probably his grandchildren. The will went on to name his white children – three sons and two daughters – each of whom received a small bequest.

And Alsey, who was the common-law wife of the will's executor, John B. Bosley, was probably a daughter of William Cloud as well. She was likely the unnamed beneficiary of property referred to later in Cloud's last will and testament. "It is my will that all the property I possess… in the State of Tennessee remain… in the care and possession of my Executor (Bosley)… for which I have a particular reason, best known to myself…" In the 1860 Census, in which she was designated as a free woman of color, Alsey was listed as owning real estate. The property was almost certainly a 215 acre tract on the Cumberland River, not far down from Nashville, that was valued at $13,000.

William Cloud was born in the mid-1770s, as was Charles Bosley, the father of the elder John B. Bosley. The younger Bosley was close to Cloud, who was probably his father-in-law, but he was estranged from his father. who was in the process of becoming one of the wealthiest men in the region. Charles Bosley was vehemently opposed to his son and Alsey living as husband and wife and raising a family together, and he did as much as he could to bring about a separation. His anger and frustration were still evident twenty years later when he underlined parts of his will.

"It being my positive injunction that my son, John B. Bosley, is not to be counted an heir… (my) real and personal estate is to be disposed of… as if he were no kin to me… My son, not being deemed worthy of my bounty… (is) to be entirely excluded… John B. Bosley is hereby disinherited and is not to claim any thing under

<u>my will</u>." When he died in 1870 at the age of ninety-three, Charles Bosley's entire estate, with an estimated value of around one million dollars, was inherited by his only named descendant – a seven-year-old great-granddaughter.

Charles Bosley

But Bosley had other descendants. In 1855 John B. Bosley's oldest daughter, Laura Ann, had married an enterprising free man of color named George Trimble, and by the time of Laura's death in 1863 she had three sons, James, George, and John Trimble. And his unforgiving father had another grandson. In 1870, a few months before his grandfather died, John B. Bosley, Jr. married Catherine Harding. Three years after Charles Bosley died, his second great-granddaughter, the daughter of John B. Bosley, the younger, was born. She was named Minta Gwynn Bosley.

The relationship between Charles Bosley and his son must have been far different in the beginning. John Beal Bosley was born near Natchez, Mississippi, in 1808, and five years later his mother, Sally Hoggatt, died. Her widowed husband was a financially-driven planter and slave trader, and his only child would have likely been cared for by a female slave under the supervision of an aunt or a cousin. Charles Bosley moved from Mississippi back to Davidson County by 1817, and he was in his early forties when he married his second wife, nineteen-year-old Eliza Childress, in 1818. John B.

Bosley, who was only nine years younger than his step-mother, was raised three miles southwest of Nashville on what would become the site of Aquinas Junior College on Harding Road.

Charles Bosley fathered four children by Eliza during the 1820s, but two of those children – John B. Bosley's half-siblings – died in infancy. Another died at sixteen, and only Charles Bosley, Jr. lived long enough to marry. By the time he died in 1847, his half-brother John B. Bosley had been living for more than a decade with Alsey, who had given birth to her sixth child, John B. Bosley, Jr., only three months before his uncle's passing.

The deaths of children, which were so frequent on Charles Bosley's plantation, took place just as often on the farm several miles to the northeast, where his first-born son was living with Alsey. Three of her first five children were dead before John B. Bosley, Jr. was a year old. Of the nine children she ultimately had, only John B. Bosley lived past the age of twenty-seven.

But Alsey was considered to be a gifted midwife, and seventy years after the birth of her last child, she was still remembered for the assistance she provided – presumably to white women as well as to black women – as they went through the dangerous ordeal of childbirth. "(Alsey) was a midwife who had many calls. She went about the city driving a good horse to an old, high up, mammoth-topped gig – the only one of the kind I ever saw. She wore a gorgeous, high black bonnet and a white lace cap… She lived across the river near Hyde's Ferry."

Another recollection of Alsey came from local black leader, James C. Napier, in the 1930s. "Her husband was white, and her family owned two large plantations south of Nashville, and another north-east of Nashville. They owned about twenty-five or thirty slaves. She was a thoroughly religious woman and every Sunday would have her slaves and children attend church."

In 1850, when young John B. Bosley was three years old, he was living in Nashville with his parents and two older sisters. The household included eight of those who had been mentioned by William Cloud in his will. The federal census was taken that year, and the individuals who were listed, including the slaves that had been left in trust to John B. Bosley, Sr. were all designated as free people.

Most of John's childhood was spent on the family's 350-acre farm on the Cumberland River. By 1860 the farm was also home to twelve slaves, two of whom were close to the same age as John, who turned thirteen that summer. No record indicating how the Bosley slaves were treated has been found. The Civil War swept in and Nashville fell to Union forces early in 1862, and it is uncertain whether John was still at home when a series of deaths took place the following year.

John's oldest sister, Laura Bosley, the wife of George Trimble, died in mid-July, 1863, two weeks before the death of her only daughter, and in December Alsey died as well. It may have been around that time when John, along with a dozen or so other young Nashvillians of mixed racial heritage, was sent to Ohio to attend Wilberforce University. He returned to Nashville at some point following the war – possibly before the death of his father, John B. Bosley, in 1867. John and his two brothers each received a sizable inheritance, and at the age of twenty, John resumed his life as a college-educated young man of means.

Being young and independent, there were times when he behaved injudiciously, and an incident that took place in 1869 was reported in a local newspaper. The brief article was a stark reminder of how those of mixed race were seen by the ruling class. "One of the aristocratic darkies of the town, Coon Bosley by name, was jerked up by the police about ten o'clock last night in a beastly state of intoxication, while riding with a saddle colored *nymph du parc* (a prostitute) of Gay Street." The case was quickly dismissed, but the nickname, "Coon" would continue to label him for years to come.

In 1870, just after he turned twenty-three, John Bosley married nineteen-year-old Catherine Harding, the light-skinned daughter of Henry Harding, a former slave of the Francis McGavock family. Harding was one of the area's most economically-driven men, and Catherine's mother, Minta White Harding, had been a slave at Belle Meade, the plantation of William Giles Harding. John and Catherine Bosley lived with her parents in the three-story hotel her father had built on Cherry Street. Along with Henry and Minta, the household included George Trimble, who had been married to John's deceased sister, Laura Ann, and also John's younger brother, James, who would study at Fisk University.

John Bosley's wife, Catherine, died after only three years of marriage, but she left behind their daughter, Minta, who was named for Catherine's recently-deceased mother. John and his father-in-law, Henry, would see to it that little Minta Harding was, unlike most children of color who grew up in the closing years of reconstruction, raised in comfortable circumstances. They were partners in at least one business, and Henry, who was active in the local Republican Party, became John's political mentor.

John Bosley was heavily involved in raising thoroughbreds. One of his horses won the feature race at the Colored Fair in 1871, and another thoroughbred was awarded a premium in a livestock competition. A newspaper article many years later referred to his passion for an activity typically associated with aristocratic white men.

"Bosley was a lover of horses during all of his life. He worked with them and never allowed anyone to have a horse that surpassed his in speed."

As one of Nashville's most active and conspicuous figures, there were times when John Bosley had problems with the law. On one occasion he and a friend were involved in a violent fight at the Colored Fair. Bosley was not ultimately punished, but he received a number of subsequent fines for such minor violations as chicken fighting. His financial situation and his deep involvement in politics would ultimately be mentioned in a local newspaper article.

"A large fortune was left him by his parents, but misplaced confidence in his friends caused the greater part of it to vanish before he reached the age of sound discretion. He was naturally a politician, and early in life took an active part in the counsels of the Republican Party. He has been a number of times a delegate to the National Convention, has almost continually been a member of the county and state Republican organizations, was a candidate for a seat in the House of Representatives, was a candidate for Sheriff of Davidson County, served in the Registry Department of the Post Office, and served in the Internal Revenue Service. He was a man of great force of character, having strong opinions and convictions which he never hesitated or feared to express."

Although he experienced financial disappointments he persevered, and along with investing in real estate, he owned a furniture business in partnership with his father-in-law, Henry Harding. In the late 1880s his political involvement led to a fairly lucrative appointment as head custodian of the Customs House, and in 1896, after serving as a delegate to the Republican National Convention, he and James C. Napier, who had been students together at Wilberforce during the Civil War, campaigned across the state on behalf of William McKinley.

His daughter, Minta, was a superior student, and following her 1894 graduation from Fisk, she married Henry Allen, an industrious young Fisk alumnus who had a career as a mail clerk on the Louisville and Nashville Railroad. Minta had a daughter – John Bosley's first grandchild – by the time he finally remarried in 1898. When his wife, Susie Williams, who was some twenty-three years younger than John, began attending classes at an all-white local college in 1900, the event made national news. A local article circulated to newspapers across the country, and it illustrated the position to which those not considered to be of pure Caucasian ancestry had been relegated.

"It was found yesterday that a colored woman, the wife of "Coon" Bosley, a Republican politician, was one of the students at the Peabody Normal College. About two months ago she applied for admission to the art department, satisfied all the requirements, and was admitted. She is twenty-one years old (she was around thirty) and would pass anywhere for a white woman. On Tuesday she was seen by one of the professors talking from a studio window with a Negro, and later

When Mrs. Bosley Was Seen with Her Husband Chancellor Took Action.

Nashville, Tenn., April 27.—It was found yesterday that a colored woman, the wife of "Coon" Bosley, a Republican politician, was one of the students at the Peabody Normal college. About two months ago she applied for admission to the art department, satisfied all requirements and was admitted. She is twenty-one years old and would pass anywhere for a white woman.

On Tuesday she was seen by one of the professors talking from a studio window with a negro, and later was seen upon the street with him. When called before the chancellor to account for her conduct, she explained the man was her husband and that she was a negress. Realizing that this meant dismissal, she withdrew from the college before any action was taken on the part of the faculty.

Elmira, New York Star Gazette, April 27, 1900

was seen on the street with him. When called before the Chancellor to account for her conduct, she explained that the man was her

182

husband and that she was a Negress. Realizing that this meant dismissal, she withdrew from the college before any action was taken on the part of the faculty."

Bosley continued to be a leading member of the black community, and along with his other activities, he served as a director of the One-Cent Savings Bank, a local black-owned institution. The first part of his life had been a time of loss, as one family member after another was claimed by death. Then there was a long period that was devoid of tragedy until Minta's husband, Henry, was killed in a railroad accident in 1903. Minta had three children by then, and after their home burned down less than two years later, she and her children moved to New York, where Minta must have hoped to find a more progressive racial atmosphere.

John Bosley's daughter and grandchildren were traveling in Europe when he suffered a stroke in 1910, but they were able to reach Nashville in time to attend his funeral. John B. Bosley, Jr. – raised in the South by a white father and a mulatto mother before the Civil War – lived through a time of great change.

The possibilities that had accompanied Reconstruction had been largely blotted out, but because of his economic advantages and his hard work, Bosley was not only able to lead a noteworthy life, his daughter and her children – his granddaughters – went on to live distinguished lives as well. Minta worked tirelessly to benefit the Brooklyn community where she raised her three children, and was a successful political activist. Her daughter, Catherine, not only became the first black individual to be hired as a reference librarian for the New York Public Library, she played a role in the Harlem Renaissance, a black intellectual movement of the 1920s.

13

Minta and Henry W. Allen

The woman on the right is Minta Allen when was twenty-five or twenty-six years old. She and her husband Henry had married some four years earlier – just before Christmas in 1894. They lived west of Nashville on Church Street, and all their neighbors were white. The home where their daughter Catherine was born on January 22, 1896, was owned by Minta's father, John B. Bosley.

Minta had graduated six years earlier from Fisk, where she was not only a superior student, but also an accomplished vocalist and public speaker. When the photograph was taken, Henry and Catherine were both staring into the camera, but Minta was gazing past Henry. She was aware of the camera, but she looked like her mind was someplace else. She probably looked the same way when she thought about the family into which she was born.

Her great-great-grandfather, Captain James Bosley, was a cavalry captain during the Revolutionary War. In 1784 Captain Bosley left Maryland and brought his family, which included his seven-year-old son, Charles, to the struggling frontier outpost that would become Nashville. Charles grew up and fought in the Indian wars and eventually became a slave trader, and by the time of the Civil War he owned a 2000 acre plantation on Harding Pike just west of Nashville. When he died in 1870 at the age of ninety-three, he may have been the richest man in Davidson County.

When Charles Bosley wrote his will during the Civil War, he disinherited his eldest son – Minta's grandfather, John B. Bosley. The younger Bosley had a mulatto common-law wife named Alsey. They had been together since the 1830s and raised their family on a farm six miles west of Nashville. John B. Bosley, who owned a number of slaves, had consistently refused to leave Alsey, and his father never forgave him.

Alsey was born in 1813 and in addition to giving birth to nine children, she eventually became a well-known figure in the community. Over 60 years after her death in 1863, the mulatto woman whose husband chose her over the fortune he would have otherwise inherited, was still well remembered for the services she had rendered as a midwife.

Minta's father, John B. Bosley Jr., was the oldest of the three surviving Bosley sons. Despite being born to a mixed-race mother during slave times, he had received a good early education. During the Civil War, along with thirteen other young Negroes from local families of means, he was sent north to attend Wilberforce College in Ohio. He returned to Tennessee, and in 1870 he married Catherine Harding, a light-skinned former slave who was raised just beyond Charles Bosley's sprawling plantation on Harding Pike.

There must have been times when Minta, especially after she became a mother, thought about her own mother, Catherine Harding, who had died when Minta was only seven months old. Catherine, like her husband, had been of a mixed racial heritage. Catherine's father, Henry Harding, whose complexion indicated a recent Caucasian bloodline, had been the slave of David H. McGavock when the Civil War began. Catherine's mother, Minta, after whom her daughter would be named, was a slave at Belle Meade, the plantation of William Giles Harding.

One of her grandfathers and both of her grandmothers were dead before Minta was born, and she could not remember her mother. But both her grandfather and her father – Henry Harding and John B. Bosley – were intelligent and well-informed men, and they would have passed along the details of their family origins.

Minta would have been told about the 1823 marriage between Amanda Harding, the daughter of John Harding of Belle Meade, and Frank McGavock. She must have known why Henry had the surname, Harding, despite being a slave of the McGavock family. And she must have known that when he was a boy he had carved

186

wooden combs and sold them to other slaves, and that there were times when he had loaned money to his master, Mr. McGavock.

She knew that her grandfather had learned to be a wheelwright, and that not long before the war, city authorities whipped him with a leather strap after he was convicted of purchasing stolen goods from a fellow slave. When his cabin was searched, promissory notes from those to whom he had loaned money – both white men and black men – were found, along with a significant amount of cash.

And Minta knew whether Henry was fathered by one of the Harding men, or by a member of the McGavock family. John Harding was suspected of being the father of a local mulatto woman named Rachel Norris, and his younger brother, Morris Harding, who owned a nearby plantation, had sired a number of children by his slave, Priscilla. Or Henry's father might have been Frank McGavock, whose son David Harding McGavock, was nearly the same age as Henry.

Both Henry Harding and David H. McGavock, who at some point had become Henry's master, were in their mid-thirties when Nashville fell to Union forces in the first year of the Civil War. Minta probably knew that some of the McGavock slaves were seized by Federal authorities and put to work building fortifications to protect the city, and that David McGavock had planned to ship his remaining slaves further south so they would not be seized. But after a slave woman who was suspected of planning to escape was chained to a tree near the McGavock's Richland Creek home for ten days, the others fled to Nashville. The McGavock family went south in October, 1862, and Minta would have known whether her grandfather accompanied them, or if he came to Nashville to live.

Henry Harding had a considerable amount of money at the time of emancipation, and he soon started buying real estate. Over the next twenty years he not only built a three-story hotel and owned several businesses, he played a crucial leadership role in the local Negro community.

In the wake of the war, a struggle took place between those who wanted to restore as much of the old order as possible, and those who were trying to bring about a new order that included basic civil rights and human rights for Negroes. In October, 1866, as the Ku Klux Klan was becoming more powerful, Minta Allen's grandfather, Henry, along with other local black leaders, managed to defuse a false rumor that the Negroes of Nashville were planning a dangerous uprising.

In the spring of 1867, a petition – signed by a number of prominent whites and asking that the mule-drawn streetcars be integrated – was circulated throughout the city. After a few years segregation would prevail, but many of those who had supported the Confederacy were temporarily prevented from voting, and local elections were hotly contested for a time. When the first statewide election in which Negroes were allowed to vote took place that August, Henry Harding was accused by those who were referred to as Conservatives of being a central figure in a widespread conspiracy of voting fraud.

Whether or not he was innocent or guilty of election misdeeds, Harding had more than his share of run-ins with the law. Over the years he was in court for a number of relatively minor offenses, and although he was once accused of assault with intent to kill, in the end he only paid a small fine.

Minta would have known about her grandfather's continuing efforts to improve the lives of Nashville's black community. In 1870 Harding helped found the Tennessee Colored Agricultural and Mechanical Association. He took the lead in purchasing land for the

Colored Fairgrounds, and he was a founder of the Nashville branch of the Freedman's Savings Bank. He also worked tirelessly to bring political power to the black community.

And even though she had only been eight years old at the time, Minta would have remembered her grandfather's lawsuit on behalf of his second wife, Maggie, when he sued the Louisville and Nashville Railroad in 1881 after Maggie tried to enter a car reserved for white women. Until his death in 1888, Henry Harding continued working to deliver Negro votes to the Republican Party, which he regarded as the only hope for the black race to advance.

As Minta sat with her husband and daughter for their family portrait, she probably wasn't thinking about her father, John B. Bosley Jr., but he had probably been on her mind more than usual. Only a few months earlier, after twenty-five years as a bachelor, he had remarried. Despite his father's disinheritance, John B. Bosley Jr. had become a fairly wealthy man. As one of four surviving children, he had shared in a valuable estate after his father died in 1867.

Following the death of his wife, Catherine, John B. Bosley had raised Minta in circumstances that were unusual for a girl with a mixed racial background. He had gone into business with his father-in-law, Henry Harding, and like Henry, he was brought into court from time to time. He was also heavily involved in politics. He was a frequent candidate for public office, and when he served as a delegate to the national Republican Convention in 1896, he had voted for William McKinley.

Local newspapers, never mentioning his college education, continued to refer to John B. Bosley Jr. as "Coon Bosley," but he seemed to ignore attempts to deride his racial heritage. He was noted as "a man of great force of character, having strong opinions and convictions, which he never hesitated or feared to express."

As Minta posed for the photograph, her husband, Henry W. Allen, stared straight into the camera. Like Minta, he was successfully navigating the oppression of the Jim Crow era. He had grown up under less-privileged circumstances than Minta had experienced, but his parents were still able to raise an extraordinary family.

Henry was born in 1870 – the oldest son of Charles Augustus and Sarah Cole Allen. Henry's father was born into slavery in Fauquier County, Virginia in 1846, and he arrived in Nashville well before his marriage to Sarah two days after Christmas in 1866. Charles and Sarah would ultimately become the parents of 13 children, and Charles supported his family with what he earned working at the Nicholson Hotel, which was later renamed the Tulane Hotel.

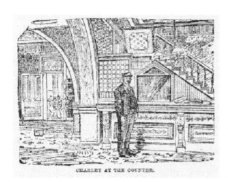

CHARLEY AT THE COUNTER.

The hotel where Charles Allen went to work in 1868 was on the corner of Spruce Street and Church Street, two blocks from the railroad depot. One of the responsibilities Charles had was described in a newspaper article in 1888. "Most conspicuous among the servants is Charles A. Allen, well known as 'Charlie.' His splendid, assuring voice rings clear above the din at the Union Depot three times a day, announcing 'twenty minutes' for breakfast, dinner, and supper." The outstanding reputation he had might have stemmed in part from an 1873 episode when he nearly died from a stab wound he received while trying to help capture a drunken white criminal who had almost killed a policeman.

By the time Henry Allen sat in the Calvert Brothers studio – awaiting the flash of the camera – he had earned a distinguished reputation of his own. Like Minta, he had been educated at Fisk

University. He was noted for his dependability and high intelligence, and he had held a position as a mail clerk for ten years. Henry and Minta and their daughter lived in her father's home, which stood just west of town. Several years later, the noted local black leader, James C. Napier, who had been a schoolmate of John B. Bosley Jr. at Wilberforce, would write an article about Henry.

"Fourteen years ago, after passing a most creditable civil service examination, he was appointed to a position as Railway Mail Clerk between Nashville and Montgomery, Alabama. He had been continuously in the service since his appointment, and he has never lost a day or missed a trip... Though a colored man, his efficiency, courteous bearing, and genial manners won for him friends among all classes of men."

When the photograph was taken, Minta Allen was pregnant with her second child. Their daughter, Marian, was born in June, 1899, and their son, Henry Bosley Allen, would be born three years later. For all the times Minta had thought about the past when she was growing up, she would have thought about the future much more often after becoming a mother. The photograph was taken, and it probably wasn't long before Minta was thinking about the times that lay ahead for her growing family.

The morning of December 23, 1903, was cold. The temperature was still in the twenties at 8:10 when what was called "The Fast Train" from Cincinnati to New Orleans was due to arrive at Union Station in Nashville. But Engine 253 pulled in late. Henry Allen had made hundreds of runs to Montgomery over the previous decade, and for the past year he had come to know his counterpart in Alabama, James Julian, a black mail clerk for the railway who also had young children at home. Julian's eldest son, four-year-old Percy, would grow up to attend Fisk, and later become an internationally-noted chemist.

That morning wasn't the first time an engineer was running behind schedule. Henry would get off in Montgomery and take another train back to Nashville, while the train that took him to Montgomery would turn west and continue to New Orleans. When the locomotive finally rolled south out of Union Station, Henry was in the mail car, which was in front of the express and baggage car, the dining car, and the two sleepers that carried a large number of passengers.

Union Station, Nashville

Number 253 was more than an hour late and the engineer was trying to make up time. He ignored a major safety protocol, and when the train was fifteen miles north of Birmingham it ran head-on into a northbound train. The mail car was telescoped and Henry died a few minutes after he was pulled from the wreckage. Several people were badly injured, but only Henry Allen and the engineer were killed in the crash.

Less than two days before Christmas, Minta had become a widow and her children had lost their father, but only Catherine, who would turn eight in less than a month, was old enough to understand the tragedy. Her father, John B. Bosley, and his second wife moved into the Church Street home, but more dark times lay ahead. In April, 1905, burning debris from the fire that destroyed the main building at Vanderbilt University, ignited the family home and burned it to the ground. Although no one was hurt, a new piano, John B. Bosley's extensive library, and the family carriage were all lost.

Around 1907 Minta and her children went to New York and settled in Brooklyn, where one of her black cousins from Nashville, Dr. James G. Trimble, had moved after his graduation from Harvard Medical School. Minta and the children spent 1909 and part of 1910 in Europe, but in the spring of that year she got a telegram in Paris that her father was seriously ill. Before she and the children made it back to America, John B. Bosley was dead, but the funeral was not held until they reached Nashville.

Minta Allen and her children returned to Brooklyn, where Catherine and Marian and Henry grew up in an intellectually stimulating home. In 1911 Minta married William Frederick Trotman, who was active in real estate and manufacturing. Over the coming decades she would reflect the same dedication to politics and civil rights that had been displayed by her grandfather, Henry Harding, and by her father, John B. Bosley Jr.

Minta enrolled at the New York School of Social Work, and was soon involved in a variety of community initiatives. Through the National Association of Negro Women, she worked to bring about suffrage for colored women, and was instrumental in preserving the historic home of Frederick Douglass near Washington. She was a leader of the Brooklyn YWCA, which established programs for girls and created housing for single working women. She also worked to advance programs for girls through the Urban League, and pushed for health programs that served the local community through the Circle for Negro Relief. While serving as president of the Women's Civic League of Brooklyn, she stressed the importance of voting, and she was later active in the NAACP.

Minta also became an avid collector of African art, ultimately donating her collection to her alma mater, Fisk University. And seeking a religion that might promote more theological unity in the world, she turned some of her energy toward the Baha'i faith.

Her oldest child, Catherine, had been fifteen when Minta remarried. Catherine was fluent in French and could read German, and was an excellent student. After high school she attended Howard University and focused on library science, and went on to do graduate work at Columbia University. In 1920 she became the first individual of color to be hired by the New York Public Library as a reference librarian.

Catherine Allen Latimer (back left) at library

The next year Catherine married Benton Latimer, a college-educated veteran of World War One, and over the next three decades she played a central role in establishing and developing the library's Division of Negro History, Literature and Prints – one of the nation's premier collections of African-American culture – which was housed in Harlem at the 135th Street Branch of the library. The intellectual movement known as the Harlem Renaissance was underway in New York City during the 1920s, and during the period when she was helping those researching Negro history, Catherine interacted with such luminaries as Langston Hughes and W.E.B. Du Bois.

While Catherine continued to work at the library, Minta's other children dealt with the racial attitudes of New York. Henry married in 1933 and was an electrician for the city, while Marian became a math teacher in Brooklyn.

Henry's race had been listed as Negro by the census taker in 1930 and 1940, but when he registered for the draft during the early months of World War Two, the registrar listed him as having blond hair, blue eyes, and a fair complexion. Marian married in 1940 to a dynamic businessman named Probyn Thompson, a future fund raiser and recruiter for the NAACP. Thompson had founded an insurance company, and also established the real estate firm where Marian would become an executive.

Minta's children lived in New York, but their ties to their relatives, both to those who had stayed in Nashville and to those who had moved away, were maintained. Their grandfather, Henry's father Charles Allen, lived until 1928, having been married for sixty-two years to Sarah, who survived until 1934. The exceptional children they raised in the deep shadow of the Jim Crow era, along with the ten grandchildren who survived them, included two doctors, an attorney, a pharmacist, and the proprietor of the only hotel for blacks in Oregon.

Although Catherine experienced her share of race-related discrimination at the library, she continued her work until failing eyesight forced her retirement in 1948. She died soon afterward, leaving her husband and one child, Bosley Latimer, an alumnus of Bard College and a future artist. The next year, a half-century after she sat for a family portrait with her husband and her daughter in a photographic studio, Minta died of a heart attack.

Her daughter, Marian, who was forty when she married, died without children in 1975, and Henry was in his late-forties and apparently without children at the time of his mother's death. Unless Minta's grandson, Bosley Latimer, fathered children, or unless her son

Henry sired a child at some point, Henry and Minta, who had posed for a family portrait so long before with Catherine, have no living descendants.

But Charles Augustus and Sarah Cole Allen are well-represented in posterity. The last of their children, Lillian, died in 1983 at the age of 96. In her later years she had been asked about her father. "Papa was a head waiter at the old Tulane Hotel in Nashville, and that was thought to be a good job for a black man in those days. It was a time when your people seemed to do so much for you with so little."

Henry and Minta and Catherine may not have any descendants, but their lives continue to resonate through the influence they had on society, and that influence is intertwined with the lives of their predecessors.

Early in 1960, student activists began a series of sit-ins in downtown Nashville department stores. When they sat at the segregated lunch counters they hoped to integrate, they were close to the place where Henry Harding had been whipped with a leather strap a century earlier. They were close to where blacks and progressive whites had tried to integrate local streetcars in 1867, and where a few months later, Henry Harding had opposed the old political order as blacks voted in their first general election. The student protesters were close to the place where, in 1881, Henry Harding's wife, Maggie, had refused to be dragged away after trying to occupy a railroad car reserved for whites.

And when black students known as the Freedom Riders boarded a Greyhound bus to leave Nashville in the spring of 1961, they were less than a half-mile from where Henry Allen had boarded a train at Union Station at the close of 1903. None of them would have heard of Henry Allen, but they were, like Henry had been, bound for Montgomery by way of Birmingham. The Freedom Riders, comprised of blacks and a few whites, rode their bus down into Alabama, toward the collision they would have with the vicious mob that awaited them.

Given his combination of intellect and character, if he had lived in another time or in another place, Henry Allen would almost certainly have risen beyond the mid-level duties he was performing at the time of his death. Considering the gifts he had, he would not have been riding in a mail car on the day of the wreck.

But he lived in the south in the early 1900s, and what his sister would say some seventy-five years later about their father's job – "that was thought to be a good job for a black man in those days" – also applied to Henry's employment as a mail clerk. Not knowing that they were reflecting times that would come a few decades later, or that the collision they were about to experience might eventually serve as a metaphor, Henry Allen and his fellow mail clerk, a white man, rode their integrated mail car down into Alabama, as another train rolled up the same track from the deeper south.

14

Nelson Merry

Nelson Merry

Nelson Glover Merry came from a background that has been largely obscured by the passage of time. What can be pieced together reveals that his origins were nearly as unusual as the life he went on to live. The most important figure in shaping the man he would become was his mother, a light-skinned slave woman named Sydney. And another woman played a substantial role in his development – an aging white spinster named Elizabeth Merry.

Elizabeth was one of ten children born to Prettyman Merry and his wife, Catherine, in Buckingham County, Virginia. Merry had served as a lieutenant in the militia during the Revolutionary War, and when a vast section of Kentucky opened up for settlement, he became one of the region's most significant early landowners. His wife died in 1814, and following the death of Prettyman Merry in 1817, most of their children left Virginia. In 1820 forty-eight-year-old Elizabeth Merry and three other unmarried sisters were living in Hopkinsville, Kentucky, with twenty-seven slaves they had inherited from their father.

Elizabeth's sisters soon began to marry and leave home. In 1821 thirty-five-year-old Catherine married William Glover, a widower with three small sons, and she moved some eighty miles to the southeast – to Sumner County, Tennessee. And her other two sisters, forty-six-year-old Ann and forty-two-year-old Jemima, found husbands as well. Elizabeth was still living in Hopkinsville when Sydney Merry, who had been bequeathed to Elizabeth by her father, gave birth to Nelson in the summer of 1824.

Sydney already had at least six children, and by the time another son, Liverpool, was born in 1826, Elizabeth and her slaves were living in Sumner County. Her sister, Catherine Glover, had died at the end of 1825, and within a few months Elizabeth joined the household of her brother-in-law, William Glover. It was probably a tranquil time for Sydney, her children, and the other family slaves. The benevolent nature of Elizabeth Merry was recorded in a document in 1843.

"Their mistress was old and had never married. The slaves faithfully served their mistress, and she treated them with great kindness and was much attached to them. She was conscientiously opposed to slavery, and for many years had come to a fixed determination to emancipate them at her death."

One explanation of why slave owners who opposed slavery did not immediately liberate their slaves is that as free Negroes, they were exposed to threats that ranged from being taken by slave traders and sold back into slavery, to the possibility of laws being passed that could force them to leave the state.

Nelson Merry was likely the son of Abram, or Abraham, Glover, who may have been a slave, and possibly a relation, of William Glover. Nelson's younger brother, Liverpool, named Abram as his father, and although there seems to be no record that Nelson made a similar identification, his middle name was Glover, and the two brothers seem to have been especially close.

Nelson, like his mother, had a light complexion, but the identity of any Caucasian forbearer appears to be unknown. And it is unclear how many of Nelson's other siblings – from his oldest brother, Reuben, to his youngest brother, Jackson – may have been fathered by Abraham Glover, but his older sister, Frankey, had a son named Abraham.

Regardless of their heritage, because of Elizabeth's attitude toward her slaves, Sydney's children were likely raised under circumstances that few black families experienced in the South during that time. While Nelson did not receive an education when he was young, both he and Liverpool became pastors, and it is reasonable to suppose that Sydney's children may have been influenced by religion when they were growing up.

William Glover died in 1830, and he stipulated that, "my will and desire are that my sister-in-law, Elizabeth Merry, have the right and privilege of occupying the place where she now lives." Elizabeth Merry remained in Sumner County until around 1836, when she returned with her slaves to Hopkinsville. She died in the spring of 1840, and her will focused on how she wanted her executor to deal with her slaves.

"I wish it distinctly known that all my slaves are to have their freedom at my death, this being my most anxious wish. At my death I hereby commit Sydney and her children, Reuben, Eliza, Frankey, Lucy, Elvira, Stephen, Nelson, Liverpool, and Jackson; also Manda and her children Barnett, Inda, and Fanny; also Clarissa and George, the children of Eliza; also Frankey's child Elizabeth, to the care and protection of my executor Joel Parrish of Sumner County, to be taken by him, or by his order, to his residence and there to be set free or manumitted by him so soon as it can legally be done. I hope my friend Joel Parrish will suffer no legal difficulty to prevent it."

In July, 1840, Elizabeth Merry's fifty-nine-year-old former neighbor, Joel Parrish, travelled to Kentucky and brought the slaves back to Sumner County. Her will had made her intentions perfectly clear, but instead of setting the individuals free, Parrish hired out those who were old enough to work. Each slave had been left $15 by their mistress, and Parrish may have believed that more money was needed for them to economically establish themselves. He decided to hire them out, and explained that when they were emancipated after a few years, he would pay them what they had earned.

In 1842, eighteen-year-old Nelson and Liverpool, who was sixteen, were hired out at the rate of $100 each per year to the owners of a Sumner County sawmill on the Cumberland River near the Glover farm. Other members of the family continued to work at their various jobs, but three years after the death of Elizabeth Merry they retained a highly-respected attorney, Josephus Conn Guild of Sumner County, and a lawsuit was filed in Chancery Court. Their feelings were summed up in one part of the bill of complaint.

"Although it is believed that he ultimately intends to have the will executed, the executor has failed to apply to the courts for the purpose of having the complainants emancipated. They have been a long time in bondage, some of them advanced in years, and they are extremely anxious to enjoy the blessings of freedom."

Nelson Merry, likely accompanied by several members of his family, came to Nashville as early as 1843. They were still waiting to be emancipated, and they may have simply decided to leave Sumner County. Joel Parrish had kept a record of what they had earned, but it is unclear if they were paid what they were owed. Nelson bought a carriage and was able to make a living as a hack driver, and during that time he met Mary Jones, a highly intelligent sixteen-or-seventeen-year-old daughter of a free black couple – Edward (or Edmond) and Lizzie Jones, from Gallatin, in Sumner County.

Nelson became Mary's husband when he was around twenty-one, close to the time he became affiliated with the First Baptist Church in South Nashville. Like many local churches of that period, the congregation included blacks as well as whites, but the blacks were confined to the balcony when services were conducted. In later years Merry described the reception he received from the minister of First Baptist.

"I formed an acquaintance with Dr. R. B. C. Howell in 1844. I made it my business to go and hear him preach nearly every Sunday. He buried me with Christ in baptism, so I got very near to him. He was the first white minister that ordained a colored man in Tennessee – Rev. Edmund Kelly of Columbia. I visited Dr. Howell and received such courtesy that I was often astonished. When I would walk to the door of his study the first word was, 'Come in and have a seat.' He would lay down his pen and commence conversing and giving me lessons for my welfare and success. I never had a better friend in Nashville than Dr. Howell."

By the time Dr. Howell baptized Nelson Merry in the Cumberland River in 1845, Nelson may have already been employed as the church sexton, which involved such duties as maintaining the building and the grounds. By then Merry was experiencing a spiritual transformation that was described many years later.

R. B. C. Howell

"From his conversion he was impressed that he must preach the Gospel. He commenced to exhort, although with great fear and trembling. He tried to shrink from duty, but the more he tried, the stronger the conviction became that he must preach."

But the way Reverend Howell generally regarded Negroes, who comprised 99 of the 354 members of his congregation in the early 1840s, could have become an obstacle for Merry.

"Colored people require special teaching. Their minds are of a peculiar caste. Their temptations and trials are unlike those of others. They are generally dull of apprehension... A sermon which to a cultivated white congregation would be highly instructive and useful, is of little worth to colored people... because the amount of thought is more than they can grasp."

Despite his racial beliefs, Howell recognized the superiority of Merry's intellect and the positive nature of his character, and at some point he began to instruct his sexton in Baptist theology. Some thirty years later, Nelson Merry spoke about Howell's relationship with the black members of his church.

"When the First Baptist Church moved to Summer Street, special provisions were made for the colored members. The basement was assigned them, with the privilege of holding services on Sundays in the afternoon, and one night in

First Baptist Church

the week. Dr. Howell often met and preached. He also visited the colored members when sick, and pointed them to Jesus. He was kind and gentle in all his ways – ever ready to instruct those who would ask the way to Jesus."

There had been sentiment for creating a separate church for the black congregants since the 1830s, and while Nelson Merry was immersed in learning Baptist doctrine, there was continuing support from both blacks and whites for such a change. In 1847 a colored mission church, still under the control of the white congregation, was established in an old school house on Summer Street, and First Baptist provided a white preacher who was paid by the black members. Attendance rose at the mission church, which became a center for several aspects of black life. By 1849, along with regular services and Sunday school classes, there were business meetings, and some white church members taught black members to read.

In 1850 Nelson and Mary Merry had a one-year-old son, and Sydney was living with them in what was an otherwise white section of the town. His younger brother Liverpool, who had started going by his middle name, Napoleon, was living nearby and may have been working as a stonemason. Their youngest brother, Jackson, was also living in Nashville, where he was a well-known hack driver.

Another child was born to Mary, and in 1853, after years of

theological instruction, Nelson Merry sat for an examination by church leaders. News of the ordination of a black minister was announced in a local newspaper.

"An ecclesiastical council was convened… for the examination of Brother Nelson Merry with reference to ordaining him to the work of the gospel ministry. The council was opened with a prayer. Brother Merry, a colored brother who is a member of the First Baptist Church in Nashville, then related his religious experience, his conviction of duty with regard to the ministry, and his views on Bible doctrine. The council being satisfied with the narration of the candidate and the evidence of his call to the ministry, voted to proceed to his ordination. Services of ordination were performed, and Brother Merry solemnly set apart to the work of the ministry."

Nelson Merry became the pastor of the mission church, and his congregation grew steadily over the next decade. Although a lot was purchased and a building was constructed, the deed was held by the white church, to which the mission church was answerable. But Reverend Merry was largely able to operate as he saw fit. His ties with First Baptist Church were maintained, and along with some twenty-five other young black men, he attended a Bible class taught by Matthew B. Pilcher, who oversaw the black church.

In 1860 Nelson and Mary had five children, and Sydney was living in Nashville with Napoleon, who was working as a stonemason to support his wife and two children. By then Napoleon may have also been serving as a pastor in the African Methodist Episcopal Church – a denomination in which he would be a leader for much of his life. And their sister, Frankey, whose name had become Frances King, was living with her five children on a piece of property she owned a little west of Nashville.

The Civil War brought significant changes to Nashville churches, including to First Baptist Church. After many of the male members of First Baptist joined the Confederate military, and after a number of women and children from the church fled south when Nashville was taken by Union forces early in 1862, the church building was seized for use as a Union hospital. When Matthew B. Pilcher, a captain in the Confederate army, was mistakenly reported as having been killed in battle, Nelson Merry and the other black members of his Sunday school class wore black crepe to mourn his passing. In the mid-1880s a respected Nashville educator remembered the way Reverend Merry negotiated the war years.

"He urged his people to keep out of the war, to live in peace with all men, and to do their duty in fear of God. He stretched forth his hand to still the troubled passions of those around him. His influence with the colored people was superior to that of any man. He was in a condition to do much harm, but he did much good. His laborers cannot be overestimated."

The black population in Nashville more than doubled during the course of the war, and Merry took the lead in addressing some of the resulting poverty. At the close of 1865, a newspaper took notice of his efforts.

"The colored clergymen of this place, having Elder N.G. Merry as president, have organized the "Nashville Provident Association." Yesterday they raised over $500 among their brethren for the sake of charity. Their object is to relieve the poor without distinction of color. They have established a wood depot, and will open a soup house. We fear that these colored clergymen will put some white clergymen to the blush. The colored man is generally warm-hearted and confiding, but we dishearten and degrade him until he becomes a poor copyist of our own vices, and then we upbraid him for the degradation we have forced upon him. We admire the spirit which prompts this colored benevolent society to return good for evil."

In first decade of its existence, Reverend Merry's Church had seen only modest growth, but as more and more former slaves made their way into Nashville, membership in the mission church expanded. In 1865 the deed to the church property was transferred, and what became known as the First Colored Baptist Church was established as an independent institution. But less than a year later, Reverend Merry was arrested after being accused of committing what was seen as an egregious crime. One Negro witness testified about what occurred at a Thursday night service in 1866.

"The audience was dispersing when all at once they sat down, and I noticed a white man walk up the aisle, holding a colored woman by the hand. I heard several people laugh, with the remark that a white man was going to marry a Negro woman. Mr. Merry was not more than five minutes performing the ceremony."

The groom, William A. Johnson of Ohio, testified about his marriage to Josephine McConnico. They had known each other for about a year.

"I went down on Sycamore Street for the purpose of finding Mr. Merry, as I understood that he was a person who married colored people and white people, and that he was a minister of the Gospel. The first time I saw Mr. Merry was just about the time of the breaking up of the service. I went up to the pulpit and presented my license, and he solemnized the rites of matrimony. There were four gas lights near the pulpit. The lights were not dim. I paid him fifty cents for performing the ceremony. There was considerable laughing in the church. I suppose that were laughing at me."

The newspaper article closed with a summary of the hearing.

"The prosecutor held that the accused had violated the statutes of the State – that any person, clerk, magistrate, or minister who performed such a marriage was guilty of a misdemeanor and liable to a fine of $500. The presiding justice remarked that the case had been made, and that the crime was an aggravated one. He directed that the accused give bond in the sum of $1000 for his appearance at the next term of Criminal Court."

A New York newspaper reported that the offending couple was found guilty, and being unable to pay the $50 fines that were assessed, they were sent to the county workhouse. How the case against Nelson Merry was settled is unclear, but the favorable reputation he had with leading whites in the community likely came into play. And three months later his relationship with prominent whites was crucial in keeping the peace. A politically-motivated warning had been circulated that a Negro uprising was being planned, and Reverend Merry took the lead in dispelling the false rumor.

On a Saturday afternoon in mid-April, 1867, 4000 black citizens attended a political rally at the eastern portico of the State Capitol. The gathering of progressive Republicans – in which conservative Democrats were castigated – was to celebrate the new amendment to Tennessee law extending the right to vote to Negroes. Nelson Merry was one of the principal speakers.

"I have been opposed to the Democratic party – just as I would be opposed to an infidel – for that party taught doctrines contrary to the teachings of my God. Some of that kind will run for office – for Governor or for Congressman. They will drift around with big promises, and be full of honeyed phrases.

"The Devil has always been fond of making promises. Once he took Christ up on a high mountain, and promised him all he could see if he would only fall down and worship him. Well devils are about now, big with promises just like their Father. Don't believe them. As soon as they get into office and have the power, they will cry, 'Press them' – not only press them from the ballot box, but press the life out of them. Don't vote for anybody of that sort.

"We see a great many Conservatives soliciting colored men to vote for them. I want to hear them make a speech like this. 'I was a slaveholder, but I am convinced I was wrong. I tried my best to keep you in slavery, but the United States whipped me into letting you go free. I didn't use you just right. I am sorry for that and want you to let bygones be bygones, and vote for me.'"

Thanks to leaders like Nelson Merry, local black people were acutely aware of the crucial nature of the right to vote. Their interest was reflected in an account that had appeared in a local newspaper in January, 1867.

"In the splendid galleries of the House of Representatives yesterday, there were 160 Negroes and no whites. The Negroes had been attracted to the Capitol by the debate of the franchise bill. Speaker Mullins promptly stopped their noisy demonstrations of applause at the close of the first remarks made in favor of the bill."

From 1864 until early 1868, Nelson Merry had performed over 1000 baptisms, over 800 marriages, and he had assisted in the ordination of fourteen ministers. During the same period, First Colored Baptist Church expanded from 120 members to 780. Merry was among the most noted preachers in the region, but in an account of his life he wrote in 1868, his achievements were scarcely mentioned.

"Friends have often asked me for a sketch of my life and labors. I lived the life of a slave for twenty-four years. I had no time nor chance to educate myself. Many, like myself, were left without an education. My work has been uphill and my way gloomy all through the past, especially since I professed a hope in the Savior. But my trust has been in Him, and I hope to continue to the end."

The first child he and Mary raised was a son born around 1849. At least four daughters were born in the 1850s, and another son, their last child, was born around 1865. In 1870 four children were living at home, and Sydney Merry was living with the family as well. And Nelson worked tirelessly to meet the needs of his congregation, the First Colored Baptist Church, which had grown year by year. Information about the economic affairs of the church was contained in a letter written in 1872.

"Nelson Merry has a salary of $900. He takes up three collections every Sunday, averaging from $32 to $35. He gives about $100 to the sexton, leaving about $700 for missions. He said to me, 'We beat you white people when it comes to making up money.' Is this not praiseworthy?"

After living in Nashville for over a quarter-century – a period when she had watched her son Nelson become more and more prominent – the long life of Sydney Merry came to a close in the early summer of 1873. Nelson likely officiated at her funeral, where her remaining children, as well as her grandchildren and perhaps some great-grandchildren, must have attended the service.

At the time of his mother's death, Nashville was in the midst of a cholera epidemic. A decade later, William Stockell, a community leader and fervent Confederate supporter, would recall the role Reverend Merry played in giving comfort to suffering families in the 1873 outbreak, as well as during earlier epidemics.

"Nelson Merry was the chief man of his race to dispense charity. In the cholera days of 1849, 1850, 1866, and 1873, he was a great worker. More than once I found him on errands of mercy among the sick and suffering. He never shirked any duty."

Nelson Merry, always with the support of his wife, continued his work, but his efforts were not confined to members of his church. Those he baptized during his first twenty years of service included a number of convicts, and a 1874 newspaper article gave an account of how he ministered to a pair of condemned prisoners.

"Since Progue Bryant and Walker Ingram were condemned to death they have yearned for spiritual comfort. The other day they both made a confession of their faith to Rev. Nelson Merry, and were told by jailor Patterson that they were permitted to receive the rite of baptism at the First Colored Baptist Church. They were taken out of jail yesterday morning and conveyed to the church in hacks. The church was thronged with the colored population. Soon the prisoners and their escort filed up the aisle, and took seats at the altar.

"Rev. Merry said, 'We meet here for a purpose which ought to place every unbeliever in fear of death and hell. They ought to prepare to meet their God. The time of these two brothers is limited. They expire on the 10th of April. They have confessed their faith in the Savior.'

"Bryant became greatly affected, and there was weeping all over the house and shrieks from the women. Merry said, 'Be quiet, sisters. They said in response to questions I put to them that they had acknowledged and confessed to God every sin of which they were guilty.' The whole audience now joined in singing, as lined out by Rev. Merry. The singing was magnificent, the voices swelling into a grand chorus, which had such a powerful effect that while many men shouted, the women shrieked out, 'Glory be to God.' While Ingram joined in the singing, Bryant was much affected and the whole church melted into tears.

"The prisoners were then led into the baptistry, Bryant being baptized first. He arose from the water shouting and throwing up his hands. Ingram was next immersed, and acted in the same manner. They moved out of the church shaking hands with weeping men and women, and then entered hacks and were taken back to jail."

Five weeks later Reverend Merry accompanied Progue Bryant to Pulaski, Tennessee, where he had been convicted of killing an old white man with a rock during a fight. Merry stood on the scaffold with the condemned man and prayed, and few hours after witnessing the execution, he conducted the funeral.

Church membership kept growing under Merry's guidance, and soon afterward a newspaper article reported how he had met the ongoing challenge of providing space for his congregation.

"The First Colored Baptist Church first worshipped on Pearl Street in a small church accommodating 300 people. The congregation increasing to 800, the present building on Pearl Street was built. And now the new church on Spruce Street has been erected for the accommodation of its 1400 members. Reverend Merry has remained pastor of the church throughout its existence, preaching almost every Sunday and sometimes holding revivals that have lasted for months at a time.

"The church has an ornate front, with a spire running up nearly 100 feet and a roof covered with slate. Its dimensions are 57 by 92 feet, with a large choir loft in front, and perhaps has a greater capacity than any colored church in the South, seating 1500. The new church cost $21,000, of which $10,000 has already been paid. The membership having shown a willingness to help themselves, many whites have assisted in assuring their success."

By 1880 Nelson and Mary Merry only had two children living at home, but church membership had grown to around 2000. The challenges of leading his congregation became much greater on the night of February 12, when an especially violent storm – one that spawned a tornado that struck East Nashville – blew down the steeple of his church and left some $9000 in damages in its wake. The destruction would not be repaired for a time, and Reverend Merry held services that Sunday in the church basement.

First Colored Baptist Church

The building was ultimately repaired, but by the time of the storm Nelson Merry, who was in his mid-fifties, may have already been wearing down. Four years later, on July 14, 1884, he died at the age of sixty. The following day newspaper articles praised the deceased minister.

"Nelson Merry was a wonderful man. He did a great deal of good, not only in his own denomination, but in the community generally. He was the pastor of the colored Baptist Church on Spruce Street for about twenty-eight years. The membership of this church is much larger than any in Tennessee, or in the South. He was the shepherd of this large flock. This good old man attended his church services on Sunday night, and led the congregation in one of his favorite hymns, commencing with, 'I am bound for Canaan.' He then pronounced the benediction. At one o'clock he was struck with paralysis – never spoke a word more – and died in the afternoon."

Members of his church wrote a brief biography of Reverend Merry that included the role he had played in Baptist organizations as well as a description of his selflessness.

"He was the lifetime president of the State Baptist Convention, and president of this city's Colored Preacher's Union. No day was too stormy and no time of night was too late for him to visit the sick and afflicted of his flock."

The tributes and expressions of respect came from white people as well as from blacks. Bishop H.N. McTyeire, the founder and president of Vanderbilt University, had known Reverend Merry for a number of years.

"I have long regarded him as one of the strongest factions for good in the city. It is not easy to estimate the amount of evil repressed and the amount of good done by his influence – exerted through so many years. It is largely due to what the Baptist and Methodist churches did for colored people, in this way, that this country made the tremendous transition from 1861 to 1866."

Local newspapers provided extensive accounts of the Merry funeral.

"From six o'clock yesterday morning until late in the evening, thousands of colored people wended their way to and from the First Colored Baptist Church, where the remains of the deceased were laid out. Not a few of the people who attended the funeral came from the country early in the morning, They brought their lunch in baskets and ate their dinners while sitting on the curbstone on Spruce Street, waiting for the funeral to commence.

"The funeral services were yesterday afternoon – the largest assembly of the kind ever witnessed in Nashville. The interior of the church was heavily draped, while the large pulpit chair, that had for years been occupied by Reverend Merry, was covered with crepe. Mourning and genuine grief took possession of the congregation, and attested to the powerful hold the deceased had acquired. The church was filled to capacity, and the crowd outside extended several hundred yards, almost to Church Street.

"There were 140 carriages in the funeral train that followed the remains to the cemetery. The streets were lined with thousands of colored people, many of whom had waited for hours to catch a glimpse of the long procession. The horse drawing the buggy that Reverend Merry had driven around the city for so many years, was followed by the hearse. Instead of being driven, it was led, and on the vacant seat was the saddle bag in which he used to carry around medicine. He used to distribute the medicine among the poor of his congregation without price."

After the body of Nelson Merry had been lifted from the hearse and was being carried to his open grave in the City Cemetery, the vehicles in the rear of the funeral procession had still not left the church. Mary, along with her six children, left the cemetery after final words were spoken, and over the next thirty-three years she remained a member of the church that she had done so much to sustain.

Mary Merry saw the First Colored Baptist Church become Spruce Street Baptist Church, which would then split into several other local congregations – all of which could be traced back to Nelson Merry. Mrs. Merry lived long enough to bury four of her children, and while her body grew frail, her mind stayed sharp until her death in 1917.

The impact of the life of Nelson Merry continued to be felt through the various branches of the church he founded. The most notable of those branches is probably the congregation that would, in 1965, become First Baptist Church, Capitol Hill. Led by its pastor, Dr. Kelly Miller Smith, the church played a crucial role in the struggle to desegregate Nashville during the late 1950s and early 1960s. And as acts of grace roll into the future like carriages in a procession, the influence of Reverend Merry continues to shine from the churches to which he gave rise.

15

The McKissack Family

Miriam and Moses McKissack

Tradition holds that one of the McKissack family ancestors was a member of the Ashanti tribe in West Africa. He was thought to have been born around 1790, and after being enslaved and sold in a market on the Atlantic coast of what was later Ghana, he was brought to America on a slave ship. He later became the property of William McKissack, a North Carolinian who was born at the close of the Revolutionary War near the border of Virginia. At some point the slave's African name was replaced by the name Moses McKissack.

The father of William McKissack, with several members of his family, eventually left Person County, North Carolina, and moved to Middle Tennessee. A number of years later William and his wife and children, along with Moses and around thirty-five other slaves, migrated west to Maury County, where they settled a little to the south of Spring Hill. Family tradition relates that Moses had married Miriam, a Cherokee woman, around 1822, and they likely had several children by the time they came west.

The 1840 census lists William McKissack as having ten people in his family and owning forty-two blacks. Twenty of his slaves were employed in agriculture, two were engaged in commerce, and six worked in manufacturing or trade. Moses McKissack was almost certain to have been one of the people who worked as a tradesman.

His owner, William McKissack, was the owner of a brickyard, and tradition maintains that after Moses learned to make bricks, he went on to become a talented builder. That tradition is somewhat supported by information included in a legal proceeding filed in the 1850s, which reported that some of the McKissack slaves worked as brick masons and carpenters. McKissack may have been involved in a construction business, and along with other family slaves, he may have been hired out to builders.

Other McKissack slaves were sent to work in a cotton mill of which their master was part owner, and a slave named Theodore was hired out for a year to Thomas Hodge and Nelson Walker, a pair of black men who operated a barber shop eleven miles away in

Columbia. After Hodge announced that he was moving to Nashville and taking Theodore with him, William McKissack sued to have the contract set aside. He made his complaint in a court document.

"The boy, Theodore, is a mighty good boy, and I have always been disposed to treat him as though he were one of my own children. I have been in the habit of letting him do almost as he pleases, and have always had an eye to the boy's morals and his own wishes. I do not think he would be safe in Tom's hands, or that Tom would see to his physical needs."

The nature of McKissack's relationship with Theodore may pertain to McKissack's relationship with Moses. The family tradition is that William McKissack was helpful to Moses, and that Moses was ultimately emancipated.

Theodore, who appears to have been hired out at $275 per year, was returned to the family, and he would ultimately be inherited by William McKissack's daughter, Susan. The elder McKissack had other sources of income, but some of his money came from what was grown on his Maury County farm. There is no indication of whether the people who worked in his fields were treated as well as Theodore and Moses were supposedly treated.

Miriam is thought to have had fourteen children over the years, and although only a few of the births have been verified, one of her children was Gabriel McKissack. Gabriel, who was born in 1840, may have begun serving as an apprentice when he was old enough to work, and the tradition is that he learned a great deal about building techniques from his father.

William McKissack had a daughter named Susan who married Nathaniel Cheairs, and there was an oral tradition that Moses helped build *Rippavilla*, the grand brick mansion belonging to Nathaniel Cheairs. Work on the structure began in 1852, and Moses may well have worked as both a brick mason and a carpenter during the three years it took for the residence to be completed.

William McKissack died in 1855, the year the Cheairs family moved into their stately new home, and it is very likely that both Moses and Gabriel attended the funeral. And before he was lowered into the ground, they may have looked through the glass faceplate of  Rippavilla the iron coffin in which Mr. McKissack was buried.

The oldest McKissack son, James, became head of the family following the death of his father, and the McKissacks moved some thirty miles south into Giles County. There seems to be no record that Moses, or Miriam and their children, were emancipated, but one way or another, they moved onto the 660 acre McKissack farm along with the rest of the family slaves. They lived near Vale Mills on Richland Creek, just west of Pulaski, where there must have been building projects on which Moses and Gabriel worked together.

In whatever manner Moses and Theodore and his other slaves were treated when William McKissack was alive, the worst evils of the slavery remained as a threat. In early May, 1858, one of the brutal outgrowths of the slave culture took place, presumably on the McKissack farm. Moses and Miriam and Gabriel would have been intimately associated with the victim of that brutality – an individual who may have even been a member of their family. James McKissack employed an overseer, and news of what took place appeared in the *Pulaski Citizen*.

"A negro man belonging to Mr. McKissack near Vale Mills in

this county, was shot a few days since by his overseer, Mr. Robert Howard. The negro refused, when ordered by Howard, to take off his coat and receive a chastisement, whereupon Howard attempted to force him. The negro resisted, and Howard shot him, killing him almost instantly."

Whether such acts of violence were typically concealed, or whether they were newsworthy because of how unusual they were, the Civil War would soon make violence commonplace across the region. The war came and went, but the Ku Klux Klan was founded in Pulaski on Christmas Eve, 1865 – only four months after the death of Moses, and just five days before the death of Miriam. Their son Gabriel remained in Giles County, and in 1869 he married Dolly Maxwell, a light-skinned young woman of color. The next year they were living in Pulaski, where Gabriel was employed as a carpenter. In 1870 he not only owned real estate worth $500 – likely the value of the house in which they were living, but he also owned personal property – probably his tools – which were valued at $100.

Dolly and Gabriel McKissack

The first five children born to Gabriel and Dolly McKissack were daughters, but then a son, initially named Gabriel but later called Moses, was born in the spring of 1879. A succession of boys was born to the McKissack family in the years that followed. Moses was educated in Pulaski schools until he was eleven, and in 1890, the year in which his brother Calvin was born, he discontinued his formal education. Gabriel and Dolly were likely involved in the decision that led Moses to leave school and go to work for a white architect who lived in Pulaski.

In 1890, the same year that Moses went to work, the well-preserved remains of William McKissack were exhumed from the family graveyard and moved to a larger cemetery in Spring Hill. The world outside of his hermetically-sealed coffin was vastly different from the world that McKissack had known during his life, but the Jim Crow era was burying the potential of black Americans under an increasingly heavy layer of restrictions.

Moses gained experience in home construction, and in addition to becoming a construction supervisor at the age of sixteen, he was becoming more and more adept at making architectural drawings. In 1900 he was twenty-one years old and living in Pulaski with his parents. His father, Gabriel, was still working as a carpenter, and of the fourteen children that had been born into the family, nine were still living.

In 1905 Moses McKissack moved to Nashville and established himself as a contractor, and the next year he was hired by Granbery Jackson, an engineering professor at Vanderbilt University, to build a home on Farrell Avenue. As a result of the work he did, he began to receive contracts for other homes in the West End section, and project by project, he developed his reputation as a quality builder.

When McKissack was awarded the contract to build the Carnegie Library at Fisk University in 1908, the Nashville Banner referred to him as "a very capable and responsible colored architect, contractor, and builder." Over the next few years he designed and built three major structures for black schools in the state, and his reputation continued to grow. A 1921 state law required Tennessee architects to be licensed, and the following year, despite resistance from some local authorities, Moses McKissack and his younger brother, Calvin, were allowed to sit for the examination. Both passed the test and after they were awarded licenses, they formed McKissack and McKissack, the first black-owned architecture firm in the state.

Morris Memorial Building

In 1924, two years after the death of their father, the McKissack brothers won a contract with the National Baptist Convention, USA, to design the Morris Memorial Building on Charlotte Avenue, where they would locate their offices. Along with designing churches and a number of other structures across the South, the company went on to design several buildings in Nashville – Tennessee A & I Memorial Library and Washington Junior High School in 1927, Pearl High School in 1936, and Ford Green Elementary School in 1937.

Adapting to the Depression, McKissack and McKissack was awarded projects in several southern states, and with the coming of World War Two, the company made a major contribution to the war effort. In 1942 the McKissacks were awarded the contract to build the air base for the 99th Pursuit Squadron in Tuskegee, Alabama – the home of the Tuskegee Airmen. It was the largest contract ever won by a black business, and led to McKissack and McKissack being named America's outstanding black owned and operated company.

A long succession of subsequent accomplishments included the College Hill public housing project near Tennessee A & I, and with the death of Moses McKissack at the age of seventy-three in 1952, control of the firm passed to Calvin McKissack. Calvin led the company until he passed away in 1968, thirty-three days before the death of Martin Luther King. William DeBerry McKissack, son of the company's founder, Moses McKissack, then assumed control of the family business. In a 1981 interview, Leo Sam, a company vice president, diplomatically illustrated a local obstacle with which the company had long been forced to contend.

Moses McKissack III

"As a small minority firm, we have the problem of having very few clients in the private sector. We designed the Morris Memorial Building, but we have never participated in a major building downtown, or in Metro Center. People on boards who are responsible for these buildings have never looked to us in subcontracting. Most minority businesses depend heavily on government contracts, because they are awarded on the basis of credentials."

DeBerry McKissack led the firm until he suffered a debilitating stroke in 1983, and his wife, Leatrice – declining to sell the company – stepped in to lead McKissack and McKissack. With an undergraduate degree in mathematics and a graduate degree in psychology, Mrs. McKissack compensated for her lack of experience in architecture and construction with her deep reservoir of intellect, intuition, and leadership ability, as well as with a fierce work ethic. And after receiving initial help from her oldest daughter, Andrea, who was leading an engineering firm in Detroit, she received support from her twin daughters, Cheryl – who had a degree in civil engineering, and Deryl – whose degree was in structural engineering.

Calvin McKissack

After overcoming significant early challenges, the company prospered under Leatrice McKissack. The signature project under her leadership was the design of the National Civil Rights Museum in Memphis, which included the Lorraine Motel where Dr. Martin Luther King was murdered. The company continued to be awarded substantial contracts, including a substantial complex at Howard University in Washington, but Cheryl and Deryl eventually decided to branch out on their own, and each established a separate business.

In 1990 Deryl opened McKissack and McKissack of Washington, a firm focused on architecture, engineering, and construction management. The company handled such projects as the renovation of the US Treasury Building, was the lead architect on the Martin Luther King Memorial, and designed and built the Smithsonian National Museum of African American Culture and History – all in Washington DC. With offices nationwide, including in Chicago,

Dallas, and Los Angeles, it grew to manage a portfolio of billion-dollar projects.

The company established by Cheryl McKissack in New York in 1991 focused solely on construction management, and grew exponentially as well. She had been in business for a decade when her mother was ready to retire. Cheryl bought the company that her grandfather, Moses McKissack, had established some ninety-five years earlier, and she relocated the Nashville office to Philadelphia in 2001. McKissack

William DeBerry McKissack

and McKissack, the oldest black-owned construction company in America, grew to have over 150 employees. It played a crucial role in such high-profile projects as the JFK Airport Terminal One project and the Long Island Railroad Hub, and won contracts to oversee a succession of multi-billion dollar construction projects.

Moses and Miriam McKissack could not have imagined the lives their descendants would experience, or what they would accomplish. And those lives and accomplishments would have also been beyond the dreams of their son, Gabriel, or of their grandsons, Moses and Calvin. From West Africa to America, from slavery to freedom, and from making bricks to designing memorials of global significance – the journey of the McKissack family is still underway.

16

Sampson W. Keeble

Sampson Wesley Keeble was born in northwest Rutherford County in 1833, a half-mile from the village of Jefferson. His mother, Nancy, had been born in 1805 in Virginia, and came to Tennessee with her master, Walter Keeble, when she was around six years old.

Sampson had several brothers and sisters, and they grew up in an environment that may have been more humane than what many slaves experienced.

After Walter Keeble died in 1844, eleven-year-old Sampson and his sixteen-tear-old brother, Marshall, were inherited by Horace P. Keeble, his deceased master's twenty-two-year-old son. Sampson was likely engaged in farm work for the next few years, and in 1851, when he was eighteen, he began working – possibly after being hired out – at a local newspaper, the *Murfreesboro Telegraph*. As a roller boy, he was responsible for applying ink to the printing plate. After holding that job for about three years, he became a pressman, and some years later he was described by a long-time newspaperman.

"Sampson used to be our pressman when I was a journeyman printer in Murfreesboro in 1855. He could read and write then, and was an active, intelligent, and obedient servant. His master thought highly of him."

It was apparently in the mid-to-late 1850s when Sampson married a light-skinned slave woman named Harriet, and she gave birth to their son in southeastern Rutherford County around 1859. As was frequently the case with slave couples, Harriet and Sampson probably lived apart, and the Civil War would take them even further away from each other.

Sampson's owner, Horace Keeble, traveled to Georgia and enlisted in the Confederacy, and Sampson would be with him for much of the conflict. Along with cooking and doing laundry, his duties as a servant would have included barbering. Sampson returned to Tennessee before the end of the war, and in February, 1865, he established a barber shop on Cedar Street "under the Commercial Hotel," near the site where a slave market had been in operation only a few years earlier.

Sampson Keeble – literate, intelligent, and energetic – soon became a leader in the local Negro community. In 1866 he attended the Colored Convention in Nashville as a delegate, joining such men as Nelson Merry, Peter Lowry, Daniel Wadkins, and Frank Parrish. The next year, as a leading man of color, Keeble

Fashionable

BARBER SHOP

AND SALOON,

No. 14 Cedar St., under Commercial Hotel

SAMPSON KEEBLE, Proprietor.

CITIZENS and strangers wishing anything in this line, are invited to give this popular establishment a call. The most experienced practical barbers only are employed, and none but the best and most elegant materials used. Every department is under competent supervision, and cleanliness and neatness strictly observed. Call, be shaved, and satisfy yourselves.

Nashville Daily Union, February 28, 1865

was one of fifteen blacks who felt compelled to publicly dispute a dangerous false rumor being spread that Negroes were plotting to rise up against local whites.

Prominent white men went exclusively to black barbers, and the relationships that developed over the years between barbers and their customers created an invaluable avenue of communication between the races. In describing his profession as it was in the 1840s, James Thomas, a former slave who had been a barber in Nashville in those years, explained the racial attitudes that continued to govern many barber shops in the late 1860s.

"In those days nobody seemed in a great hurry. They had time to talk in the barber shop. Everything was discussed – social, commercial, political, and financial. The old time barber not only learned the gentleman's ways, but was often called to gentlemen's houses – sometimes professionally, or sometimes to care for a guest when there was a social gathering. The free Negro was tolerated around the gentleman's home as his barber, and frequently waited on the table in case of a gathering, or to make music for a dance.

"But I have not seen a poor white man anywhere about the

premises. If a white man attempted to wait on a southern country gentleman in the capacity of a barber, he would go into spasms. If a white man came toward him to shave him, he would jump out of his chair. It was not the white man's place to play the part of servant. The true southern gentleman had no use for poor white people."

According to family tradition, Sampson Keeble supplemented his income by working as a janitor in a law office, where, after expressing an interest in studying the law, he was provided with instruction by one or more of the lawyers. The political structure of the state was muddled in the wake of the Civil War. For a few years – with those who had supported the Confederacy not allowed to vote, and with freed male slaves allowed to vote for the first time – a number of changes took place. In 1867 an act of the Tennessee General Assembly granted black men over the age of twenty-one the right to vote, and at the end of the year Keeble was appointed as a delegate to the State Republican Convention.

Keeble was highly involved in political and community affairs during the period of reconstruction. In 1869 he attracted significant support, but fell short of becoming the Republican nominee for the State House of Representatives. In 1870 he was a leader in the effort to establish a Colored Fairgrounds and he helped plan a massive celebration in May that was of great importance to local Negroes.

"The colored people of Nashville celebrated the ratification of the Fifteenth Amendment yesterday. The whole affair was conducted in a very praiseworthy manner. At ten o'clock, with flags and banners, the procession commenced to move up Broad to Vine Street, and along the line of march. The African population was out in force, and women and children lined the street. Not including the crowd who went in droves to the grounds, the procession numbered not less than 1500 people. One notable feature was the large number of banners and mottos – 'This Is My Native Land;' 'United We Stand, Divided We Fall;' 'Equal Rights for All;' 'Tell Them We Are Rising;' and 'We Live in the Future.'

"The grounds consisted of around five acres, and there were about fifty refreshment stands scattered in every direction. No intoxicating liquors were allowed, and in consequence, everything passed along in an agreeable manner. Nelson Walker opened the exercises of the day, and a prayer was offered by Reverend Merry."

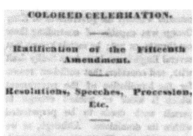

Union and American, May 5, 1870

A speech was made, and then a long resolution was read. The crowd was large and it would have been difficult to hear, but much that was said must have resonated with those standing close enough to where the speaker stood.

"We greet with joy and heartfelt satisfaction the ratification of the Fifteenth Amendment. It is declared to be a part of the Constitution of the United States, and we recognize the onward march of justice and the fulfillment of our country's mission as a republican form of government. We recognize the principles of true and enlightened Christianity… While we, as Americans, may differ in complexion, we are one, and while we may differ in politics, our interests are one and we owe allegiance to our country."

A few weeks after the celebration, Sampson Keeble's wife Harriet died at the age of twenty-nine. She left her only child, Samuel, to be cared for not only by Sampson, but by his mother and his sister, who were both part of the household. A second major change in his life took place at the end of the year, when he purchased Nashville's leading hotel for people of color from Henry Harding. It was known as the Harding House, and would have added to his prestige in the community. But only a few weeks after he took over the Harding House, Sampson was involved in a bizarre incident that nearly cost him his life. The altercation was reported in a local newspaper.

"Byron Jackson was tending a stall at the Market House yesterday, and he sold a turkey to Sampson Keeble. Keeble handed him some money, took the turkey, and walked on. Jackson was busy waiting on customers. In a few minutes the amount only proved to be a dollar, and when Keeble passed that way shortly afterward, Jackson stated that he had only paid one dollar. Keeble insisted that he had paid a dollar and a half. When "the lie" was exchanged, Keeble struck Jackson and a fight ensued. They were separated, and Keeble ran out and got a rock. He came rushing back in to demolish his antagonist, but he was prevented from striking by the bystanders.

"Going directly home, he got a cane with a loaded head, and again made his appearance at the Market House. He commenced a furious assault on Jackson, but Jackson rested the cane from Keeble and struck him a fearful blow on the head which laid him out. Keeble was taken home, and it was discovered that his skull had been broken in. Several pieces of the skull were removed, and Keeble is lying in very critical condition."

Sampson had recovered enough by November to travel some 95 miles to work as a waiter at a wedding in Winchester, Tennessee. While he was there he encountered an old acquaintance, who wrote brief a brief account of Keeble.

"Sampson has made money, owned several barber shops in

Nashville, and now owns a hotel for the accommodation of the colored people. He is a worthy "amendment," and we were glad to see him. We would give him some of our advice as to the influence he could, and ought to, exert with his race, but this would be out of place in connection with a wedding."

The undispensed advice would have probably been paternalistic and demeaning, as well as unnecessary. Less than a year later, he was nominated by the Davidson County Republican Party to be one of its candidates for State Representative. There were nine candidates, and the four men who received the most votes would be elected to office. In the same election that gave President Grant a second term in office, Sampson Keeble – who got over 5000 votes and finished fourth – became the first black man elected to the Tennessee General Assembly.

Late in 1872 a local newspaper presented what was meant to be a brief biography of Keeble.

"S.W. Keeble, one of the Representatives-elect from Davidson County, is the first colored man ever elected a member of the General Assembly of this State. He is by no means a "bigoted nigger," as might be expected. Upon the contrary, while he knows the laws guarantee him equal political rights with the other members, he is fully conversant of the fact that there is a social difference between them – as great as the difference between day and night. He was the slave of H.P. Keeble, and he holds in grateful remembrance his former master. He has a barber shop in Nashville, is very attentive to his business, and is one of the best and most industrious of our colored citizens."

But a second newspaper article – written a month later in January, 1873, just after he had assumed his legislative duties. – gave a better indication of the environment in which he found himself.

"The present General Assembly of Tennessee will long be noteworthy as its members include the first and only negro who has ever attained legislative honors in this State. In the House of Representatives, solitary and alone, sits the Honorable S.W. Keeble of Nashville, representing Nashville. He is of low stature, rather heavy set, and while he can undoubtedly claim an unmixed African descent, he is of a ginger-cake complexion. He bears his honors with meekness bordering on timidity. Generally four members from the same county occupy two double desks, however in this case the colored member has a 'bunk' all to himself.

"He is evidently very lonesome, and looks as if he thought he was doing something wrong. As a voter he has scarcely an equal – jumping up and voting 'yes' or 'no,' and sitting down and looking around as if he had shot off a decree which was to shake empires and was timid of the result. Keeble can read and write, after a fashion, and is less obnoxious on this account. Formerly a slave in this State, he shouldered his cooking utensils and went into the Southern Army, and after the war he settled in Nashville and became a barber. The ex-Confederate members of the legislature declare their intention to hear what he may have to say, and make him feel as easy as his position will allow. He will make little headway as a legislator."

At the close of the legislative session, another derisive article appeared in a Memphis newspaper.

"The Tennessee legislature has adjourned, and Sampson Keeble – accused of no grievous folly and suspected of no crime – is well esteemed. Two years ago he was knocked on the head by a black Philistine, and he lost a tin-cup-full of brains. With a hole in his cranium as big as a woodpecker's retreat in a stump, Sampson constitutes a curious figure, standing forth in black solitude in the midst of the General Assembly."

In the one term he served, Keeble introduced a handful of bills that were intended to improve the lives of those in the black community. None of his attempts to pass legislation succeeded. He was not a candidate for reelection, but he continued to be an influential local figure. He remained active in the Republican Party, and in 1876 he was elected to serve as a magistrate, narrowly defeating a white opponent. On two occasions that may or may not have been politically motivated, he would be accused of using his position for extortion, but he continued to serve as a magistrate into the early 1880s.

A widespread lack of other economic opportunities resulted in more and more young black men going to work as barbers, and their rising numbers caused a decline in the pay received by those already in the profession. A meeting, attended by both shop owners and their employees, was finally held at Sampson Keeble's office. The grievances that were aired were not resolved, and along with a threatened strike, a list of demands was generated.

"We, the journeyman barbers of Nashville, met July 31, 1877, at the office of S.W. Keeble to consult on our interests. We are doing ourselves and our families injustice to work for one-half of what we make at the prices now charged. Our employers, having cut prices down, are the cause. We are crowded with more barbers in shops than there is work for them, thereby curtailing us of making a living. We protest against the employment of itinerant barbers, which are an injury to the steady working journeyman. While this is beneficial to our employers, it is an injury to us. Therefore we will not work for less than 65 cents on the dollar. We recommend to our employers to put the price of shaving at fifteen cents. We will not work for less than seven and a half cents on shaving, seventeen and a half cents on hair cutting, and seventeen and a half cents on shampooing."

The ultimatum was rejected by barber shop owners and the strike fizzled, but changing economic conditions helped bring an end to the once-relaxed atmosphere of the barber shop. Beyond his work as a barber and a magistrate, Sampson Keeble had the responsibility of providing for his family. After having been a widower for several years, he was in his early forties when he married Rebecca Gordon in the mid-1870s.

By 1880 they had two young children – a son and a daughter – and the household included Sampson's aging mother, Nancy, as well as a niece and an adopted daughter. Other children were born, but only two would survive into adulthood. Sampson continued to work as a barber after Nancy Keeble died in 1883, but in 1886, after apparently taking up a new profession, he was identified as a teacher in the city directory. In 1887, perhaps while he was away on a visit, Sampson Keeble died in Texas at the age of fifty-four.

His daughter, Jeanette, went on to graduate from Fisk and became a highly-respected teacher. She married an eminent educator and raised a large family, and when she died in 1956 – with the most intense period of the Civil Rights era only a few years away – her five children and six grandchildren were poised to experience the next chapter of the movement in which her father had once played a highly visible role.

17

The Napier Family

In the early 1800s an enslaved girl named Rebecca escaped from her owners in Frederick County, Maryland. She was around ten years old, and she was taken in by a Quaker family in Pennsylvania. Rebecca remained with them for about a year, but then she was recaptured and taken back to Maryland. She was soon transported to Nashville, where she was apparently bought by William Watkins. Watkins, an aging Revolutionary War veteran and small scale land owner, lived near Richland Creek, a few miles west of Nashville. At some point Rebecca became the property of the old man's son, William E. Watkins, who was only three or four years older than Rebecca. The depth of Rebecca's relationship with the younger Watkins is no longer known, but sometime between 1817 and 1826 he sired a daughter by Rebecca.

Rebecca may have had other children fathered by William E. Watkins, who was in his early thirties when he married a Caucasian woman in 1819. While Watkins had children with his white wife, Rebecca raised their daughter, Jane, on the Watkins farm. It was probably around 1841 when Jane first met Carroll Napier, a young, light-skinned man who lived about two-and-a-half miles closer to Nashville on Charlotte Pike, on a place that had recently been bought by Elias Napier.

When Colonel Richard Napier, a former officer in the Revolutionary War, came to Tennessee in the mid-1790s, two of his sons, Elias and Richard Claiborne Napier, arrived along with the rest of the family. The Napiers eventually settled in what became Dickson County, where young Richard Napier became a highly successful iron master. His brother Elias left home and attended medical school at the University of Pennsylvania, and after graduating in 1811, he served, along with both his brother and his father, in the Creek War.

Over time, Elias Napier became more and more involved in the iron business, and after the death of his brother in 1833, he took charge of the two furnaces and three forges, as well as the sixty or so slaves who operated the various ironworks. Although he was highly successful when it came to running his iron concern, his controlling personality, his unwillingness to adhere to social convention, and what appears to have been the nature of his sexual interactions led to a somewhat unusual domestic situation.

His only marriage – to a white woman – ended in divorce after only a few months, but he would eventually father a number of children. Having already been named as the father of a white child in an 1819 court case, from 1822 to 1830 Napier sired five children, a daughter and four sons, all born to his slave woman, Judy, who was also known as Judah.

His oldest son of color, William Carroll Napier, was born in Dickson County in 1824. Carroll and his younger brothers were slaves, but due to their father's influence, they were all educated with the white children of the neighborhood. Carroll worked on the family farm, and from an early age he was given important tasks, including driving large loads of iron products from the forges all the way into Nashville, collecting payments, and then returning to Dickson County with the money.

When Elias Napier came to Davidson County in 1841, the fifty or so slaves he brought with him included Carroll and his four other children by Judy, along with two or three grandchildren and a number of aging slaves who had spent long years producing iron. Sixty-five or so other slaves were left behind to continue their work at the furnaces and the forges.

Carroll Napier must have met Jane Watkins soon after the arrival of his family on the outskirts of Nashville. The Napier Place was a little to the northeast of where Charlotte Pike crossed Richland Creek, and the Watkins Place was only two-and-a-half miles to the southwest. Few other details of their early relationship were recorded, but in 1844 Carroll and Jane rode horses to Nashville, where they were married by an elderly black preacher named Andrew Chapman. They rode back the same night – he to the Napier Place and she to the Watkins Place – and they went back to work the following day.

They may not have had a wedding night, but their first child, James Carroll Napier, was born in a slave cabin on the Watkins Place in early June of the following year. By the time Elias Napier, the family patriarch, turned sixty-five in March of 1848, his health may

William E. Watkins residence

have already been failing. Being a scrupulous businessman, he prepared a highly detailed will that not only stipulated how his possessions were to be distributed, it contained specific instructions regarding Judy and the children he had fathered.

"I hereby emancipate and set at liberty the following named slaves, Judy, my seamstress, and her five children, to wit, Fanny, William Carroll, James Monroe, Thomas Benton, and Andrew Jackson… And all my household and kitchen furniture I give to Judy and her four sons and to Lizzy, my cook, a yellow girl, to be divided between them…

"And I hereby give to Judy and her five children, the use and possession of my farm on Richland Creek in Davidson County, together with the crop now growing on the same, and all the stock of every kind at said farm. The stock and crop are to be subject to their entire control and disposition. I also wish the Negroes which I have emancipated, to be furnished out of my smokehouse and other places with bacon, corn and meal, sugar, coffee, and salt, sufficient to last them for provisions for twelve entire months after my death. And they are to enjoy the possession of said farm until the 1st day of March next, and on their leaving said farm, my executors are to take possession and rent it out or dispose of it as they may think proper until it is sold."

And Elias provided a way for them to transport the household furnishings, clothes, and food they would need to establish a new home. At his death two of his experienced servants were to "select my box wagon and eight of my best mules and gear, which my executors are to place in the possession of those slaves that I have emancipated for their own use and benefit, all of which are to be and remain their property."

And he was determined that the wagon he provided would take them on a long journey. "Now, it is my will and desire that should any of those negroes that I have emancipated, choose to live in Davidson County or make that their general home, then my executors are to send an officer and take possession of said emancipated slave and put him or her on the block in the town of Charlotte (in Dickson County), and hire him out... until he may quit Davidson County and choose some other place for a home, and the money arising from said hire, if any, is to be equally divided among the other slaves that I have emancipated."

Napier also liberated the five grandchildren he had by Judy's daughter, Frances, and then he went on to free two other slaves who appear to have been his children as well.

"I hereby... emancipate and set at liberty Caroline and her child, who are to go with Judy and the other emancipated slaves, and are to be subject to the control of Carroll and James. If her conduct deserves it, they are to expel her from the company and send her back to this county with her youngest child. And should Caroline indulge

240

excessively and notoriously in drunkenness and debauchery, she is to be expelled and sent back to the country by Carroll and James, two of my emancipated slaves.

"And I do also hereby emancipate and set at liberty a yellow boy named Solomon, about six years old, the son of a mulatto girl called Angeline... And Solomon is to be furnished by my executors with fifty dollars per annum for his schooling, etc., until he is fifteen years of age, then he is to be put to some trade which my executors may select, giving due to his genius and capacity, and when he is twenty-one years of age, they are to pay into his hands the sum of five hundred dollars, to commence his trade on... provided he may be of sober and steady habits... "

But Napier did not liberate an additional child he may have fathered. He directed that the son of a friend was to receive, "my negro infant child of my negro woman Clary. Said child is a girl and is named Kitty, and is now at the breast of its mother. The said child Kitty is to be delivered... as soon as it can be taken from the breast of its mother... I have this day executed a bill of sale."

The section went on to emancipate a number of other individuals, and he acknowledged the role they had played in his financial success. "Many of these servants are of advanced age, and have with faithfulness aided me in making what property and money I have..." Elias Napier died on August 4, 1848 – three days after completing the final codicil of his will.

It is not clear whether Jane was purchased from her father, William E. Watkins, or if he set her free, but she left Davidson County with her husband, Carroll, their son, James, and the other emancipated Napier slaves. Carroll and his younger brother led the entourage, which included their mother, Judy, as well as their sister and her five children, and six-year-old Solomon. Riding in the wagon or on horseback, or driving their livestock on foot, they headed north, concluding their trip when they reached the free state of Ohio. A farm was bought, Jane gave birth to her second child, and the family stayed together for a time. But after eighteen months, Carroll and Jane decided to return to Tennessee, and despite the instructions contained in Elias Napier's will, they settled in Nashville.

Carroll opened a livery stable, and year by year, the number of horses, wagons, carriages, and buggies he could rent out slowly increased. He was

Republican Banner April 17, 1856

popular with whites as well as with blacks, and he became a well-known community figure. Jane Napier gave birth to four sons and a daughter during the first fourteen years of their marriage. Although their second son, William, died in 1851, the rest of the Napier children grew up to reflect, in various ways, both their heritage and the times in which they were living. And by the time Nashville was taken by Union forces early in the Civil War, Jane – with the responsibilities of motherhood largely diminished – was able to attend school and finally learn to read.

Carroll and Jane Napier's son, Henry Alonzo Napier was born in Nashville in 1851, and during his years in school he showed considerable intellectual promise. He attended Fisk during Reconstruction, and with progressives running the government, traditional racial restrictions were relaxed. In 1870 Alonzo, the great-grandson of two Revolutionary War veterans, received an appointment to the United States Military Academy. In order to prepare for the academic rigors he would face, he attended Howard University, graduating in 1871 at the head of his class and as leader of the cadet corps.

The appointment of Alonzo Napier – the second black to be nominated to attend the Academy – was reported in newspapers across the country. The first cadet of color to attend West Point, James Webster Smith of Charleston, had been shunned and abused after his arrival in 1870, and a periodical in Ashtabula, Ohio, anticipated what Alonzo might face.

"A second colored cadet, named Napier, has arrived at West Point. He stands about five feet nine inches in height, is square-built, and if attacked by any of the white trash, would be very apt to give them hot work, preparatory to annihilating them."

But before a nominee could become a cadet, he was required to pass both a physical and an academic evaluation. The Nashville Union and American carried an update written on June 7.

"President Grant arrived here last evening and was received with a national salute. Very nearly all the applicants for admission to the Military Academy have come forward for the present examination. Of the ninety-six that have been examined, thirty-one have been rejected. Among those who passed were a son of Brigham Young, and Napier, the colored boy from Tennessee."

Grant had come to West Point for the graduation of his son, Frederick, and although the president's appearance received considerable attention, an article in the New York Tribune included a description of the incoming cadets and the reporter's appraisal of what set Alonzo Napier apart from his classmates.

"The examination of the newcomers preceded that of the graduates. Most of the aspirants are very young, and generally hailing from the backwoods, they are not – to speak mildly – models of manners or mirrors of bearing. They are a rugged, sober, honest set of lads, very eager, very bashful, and dreadfully awkward. It is not conducive to a complacent state of mind to be thrust into lofty barracks, unknowing and unknown.

"Tennessee sends a colored lad of marked capacities named H. A. Napier. He was educated at Howard University and is excellently grounded in the common branches of academic education. He repeated to me the substance of the examination, and rattled off question and answer with astonishing readiness. Astonishing – for not one boy in ten can make a clear story of English grammar. This lad solved the relation of words with incredible facility."

A newspaper in Fall River, Massachusetts, contained a very complimentary article. "The new colored cadet, Henry Alonzo Napier, is a native of Nashville. Rumor says he has the blood of the ancient and honorable English family of Napier in his blood. He is dignified, ready-spoken, and quite charming as a conversationalist. He is said to be very patient and even-tempered, but not at all likely to suffer being trampled upon unjustly. He has a very natural and becoming military bearing – acquired at Howard University, where he was Quartermaster and Adjutant of Cadets. He has the reputation of being a good scholar and a conscientious gentleman."

Although he passed the West Point entrance examination with flying colors in the summer of 1871, he was soon being called, "Lord Napier." General Robert Napier was the commander of the British army in India at the time, and the nickname was meant to demean Alonzo Napier.

The following spring a Nashville newspaper, the Republican Banner, reported that Napier had finished the year at the bottom of his class. It was not until years later that details of his departure from West Point were reported in a St. Louis newspaper. "His treatment there was characterized by all the persecutions of which young army roughs are capable. Having put up with this treatment as long as he could, he finally knocked one of his tormentors down. He was tried and all the testimony given was against him."

West Point Cadets, circa 1870

Nashville newspapers failed to carry any explanation of why such a formidable young man had floundered as a cadet, but a decade later Alonzo Napier wrote an eloquent account of what he had experienced at West Point.

"During that time I failed to discover a single trace of honor. It would be hard to find a set of men who would do more dastardly deeds, and take more contemptible means to hide them. While sitting at the table (with the only other black at West Point, Cadet Smith), we would ask for 'bread, please,' or 'butter, please,' or 'coffee, please,' or 'water, please.' Then we would hear 'Pass that damn nigger the bread and let him shut his mouth,' or 'Why don't you give that damn moke the butter.' When Smith and I were passing along the walk, we would hear, 'Here come the damn mokes. Let these damn stinking niggers pass.'

"Cadets are the officers of the battalion. Some corporal or sergeant would stand behind me and jot down such charges as, 'Hat not on properly,' or 'collar not adjusted,' or 'feet not at proper angle while in rank' – nearly all of which were unmitigated lies. Sometimes I would receive twenty-five or thirty reports a day. I received about 500 demerits in the first six months.

"When falling in at roll-call, for meals, parades, or anything else, there was always a struggle to keep from being next to the niggers. The officer in charge, a United States officer, would see this and never say a word. And I have known cadets to enter our rooms and throw a bucketful of slop (human waste) on our beds. The United States officers encouraged and abetted the deeds of the cadets.

"Under these circumstances what could be done? Complain of such treatment to the commandant of cadets? You go to the commandant and lay before him your grievances. He is 'very much surprised to think that a cadet would be guilty of any such unbecoming conduct!' He promises to investigate the matter and punish the guilty parties. You name your men and leave feeling that the honor of the school will secure to you your rights, and that the distinctive character of American citizenship is intact.

"The cadets against whom you brought charges are summoned before the commandant, put on their honor, and they testify – to a man – that what you state is false, and that *they* are the aggrieved parties. These men will swear to this and, if necessary, have a dozen others who were not present swear to the very same thing. Then the commandant sends for the cadet who, a short time earlier, left under the impression that the Government would protect him. The commandant delivers a lecture on the vice of lying, and tells the cadet that if he wants to get along at the academy, he must 'pursue quite a different course.' The cadet is then sent to his room under close confinement, or with a demerit, and cautioned never to be guilty of lying again. Such is an affair of honor at West Point.

"Honor at West Point is a myth. Deception, hypocrisy, and cruelty run riot. Fair play is unknown. Officers and cadets unite to crush every colored man that dares to darken the door of the Academy, and if he has nerve enough to stand it the whole term, they will conspire to disgrace and dismiss him. The infernal abuses should be cured, or the institution ground to powder, for it is a standing disgrace to the flag it is designed to honor and perpetuate."

After leaving West Point, Alonzo Napier, still reeling from what he had just experienced, took a steamship from New York to Charleston, arriving in early July. He soon made his way to Tallahassee, where he accepted a position in the office of the Florida Secretary of State. Within a few weeks he married Venus Bond, an illiterate light-skinned eighteen-year-old cook. He worked in Florida until he became infected with swamp fever (malaria, typhoid, or encephalitis). He was dangerously ill, but he was able to return to Nashville in a private car provided by the Louisville and Nashville Railroad. It is unclear whether his young wife came with him. A divorce would be granted in 1877, but his marriage to Venus may have fallen apart long before that time.

Regaining his health, he not only became principal of a Negro school in the suburbs of Nashville, he enrolled in Meharry Medical College. By late summer of 1874 he announced that would be a candidate for City Council, and in early fall he received the award for most graceful rider at Davidson County's Colored Fair.

Just after the Civil Rights Act was passed by the House of Representatives on February 4, 1875, and before it was passed by the Senate on February 27, a contingent of some 500 blacks – emigrating from Giles, Maury, and Rutherford Counties – passed through Nashville on their way to Kansas. By the time the bill was signed by President Grant on March 1, a local newspaper had published an overview of the new law.

"It provides that all citizens, black as well as white, shall be entitled to full and equal enjoyment of the accommodations, advantages, facilities, and privileges of inns, public conveyances, theaters, and other places of public amusement, and that no citizen, on account of color, be disqualified from serving as a juror."

On March 10, less than two weeks after the bill was signed into law, a Nashville newspaper article described a local repercussion of the act.

"The civil rights agitation is increasing rather than diminishing. Mr. J. T. Rundle, the proprietor of the restaurant at the corner of Deaderick and Cherry Streets, says he has been forced to close his establishment on account of the frequent invasions of Negroes who have set upon him. He believes that they do it with a view of obtaining, by force of law, $500 should he refuse to permit them to eat. He says the Negroes who visited him had seriously damaged his business, as they had caused many white people to leave him."

The next day there was another account of the local situation.

"Groups of colored people were seen standing at various points in the city yesterday, evidently discussing the absorbing topic of the day – the Civil Rights Act. No concerted raids were made yesterday on the restaurants or saloons. The sentiment of a large portion of the colored community emphatically condemns the conduct of the raiders. Probably not more than a dozen Negroes have engaged in the experiment that has been made in this city. Those that were recognized were Jake Waddleston, John Phelps, and Marion Reed, hotel servants; Jesse Bransford and John Trimble, hackmen, and John Hooper and Alonzo Napier. Most of them have got their reward by losing their situations."

Less than two months later, on April 30, 1875, the local Negro community was rocked more directly. After being arrested for killing a policeman, a local black laborer, Joe Reed, was taken by a mob from the Nashville jail and then shot in the head and hanged by the neck from a bridge. With the failure of authorities to enforce the Civil Rights Act, with the lynching of Joe Reed, and with the political tide changing from progressive to repressive, twenty-three-year-old Alonzo Napier was one of those who took the lead in trying to address the situation.

Although he was misidentified as "N. A." Napier in some local news accounts, he became a driving force behind what was intended to become a statewide movement. A convention was held in Nashville, and a document was produced that was clearly meant for white readers as well as for blacks. Given how similar it was, both stylistically and grammatically, to other samples of his writing, Alonzo Napier, one of five individuals who signed the manifesto, was very likely its author.

"Grievous and afflictive dispensations have been visited upon the people of color of the State of Tennessee. They are of so grave a nature as to excite fears as to the safety of life and the enjoyment of the inestimable boon of liberty. These evils being constantly on the increase, the condition of the race being less favorable, even in the first days of our citizenship, therefore conventions were called in the several counties of the State. Delegates were elected to hold a State Convention at Nashville on the 19th of May, 1875, to inquire into the causes leading to those grievances, and to recommend some method by which we may be relieved of the distresses that now burden us.

"Delegates met together in convention, and have carefully weighed these questions. They state it as their firm faith, based on observation and actual suffering, that to the white people and to them alone is due the ills borne by the colored people of the State. The

General Government has enacted laws looking to our protection and the enjoyment of our privileges as citizens, yet these enactments are a dead letter."

Only four years earlier the proud and promising young Nashvillian had been preparing to enter the United States Military Academy. What he had experienced at West Point must have been between each line he wrote.

"The color line is so closely drawn as to not only prevent us from sitting on juries when whites are interested, but also from sitting on cases where only we are interested. While it is true that the laws of the State promise justice to all, without distinction as to race, yet it is an established truth that no colored man appeals to these courts for a redress of his grievances, knowing that the appeal would be but a mockery and altogether in vain.

"Though it may be claimed that the more respectable white people are disposed to accord justice, yet none will dare say that they have ever made a single effort to prevent outbreaks against people of color. Reference can be made to David Jones, who while in the County Jail of Davidson, in the city of Nashville, was taken out by a mob and hanged, in front of the police station and within 50 yards of the court house. And reference can be made to Miss Julia Hayden, an accomplished young teacher in Trousdale County, who was murdered by assassins while in her own house, or to the six men who were shot to death by armed banditti at Trenton.

"And recently, Joseph Reed, after he was incarcerated in the County Jail, was murdered brutally by an armed mob in the presence of at least 4000 citizens of Nashville. This was one of the foulest blots that ever stained any city. The Mayor of the city, and the Governor of Tennessee, refused to prevent the crime although they had at least six hours' notice of the outrage. These are but a few of the many horrible crimes that have been perpetrated against us, and in no instance has one of the miscreants been brought to justice. These wrongs going unredressed rest like a cloud upon the race, and have given us the undoubted assurance that the whites are determined that the colored people shall not remain at peace in their midst."

The promising young man who once expected to serve his country as an officer in the army, had a great deal more to say.

"In addition to the foregoing, the whites have evinced a purpose to hinder the blacks in all their efforts at advancement. In many counties where schools are to be found, they are always inferior to those of the whites. School houses have been burnt, teachers whipped and driven from many localities, and ministers of Christ have been whipped and killed, and their churches burnt to the ground.

"Even that inestimable privilege of citizenship, the elective franchise, has been denied to a number of the race; in many sections the right to vote is being virtually denied them, in others they are made by pistol and knife to vote contrary to their honest convictions.

"Recent partisan legislation – a vagrant act by which a colored man out of employment shall be incarcerated in the County workhouse, and the labor law, which compels the laborer to remain with his employer under any and all circumstances – was passed by the Thirty-ninth General Assembly. Either would alone be sufficient to make personal liberty an utter impossibility, and is calculated to place the race in a condition of servitude scarcely less degrading than that endured before the late civil war. It is true that these laws are applicable to whites also, but a single instance of punishment of whites under these acts has never occurred and is not expected to occur.

"The price of work is reduced so low through the introduction of convict labor on the farms, on the railroad, and in the mines, that it is impossible for a man to support his family on the wages promised, even if he were paid for his labor, which too frequently is not done. And when laborers work on shares, unprincipled whites usually bring those at work into debt before the days of harvest."

What he had encountered at West Point – as putrid as what had been poured onto his bed from the slop jar – continued to weigh on him. Of the hope he once had, very little was left.

"These are but a few of the many difficulties under which the colored people labor in this State, and time but adds to the weight. We despair of relief so long as we continue within its limits. In the patience that has ever characterized our race, these wrongs have been endured with Christian submission. Trusting to a sense of justice, which we had a right to believe dwelt in the breast of every man made in God's image, we hoped that time might repair the evils we bear. But now, after so long a time of waiting, forbearance has ceased to be a virtue.

"Unable to cope with our adversaries, even if so disposed, by reason of our inferior numbers, and surpassed by them in wealth and education, this convention, with God before their eyes and with no malice in their hearts, recommends that the entire colored population take steps, looking to the early emigration from the State – believing that only in this way may they attain full measure of their manhood, and bring the enjoyment of liberty and happiness to themselves and their children."

Alonzo Napier was one of three men selected to locate a region suitable for a mass emigration of black people, but he appears to be the only one who made the journey. In early August, 1875, a Kansas newspaper carried a brief account of Alonzo during his travels.

"H. A. Napier passed through this city (Topeka) yesterday, on his way home to Nashville, Tennessee. He is acting as agent to hunt up lands for 600 colored people to settle on. He thinks that Barton County is the place for them, and that they will be here in October."

Soon after he reached Nashville he presented his report to those who attended a mass meeting. It was written with the same eloquence and style as the manifesto produced at the convention. After he described the fertility of the soil and the availability of water in the Great Bend of the Arkansas River, he added that, "politically, there is no better State for colored people than Kansas." But then he pointed out that individuals needed to have around $1000 to establish a settlement. Although considerable numbers of blacks continued to move away, the mass migration from Nashville that had been envisioned did not take place at that time.

Alonzo Napier finally revisited the military inclinations that had brought him to West Point. In 1877 he founded and served as Captain in a black military company called "the Key Rifles," named after Postmaster General David M. Key, a former Confederate officer and political figure from East Tennessee. The organization was connected to the Langston Rifles – a forerunner of the unit, "Company G, Unattached," which became part of the Tennessee National Guard. For a time Company G was the only Negro unit in the South, and went on to do heroic service in France during World War One as part of the 372nd Infantry regiment.

After receiving his medical degree from Meharry, Alonzo Napier chose to pursue a career in education, eventually becoming a noted educator in St. Louis, where he married Elmira Copeland, a Wilberforce graduate and a teacher. He moved back to Nashville early in 1882, and quickly became a highly respected principal at the Vandavell School in East Nashville, but an accident occurred in December of that year. While he was on his way to school, with his father sitting beside him, he was horribly injured in a carriage accident. The event was reported in newspapers in both Nashville and St. Louis.

"His horse was frightened by a locomotive and made a sudden plunge to one side. In crossing a street railroad track, the axle of the carriage broke and he and his father were thrown out. The young man caught his ankle between the wheel and the street rail, breaking the bones so that they protruded. In that condition he was dragged along the ground for some distance. The best physicians were called in and the foot amputated, but he will probably die."

A former cadet, a medical school graduate, and a gifted educator, Alonzo Napier – after whom Nashville's Napier School would be named – was thirty-one-years-old when he died nine days before Christmas, 1882. Local newspapers listed his achievements and described his funeral, and his character was eulogized.

"He was highly esteemed here and was doing fine work. He was naturally bright and intelligent, and won the esteem of all with whom he came in contact. The young men of his people can find no one whose example is more worthy of imitation, whose energy and perseverance are more to be commended."

But following his death there was no mention of the campaign that had been waged against him while the military officers in charge of West Point looked on – no mention of the treatment he received at the hands of his fellow cadets, who had tried to break his spirit in the way the carriage accident had ultimately broken his body.

Elias Napier, two years old than his brother, Alonzo, was born in Cincinnati in 1849, during the time the family was away from Tennessee. His family had returned to the Davidson County farm of his maternal grandfather, William E. Watkins, by November, 1850, and he spent his early childhood there and in Nashville, where his family had moved by 1857. There were laws outlawing schools for blacks, but Elias, along with his older brother, James, was educated at home and then at a local school his father, Carroll, helped establish.

After the school was shut down following threats from white authorities, his father sent Elias and James and their baby sister, Ida – all under the care of his wife, Jane – to Ohio where the two boys took preparatory courses at Wilberforce University. Elias was not the student that his brother James was. At some point Elias Napier came back to Nashville, and in addition to attending the high school associated with Fisk University, he worked in his father's livery stable.

Elias was involved in a number of physical altercations, and he was sometimes charged and brought into court. One of his earlier fights took place in 1871 at the Colored Fair, where his horses had been awarded a pair of awards. After John B. Bosley, a friend of Elias, became involved in a heated dispute with another man of color, Napier became involved. The other man, a magistrate, ended up in critical condition, and Napier ultimately paid a fairly heavy fine for assault and battery. And in 1875, when a black man named Joe Davis insulted Napier by saying, "he had rather work for white people than darkies," Elias apparently broke the man's nose.

The Civil Rights Act was passed several weeks later, and shortly after his brother, Alonzo, attempted to test the effect of the new law, Elias placed a notice in a local newspaper.

"I desire to correct the false impression that I had gone into a restaurant and demanded admission. Since my business is likely to be injured by such impressions, I want the public to know that I am not the man who is reported as having gone to the restaurant. I do not wish to intrude myself on any man, and as for civil rights, I want all to know that I was opposed to the passage of the civil rights bill from the first."

In 1876, at the age of twenty-seven, Elias Napier married

nineteen-year-old Maggie Mitchell. The following year he clashed with the high-spirited young wife of Henry Harding. An argument over one of his rented carriages led Elias to condemn Mrs. Harding.

"I told Harding that if I had such a wife, I would kick her until she should know how to behave herself, and if he could not do it, he should send for me and I would do it for him. Mrs. Harding came to my house and called me out. She told me to repeat what I had told her husband, and told me if I did not swallow what I had said about her, she would shoot the top of my head off. I caught her hand as she was about to raise a pistol, and it was discharged in the air. She pulled the trigger again, but the weapon did not go off. She proved to be a good deal stronger than I supposed she was. I threw her to the pavement when I was trying to wrest the revolver from her hands, but assisted her to rise again. Then she ran for her barouche and got her whip. I told her she had better not use it, and were it not for the respect I had for Mr. Harding, I would give her a good beating."

The case would take some time to resolve, but the next week Elias took his hunting dogs, which were considered to be "the best pack of hounds in Davidson County," to participate in a fox hunt and deer chase. His livery stable, located on what would become the site of Hume Fogg High School, grew over the next two decades, as did his family. His first child, Ida, was born in 1877, and his wife had two more children and a son by the mid-1880s. Along with his stable, Elias took on additional work. He was the proprietor of the "Red Light Saloon" as well as a billiard hall on North Cherry Street, and for a time he also worked as a fireman.

Although he had widespread business involvements, he continued to appear on court dockets. He was periodically charged with such offenses as "fast driving," using abusive language, and assault and battery. There were times when violations were dismissed, but he also paid a number of fines. In early 1888 the Nashville American reported a violent altercation which did not lead to Napier appearing in court.

"Carter Thompson's little boy, who it seems has been neglected by him, obtained employment at Elias Napier's stable. Thompson, colored, went to the stable on Saturday night to get some of the boy's wages. This Napier refused to give him, telling him that he ought to take care of the boy. Thompson began cursing and finally drew a knife, when Napier knocked him down."

In the summer of 1889, when a physician's carriage was stolen, Elias Napier was informed that a noted local criminal was fleeing in the carriage along Nolensville Pike. "Elias Napier started at once in pursuit. About seven miles from town he came up with the miscreant, and after some difficulty arrested him and turned him over to Detective Porter."

And less than a month later, at a bar close to his stable, Napier was involved in yet another conflict.

"Elias Napier, colored proprietor of the Custom House livery stable, today struck a white man named R. M. Dugger and knocked him out of Woods' Saloon. Napier said, 'I was taking a drink with a couple of gentlemen when that fellow said he would not take a drink with any nigger, and I knocked him out of the door.' Napier struck him three times. Dugger started to the police station for the purpose of having Napier arrested." Two days later Napier appeared in court, where he pled guilty and paid a five dollar fine.

There were other run-ins with the law over the next several years, but there were also economic advancements, including in 1896 when Napier was awarded a lucrative contract to carry mail back and forth between the post office and the mail trains.

In 1897, not long before a Confederate convention was to be held in Nashville, Napier endeared himself to the old guard of the local community. A large parade was being planned, and in making a well-received gesture to a wealthy matriarch, Harriet Maxwell Overton, president of the Nashville chapter of the United Daughters of the Confederacy, the scope of Napier's stable was revealed.

"Yesterday Elias Napier, proprietor of the large livery stable on Broad Street, opposite the Customs House, called on Mrs. John Overton and tendered her the use of his entire livery outfit for the parade, free of charge. He said that the Southern people had always been his best friends, and he had long wanted an opportunity to show his appreciation of their kindness. The stable contains a large tally-ho (a six-horse observation coach), a trap (a sporty carriage) for eight, and twenty or thirty other vehicles." And along with the vehicles, Napier made forty horses available to Mrs. Overton.

The next several months were devastating. Elias and his family lived five miles south of Nashville on Granny White Pike, and in December the Napier home was destroyed by fire. Late the following May he died of pleurisy, leaving his wife Maggie and their four children.

Despite the rough-hewn nature of his character, Elias Napier left behind some highly-successful descendants. His son, Dr. James Alonzo Napier, was trained at Meharry and became a prominent local dentist, and Elias' daughter, named for his sister Ida, managed to live an extraordinary life. She was educated at Fisk, where she was a soloist with the Jubilee Singers. At Fisk she met her future husband, R. Augustus Lawson, who would be recognized as "the foremost pianist of the Negro race in America."

Ida ultimately moved to Hartford, Connecticut, and became both a nationally-recognized expert in daycare nursing and a prominent civic leader. She and her husband, a long time music instructor and pianist with the Hartford Philharmonic Orchestra, raised two accomplished children.

Their daughter, Rosalind, returned to Nashville and after graduating from Fisk, she received advanced degrees in education and social work, teaching for a time at Hong Kong University. Their son, Warner, who would later study in Berlin under the noted Austrian pianist, Artur Schnabel, graduated from Fisk and went on to earn music degrees from both Yale and Harvard, and was dean of the School of Music at Fisk before

R. Augustus Lawson

becoming head of the School of Fine Arts at Howard University.

Ida Morgan Napier, the youngest child and only daughter of Carroll and Jane Napier, was born in Nashville in 1858 – ten years after the emancipation of her parents. Her family lived downtown during the Civil War, and in 1867 she was enrolled in the elementary school at Fisk University. She received a superior education at Fisk, and subsequently attended Oberlin College in Ohio. In 1878, after returning to Nashville, she married Arthur Langston of St. Louis, a young graduate of Oberlin whose family background was similar to her own. The event was described in a local newspaper article.

"The event of events in colored society since the war occurred last night at the residence of Carroll Napier, just north of the Opera House. It was the marriage of Arthur Langston, son of John M.

Langston, Minister to Haiti, to Ida Napier, daughter of Carroll Napier. By 5:30 PM the large double parlors were pretty well filled. Those present represented the intelligence of their race. The men were neatly attired, while the dresses of the women were of the most elegant and expensive character, made after the latest fashions. Quite a number of the students of Fisk University were present, and the teachers in the University were also there.

"A little after six o'clock, Carroll Napier appeared upon the scene bearing upon his arm his daughter, and with Arthur Langston escorting her mother, Jane Napier. The bride bore in her left hand a magnificent bouquet made entirely of camellias and tube roses. She was attired in a cream colored silk dress, with white tulle skirt and tulle and lace trimmings. A tulle veil, trimmed with hyacinths, fell from her head to the long trail.

"The bride has large, lustrous eyes, regular features, dark hair, and a fair complexion. In any assemblage she would attract attention by her style and *distingue* air. She graduated from Fisk, and is said to have a decided talent for music. A stout white man named Boyd, in offering his congratulations, said that he had known her for a long time and was therefore entitled to kiss her, which he did.

"The bridegroom has a light brown complexion and an intelligent face, much resembling his father, who ranks with Frederick Douglas in prominence as a colored leader. The groom came here from St. Louis, accompanied by Alonzo Napier, both of whom hold positions as teachers in the public schools there."

Like both of Ida's parents, John Mercer Langston, her new father-in-law, had been sired by the wealthy white man. And the Napiers and the Langstons were already well-acquainted. Two months earlier, Ida's oldest brother, James, had married Arthur's sister, Nettie.

Ida Napier Langston would live in St. Louis for the rest of her life. Arthur continued to teach and later became a school principal, and Ida raised their two sons. John Mercer Langston was named for Arthur's father, and Carroll Napier Langston was named for Ida's father. Arthur died in 1909, but had seen both boys graduate from Oberlin.

John, who never married, went back to St. Louis and became a respected educator, but Carroll, following his graduation in 1903, moved to Nashville where he worked as cashier in the bank that had been founded by his uncle, James Napier. Carroll eventually married and fathered a son, Carroll Napier Langston, Jr. After a few years the elder Langston moved to Chicago, where he became president of a

Carroll Napier Langston, Jr.

bank, and after the bank closed as a result of the Depression, he became a lawyer in Chicago. Young Carroll Langston grew up to attend Oberlin – the fourth generation of his family to be educated there. In 1937, just after the beginning of his senior year, his mother, Ida, died in St. Louis.

After his graduation from Oberlin, young Carroll Langston went on to get his law degree from the University of Michigan, and he was practicing law in Chicago when World War Two began. He volunteered for service in the Army Air Corps early in the war.

He was later assigned to the Tuskegee Air Training School in Alabama – a facility and airfield that was designed and built by

McKissack and McKissack, a black-owned architecture and engineering firm located in Nashville. While Carroll was receiving his training as a pilot, he married. An article in the Chicago Tribune in May, 1944, touched on his time as a Tuskegee airman.

Lieutenant Carroll N. Langston

"The first all-Negro air fighter group in any war theater has been in action in Italy for two months. It has flown 307 missions with over 4000 sorties. The Negro flyers have been using P-39 Airacobras. More than 90% of the officers are college men. A recent incident happened when a B-26 Marauder crew, forced to bail out, was in a dinghy off Gaeta. The Negro pilots hovered protectively above, drawing heavy German anti-aircraft fire, and soon a British boat rescued the crew. One of the pilots in the group is Carroll N. Langston, Jr., who practiced law in Chicago."

The next month twenty-six-year-old Carroll Langston – who would have known all about the persecution experienced by his great-uncle, Alonzo Napier, at the United States Military Academy – was killed when his plane crashed into the Adriatic Sea. He was Ida's only grandchild.

"Carroll was a lanky, disarmingly handsome man with straight hair and a movie-star smile… He was a philosophical soldier, reading

Plato's Republic and law books in his spare time, and copying his wife's love-struck letters into a book."

While their children and grandchildren were living their lives, Carroll and Jane Napier continued to reside in Nashville. They cared for Jane's mother, Rebecca, until she died in 1885 at the age of ninety-four. After turning over operation of the livery stable to his son, Elias, Carroll was custodian of the Nashville Medical College for many years, and was a well-known community figure. He suffered from rheumatism, but there was a celebration of his and Jane's golden wedding anniversary at the home of his oldest son, James C. Napier. A newspaper article described the aged couple.

"Carroll Napier is old and feeble, but his wife seems much more active, and few would take her for the elderly woman she is. The residence was elaborately decorated with palms and tropical plants, with a profusion of cut flowers, including some from white friends of long standing. Beautiful and costly presents filled a large table and made a most beautiful display.

"The assemblage was composed of the very best elements of the colored population of Nashville – physicians, lawyers, dentists, merchants, teachers, editors, and their sons and daughters, as well as a number of white friends of himself and his wife. After the older ones had gone, the younger element danced for a time to the splendid music of the string band in attendance."

The celebration not only marked the fifty years Carroll and Jane had been together – it was a goodbye. Carroll died late the following year, and the *Nashville American* noted his passing.

"One of the best-known citizens of Nashville passed away Friday morning when William Carroll Napier died at the residence of his son, J.C. Napier. No man in Nashville was better known or more highly esteemed, and no man had more friends. He was one of the most industrious men of his time, and the quiet influence of his Christian life will be long remembered and felt in this community. Generous and unselfish, he was always forgetful of himself when he saw an opportunity to perform an act of kindness or charity for others."

Jane, who would live until 1909, was at her husband's bedside when he died, as were his surviving children Ida, Elias, and the eldest, James – who was referred to as J.C. outside of the family.

At the time of his father's death, J.C. Napier was in the process of becoming one of the most noted citizens Nashville ever produced, as well as one of the nation's most influential black leaders. Much of his life would eventually be captured, at several different times, in his own words.

"My father's father was Dr. E.W. Napier, who graduated from the medical school of the University of Pennsylvania. He was also a pioneer iron man in Middle Tennessee. He was a man of considerable force of character. He had four colored sons, and he had his sons go to school along with the white children. He had great political influence and it was through his influence that one of the governors of Tennessee was elected.

"My father was William Carroll Napier, named for Gov. William Carroll. As a boy he attended school in Dickson County, and received such education as was, at the time, within the reach of the average youth of the state. Race prejudice did not run so high then as now, and no objection was raised to his attending school with the white children of the community. My mother was Jane Elizabeth Watkins. They were exceptional people. They always taught us children that we must be honest and truthful and law-abiding.

"When my father's father died, his will provided that his children should leave Tennessee, and go to a free state or to Liberia. When I was a little child, my father and mother took me to Cincinnati, where they bought a farm. They traded it for a farm at New Richmond, Ohio, and although two of the sons went to New Richmond with my grandmother, another went to St. Louis and my father – not satisfied there – soon sold out and came back to Nashville, establishing a livery stable.

James C. Napier

"There were three or four (Negro) schools in Nashville, before the war. One was… in an old church right over a branch. It was built up on stilts, and was a place of worship built for the slaves by their owners. Another one was taught by a Mrs. Tate, who was of a very excellent family. Mrs. Sallie Player, a most delightful teacher, taught another one of these schools. Mrs. Player was a free woman, but her husband was a slave. He belonged to a very excellent family of white people, whose slaves enjoyed every privilege that free people enjoyed. They were protected by their owner. She was a woman of some education. Her husband also had some education, although a slave.

"There was another school taught by a white man and his wife whose name was Westbrooks. They came to Nashville from St. Louis, Missouri and organized a school. These two gathered considerable money from the free and slave people who wanted to send their children to school. They taught school for about three weeks when they suddenly disappeared.

265

Rufus Conrad

"My father and a number of other free men of color who lived in Nashville concluded to start a school. They had a young minister named Rufus Conrad come down from Cincinnati, Ohio, to teach their children. I was one of his pupils. Classes were begun in a small house which stood on North Vine Street near Jo Johnston Avenue, and both free and slave children went to the school. This was in 1859.

"The school had been open two or three months when one day, while the class was spelling the word 'baker,' an abrupt knock on the door interrupted the class, and a man entered without waiting to be admitted. He said to the teacher, 'What is your name' The teacher answered, 'Rufus Conrad.' The man said, 'I have been authorized by the powers that be in Nashville to send these children home, to close the doors of this school and give you just 24 hours to leave this town.' This ended this school. I felt very resentful. The next week my father placed my mother, me, my brother, Elias, and our baby sister, on a small steamboat, the Winona.

"Although we were free Negroes, it was hard to get permission for my mother to take me and my brother to Ohio. Mayor Polk Brown, who was a great friend of my father in antebellum days, interceded for us. I can remember boarding the boat. We traveled to Ohio, where we joined a colony of free families, which my father and his brothers had formed some years before near Xenia. At this place a

266

school, Wilberforce, had been organized for Negroes, and Elias and I attended."

The Civil War caused enrollment at Wilberforce to plummet, and Napier made his way back home.

"Nashville was then still in the hands of the Southern army. When the battle of Fort Donelson was fought, I had just been returned from Ohio. I witnessed the entry of the federal troops into Nashville in 1862. I was one of a great crowd that gathered at the lower landing when the Mayor of Nashville, Richard Cheatham, took a skiff and rowed across the river to where the federals had bivouacked. When Mayor Cheatham came back, I clearly remember the only words he uttered, 'Now folks, go home. Be quiet and peaceable. Be assured of one thing – the Negroes are safe.' After leaving Wilberforce, I went to Oberlin College, one of the first colleges in the nation to invite Negro students. I remained there until my junior year, when I returned to Nashville.

"I got a job as messenger in the state senate, and upon the adjournment in 1867 I was appointed by Gov. Brownlow as one of the three commissioners for Davidson County to audit the claims of loyal citizens whose property had been destroyed by the Federal and Confederate armies."

In each position he held, J.C. Napier had relied on both his dignified bearing and his superior intellect, and his leadership qualities soon became apparent. At the age of twenty-four, after what was referred to as the Colored Convention was held in Nashville in 1870, he was selected by convention leaders to be one of the five individuals who would travel to Washington and meet with President Grant on behalf of black Tennesseans.

At the meeting, Grant was informed of several areas that were of great concern to the black community. The most pressing issue was the violence being used in various parts of the state against Negroes and their allies, and the failure of the State Legislature to protect those citizens. The president responded that he would consider sending Federal troops to Tennessee to quell the violence.

John Mercer Langston

John Mercer Langston, who established the Law Department of Howard University and who would be a member of Congress, became a significant force in the life of young Napier. Langston persuaded Carroll and Jane Napier to allow their son to travel to Washington, and attend law school at Howard. In order to support himself, he took a position as a clerk in the State Department, becoming the first Negro to work in that branch of the government.

And Napier thrived as a student. At his graduation ceremony he delivered a well-received oration from the platform of the Congregational Church in Washington D.C. He closed with an observation that did not directly mention race, but spoke to the intrinsic connection between citizens and the law, and to the racial challenge America was yet to meet. "To be free is to live under a government by law. Miserable is the condition of individuals – dangerous is the condition of the State – if there is no law, or no certain administration of law to protect individuals or guard the State."

Having earned his law degree, he was poised to become an attorney.

"In May, 1872, I came back to Nashville, stood examinations for the Nashville bar, and upon the motion of Thomas Smiley, who had served as an officer in the Confederacy, I was admitted to practice law in Tennessee. I was admitted to the bar, but there was not much opportunity for a Negro lawyer, and I entered the Internal Revenue Service."

It was through his role as a leader in the state Republican Party that Napier received his Revenue Service appointment in May of 1874. As a highly intelligent young man of color, Napier must have known that holding a federal position with a substantial salary might create problems, but he made no attempt to keep a low profile. Less than two weeks after his salary of $3000 a year was publicly reported, he was ridiculed in a local newspaper article.

"Napier, colored, the recently appointed agent in the Revenue Department, seems to be making up an interesting history of himself in these times of civil rights agitation. He had hardly received his commission before he went to Memphis. Preferring to go to that city in a sleeping coach, he entered one at the depot. When a short distance out, he was invited into the car set apart for the exclusive use of men.

"As the excitement in regard to the bill now pending in Congress had just spread all over the land, this was considered as an attempt on the part of Napier to break down old customs, and to force the privileges contemplated in that measure. He thought it hard that a government official could not occupy a berth, but he having readily yielded, very little was said about it at the time.

"Napier and Lotz, a white man in the revenue service, went to Chattanooga on Sunday. Napier registered at the Read House, and ate his dinner there with the white guests. He moreover called for a room, and he was so nearly white – the clerk failing to detect that he was a lineal descendant of Ham – that it was granted him. But the clerk found out, and told Napier that he could not remain under that roof. Those who had eaten dinner in the same room with Napier, on discovering that the blood of the Negro coursed through his veins, became enraged and then indignant. The little affair was soon the talk of the town.

"Napier and Lotz subsequently took the train for Murfreesboro. On arriving they registered at the Willard House, and went to bed. Not long after, someone, in looking over the register, discovered Napier's name, and informed the clerk that he had a Negro in the house, at which the clerk was greatly astonished. A delegation of ten men went to the rooms occupied by Napier and Lotz, led them down to the depot, and told them to run toward Nashville. They walked to Lavergne, where, procuring a buggy, they came into Nashville yesterday near noon."

There were racial obstacles to be overcome, but Napier managed to perform his duties in a highly professional manner – on one occasion going into the wilds of DeKalb County to investigate the murder of a federal agent who had been killed by moonshiners.

In 1878, just after his election to his first term in Nashville's City Council, J.C. Napier traveled to an environment that was entirely different from the wilderness haunts of moonshiners. In October he arrived in Washington DC, where he married Nettie Langston, the daughter of his law professor and mentor, John Mercer Langston. Langston was serving as the nation's minister to Haiti. Accounts of the event were carried in newspapers across the country.

"Nettie Langston, only daughter of our minister to Haiti, was married to James C. Napier, an educated and fine-looking colored gentleman of Nashville, Tennessee. The bride, who is almost white, wore satin with tulle, and the gifts, which were numerous and rich, will aggregate in value to several thousand dollars."

Nettie and J. C. Napier

An article from the Cincinnati Gazette, reprinted in Nashville, provided a more detailed report.

"The Langstons, their complexion being a yellow-brown, are what the Negroes call 'bright.' Professor Langston's father was a Caucasian, who was conscientious enough to give his son an education at Oberlin University. At Oberlin Langston met a girl being, like himself, educated by her white father, and the girl became his wife. Their daughter, Nettie, was sent to the institution which educated her parents. The Professor gave his daughter – quite an accomplished musician – a grand piano.

"The bride is to be taken to Tennessee, where a handsomely-furnished house awaits her. 'But where will she find an opportunity to wear her velvet dress?' I asked a stylish 'bright' woman. 'Oh, she will mix with the white people, of course. Things have changed over the last few years, I assure you. And why shouldn't the educated daughter of the Minister be good enough to mix with white folks?'

"I remained silent, especially as I recalled the vision of Mr. Napier and Miss Langston dashing by my window – he with his silk hat and holding in his light-gloved hand the whitest of reins, while she was dressed, from shoe to bonnet, in the latest style."

While he continued in his Internal Revenue Service position, J.C. Napier proved to be an exceptionally able councilman. During eleven years on the Council – he was the first man of color to preside over a council session – his manner and diplomacy allowed him to win major concessions for the Negro community. In 1881 he was almost certainly responsible for calling attention to the condition of the Vandavell School, of which his brother, Alonzo, would briefly serve as principal. He also spearheaded the establishment of Pearl High School, Meigs School, and Napier School – which was named for Alonzo, and he successfully pushed for black school teachers to be hired for the first time in Nashville. Napier was also largely responsible for the establishment of the two black fire companies, including William Stockell Engine Company No. 4.

He was a political appointee, and years later he summed up the federal work he did until 1884, when the Republican Party lost the national election. "Except for the chief post of collector of internal revenue for Tennessee, I held every post in the office – surveyor, bookkeeper, storekeeper, inspector of stills, and clerk."

Napier usually chose to be uncontroversial, but there were times when he spoke his mind. In August, 1891, he made a speech at Nashville's baseball park, Sulphur Dell, and the directors of the professional team, the Athletics – forerunners to the Nashville Vols – took offense. A local newspaper carried the story.

"The directors of the Athletic Club held a meeting last night, at which the park commissioners were instructed not to rent the park to colored organizations hereafter for any purposes whatsoever. This action was taken on account of an incendiary speech made by J.C. Napier at the park a few days ago, in which he said that he had noticed the short accounts of colored ball games in the papers, and long accounts whenever white clubs contested. He said he knew the colored players could beat the whites at baseball, as they had done in everything else when given half a chance."

Napier had become a nationally-recognized black leader by the turn of the century, and in 1901 he was interviewed for an article in a Washington newspaper.

"The colored people of the country need more than anything else to be left alone. There are those whose sole business seems to be to parade his every movement before the country, to his detriment. If he stands still they say he is indolent and not progressive. If he moves forward they criticize his aggressiveness. If he moves backward they condemn him for not keeping pace with American civilization.

"He has no inclination to disturb the social relations of whites. His own social relations are pleasant and highly satisfactory to him. What he most desires is for others to refrain from disturbing his relations. But there is a distinction between social rights and civil rights. The former are matters of choice between individuals and classes, and they regulate themselves. The latter are prescribed by laws and by the Constitution, and colored people are entitled to all which their citizenship and laws guarantee them. The execution of laws in the South should be in the hands of courageous men. We need men who are imbued with a sense of justice for all mankind, not caterers to public sentiment."

Napier had become increasingly involved in politics during his time as a government official, and his involvement grew more intense after he went back to practicing law. He was a delegate to every Republican National Convention from 1876 until at least 1912, and he was elected Secretary of the Tennessee Republican Party in 1882. The high point of his political activity came in 1898 when he was nominated by his party to run for Congress. An editorial in the Nashville American reflected the prevailing attitude of that period.

"The nomination of J.C. Napier as Republican candidate for Congress in the Sixth District... shows such a marked indication of the composition of the party in the State, that we cannot fail to call attention to it. It is trite and stale to talk about this being a white man's country, because that fact is established as firmly as anything can be. Napier is a very worthy and respectable Negro, but the people of this Congressional district do not relish the idea of having the brother in black occupy an elective position of public trust. It is a precedent they do not wish to establish."

Napier's loss in the election was overwhelming. The Democratic candidate, J.W. Gaines, received 4583 votes while only 330 votes were cast for Napier. But Napier's political activity continued, as did his business involvement. Locally he was a driving force of the Nashville Negro Board of Trade, and nationally of the National Negro Business League, serving as president of each organization. And he was acutely aware of how business and politics and the social fabric of the nation were interconnected. In 1917, when he was addressing the National Negro Business League, he criticized many of the conditions his brother, Alonzo, had fought against over forty years earlier.

"Mob law, the 'Jim Crow' system, poor housing, poor and short-term schools, inadequate education, disenfranchisement, and a general abbreviation of citizenship are the things with which none of us are satisfied. Discrimination and humiliation are thrust upon us at all times and on every hand. Although the laws provide for it, we do not receive the same accommodations for our money as our fellow white citizens. These conditions, as well as present temporary high wages in the north that have lured some of us away from our homes, are driving colored people out of the south."

Napier said that it was economically harmful to all parties, and he implored the League to work with white southern leaders to help end the mass migration of blacks from the South. By the time of his speech, he was deeply familiar with the struggles of working-class blacks and the perceptions of the business community. His real estate holdings included a three-story structure called Napier Court, and along with several other tenants, it housed the One Cent Savings Bank, an institution founded by Napier

Napier Building

and several other local black leaders in 1904. Some years later Napier described what had led him to establish the bank, and he described the local economic environment at the close of the 1800s, when he was practicing law.

"The need for a bank for Negroes presented itself. Out of my own savings I could lend small amounts, but there was no ready credit source for the average poor Negro. Negro workmen often had difficulty finding a creditor for even as small an amount as $5 or $10. It was from my experience as a lawyer and lending from my own savings that I had the idea of organizing the first Negro bank in Tennessee, the One Cent Savings Bank. At first the bank was located in the Napier Building, which I had erected on Fourth Avenue North, and which I rented to Negroes needing offices. The first day we had deposits of something more than $7000. Today, of course, our deposits are much larger."

In 1911 another local black leader, Dr. Richard F. Boyd, addressed the importance of the bank, which would become Citizens Saving Bank and Trust Company in 1920, and he spoke of Napier as a "financial genius."

"Unwavering in his determination for the uplift of the financial reputation of his race, he gathered with his Negro fellow citizens and organized a banking institution, and he has skillfully managed it as custodian and cashier. The institution has proven a helper and blessing not only to the Negroes of Nashville, but to the entire State of Tennessee. Within the last eight years something over four million dollars have been trusted into the custody of this bank without the loss, misappropriation, or mismanagement of a single dollar, causing three other banks to be organized in this state."

J.C. Napier was most noted for his service as Register of the United States Treasury. He was appointed to the post – with the recommendation of Booker T. Washington, with whom Napier had a close relationship – by President William Howard Taft in 1911. His staff numbered over seventy individuals, and the duties of his office included accounting for all public funds coming into the United States government and the money being expended, as well as overseeing both the funds owed to the nation and its debt obligations. And as Register, Napier's signature, along with the signature of the Secretary of the Treasury, appeared on some of the nation's currency.

He used the influence of his office to help black Americans receive the benefit of the funds that federal laws intended that they receive. Although some of his initiatives were unsuccessful, Napier led efforts in Tennessee that culminated in the establishment of what was initially called the Tennessee Agricultural and Industrial School – later known as Tennessee State University. But soon after Woodrow Wilson, a decided segregationist, came into office in 1917, a directive was issued requiring blacks and whites working in the Treasury Department to use separate bathrooms, leading Napier to object and then resign.

He was nearing the age of seventy when he and Nettie returned to Nashville. The couple had remained childless, but in the mid-1890s they adopted Nettie's niece, Carrie, the biological daughter of Nettie's brother, Frank. Carrie died in 1918, and the aging couple continued to serve the community and remain active in the Congregational Church. In 1934 a newspaper reporter interviewed eighty-eight-year-old J.C. Napier about his long and full life. After covering his career and relating a few stories, he talked about race relations.

"I realize that the old ties which existed between the white and colored races have been largely severed. The bonds of affection that prevailed until the older generations passed away, no longer exist. The younger generations of both races realize that an altered condition is now at hand. They seem to be farther apart, and to have less sympathy for one another.

"We breathe the same air. We tread the same paths. We eat the same food. We drink the same water. We educate ourselves according to the same standards. We are ready to make the supreme sacrifice for our flag and for our country. We worship the same God. How long can we permit the small matter of race and color to prevent a unified and everlasting friendship? It is the cherished desire of my advanced years to do all within my power to lessen the friction between the white man and the colored man, and to bring them together. We cannot exist at cross-purposes. Since we must live here together, let it be as Christian friends with a common purpose, and not as foes with sword and a dagger."

In 1937 a newspaper reporter met Napier at the bank and his article described a man who was more active than men half his age.

James C. Napier

"Except for a slight deafness, Mr. Napier shows few signs of his ninety-two years. Since his retirement, Mr. Napier has remained in Nashville, resuming his practice of law and his work as bank cashier. He is a member of the board of trustees of Meharry Medical College, Howard University, Fisk University, and the Jeanes Foundation, a million-dollar trust fund for advancing the rural education of Negro children in the South. And he is senior deacon of the Howard Congregational Church, which is largely composed of men and women who had their educational opportunity through the aid of Oberlin College or Fisk.

"He has been reading Gone with the Wind to his wife, and together they have enjoyed this study of Civil War and what it did to a special type of social structure. They are wise enough to know how much their lives are a product of such a civilization, and they observe that some of the strongest characters are Negroes."

Old school house where Rufus Conrad taught Napier (Fisk Special Collections)

The following year he was interviewed on his birthday, and he had some thoughts about slave times. He did not mention that on one occasion, years earlier, he went inside the old building where, before the school was shut down, he had been taught by Rufus Conrad prior to the Civil War. And didn't say anything about going out Charlotte Pike and visiting what had once been the old Napier Place. The slave cabin where he was born was still standing, and he had his photograph taken in front of the dilapidated old structure.

Earlier in the decade he had been asked about slavery.

"On one occasion I saw a number of slaves chained in line and being marched west on Cedar Street. There were three slave yards in the area. One was located at what is now the Colored YMCA building. Another was on the north side of Cedar Street between Fourth Avenue and the Square. And another was on Fourth Avenue,

279

running north toward Deaderick Street. I only remember the name of one man who operated these slave sale yards. His name was Bill Boyd. He was reputed to be a very kindly-disposed man, but he finally committed suicide."

J.C. Napier (right) at his birthplace (Fisk Library, Special Collections)

In 1938 his wife, Nettie, who was known for her grace and for her devotion to the community, died five days before their sixtieth wedding anniversary. J.C. Napier died in 1940. His mind had stayed sharp, and he probably spent much of his final two years remembering.

He was the last surviving child of Carroll and Jane, who had both been dead for decades. From time to time he must have thought about how his parents had ridden their horses into town and married, and begun their lives in a world that seemed like a distant dream.

And he must have thought about the children his parents brought into the world. His sister Ida died the year before Nettie, and his brothers had been dead for years. How much did he allow himself to relive Alonzo's death – or his life? Were there times when he smiled about his brawling brother, Elias?

He might have remembered back to 1884, when a major snowstorm had blanketed Nashville. He and Elias and John B. Bosley, along with two friends, had gone at night to the top of Cedar Street, back before the name was changed to Charlotte. A big crowd was watching the sleds – most carrying at least five men – race each other down in the direction of the river.

The other sleds were manned by whites, but the Napier brothers and Bosley were prominent and well-liked men, and on that night, as if made irrelevant by the snow, matters of color were not a consideration. The fastest sled on the hill was thought to be the one called *Cowboy*, but it was challenged by James and Elias and their crew – manning the sled they named the *Susie B*. A newspaper article appeared the next day describing the race.

"The *Cowboy* had just run the course in eight seconds and three-quarters, and was taken back up to be run against the *Susie B*. Soon after the two sledges passed the Cathedral – neck and neck, with tin horns blowing, cow bells ringing, and the crews hallooing – the *Cowboy* caught a billow on her starboard bow, throwing her whole crew into the icy element."

But James and Elias Napier, aboard the *Susie B*, continued to fly down Cedar Street – toward the site of the old slave markets from which the heart of Nashville's black business district would rise, and toward the Public Square where, seventy-six years later, African-American students would prevail after demanding the integration of downtown department store lunch counters.

18

Preston Taylor

Like many prominent men of mixed blood who had once been slaves, Preston Taylor may have chosen to keep some details of his ancestry to himself. When he died in 1931 a local newspaper article mentioned that, "he was born a slave on November 7, 1849, in Shreveport, Louisiana, and he was owned by the family of Zed Taylor, the brother of former President Zachary Taylor." While the details of Preston Taylor's ownership were incorrect, it seems doubtful that his connection to the well-heeled Taylor family was without some basis in fact.

An account written in 1907, nearly a quarter-century earlier, confirmed that Preston Taylor was born in Shreveport in 1849, but it went on to say that he was born "of slave parents." That Zed was not his owner but his slave father, and that his mother was named Betty, had already been established in a detailed biographical sketch of Preston Taylor that was published in 1895. After noting that "he was born in slavery," it named Preston's parents as "Zed and Betty Taylor."

Richard Taylor, the father of President Zachary Taylor, had five historically-recognized sons – none named Zed – but the possibility remains that Richard Taylor, who owned a considerable number of slaves, could have fathered Zed, making him not the brother, but the half-brother of President Taylor.

But Richard Taylor was born in 1744, and while it is possible for 105 years to have spanned the interval between the birth of a grandfather and a grandson, it may be that the details of family relationships became blurred over time. If there was a connection by blood, it seems more likely that instead of being Zachary's brother, Zed could have been sired by one of Zachary's brothers. Despite the uncertainty surrounding Zed's paternity, there is another possible indication that Preston Taylor was related to the family of the twelfth president.

The 1895 account conveyed that Preston "was carried to Kentucky when a year old." At the age of four, Preston and his mother, and perhaps his father, were apparently living in Lexington, some eighty miles away from where Richard Taylor's family had settled in the 1780s. It is plausible that a family connection could have brought Preston and his parents to northern Kentucky in 1850 – the same year President Taylor died during his second year in office.

Aside from the 1931 newspaper article that mentioned a relationship between Preston Taylor and the family of Zachary Taylor, there is another detail to consider. Fairly early in his life, Preston Taylor, whose complexion indicated a substantial amount of white heritage, appears to have had access to one or more individuals of wealth.

Preston Taylor, 116th Colored Infantry

He was well cared for as a child, and was bright and impressionable. After attending a church service in Lexington around 1853, he was so taken with the pastor that he told his mother he wanted to become a preacher. Preston was eleven when the Civil War broke out, and when he was fourteen he joined the Union Army, serving as a drummer in the 116th Colored Infantry. His unit was in Virginia during the final months of the war, and after being present during the siege of Richmond and Petersburg, Taylor was at Appomattox when General Lee surrendered to General Grant.

Returning to Kentucky after mustering out, Preston Taylor learned to be a stone cutter, and became skilled in crafting monuments and engraving marble. He went to Louisville and found employment in a few marble yards, but the white workers soon refused to work with a young man of color. He then secured a position as a railroad porter, and in 1870, the year he married Ellen Spradling, he was living in Louisville and was the owner of personal property valued at $600. His work was so highly regarded that when he resigned after four years, he was given a railroad pass that provided him, and perhaps his wife, free travel throughout much of the north.

Following a prolonged trip, he went back to Kentucky and became the pastor of a Christian Church in Mount Sterling, Kentucky – 100 miles east of Louisville. Over a period of more than a decade, his church not only grew into the largest black Christian Church in the state, Reverend Taylor helped found additional churches across the region and became his denomination's leading minister. And years later he would establish a Bible College at New Castle, Kentucky, raising some $20,000 to purchase the property.

Reverend Taylor's organizational and financial ability also served him well when he became involved in business. Around 1881 the Big Sandy Railroad, which ran between Lexington and Mount Sterling, sought to expand to the east. When the contractors would not hire Negro laborers, Taylor submitted and won a bid to build two especially-difficult sections of the road. It is unclear how he was able to pay for the substantial operation he pulled together.

After building a large structure where his crew would be sheltered and fed, he purchased 75 mules and horses, as well as wagons, carts, tools, and construction implements, and he assembled an all-black force of 150 workers. The section was completed in fourteen months – well ahead of schedule – at a cost of $75,000, and after being praised by the supervisor of the railroad, he was asked to take his crew to supplement white crews that were behind schedule. Unwilling to take more time away from his church duties, he refused that opportunity as well as a number of subsequent business offers.

Along with his formal pastoral duties, Reverend Taylor was highly active in advancing the Republican Party, which was, on occasion, helpful to black people. In 1885 Reverend Taylor moved to Nashville, but it is unclear whether he and his wife, Ellen, were still together by then. A lone and uncorroborated claim of domestic discord had appeared in a newspaper in 1884, a few months before he came to Nashville.

Taylor became the minister of the Gay Street Christian Church, and in 1886, only a year after his arrival, the power of his personality came into play. The church choir had become recognized as an outstanding musical ensemble, and a committee of leading white Nashvillians requested that the choir give a concert in the Opera House. An account written several years later gave details of what took place.

"When Mr. Taylor met with this committee, they informed him that on the night of the concert, the colored people would be expected to take the balcony, as usual. Mr. Taylor refused to have anything further to do with the matter, and publicly denounced the whole crowd in his church, which was very satisfactory to the colored citizens, who urged him to give a concert nevertheless, and he consented. On the night of the concert, there was scarcely standing room for the people, who said they desired to show their appreciation for the manly stand in resenting such overtures."

The concert took place the next week and on the following day received glowing praise in the Nashville American.

"The grand musical and literary entertainment by the Gay Street Christian Church choir, at the Grand Opera House last night, was unquestionably one of the grandest successes of the season. The choir, assisted by a splendid orchestra, rendered as fine music as any audience would wish to hear, and could not have been excelled by the Jubilee Singers themselves."

Reverend Taylor's reputation was spreading, and one factor in his rise to prominence was his membership in a variety of organizations – from the local Masonic Lodge for Negroes to the Odd Fellows to the Knights of Pythias. And three years after coming to Nashville, he became part of the business community. In 1888 he established Taylor and Company, a funeral home that would bring him into even closer contact with the local black community.

Georgia Gordon

But the dominant nature of Reverend Taylor's leadership gradually led to discord within his congregation. A lawsuit seeking to remove him from the church was filed in Chancery Court in 1889, and in early May, 1890, in the wake of the lawsuit and five months after the death of his first wife, forty-year-old Preston Taylor married Georgia Gordon, a twenty-five-year old native of Nashville and an early member of the world-renowned Fisk Jubilee Singers.

Reverend Taylor had managed the Jubilee Singers in 1887, and he and Georgia must have worked closely together. She gave birth to a son six months after their 1890 marriage, but the couple suffered a devastating loss seven months later when the child, Preston Gordon Taylor, died of a bowel ailment.

The following year, in 1891, he started the Lea Avenue Christian Church. It was located just south of downtown Nashville, and although he would serve as its pastor for the next quarter-century, he continued to supervise his business, which was described in 1895.

Lea Avenue Christian Church

"It is said that Preston Taylor does the largest business of any man of his race engaged in the same business in the country. He owns and occupies the large two-story brick structure at 449 North Cherry Street. The building is 42×180 feet and it is divided and furnished in the most convenient style, with reception hall, office, chapel, show rooms, supply rooms, trimming rooms, dry rooms, carpenter shops, paint shops and a morgue. In the rear stands a large stable occupied by eighteen head of horses, seven carriages, hearses, and all kinds of vehicles used in the undertaker's business. The entire building is lighted with electric lights and fitted up with electric bells. He is the only one in the city that manufactures his own goods. He works sixteen men in his establishment, and often is compelled to call in extra help."

By the time Tennessee's belated Centennial observance took place in 1897, Reverend Taylor was not only one of the state's leading black citizens, he was widely recognized for his oratorical ability. Booker T. Washington, the noted Negro leader, educator, and author, was to give an address on the Centennial grounds in celebration of the Emancipation Proclamation, and Preston Taylor was selected to introduce Washington. In addressing the need for black people to strive for economic advancement, there were times when Washington's words of applied directly to Reverend Taylor.

Booker T. Washington

"As bad as slavery was, for 250 years it taught the southern white man to do business with the Negro. If a white man wanted a house built, he consulted a Negro mechanic about the building of that house. If he wanted a suit of clothes made, he consulted a Negro tailor. In a sense, every slave plantation was an industrial school. On those plantations we had thousands of young men being taught farming, blacksmithing, carpentry, wheelwrighting, brick masonry, and so on. The great problem that is pressing upon us more and more as a race is – can we hold onto the legacy that was purchased by our forefathers at the price of 250 years of slavery? During slavery we had more young men learning trades in a single county than we have today in the whole city of Nashville."

Washington went on to address the white people who were part of the vast audience – as well as whites in general – about a subject that Preston Taylor had faced before, and would face again.

"My friends of the white race, we are one in this country. Unjust laws or customs that inconvenience the Negro, injure the white man. No race can wrong another race without being dragged down in its moral status. Character, not circumstances, make the man. We rise as you rise. When we fall, you fall."

The success of his funeral business allowed Taylor to pursue opportunities that not only made money, but also strengthened the black community. In 1899, eight years after his infant son was buried at Mount Ararat Cemetery southeast of downtown Nashville, Taylor purchased a large nearby tract of farmland and announced his plan to establish a cemetery for Negroes there.

City Cemetery had been Nashville's principal burial ground since 1822, and although black people and white people had been buried there in near proximity to each other for decades, recent restrictions banned black burials in newer cemeteries like Mount Olivet. With Mount Ararat, an early black cemetery, running out of space, Reverend Taylor took action, but a campaign was soon launched against the burial ground he was trying to establish. He named it Greenwood Cemetery, and the legislative response by Davidson County's senators in the Tennessee legislature was reported in the Nashville American in 1899.

"A bill passed the Senate yesterday making it a misdemeanor to bury dead bodies or establish a cemetery within ten miles of a large city on a stream or on a tributary of a stream from which a city receives its water supply. This bill is directed against a cemetery which has been established by Preston Taylor, a Negro undertaker and preacher. The mouth of Mill Creek is just above the pumping station, and the interment of bodies there, it is believed, will contaminate the waters from which the city receives its water supply. The bill was inspired by the City Board of Health, and will likely become a law."

But the same day a letter from Reverend Eugene Harris, a local pastor and a professor of theology at Fisk, appeared in the Banner.

"Regarding the cemetery as a menace to public health by contaminating the city's drinking water seems groundless. Between Mill Creek and the nearest burial plot lie the Lebanon Railroad and several acres of field. The cemetery is on a high bluff sloping away from the creek, while the opposite bank is low and drains into the stream. West of the railroad, right on the bank of the stream, an old cemetery has been standing for years. It is strange that no fear of contamination arose until Greenwood appeared on the scene."

Preston Taylor was almost certainly the author of a letter that was signed, "Taylor and Company." The letter indicated that much of the opposition to the new burial ground came from the proprietors of Mt. Ararat Cemetery. The letter accused the managers of Mt. Ararat of merely trying to maintain their monopoly, and it cast aspersions on the quality of the burials.

"So long as they have the only graveyard where colored people can bury their dead, they can say, 'take what we offer you or go elsewhere,' which is to say, 'go to a potter's field.' We bury the dead of 147 benevolent societies. Representatives came to us eighteen months ago and demanded that we find a place where they could bury their dead deep enough to prevent the dogs from scratching them up overnight."

Other objections were addressed in the letter, and after opposition to the new cemetery was ultimately overcome, Greenwood Cemetery was officially dedicated on June 11, 1900. Reverend Taylor had invested over $20,000 in the property, and it took him just over three years to pay off the debt on the graveyard, which would ultimately become part of a much larger vision.

The winter of 1905 was especially cold, and understanding the suffering of Nashville's poorest black citizens, Taylor not only rented "a large hall" to shelter those who were exposed to the frigid temperatures, he had connections with a coal mining company in Kentucky and saw to it that a train-car-load of coal was provided to those who had a place to stay. His generosity was recognized by Booker T. Washington two years later.

"His philanthropic spirit is strong, and through his feeling for suffering humanity, his individual help, and his solicitations from friends, he was able to feed, warm, and clothe almost a thousand suffering people and shield them from the cold."

Later in 1905 Preston Taylor incurred the wrath of a number of prominent white Nashvillians when he bought property one street west of his undertaking business.

"Residents of Fifth Avenue North are greatly aroused over the purchase of the old Jungerman residence, at the corner of Gay Street and Fifth Avenue, by Preston Taylor and other Negroes. It is understood that the Negroes intend to make this building the center of their social life, and to make of it their clubhouse. As soon as the purpose for which the property had been acquired leaked out, there was a storm of indignation.

"There are many fine residences along Fifth Avenue from Cedar Street north, to beyond Gay Street, and some of the oldest and best families of Nashville reside there. The encroachment of the Negroes upon Fourth Avenue from Cedar Street north has been watched with apprehension for several years, but it was not thought they would invade Fifth Avenue. The depreciation in realty values is not the only cause of indignation, although it naturally contributes to it."

Opposition faded after Preston Taylor's plan for the $10,000 property was communicated. While the upper floor would indeed be rented to Negroes – for use of the Knights of Pythias as a lodge – the two lower floors would be leased as offices to white tenants.

Taylor was exposed to more controversy three weeks later when a newspaper story listed him as the president of a recently-established company. The company had been organized by a number of local black leaders in response to a new law requiring the segregation of Nashville's streetcars. A few years earlier Taylor had been central to another effort that was undertaken on behalf of the black community when, along with James C. Napier and several others, the One Cent Savings Bank was founded.

"President Preston Taylor of the Union Transportation Company, the new automobile line for colored people, stated that within a few days cars would begin to run in the four sections of the city. A new two-story brick garage is being erected in the rear of the Taylor and Company undertaking establishment. Part of the building already occupied by Taylor and Company will be converted into a waiting room, while there will be room for a café."

Although the transportation company did not succeed, three years later the Nashville Globe took note of Taylor's contribution.

"When the legislature passed laws separating the races on the streetcars, the Negroes of Nashville resented the insult. After much discussion it was decided to purchase cars and conduct a transportation company of their own. Preston Taylor was one of the few men who spent their money freely – that the race might keep off the streetcars. No one except the few who bore the brunt of that ordeal will ever know what they spent."

By the spring of 1907 Preston Taylor had begun to provide the black community with a place that would be the culmination of both his far-reaching-vision and his deep creativity. It adjoined Greenwood Cemetery and he named it Greenwood Park. Preparations for the official opening were nearly complete, but there was heavy neighborhood opposition to the park, and the Tennessee Assembly quickly passed a law in order to thwart Taylor's plans. A strong response – likely written by Henry Allen Boyd – appeared in Nashville's only newspaper for Negroes, the Globe.

"A meaner piece of legislation was never railroaded through a law-making body than the one aimed at the existence of the only park for colored people in this vicinity. A local bill entitled 'To Regulating the Location of Parks and Places of Amusements' was passed by the legislature of the State of Tennessee on April 4. The bill was hatched up solely to affect Greenwood Park. It was railroaded through in one night.

"It was worded so as not to affect any of the amusement places or parks of the whites. It provided that no park or amusement place outside the corporate limits of Nashville shall be maintained, used, or operated within two miles of a cemetery, or within a quarter mile inside the city limits. It was a gerrymander of the worst kind. The colored people have been shut out from the places frequented by the white race, and now they are forbidden by law to have one.

"One race has as much right to parks and places of healthful amusement as another. Six hundred trees have been planted, which add to the beauty of the landscape and make an ideal place where colored people could do as the whites do at their many parks – meet and enjoy themselves.

"The law says for its authors: 'If you Negroes take any amusement, you must take it on the curbing under police surveillance, or sweat it out within your homes. You shall not have a park inside the corporate limits, nor shall you have one outside of it, and you better not think of peeping through the fence at ours.' What will be the next curtailment inflicted upon us by that class of prejudice-ridden whites who are having nightmares over what the Negro is doing?"

But the bill had not yet become a law. A few years later, Preston

Taylor described the help he had received from some of Nashville's most influential citizens.

"Some of our white friends did not want Greenwood Park, and some of our colored friends were of the same opinion. They got together and had a bill drawn and introduced. One of the Street Railway officials, Mr. (Percy) Warner, called me up one morning and asked if I had read the morning paper. I told him no, and when I got it I saw that the bill had been passed in both houses. It was on the Governor's desk for his

Ben Carr

signature. Mr. Warner said, 'Get to work at once. Get your friends together and then go to see the Governor.'"

Taylor went to the capitol, and the first man he recognized was Colonel Duncan Cooper, a former Confederate officer. Cooper was an ex-state legislator and a controversial political ally of Governor Malcolm Patterson, who had recently pardoned Cooper for the murder of newspaper editor, Edward Ward Carmack. After listening to Taylor, Cooper introduced him to Ben Carr, a widely-known and well-connected Negro porter at the capitol. As soon as Carr understood the situation, he agreed that the bill should not become a law, and he took Taylor to see the Governor. Taylor made his case, and "by the aid of Carr and other influential citizens, the Governor was induced to veto the bill."

The day before it officially opened, the park was described in an article in the Globe.

"Greenwood Park, the new park for colored people, will be thrown open to the public on the Fourth of July. Preston Taylor, seeing the need of a park where his people can take their outings during the heated season, and with the pluck and

Greenwood Park

energy which has made him successful in other enterprises, determined to supply the need. He purchased a forty-acre tract of land on Lebanon Pike, just beyond Mount Olivet, and has equipped it with the amusements of a modern park. About twenty acres are rolling land and the rest consists of cool lawns. Large trees furnish ample shade for patrons of the park.

"There are four large springs, and the brooks are spanned by beautiful bridges. Approaching the park from Lebanon Pike, one's eye is greeted by a spacious lawn – covered with flower beds, walks, and nicely painted seats – in front of a clubhouse. The clubhouse consists of a six-room cottage with broad porticos on two sides and a spacious veranda in the rear. The veranda is arranged so that 100 guests can be served from the café.

"In the rear of the clubhouse is a large covered skating rink, with seats on four sides for spectators. In a shady valley 100 yards away is an unusually large merry-go-round. It is run by steam power and is equipped with fine horses – two abreast – and all manner of chariots. It will carry 150 passengers each trip.

"The bandstand is a circular pavilion located on a hill, but the chief feature of the park is the theater and the attached moving picture hall.

The theater has a seating capacity of 1000 and handsome oak settees, and is equipped with electric lights in abundance. Every preparation has been made for a great day at Greenwood Park on the Fourth. In the theater there will be old plantation concerts, interlarded with moving picture exhibitions."

The size of the opening day crowd was estimated at around 8000, and the only reported difficulty was the appearance of three unanticipated white vendors. There were numerous complaints, and while it was announced that there would be no more white people in the park, Preston Taylor merely conveyed a brief message.

"Please say for me that Greenwood Park is owned by colored people, and run by colored people for colored people."

The park was embraced by the black community, and a month after it opened the Globe reported that Taylor considered his project far from complete.

"Elder Taylor told of his plans to further beautify the grounds. He showed where he was going to put different buildings and where flower beds would be laid out, and he showed where he intended to locate the field for athletic sports. One could not have listened to this big-hearted man unfolding his plans without feeling the highest admiration for this public benefactor. In after years, when what he is now doing shall be fully appreciated, no name will be more reverently spoken than Preston Taylor."

Greenwood Park grandstand

The next year a grandstand seating 5000 people was built in Greenwood Park, and baseball games were played on the new athletic field, but only two years later the grandstand would burn to the ground. Although arson was initially suspected in the 1910 fire, the Globe reported that the blaze was accidentally started by tramps.

The uninsured grandstand was valued at $10,000, but with his undertaking business thriving, Taylor was able to withstand the loss. Two decades after it was established, the Globe mentioned the founding of the business in an article.

"Twenty years ago a sign was hung out on Fourth Avenue, near Deaderick Street, which read Taylor and Company, Undertakers & Embalmers. The Negroes of the city had never seen a sign with a Negro's name on it, and while they hailed its advent with delight, many of them were skeptical as to the success of such a venture. But time has shown that a man with black skin can bury a man with black skin as nicely and as scientifically as any other man, and more satisfaction is received from the services of a man of the race than it is possible for a member of the white race to give."

In 1913 those services would be rendered to Reverend Taylor's wife of twenty-three years, Georgia Gordon Taylor. After the loss of her child, she had thrown herself into working with her husband, but according to an especially well-informed family historian, there were eventually complications.

"Georgia was heartbroken over her son's death and her husband's infidelity. He had fallen in love with his secretary, whom he married after Georgia's death."

Despite the grief she carried after

Georgia Gordon Taylor

298

the loss of her child, Georgia Taylor had been integral to the success of Lea Avenue Church, and to Greenwood Cemetery and Greenwood Park, and she had continued to share her vocal gifts in countless charitable appearances. At her funeral, after her enormous contributions to the Fisk Jubilee Singers were praised, Preston Taylor listened as his wife was honored with the Jubilee Quartette's performance of *Swing Low, Sweet Chariot* and *My Sister's Took Her Flight and Gone Home.*

Taylor married Ida Mallory in 1916, and the following year he resigned as pastor of the church he had founded. But he remained highly active. Along with his oversight of Taylor and Company and the cemetery and the park, as well as his involvement with the One Cent Savings Bank, World War One would bring an additional responsibility. Taylor, through the United War Work Campaign, led the local effort of the black community to raise money to support the war effort. He continued to be involved in a wide array of activities until his death in 1931 from a kidney infection.

One of his legacies, Greenwood Park, would benefit the black population of Nashville until it closed in 1949, and in his will Taylor left Greenwood Cemetery to the Disciples of Christ, which continues to operate the cemetery. Years before his death, Preston Taylor – a former slave with a rare combination of vision and drive, and with a deep sense of benevolence – wrote words that were intended to apply to the entire black race, but that also applied to the man who wrote them.

"Our race has always stood side by side with other races to do its duty, whether in the time of peace, or in the time of war. If our good deeds were as widely published as our bad ones, in what a different attitude it would place us before the world. I would not object to our bad being told if the good we are doing could only be known."

299

19

Richard Henry Boyd

Tradition conveys a number of details surrounding the ancestry of
Reverend Richard Henry Boyd. His mother, Indiana, the youngest

of sixteen children, was supposedly born in Petersburg, Virginia, and her parents were said to have been named Dick and Mollie. Indiana was reportedly sold away from her family at the age of seven, and taken to Georgia by slave traders.

Much of that information was drawn from a very brief biographical pamphlet, published in 1922, that included the early life of Reverend Boyd. The pamphlet went on to state that Boyd was born in Noxubee County, Mississippi, that his mother, Indiana, was a slave of the Gray family, and that during the initial years of his life, he went by the name, Dick Gray. Those parts of the account are largely supported by historical records, but other information is contradicted by military records, and by what was written in an old family Bible.

Benoni Gray, who was almost certainly the father of Reverend Boyd, was born in South Carolina in 1806, and when he was twenty he married seventeen-year-old Martha Speller, of Walton County, Georgia. After the birth of at least three children in Georgia, Gray moved his family to Alabama, where Martha had two more children. From there they migrated to Mississippi, where several more children were born in the 1840s and 1850s.

Benoni Gray's old family Bible contains the names of children – both white and black – that he apparently fathered. His white daughters and sons are listed by their full names, while his other children – apparently those that Benoni fathered by one or more women of color – are only identified by their given names. The record in the Bible of Benoni Gray includes that, "Dick was born Mar 5, 1851."

Dick Gray, who would later change his name to Richard Henry Boyd, was not born into a wealthy family. Although Benoni is listed as a "planter" in the 1850 Census, he only owned a single slave –

a seventeen-year-old female who was likely Dick Gray's mother, Indiana.

Indiana's death certificate indicates that she would have been born around 1820, making her thirty-one when Dick was born, but the death certificates of three of her ten children indicate that she must have been born over a decade later. Those children were all born after 1868 – and one was born in 1879. If Indiana was actually born in 1820, she would have had to give birth to three children when she was between the ages of forty-nine and fifty-nine. It seems likely that she was actually born in the early 1830s. But records do not contradict the tradition that when she was about seven, she was taken south by a slave trader before being sold in Georgia.

The death of a son – likely born to Indiana – was recorded in the family Bible as having taken place the year before Dick Gray was born, but the unnamed child died after living less than a day. Three more children, two identified by only their first names in the old Bible and all probably born to Indiana, appear to have been subsequently fathered by Benoni Gray. A son, Wesley Collins, was born in 1857, and the last recorded births were of twin girls, Mary Ann and Sarah, born in 1859.

Martha Gray died in June of 1859, only a few weeks after the two girls were born. Her widowed husband, Benoni, married again six months later, and by the late spring of 1860, the Grays had moved to East Texas and settled on a 600 acre tract in Grimes County. When a census taker arrived that year in the middle of June, he found the Gray family and the Boyd family – into which Benoni Gray's oldest daughter, Sarah Frances, had married in 1846 – intermingled in two adjacent houses. Benoni Gray was listed as head of a household that only included his new wife, his eldest daughter, and her husband, Thomas W. Boyd.

The head of the other household was Benoni's oldest son, twenty-eight-year-old John H.P. Gray. Eighteen individuals were apparently living together under the same roof, and those in the home included Benoni Gray's four unmarried sons and nine members of the Boyd family. And in the same household there was also a young man named John H. Wilson, who may have eventually had a significant impact on the life of Dick Gray. Wilson, a twenty-six-year-old immigrant from Ireland, was a man of some means and was following a career as a printer – the industry in which Dick Gray would find enormous success many years after he changed his name to Richard Henry Boyd.

The biographical pamphlet written in 1922 conveys that during the Civil War, Dick Gray acted as a servant when he accompanied his master and three of his sons when they left home to serve in the Confederate military. It claims that Benoni Gray and two sons were killed in the fighting that took place around Chattanooga, and that Boyd, who at the time was still called Dick Gray, brought the surviving son – who was wounded – back to Texas.

Although the family Bible does list two sons of Benoni and Martha Gray as having died while "in the army," neither was killed in the fighting around Chattanooga. They both died in 1862, a year prior to the Chattanooga Campaign – William Schley Gray in Macon, Georgia, and George Hanson Gray in Jackson, Mississippi. And John H.P. Gray, who served in the 12th Texas Infantry, died on April 30, 1864 – the day his unit fought in the Battle of Jenkins Ferry in Arkansas. No military record of Benoni Gray having served in the Confederacy was found, but family tradition gives the date of his death as also having occurred on the day of the battle in Arkansas.

If thirteen-year-old Dick Gray did bring a wounded member of the family back to Texas, it would have probably been his half-brother, Richard Henry Gray, of the 21st Texas Cavalry. But the man he accompanied may well have been Thomas W. Boyd, the husband of Dick's half-sister, Sarah Frances Gray. Boyd's unit, the 13th Texas Infantry, also fought at Jenkins Ferry, and his unit sustained fairly heavy casualties when a Confederate force pushed back a major Union offensive that had been launched in the direction of Texas.

After the deaths of three half-brothers during the war, Dick likely helped sustain the Gray family, as tradition suggests. He is said to have made money for the family by transporting wagonloads of cotton to Mexico, where one account held that he and his wounded companion took refuge at the close of the war. It was around 1867, when members of the family were going to live in different places, that Dick changed his name to Richard Henry Boyd. He may have chosen the name out of the fondness he had for his half-brother – who was only four years his senior – and because of his connection to the Boyd family.

It seems reasonable to wonder if he changed his name because he wanted to separate himself from the circumstances of his heritage. What was contained in the historical pamphlet would have primarily come from Reverend Boyd, and the information includes a detailed explanation – an explanation contradicted by the records contained in the family Bible – that his relationship with Benoni Gray had come about only after the death of Martha Gray.

But there is no explicit account of what motivated him to choose the name he took, and there is no account establishing that his early association with John H. Wilson was what led him to his eventual involvement in the printing industry. The Gray family broke up before Boyd turned eighteen, and he worked in an East Texas sawmill, and may have even been a cowboy in West Texas before he began the next phase of his life.

Although Richard Henry Boyd had not yet learned to read or write, his unusually high level of intelligence must have been increasingly evident by the time he married in 1868. His wife only lived for eleven months, and it is unclear whether her death led him to be baptized the following year in a Baptist church in Grimes County. It must have been around this time that he was learning to read and write. In 1870 Boyd entered a small Texas school for former slaves called Bishop College, and after becoming a minister, he served successfully in a several churches in Texas.

When Boyd married Harriet Albertine Moore in Grimes County in 1872, he was nearly twenty-one and she was close to the same age. By the time their first child was born the next year, Boyd's ministerial duties were expanding. Emerging as both a natural leader and a brilliant organizer, Reverend Boyd, with the help of a white Baptist preacher, not only formed the first Texas Negro Baptist Convention, he established a number of local churches.

His statewide influence as a leader continued to grow, and after he started representing the state in national Baptist organizations, his reputation spread well beyond Texas. Reverend Boyd, who was deeply aware of the importance of printed material in black Sunday Schools, saw that black churches would be better served if that material was created by blacks instead of by whites, but it would take years before he was able to pursue the opportunity he envisioned.

Despite his increasing prominence within the framework of the Baptist Church, the Boyd family lived modestly. In 1880 Richard Henry Boyd, who was listed in the census as "teaching school," was raising four children with his wife, Harriet, on their 14-acre farm in East Texas. When the census taker made a record of their possessions, he listed one horse, two cows, three hogs, seven chickens, and noted that nine acres of their land had produced ninety bushels of Indian corn during the previous year.

Reverend Boyd watched a number of black Baptist associations come and go, but in the mid-1890s several organizations consolidated to form the National Baptist Convention. He was named to a powerful position within the organization, and in 1896, despite considerable opposition, he was authorized to create a black publishing house. Five years later he explained how the opportunity came about.

"A few years ago I went to Philadelphia to see the manager of the American Baptist Publishing Society. I said, 'Doctor, Negroes want representation. They want their writings published in your papers, and their pictures printed in your columns.' He replied, 'We would lose $40,000 a year if we did that. The time has not come when the American people will read after a Negro.' I said, 'Very well, if you shut us out, we will print our own papers.' That was the origin of this publishing house.

"Our convention elected two men to establish the plant, and they failed. In 1896, when we were about to give it up, I told the convention that the plan would go through if put in the proper hands. I am just a big, backwoods Texas Negro, and my make-up made such an impression on the convention that they made me the manager of the new house."

Boyd decided that the institution would be established in Nashville, and in 1896 he came to the city. In 1907, in his book, *The Negro in Business*, Booker T. Washington not only explained the help Boyd received from Dr. James M. Frost, the Secretary of the Sunday School Board of the all-white Southern Baptist Convention, he reported that Boyd was required to pledge property he owned in Texas in order to finance a contract with a local printing company.

Then Washington gave a detailed account of how Boyd moved the new publishing entity forward.

"Secretary Boyd rented a small room at 408 Cedar Street. This room, 8 feet by 10 feet, had one small second-hand table, two second-hand chairs, one oil lamp, a bottle of ink, two pen holders, and writing paper and envelopes. How ridiculous this seemed – a backwoods, uneducated preacher with such headquarters – to call this undertaking the National Baptist Publishing Board.

Richard Henry Boyd

"Although a novice in business, he had been careful to acquaint himself with the methods of distributing church supplies, and to arm himself with the addresses of Sunday school superintendents, clerks, and pastors of Negro Baptist churches.

"The first work to be done was the preparation of covers for four Sunday School magazines. Then he prepared price lists, order blanks, self-addressed envelopes, and a circular letter. He secured the services of three young women and set them to work addressing envelopes. In one day he mailed 5000 letters to every state in the union where he knew there was a Negro Baptist Church.

"The first year's report showed an annual circulation of 700,000 Sunday school magazines, the employ of two clerks and a bookkeeper, cash receipts of $5089, and about $1000 expended in missionary and benevolent work."

In 1899 the National Baptist Convention met in Nashville. An initial speaker was Dr. Frost, and a newspaper reporter was in the audience.

James M. Frost

"Dr. Frost touchingly referred to his childhood days and his black "mammy" who had taught him how to walk, and cared for him when he was unable to care for himself. Under such circumstances he could not forget the race, and would do all in his power to help it."

Then Reverend Boyd, who thirty years earlier was still learning to read and write, addressed the large audience. He described the challenges that had faced the black race immediately after the Civil War.

"At the close of the war, 4,500,000 Negroes, about three-fourths of them in the slave states, suddenly emerged from slavery into American citizenship. They were turned loose in the world – nameless, homeless, and penniless – without experience, without education, without schools or churches, and without benevolent organizations.

"The old slave, who had worshipped in the gallery of his master's church or knelt by his master's preacher, was deprived of even this privilege. The Ku Klux Klan, the intimidators, and the mobs took the place of the old patrollers, and the old masters' or overseers' passes were not recognized by these new regulators. The shotgun, the six-shooter, the rope, and the stake took the place of the bull whip and the bloodhound."

Then he traced the role that Negro churches and Sunday Schools and associations had played, and went on to detail how the publishing concern was doing its part to uplift the black race.

Reverend Boyd did not grow the business by himself. His oldest son, Henry Allen Boyd shouldered a number of operational responsibilities, which not only allowed the venture to grow more rapidly, but also gave his father the time to pursue other objectives.

Henry Allen Boyd and Richard H. Boyd

In a 1901 newspaper article, Reverend Boyd summed up the success of his operation.

"I came to Nashville without a dollar and started my establishment on credit – publishing by contract for the first year and a half. The first year I did $5000 worth of business, and as soon as my receipts got up to $600 per month I set up my own plant. My receipts the second year netted $20,000, the third year $35,000, and in 1900 they amounted to $49,000."

The article went on to indicate how essential Reverend Boyd was to the National Baptist Publishing Company.

"There are 107 employees on the place, and every one is a Negro. Everything from the boiler room to the counting room is modern, and Dr. Boyd has new machinery coming. Dr. Boyd believes in systems, and every employee is governed by a set of printed rules. Dr. Boyd trains his employees, and all business is dispatched according to method. What Reverend Boyd has done illustrates what pluck, intelligence, and untiring energy can do."

In *The Negro in Business*, Booker T. Washington provided additional insight into Boyd's leadership.

"One of the unique features of the establishment is that it has a chapel. Thirty minutes are spent each morning in devotional exercises. All are required to be present, and are paid the same as for other work hours. Strict conduct is required, and a card of rules and regulations is furnished to each employee. They prohibit profane language, unseemly conduct, smoking, and the use of intoxicating liquors."

National Baptist Publishing Company

By 1905 Boyd oversaw a publishing concern that employed as many as 120 workers and occupied six different brick structures. The physical plant, which included printing presses, embossing machines, and a bindery, printed some 100,000 books and 7,000,000 periodicals per year.

National Baptist Publishing Company workers

Reverend Boyd and J.C. Napier, along with other black leaders, were eager to advance the prospects of the local Negro community, and at the end of 1903 they took the lead in founding the black-owned One Cent Savings Bank and Trust Company. Boyd – who would serve as president of the bank – along with Napier and a handful of other leaders, saw a black-owned bank as crucial to the individual and collective economic advancement of the Negro community, which had long been neglected and frequently mistreated by local financial institutions. The bank grew very slowly over the years, and in 1920 it was renamed Citizens Savings Bank and Trust Company.

Boyd tried to maintain good relations with white political and community leaders, but in 1905 the Tennessee State Legislature sunk deeper into the shadow of Jim Crow when it passed a law segregating streetcar lines. His analysis of the situation was expressed in a letter to the Nashville Banner.

"Negroes have regretted the "Jim Crow" car law, and believed it uncalled for. They regretted the active part taken in the making of this law by the streetcar company management. So much did they regret it that a committee of Negro businessmen called on the streetcar managers and begged them to refrain from taking such an active part.

"Thirty or forty thousand Negro citizens of Nashville and vicinity were patrons of the railway, and have refrained from giving them any trouble. They have borne the unjust and abusive treatment given themselves and their families by streetcar conductors, hence we did not feel that we should be made an object for passing this law. We were assured by streetcar management that the law was not a necessity on account of the Negroes, but because of the discontent of the white people of the South, confusion, disturbance, and riots would possibly arise.

"The statement is constantly made that Negroes are boycotting the streetcars. Negroes have never passed resolutions in their churches, or had mass meetings to boycott the streetcar company. Instead of Negroes boycotting the streetcars, the streetcars boycotted the Negroes. Thus it came about that the Negroes of Nashville felt this was a good occasion for raising the automobile as a common carrier.

"Should the Negroes succeed in this enterprise, it will stop agitation by the races on the streetcars. If the Negroes of Nashville succeed with their first five autos, they will increased to twenty or fifty cars. Then there need be no discriminating laws, for Negroes can have their own transportation lines, run by their own men. We very much regret that there is talk from our city fathers attempting to legislate against this enterprise. We hope that the powers that be will not cripple it in its infancy."

Boyd and Napier, along with Preston Taylor, another local leader, led the formation of the Union Transportation Company, which initially provided small steam-powered buses for the use of black riders, and later purchased fourteen electric buses. Instead of buying the necessary power from the

Union Transportation Company vehicle

Nashville Railway and Light Company, the local white-owned monopoly that had helped engineer the new segregation law, Reverend Boyd had the fledgling company install a dynamo in the basement of the National Baptist Publishing Company.

The Nashville City Council sought to undermine the Union Transportation Company by imposing a tax on electric buses, and the enterprise faced other challenges – some of them self-imposed – before going out of business in 1907. But one benefit of the streetcar boycott was that it gave rise to the Nashville Globe, which was founded by Reverend Boyd at the end of 1905.

In the short term, the Globe served to garner community support for the boycott, and over the next few years it became Nashville's most successful black-owned newspaper. Henry Allen Boyd, who was still in his late twenties when the Globe was founded, assumed operational control of the newspaper, and he helped provide the editorial voice that would, until the eve of the Nashville sit-ins and the Freedom Rides, speak for many in the Negro community.

In 1908 Reverend Boyd and his son were in the early stages of founding the National Negro Doll Company – an enterprise which began producing dolls of color over eighty years before similar dolls would be heralded as new to the American market. Henry Allen Boyd is the likely author of a piece describing dolls that not only resembled the little black girls who would play with them, but did not present blacks as caricatures.

Nashville Globe, October 6, 1911

"These... are not made of that disgraceful and humiliating type that we have been accustomed to seeing black dolls made of. They represent the intelligent and refined Negro of today, rather than that type... usually given to children and as a rule used as a scarecrow."

The dolls were sold over a period of twenty years, and were shipped across the country. And during the same period, the Boyds used the columns of the Nashville Globe to advocate for improving the education being provided to the colored community. The Globe carried articles that pushed for more Negro schools to be built, lobbied for the establishment of what would become Tennessee A&I, and insisted that white control over Fisk be turned over to blacks. The publishing company continued to thrive, and in 1908 the Globe described the business in a glowing article.

"The National Baptist Publishing Board is the largest Negro printing house and publishing concern in the world. They are prepared to print anything from a calling card to an encyclopedia, and print thousands of volumes of books annually."

Along with printing, there was also a music department that employed composers to write new hymns, and some six years earlier a branch of the business, the Church Supply Department, had been developed.

"They are supplying churches throughout the United State with pews, organs, pianos, bells, pulpits, lamps, communion sets, baptismal garments and robes – and are supplying homes with pianos and sewing machines."

Richard H. Boyd family

But from the beginning Boyd had detractors in the Baptist Convention. He considered the publishing house as a private business, and complaints about the money he made from the venture grew louder over the coming years.

Several of Reverend Boyd's children worked for the publishing house, and the members of his family living in Nashville eventually included his mother. Near the beginning of the Civil War, Indiana had married Samuel J. Dixon, with whom she had the last six of her ten children. After the death of her husband she came to Nashville, and in 1910 she was living with Reverend and Mrs. Boyd in their home on Second Avenue North. Nine of her ten children were living, and the final years of her life were spent in the midst of her Boyd grandchildren.

Indiana Dixon was described as having a dark complexion and African features, and a strong constitution. She often wore large gold rings on her ears, and was noted for her sense of charity. She had overcome being taken from her family as a child, and managed to raise her children through the ordeal of slavery and the disruption of

Mr. and Mrs. Richard H. Boyd

war. Along with several accomplished daughters, she had four sons who grew up to be ministers, and she lived to see her eldest son become a man of great consequence. In the spring of 1915 her long life came to an end, and her remains were taken to Texas, where she had lived for so many years.

Although Reverend Boyd had solidified his control of the publishing house in 1898 by chartering the enterprise as a separate entity from the National Board, and although he had invested significant capital in the venture, his enemies persisted in their attempts to seize control of the publishing enterprise. In 1915, a few months after the death of his mother, Boyd's struggle against his detractors reached a climactic point.

A corporate strategy was devised by Reverend Boyd's adversaries, and after he resisted, a lawsuit was filed that would have ended his control over the organization. But he had used his own money to pay for real estate and for the expansion of buildings, and the associated deeds and titles and copyrights were filed in his name, rather than in the name of the National Baptist Convention. Boyd ultimately prevailed in the lawsuit, and what came to be called "the Boyd Convention" continued to grow and prosper.

Henry Allen Boyd

Reverend Boyd died in 1922 – a few months after he and Harriet had their fiftieth wedding anniversary – and when she died in 1928, she left behind a thriving family. Along with the financial legacy he provided to his descendants, Richard Henry Boyd left a compelling social legacy, both for the black community and for the city of Nashville. Leadership of the National Baptist Publishing Board would pass to his son, Henry Allen Boyd, who, along with leading the Nashville Globe, would head both the publishing board and Citizens Bank until well after the Second World War.

Henry Allen Boyd proved to be an exceptional executive, and all three enterprises thrived under his management. The younger Boyd also became Nashville's leading black political figure, overseeing voter registration drives and leading the patriotic efforts of the Negro community during World War One, and he also led the effort to establish the local Colored YMCA.

After the death of Henry Allen Boyd in 1959, the Nashville Globe was discontinued, but his nephew, Theophilus Bartholomew Boyd, Jr., one of Reverend Richard Henry Boyd's grandsons, assumed control of both the publishing board and of Citizens Bank. T.B. Boyd Jr., who was a pastor and a veteran of World War II, not only oversaw the relocation of the publishing facility from Second Avenue North to a new complex west of downtown Nashville, he was an exceptional business and community leader, and a strong voice for black advancement. Following his death in 1979, leadership of the family's publishing and banking concerns were assumed by his son, T.B. Boyd III, the great-grandson of Reverend Boyd.

T.B. Boyd III continued the family's tradition of excellent leadership, and under his stewardship the publishing company and the bank continued to thrive. In 2000, 104 years after its founding, the name of the National Baptist Publishing Board was changed to the R.H. Boyd Publishing Corporation. T.B. Boyd III retired in 2017, and he was succeeded by his daughter, LaDonna, the great-great-granddaughter of Reverend Boyd, representing the fifth generation to lead the company.

While many of the descendants of Reverend Boyd thrived, there were a few who struggled, and the struggles of one of his grandsons ultimately reflected the resilience that seems to have existed across many branches of the family.

Richard Henry Boyd's daughter, Lula, was born in 1882 while

the family was still living in Texas, and she moved with her family to Nashville in 1896. She married Lovell Landers in 1905, and two years later she gave birth to a son, Lovell Landers, Jr. Her son was exceptionally gifted. When he was fifteen he built a battery-powered airplane which was so admired that he was featured in a newspaper article entitled, "Negro Boy May Be Mechanical Genius."

His gifts were not only intellectual. Lovell Landers Jr. was a football star at Pearl High School and an outstanding player at Fisk before graduating and moving on to New York City in 1929. He lived with his sister and brother-in-law and worked as an auto mechanic for about three years before his life was torn apart. He was accused of murder – supposedly having been hired by a woman to kill her husband for the insurance benefits she would receive.

He steadfastly denied any involvement, but he was convicted of the 1932 murder – largely on the testimony of his former girlfriend. The girlfriend was of Italian extraction, and she was said to have been outraged after learning that Landers was leaving her for a black girl. She went to the police and accused him of several different crimes before circumstantial evidence led him to being charged in the killing. Twenty-six-year-old Lovell Landers was convicted and sentenced to die in the electric chair, but two days before his execution, because of his previous accomplishments and the reputation of his family, the Governor of New York commuted his sentence to life in prison.

Landers was incarcerated at Sing Sing Prison in New York, where he soon became a star performer on the institution's football team, and where he would spend much of his time working on inventions. After devising an improved dish washing machine and then a glove making machine, Landers invented a system that was able to vaporize crude oil into a fuel that would operate an internal combustion engine, and then he offered it to the government as his contribution to the war effort.

Lovell Landers Jr. was eventually released from Sing Sing, and worked as an electrician in Nashville for a number of years. He quietly lived out the rest of his life, and he was 92 when he died in 1999 in Decatur, Georgia. The intellectual energy with which he was blessed was a reflection of his grandfather, Reverend Boyd, but the enormous resilience he displayed in the wake of what befell him in New York, reflected the resilience of his great-grandmother, Indiana, who had lived through so much during the 1800s.

In 1901 Reverend Boyd, who had been an illiterate slave boy forty years earlier, wrote about his race and his denomination, and in describing the role he expected each to play in the world at large, he disclosed the context in which he saw the work to which he devoted his life.

"The Twentieth Century is to witness a rejuvenation of the great African race. The Negro is slowly but surely awakening from his long slumber, and will soon step forward to take a man's part in (solving) the great world problems. The Negroes of the United States are in the van of the coming army. The dominating influence of this advance guard is to be religion. In religious affairs Negro Baptists, being numerically stronger than any other Negro denomination in the United States, are to largely influence the race in America. The Negro race in America is to largely determine the destiny of the entire Negro race, and the Negro race is ere long to largely determine the current of human history."

20

Annie Compton

When he climbed up to the driver's seat of a fire engine on a February day in 1907, James Trimble was fifty years old. He was an original member of William Stockell Engine Company No. 4, one of Nashville's first colored fire companies, which had been formed in 1885. Trimble was a beloved individual in the community and he clearly loved being a fireman, but by then he knew that his career was coming to an end. His rheumatism was more and more painful, and there were problems with his heart and his kidneys.

When a reporter arrived that day to interview the men at their fire station on Woodland Street, Trimble talked about the role his engine company played in the East Nashville community.

Stockell Fire Company 4, (1907)

"The white people have been our friends from the start. We have tried to deserve their good will, and show them that we are endeavoring to make good citizens. We have seen a great many of the boys and girls grow up over here on the East Side, and now we keep up with them and with their children. We have the hearts of the children. They like to come to the station, and we do not discourage their visits. We... forbid the use of any language or behavior that might in any way be hurtful to them.

"We arrange a Christmas tree every year. We buy the gifts

ourselves to some extent, but some of the white merchants are very liberal in helping us. Last Christmas we had several hundred children. When we first opened up on the East Side, it was said the station would be a rendezvous for thieves and loafers. We had to outlive that idea."

There had been other obstacles put up by those who adhered to the racial attitudes of that period. In 1874 the existence of a black fire company had been threatened when a petition was presented to government officials.

Stokely Allen, Company 4 (1892)

"To the Honorable Fire Commissioners and the Mayor of Nashville – We the undersigned members of the Fire Department of the City of Nashville, respectfully petition your honorable body to dispense with colored firemen at present employed, for reason that they do not work in harmony with the regular firemen of the city, and if white men were employed on the Hook and Ladder, it is confidently believed that there would be more good-will between all parties, and there would be more effectual service rendered when fires occur."

A decision was communicated the following month. "The charges preferred by members of the Fire Department against the Hook and Ladder Company... have been carefully examined. The Board of Commissioners has determined that the charges are not of a character justifying the action desired... This Board cannot shut their eyes to the fact of there being much prejudice existing, but...no charge, either of inefficiency or neglect of duty having been preferred...the petition is rejected."

When the reporter who interviewed James Trimble wrote his article, he also described the atmosphere at the fire station.

Harvey Ewing, Company 4 (1892)

"The children never tire of the place – of the horses and the good times they have at the station. It is claimed that many an East Nashville mother, wishing to go downtown and having nobody to leave the children with, sends them over to the fire station, knowing that the children are as safe as at home. The great delight among the little folks is when the alarm sounds. The news spreads all down the neighborhood, and the children, catching the contagion of excitement almost as quickly as the horses in their stalls, come scurrying – boys shouting, girls giggling, and dogs barking – all hurrying down to see the engine come out, Trimble on top, and reelman, pipemen, driver, stoker, and captain all off and away for a fire."

The article also covered the role that Engine Company No. 4 had played when a massive fire destroyed the buildings on the north side of Church Street between 3rd and 4th Avenues on the evening of January 2, 1892 – seventeen years after the petition was presented by the white firemen. Accounts of the fire were front-page news for a couple of days.

"Three men never met a braver or nobler death than the three colored firemen who lost their lives last night… The colored people of Nashville have good reason to feel proud over the heroic deaths of these men, and the firemen of the city, both white and black, will always pay tribute to the memory of these gallant men… Captain C. C. Gowdey was the Captain of Stockell Fire Company No. 4. He was 38 years old, and leaves a wife and a son. Harvey Ewing was the pipeman of Stockell No. 4. He was 41 years of age and leaves a wife and 10-year-old son. Stokely Allen was the reel driver of his company. He was 29 years old, is married, and has a young daughter. The other members of this gallant colored fire company worked disconsolately, but manfully, at the fire after the horrible death of their comrades."

C. C. Gowdey, Fire Company 4 (1886)

James Trimble was one of the men who kept working until the fire was under control, and he was likely among those who spent several hours the following day, recovering the scorched and mutilated remains of the three men he had known so well.

Because Trimble was such a beloved figure in the East Nashville community, the article that appeared in the February 9, 1907 issue of the Nashville Banner included details about his family. He told the reporter about how both of his children, Laura and James, had graduated from Fisk. Before marrying and moving to Colorado, Laura was a music professor at Lane

College in Jackson, Tennessee, and James Jr. had become a physician and recently opened his practice in Brooklyn.

The previous year, Trimble had taken a few days off and travelled to Boston to watch his son graduate from medical school. The elder James Trimble had gone through "the Normal Course" at Fisk, but unlike his children, he had not entered the university. He would have been proud of the education they each received, and he must have particularly enjoyed watching them graduate. But the most memorable ceremony he attended was probably when his son, James, graduated from Pearl High School in 1898.

That night several thousand people had crowded into the Union Tabernacle, which would become more widely known as Ryman Auditorium in later years. James Trimble would have surely remembered the address that was delivered by Professor W.H. Councill, the president of what would become known as Alabama A&M, and he would have remembered how much applause there was. A

W. C. Councill

newspaper article recorded what Councill told the audience.

"A state which fails to educate its children bequeaths paupers to posterity. The state which fails to give industrial training to its youths transmits to posterity criminals." He said that the South would have to educate the Negro, or buy Gatling guns to kill them. Professor Councill told the graduates, as well as the crowd, that Negroes had to prepare for the future. He said that the future would not be ruled by white men or black men, but by men with brains.

Professor Councill also said, "I have no use for a man who tries to get away from his race. I do not have any trouble with my hair, nor are my flat nose and flat feet and big black hands in my way."

James G. Trimble, Jr.

Along with answering the reporter's questions about the fire company on that day in 1907 in East Nashville, James Trimble climbed up into the driver's seat of his fire engine and posed for a photograph. Part of the reason that James and his wife, Dernice, had been able to raise two such extraordinary children in a time of severe racial discrimination must have come from their unusual backgrounds. Stories about the people Trimble had known during the course of his life could have filled the pages of a long book.

The article hadn't focused on Trimble's ancestry. His grandfather, Alexander – who had been locally known as Aleck – was in his eighties when he died in 1866. James, who was ten at the time, would have probably heard all about his grandfather and the relationship he had with his owner, James Trimble – a prominent white man. Aleck and James Trimble were close to the same age, and judging from the fact that Aleck was allowed to work for himself and keep the money he earned, if the two were not related, they must have had an unusually close personal connection.

Aleck Trimble was likely born in southwest Virginia, where the white Trimble family had been leading citizens for decades. James Trimble, who was described as "a modest man of gentle habits and much courtesy" became a brilliant lawyer, and after moving to Nashville in 1813, he instructed Sam Houston in his study of law before forming a partnership with Felix Grundy, another eminent attorney.

In his later years, Aleck Trimble told about saving his money until he bought his freedom from James Trimble for $2400, and how he was later able to buy his wife, Harriett, and their infant daughter, Sarah, from James Trimble's widow, Letitia. Aleck and Harriette's son, George, was born a free person of color in 1833, and in 1840 Aleck's family not only included Harriett and their three children, it listed him as owning one slave. When the census was taken again in 1850, Aleck owned property valued at $5000, and ten years later, along with the other property he had, he still owned a single slave.

In 1855 Aleck's son George – James' father – had married Laura Ann Bosley, the daughter of a wealthy white man, John B. Bosley, and Alsey Cloud, a mulatto former slave. When their union was entered in the marriage records of Davidson County, George and Laura Ann were not designated as persons of color. By 1860 they had four children, the eldest being four-year-old James, and like his aging father, Aleck, George Trimble also owned a single slave.

James was seven when he lost his mother in 1863, and his black grandfather, Aleck, died in 1866, the year before the death of his white grandfather, John B. Bosley. Property would be inherited from his uncle, James G. Bosley, and James Trimble grew up in relatively comfortable circumstances. He received what likely amounted to a high school education after going through the Normal Course at Fisk.

James married Dernice Compton in 1879, and the next year their household on Grundy Street included their infant son, James Jr. They were sharing their home with Dernice's three younger siblings, as well as two aging black people, one of whom may have been the slave who had belonged to George Trimble, James' father, back before the Civil War.

The article about the Negro firemen in East Nashville made no mention of Dernice, who had died three years earlier, or of the Compton family. Dernice Compton was the daughter of an emancipated light-skinned slave named Annie Allen, and a prominent white man named Henry W. Compton. Compton lived on a 1760 acre farm six miles south of Nashville, and he owned some 40 slaves at the outbreak of the Civil War.

Henry W. Compton

Henry Compton was an unusual man. He had been a sickly child, and grew up to be an introvert with a very independent spirit. Unlike most men of wealth, he remained a bachelor well into his thirties, but in the early 1850s, after purchasing a fourteen-year-old slave named Ann Allen, he underwent a change. Ann, who was usually called Annie, was born in 1836 or 1837, and records indicate that she was raised in Fauquier County, Virginia. Her especially light complexion suggested that both her father and her mother must have had especially fair skin.

The 1850 slave census lists three men with the surname, Allen, who owned Negroes in Fauquier County. That census, along with other sources, indicates that one of those individuals, Fielding Allen, was almost certainly the owner of Annie Allen.

When the census was taken in September, 1850, the ten slaves belonging to Fielding Allen included a mulatto girl who was fourteen years old, which was Annie's age at that time. A subsequent record indicates that her parents were named Henry and Viney, and that along with her sister, Maria, she had three brothers, Charles, Walker, and Lewis, all of whom may have been closely related to Fielding Allen.

The census, along with other records, contains telling details of Fielding Allen's life. He was a fifty-five-year-old bachelor living on a 220-acre-farm in a finely-furnished home with his aging mother and two unmarried sisters. In 1854 he fathered twin sons by his slave woman, Phillis, and Fauquier County records bring to light another side of Fielding Allen. When he died in 1857, the cause of death was recorded as "derangement." Could it be that Annie, when she was blossoming into a young woman, had been sent south to protect her from the man who owned her – and who may have been an uncle or cousin?

Annie probably came to Tennessee late in 1850 or sometime in 1851. Henry Compton was close to forty by then, and it wasn't long before he developed feelings for Annie.

Around 1850, with the nation's political fabric growing more and more frayed over the issue of slavery, Compton, like nearly all of the other large slave owners in the area, was active in the political organization dedicated to preserving the institution of slavery – the

Democratic Party. But in 1852, on the eve of a trip to Virginia, he engaged Return J. Meigs, a prominent attorney locally known for his anti-slavery sentiments, to draw up a highly specific and unusual will. While Annie was not mentioned in the will, it would later become clear that the document Meigs prepared was shaped by the regard Henry Compton had for her.

The will mentioned three slaves who had been liberated by Henry's deceased father, William Compton. William Compton, who died in 1846, had reflected some of the contradictions endemic to the institution of slavery. He was a slave trader, but in 1825 he had placed a somewhat unusual ad in the Nashville Whig, saying that he wanted to buy "a few Negro men and women of good character... They will not be taken out of the country...and be treated with more than the usual humanity."

Henry Compton grew up to exhibit contradictions of his own. In 1853 he would put an ad in a local newspaper to recover his runaway mulatto slave, Billy, but the will he had signed a year earlier included a long clause regarding his slaves. The will reflected the uncertainty that existed about whether free blacks would be legally required to leave Tennessee, and whether they could legally own land. It also mentioned Compton's purchase of the Shute farm, a prime 607 acre tract on Richland Creek for which he paid $18,000.

"I hereby set all my negroes free, and I charge my executors with the trust and duty of carrying this bequest of freedom into execution in such a manner as the law of the land will permit, said negroes to be permitted to remain in Tennessee if they can by law... or to be removed to such other state or country as they may choose... as free persons of color.

"And I give to my negroes my Shute place, to have and to hold to them and their heirs forever, if they are capable in law of having and holding the same... If not... I direct my executors to sell said place, and to lay out the proceeds in the purchase of a home for my said negroes in the state or country to which they may be removed, and to support them for a few years after they are sent off...

"I am now about to start to Virginia to purchase certain slaves belonging to the same family of slaves now owned by me, and it is to be distinctly understood that the provisions of... my will are to apply to any and all slaves that I may buy, as well as those now in my possession, it having been my long settled purpose to set all my slaves free."

A subsequent document indicates that Compton was unable to buy the slaves that he had expected to bring back from Virginia. That document, a codicil to his will, was written in 1858 after he had emancipated Annie. It reveals additional details about the reason for the trip on which he had embarked six years earlier.

"I give the land I purchased from Robert Boyd to my slaves in the same way in which... I gave to them the place I purchased from Shute... and I also give to my slaves all my livestock and money... In case I should not give to Annie Allen, a mulatto woman set free by me and now residing in Warrenton, Virginia, the sum of $7000 in cash while I am at that place on a visit... and on which I expect to start tomorrow, then I give to her the note which I hold on H.H. Haynes & Co. for about the same sum, together with the mortgage by which it is secured."

H.H. Haynes & Company, the business indebted to Compton, was a slave-trading firm located in Nashville on Cedar Street, and its two owners served as witnesses to

H. H. HAYNES & CO.,
AGENTS FOR THE
Sale and Purchase of Negroes,
At No. 16 Cedar street,
Between Public Square and Commercial Hotel,
dec29-tf   **Nashville, Tenn.**

Daily Patriot, December 30, 1859

the codicil. In mid-April of that year, the company had placed an ad in the Republican Banner with the heading, "Fifty Negroes Wanted," and within two weeks another ad was published with the heading, "Fifty Negroes for Sale." While the dates of the advertisements and the date of the codicil may have been coincidental, it seems that some of the fifty Negroes mentioned in the later ad may have included slaves Compton sold to Haynes & Co, and for which he was owed money.

In his 1852 will, Henry Compton mentioned that he was going to Virginia "to purchase certain slaves, belonging to the same family of slaves now owned by me." And six years later he went back again to "give to Ann Allen, a mulatto woman set free by me and now living in Warrenton, Virginia, the sum of $7000 in cash, while I am... on a visit there." A reasonable hypothesis is that when Compton initially tried to purchase the "certain" slaves he wanted to buy, Fielding Allen had refused to sell them, and that after his death, Annie went back to Fauquier County to live with her family.

Following the death of Fielding Allen, did Annie get word to Henry Compton that the rest of her family could be acquired? Had Compton presented the codicil to Annie when he arrived, and used it to persuade her, and perhaps the other members of her family, to return with him to Davidson County?

Most if not all of the mixed-race Allen family soon left Fauquier County for Tennessee. Not only would Annie's brother Charles indicate, many years later, that he had come to the Compton place as a boy in the mid-to-late 1850s, census records reveal a telling change in the number of light-skinned slaves on the Allen and Compton farms between 1850 and 1860.

The mulatto slaves on the Allen place in Virginia fell from seven in 1850 to only one in 1860, while the five light-complexioned slaves on the Compton farm in Tennessee rose from five to fourteen during the same period of time. An examination of the ages of the biracial Compton slaves in 1860 establishes that most of the increase was not brought about by individuals who were on the place at the beginning of the decade. But there was at least one biracial child born who *was* born on the place during the 1850s. Henry Compton, perhaps during Annie's absence, had fathered his son, Joshua, by a black or mulatto woman named Harriet.

Henry W. Compton residence

In his will, Henry Compton had included his intention to emancipate his slaves, but they were never liberated. It might have been the continuing threat that free persons of color could be forced to leave Tennessee that kept him from setting them free, but actions he took both before and during the Civil War signaled that he was a proponent of slavery and a staunch supporter of the Confederacy.

While his feelings about owning slaves may have been traditional for the place in which he lived, his relationship with Annie flaunted tradition. They lived together as husband and wife, and at the age of twenty-two, not long after her return from Virginia, she became pregnant with the first of their five children, William Henry Compton, who was born in September, 1859.

Henry Harding, a well-known local Negro businessman and political leader, was somewhat neutral in the way he described the living situation Henry and Annie Compton had during the war. "I occasionally visited the plantation of Compton for the purpose of seeing his wife, a concubine, a colored woman, and other black people." But nearly two decades later, a second individual mentioned how the affluent portion of the white community viewed Henry Compton. "(He) plunged his relatives into great distress, and completely outlawed himself from good society."

Dernice Compton, who would eventually become the wife of James Trimble, was conceived around Thanksgiving, 1861, when Nashville was still in Confederate hands. But by the time she was born in the summer of 1862, Nashville had fallen to Union forces and the area was under Union control. By then Annie may have joined some of the other women on the place, working at Henry's direction to make cloth and socks that would be sent to Confederate soldiers.

The Compton farm was close to Nashville, and it was visited on several occasions by Union foraging parties. Soldiers and a long line of wagons would arrive, and in addition to hauling away significant quantities of corn and hay, hams would be removed from the smokehouse and large numbers of cows and horses and sheep were taken. And along with the Federal patrols that came through the neighborhood, the farm was sometimes visited by Confederate units in need of provisions.

On the final day of 1864, two weeks after the Battle of Nashville, Annie gave birth to her third child, a daughter named Maria. Henry and Annie continued living together as husband and wife, and two more children, Mary Ann and Thomas, would be born after the war. When the next census was taken in 1870, the family was living in Nashville. That year the Compton household not only included Henry and Annie, who was not designated as being non-white, it listed Dernice and her three siblings, her half-brother, Joshua, and twenty-five-year-old Maria Allen, who was likely Annie's sister.

By then Dernice was a student in the grammar school conducted at Fisk University, where other Compton children would also be educated. Annie Compton had her fifth child, Thomas, in 1872, but the following year, at the age of thirty-six, she died – supposedly after a carriage accident – at the home she and Henry shared in Nashville.

Only four months after her death, Henry married Irish-born Anna Ward, a young woman in her early twenties who had been living with her family on a small farm in the neighborhood of the Compton Place. Henry may have still been in mourning when the marriage took place. Later, in 1874, an acquaintance described Henry Compton. "He seems to be universally known as a sullen, silent, penurious, and avaricious man, who all his life has had no love or companionship for aught but himself, his possessions, his negro wife, and his mulatto children."

And the same account provided insight into the connection between Henry and Annie. It referred to his "cohabitating with a Negro woman for many years as his wife, and treating the fruits of this cohabitation in all respects as his children. This woman retained her influence with him to the last."

It is not known how long he may have mourned the loss of Annie, but it was nearly seven

Ferdinand Augustus Stewart

years after her death before Anna Ward bore a child. She ultimately had four daughters by her husband. The last of his children was born in 1890, when Henry was seventy-six.

When he died in 1895, Henry Compton left the bulk of his estate to the four daughters he had with Anna Ward, but he had previously given property to his mixed-race children. Until late in the twentieth century, some of his and Annie's descendants would continue to live on land that had been part of the old Compton farm.

Annie Allen did not live to see her children grow up, but she would have likely been proud of her three daughters. When she was sixteen, after completing her formal education, Dernice married James Trimble, the fireman. Two years later sixteen-year-old Maria, who had also been educated in the preparatory school at Fisk, married Dr. H.T. Noel. He was a successful and highly-respected Meharry graduate, who would become president of the American Medical Association of Colored Physicians. And Annie's youngest daughter, Mary Ann, was in her early twenties when she married Dr. Ferdinand Augustus Stewart. Dr. Stewart was a Fisk graduate who went on to Harvard Medical School, where he graduated as valedictorian of his class in 1888.

But Annie might have been most proud of her grandson, James Trimble, Jr., the son of Dernice and James. He was Dr. Stewart's nephew by marriage, and young James was able to follow the trail that had been blazed by Dr. Stewart. After receiving his degree from Fisk, Trimble went on to attend Harvard Medical School, graduating with high honors in 1906.

Being from a relatively affluent segment of the local black community, some members of the Trimble, Noel, and Stewart families may have known Annie Compton during the final years of her life. But much of what would be passed down about Annie for future generations would have come from Dernice, who died in 1904.

Dernice Compton Trimble (Mortuary Photograph, 1904)

Dernice likely told them about her mother's grace and strength – the qualities that had allowed Annie to emerge from a troubled background and eventually reunite her family. She may have talked about the grace and strength that enabled her mother to make a life with a darkly peculiar old man. The family would have understood that by raising such outstanding children, Annie built the foundation on which they, and succeeding generations of her descendants, would all stand.

21

Pap Singleton

On the last Sunday evening in May, 1846, Ben Singleton was in Nashville, where he had been living since around 1831. The city was in a war fever. Congress had declared war against Mexico two-and-a-half weeks earlier, but military preparations had been underway for some time. News had just been received that as many as seventy military companies, composed of some 6000 Tennesseans, had tendered their services to Governor Aaron V. Brown. A number of those troops were to be taken from Nashville to New Orleans by river. After several days of rain the Cumberland was rising, and a pair of steamboats, the Talleyrand and the Connor, which would transport many of the soldiers, were expected to arrive at any time.

Colonel Robert Weakley

Ben Singleton, who worked as a cabinet maker, was owned by Robert Locke Weakley, a native of Davidson County who was living in Rutherford County. Weakley, who may have also been in town that weekend, was to become an officer in the Third Tennessee Infantry, which would soon be making its way toward Mexico. Robert L. Weakley grew up just across the river from Nashville. His father, Colonel Robert Weakley, had been one of the last survivors of the region's earliest generation of settlers, and prior to his death the previous year, he had probably owned Ben Singleton.

When Tennessee adopted a new constitution in 1834, Colonel Weakley, a longtime political figure, had played a key role in stripping free blacks of their right to vote, which was guaranteed in the state's original constitution. Ben, who had probably been hired out by Weakley, was working as a carpenter in Nashville while the Colonel was helping to craft the new constitution. In 1846 Ben Singleton had a wife, and their children included a daughter named Emily who was around six years old. But if his wife was slave, he probably did not live with his family.

Ben Singleton was described as a mulatto. He would mention his paternity when he was seventy, but all he had to say was, "the blood of a white man flows through my veins." When he was eighty-seven he provided some additional information about himself.

"I'se borned in 1809. I'se had three or four names. I was de servant of Dr. Shelby in Nashville, and den I went to Orville Shelby."

Dr. John Shelby was the oldest brother of Orville Shelby, who ultimately moved to Lexington, Kentucky. Ben went on to say he was living in Lexington in 1830, and it may not have been too long after that when he became the property of the Weakleys. Colonel Weakley lived near the Shelbys, east of the river, and he had known both brothers for most of their lives.

Late in his life Singleton, who was small in stature, recalled times in his boyhood when he had been a jockey and ridden in horse races. And he talked about how often he had run away from his master. He was sometimes given to exaggeration, and on occasion he would claim that he had been sold south at least a dozen times, including to New Orleans. In those accounts he always managed to escape and return to Nashville, but he eventually stated that had never been to either Louisiana or to Mississippi.

While he might not have gone to any of the states in the deep south, he may well have been a frequent runaway, which could be why he was sold by the Shelbys. While some of the stories he told about fleeing slavery were probably made up, there is no question that on Sunday, May 31, 1846, Ben was poised to leave behind his family, and the world he had known for most of his life. The following Saturday his owner, Robert L. Weakley, placed an advertisement in a local newspaper.

Nashville Union, June 13, 1846

"Fifty Dollars Reward – Ranaway from my plantation in Rutherford County on 31st ult., a mulatto fellow named Ben (Alias) Ben Singleton, aged about twenty-seven years, five feet five or six inches in height, a serviceable, sprightly fellow, has lived in Nashville for the last fifteen years, presumed to be lurking about the city or neighborhood as he was seen there on the evening of the 31st. I will give $20 for his apprehension in the county of Davidson, or State of Tennessee, or the above reward if taken out of the State, and secured in any jail so that I can get him."

Weakley correctly surmised that Ben, who was actually thirty-six, was making his way north, and he requested that the advertisement be published in a newspaper in Louisville, where individuals eager to collect rewards were always on the lookout for runaway slaves. Ben Singleton was able to cross the Ohio River into Indiana, and although Indiana was a free state, he was still in danger of being apprehended and taken back to Tennessee. Many years later he said, "I went through Indiana once. I was on my way through to Canada. They told me it was Indiana, but the way I hurried through it, I thought it was 'Hurry-ana."

After eventually making it all the way to Canada, he came back across the border from Ontario and settled in Detroit. In 1850 he was working as a cook and living with a light-skinned man named Dennis Hoover – who had been born in Tennessee – along with

Hoover's wife and children. Singleton would remain in Detroit until the end of the Civil War, having labored "as a scavenger, and keeping a sort of boarding house where fugitive slaves were fed, hidden, and helped on their way."

He traveled back to Nashville in 1865 or 1866. At the end of the decade he was living in town and staying with his daughter Emily and her daughter. By then he may have already been working at the job he would hold later in the decade – making coffins. He witnessed the brief period of hope that came about when black men received the right to vote. Candidates of color were elected and appointed to office, and Negro education was gaining momentum, but Singleton was skeptical that black progress would last. It wasn't long before he decided that unless significant changes took place, freed slaves had little future in Nashville, or in the South. He gave a partial explanation of his views in a newspaper article in 1878.

"I had studied it all out. It was cl'ar as day to me. I dunno how it came to me, but I 'spect it was God's doin's. Anyhow, I knowed my people couldn't live ther. It was ag'in nature for the masters and the slaves to jine hands and work together. Nuthin' but the millimium could bring that around. The whites had the lands and the sense, an the blacks had nothin' but their freedom.

"By and by the Fifteenth Amendment and the carpetbaggers came along, and my poor people thought they was goin' to have Canaan right off. But I knowed better and I told 'em so. I said, 'You is a-potterin' round in politics, and tryin' to git into offices that you ain't fit for. You can't see that these white tramps from the North is simply usin' you for to line their pockets. When they get through they'll drop you, and the rebels will come into power. Then where will you be?'"

In 1880 he tried to explain more about why his life had unfolded in the way it had. What he said was written down, but the way he pronounced his words was not usually reflected in the transcription.

"My race was coming down instead of going up. I was an undertaker there in Nashville, and I worked in the shop. I would have to go and bury their fathers and mothers. Well, a man would die and I would bury him, and the next morning maybe a woman would go to (the landlord), and she would have six or seven children, and he would say to her, 'Well, your husband owed me before he died.' They would say that to every last one of them, 'You owe me.' Then he would say, 'You must go to some other place. I cannot take care of you.'

"That is something I would take notice of. That woman had to go out, and those little children was left running through the streets, and the next place you would find the women was in a disorderly house, and their children was in the State's prison. Their disadvantages – that caused my heart to grieve and sorrow. We have the same heart and feelings as any other race and nation. That caused me to go to work for them."

For reasons he would make more and more clear, Benjamin Singleton, who was widely known as "Pap," was convinced that blacks needed to separate themselves from whites.

"Well, I called on white people in Tennessee about that time. The white people said, 'Old man, you are right. Take your people away.' And it was the white people – the ex-governor of the State – they felt like I did. They said, "You have tooken a great deal on to yourself, but if these negroes, instead of deceiving one another and running for office, would take the same idea that you have in your head, you will be a people.' Well my people – we needed land for our children."

In 1869, hoping to find a place where blacks could live apart from whites, Singleton took action. Despite his inability to read or write, he became the driving force behind the formation of the Tennessee Real Estate and Homestead Association.

"I was advised by my white friends to see if we could buy land in Tennessee, but the land in Tennessee was sixty dollars an acre. I proposed that we should go someplace where there was government land."

By early in 1871 he was convinced that Kansas afforded blacks a much better opportunity, and representatives of the Homestead Association, which he served as president, went west to investigate. After they came back with a positive report, a small number of emigrants left for Kansas.

In 1873 Singleton went to Kansas for the first time. A few months later, having seen the land for himself, Singleton came back to Nashville before he escorted some 300 black people to the southeast corner of Kansas, to Cherokee County – located on the border of both Missouri and Oklahoma. Seven years later he would express his pride about what that group had accomplished.

"If there is land enough, it is nobody's business where the people go. I put that in my people's heads. I jacked up three or four hundred and went into Southern Kansas, and found it was a good country. I thought Southern Kansas was congenial to our nature, and I formed a colony there. We bought about a thousand acres of ground – the colony did – my people.

"When they got there some people didn't have fifty cents left. Now they have got in my colony – Singleton colony. All of them that I carried there has got little houses – nice cabins – and their milk cows and pigs and sheep, and perhaps a span of horses, and trees before their yards and some three or four or ten acres broken up. They didn't go under no relief assistance. They went on their own resources, and when they went in there, the country was not overrun with them.

They could get good wages. They went to work, and I never helped them as soon as I put them on the land.

"This was gotten up by colored men in purity and confidence. Not a political Negro was in it. They would want to pilfer and rob at the cents before they got the dollars. It was the muscle of the arm – the men that worked – that we wanted."

For the next few years Singleton took small groups from Nashville to Kansas, and he was joined in his efforts by two colored men – an itinerate preacher from Sumner County named Columbus Johnson, and Alonzo D. DeFrantz, a Nashville barber. Singleton spent hundreds of dollars printing circulars that advertised the benefits of settling in Kansas. Blacks who travelled south – from steamboat workers and railroad porters to preachers – spread his circulars across the region. With the gradual return of conservative Democrats to political control and Negro rights in decline, and with an agricultural recession well underway, increasing numbers of blacks made the decision to leave for Kansas.

One of the many posters calling on southern blacks to leave for Kansas.

Pap Singleton was able to locate additional land he considered suitable for settlement. In 1874 Dunlap Colony was established in the eastern part of the state and Nicodemus Colony was soon founded in northwestern Kansas, and the numbers of relocating blacks continued to grow. There was an ongoing debate within the Negro community in Nashville that pitted affluent blacks – men like J. C. Napier and

Henry Harding and Nelson Walker and Alonzo Napier – against less privileged individuals like Pap Singleton.

The educated and more prominent faction was suspected of hoping, in part, to diminish the local number of impoverished, illiterate, and unemployed blacks – a group perceived as keeping back those who were more economically advanced and better able to move forward. Singleton's criticism of the rival group found its way into a newspaper article in 1878.

"They have had good luck. They are listening to false prophets. They have been boosted up, and got their heads whirlin' and now they judge things from where they stand. The fact is that the possum is lower down in the tree – down nigh to the root."

Then he explained the reason why economically deprived people chose to leave their homes.

"It's because they are poor that they want to get away. If they had plenty, they wouldn't want to come. It's to better their condition that they are thinking of. That's what white men go to new countries for, isn't it? Do you tell them to stay back because they are poor? Who was the homestead law made for, if it wasn't for poor men?"

Two days earlier the arrival in Leavenworth, Kansas, of a group from Nashville was covered by a local newspaper.

"A colony of colored people from Nashville, Tennessee, arrived in this city via the Kansas-Pacific Railroad this morning at one o'clock, in charge of Benjamin Singleton, better known as "Old Pap," and A. D. DeFrantz. The colony will sojourn for a time in Topeka while the leaders go farther west to look up a location for the colony on Government land. When they left Nashville the colony was composed of 120 persons, but they divided at Kansas City, a considerable number going to Baxter Springs."

The next year, in 1879, only weeks after he moved to Kansas,

Singleton spoke with a newspaper reporter. He mentioned those who once disagreed with him about whites being unwilling to change the way they treated blacks, and he mused about how long it might take for things to change.

"Now they say Old Pap was right. De leopard can't change his spots. De men who used to flog their slaves aint ever agoin' to treat 'em fair, now that they're free. Mebbe it'll be different a hundred years from now when all the present generation's dead and gone, but not afore. And what's agoin' to be a hundred years from now aint much account to us in this present year o' the Lord. I don't waste time botherin' about what'll happen when I'm in my grave."

Pap Singleton had become a nationally recognized figure, and in 1880 he went to Washington and appeared before a Senate committee investigating the causes of Negro emigration from the South. His testimony included a reference to himself as "the father of the exodus" and that he was "the whole cause of the Kansas migration." He also reported that he was responsible for bringing 7432 blacks to Kansas, but much of his testimony concerned the reasons blacks were leaving the South.

"There is good white men in the Southern country, but it ain't the majority. They can't do nothing. The Southern country is out of joint. The great God of glory has worked in me. I have had open air interviews with the living spirit of God for my people, and we are going to leave the South. We are going to leave it if there ain't an alteration and signs of change.

"Every year, going to work the crops, white men have said, 'I will do what is right to you.' And just as soon as that man sees cotton blooms, he will look at that negro who has been his slave, and when he sees him walk up to take his half of the crop, it is too much for him to stand. He just denies his word. He denies his contract. We will leave that country till these people refrains from this way of treatment, and gives the negro the hand of fellowship and acknowledges their wrongs.

"I have seen women and children in wagons and teams come in, and they said they was run in by the Ku Klux into Nashville. I will live in a country where the white man will lift himself to the level of justice, but when the white man thinks that equal rights to the colored man is a violation of his dignity, then I am going to leave.

"We are going to learn the South a lesson. The colored man's muscle is in her interest. And these dare devils who ride around in the night and abuse people – whenever they change from that I want to go back. We don't want to leave the South. As soon as we have confidence in the South, I am going to be an instrument in the hands of God to persuade every man to go back because that country is genial to our nature."

Later that year he was described by a newspaper reporter in Indianapolis.

"Pap Singleton is 71 years old, but still active and devoted to the work of bettering the condition of his fellow colored men. A mulatto of medium height, spare build, flowing curly hair, and gray whiskers, poorly dressed, and supported by a cane, he would not attract attention as a Moses, but when engaged in conversation, his superior mental ability and earnestness make themselves felt."

Despite his magnetic personality, the black exodus was losing momentum. Over the course of the 1870s, the black population of Cherokee County, the site of the Singleton Colony, rose from 134 to 1716. There were no blacks in Graham County in 1870, but 484 black people were there in 1880, and the cumulative number of blacks in Lyon and Morris Counties, where the Dunlap Colony was located, rose from 198 to 1559.

The continuing influx of Negro laborers had flooded the market and caused the wages of whites to fall, and the arrival of so many increasingly impoverished blacks brought about the formation of organizations such as the Kansas Freedman's Relief Association in order to prevent mass starvation. Public opinion, among some blacks as well as most whites, quickly turned against further migration, and at different times over the next few years, Singleton would consider Nebraska, Colorado, Indiana, Illinois, Canada, Liberia, Ethiopia, and Cyprus as places where blacks might resettle.

His communications received wider circulation when they were useful to politicians, and he was increasingly open in his criticism of the South. In 1883 a letter – echoing some of the sentiments he had expressed before – was written for him and published in a Topeka newspaper. It was ostensibly directed at the overwhelming majority of blacks who had remained in the South, and who were experiencing the tightening grasp of Jim Crow.

"I have shown your feet the way to Kansas, but you would not come. Now I advise you to seek a government of your own – where you can have protection. We have no arm to protect us, and no eye to pity us. You must seek a government or go to Canada, where you can be protected as a people. Go to Canada and take the oath of allegiance and be respected and protected by the British government. There are some good people in the South, but they can do you no good. We can never be respected as a people in the southern country.

"Never cast another vote in the South. Go to a country where you can have your rights as men and act your sentiments, and not be slaughtered on account of your vote. For nearly 300 years we worked for the white man and got nothing for it. When we were delivered from slavery, we were delivered with nothing. We have been trying to rise up and have some protection and be respected, and yet they still try to hold us down."

Singleton was in his early seventies when the migration of blacks into Kansas ground to a halt. Although the colored communities he had established would flourish for a time, as the years passed more and more of their inhabitants moved away – some leaving for cities and many returning home. The population of the Dunlap Colony, which had some ninety Negro families in 1885, had fallen dramatically by the close of the 1900s, and by 1905 only twelve families of color remained.

Pap Singleton lived in Topeka for a few years, and around 1888 he moved to Kansas City. Having faded from prominence, he was largely forgotten, but he renewed his association with Jo Shelby, the son of his former owner, Orville Shelby, and nephew of Dr. John Shelby. Jo Shelby, who had served as a General in the Confederacy, also lived in Kansas City, where he and Pap saw each other from time to time. When Shelby died in 1897, Singleton appeared to view his remains and his visit was reported in a local newspaper.

"In the crowd an old Negro reached the door. He hobbled with a cane. 'I'se almost blind, but I wants to see General Shelby.' A veteran took the arm of the old Negro and led him to the casket. He leaned over and gently touched the dead general. He stood up, and with tears running down his face he said, 'Dar's a friend.' And then, in a softer, broken voice, he leaned over again. 'Poor old Marstah Shelby.' He was asked, 'Did you know General Shelby?' The old man had been moved to a seat. 'I nursed him when he's a baby. I lived with his father then. He was borned in his grandfather's mansion in Lexington. I was dar. General Shelby – he's got a boy named Ben. He named him after me. He told me so.'"

Then Pap Singleton told the reporter about times when he and Jo Shelby would see each other.

"'He'd say to me, 'Ben, you want money?' I'd say, Marstah Shelby, I'se de porest man in dis town. And den he'd say, 'Ben, you got to go home wid me.' I'd say, What you want of me? I'se poor an old an blind. And he'd say, 'Man, I want you.' But I always got some money. The Shelbys is all like that. A man come hungry and destitute, and he never turn him away. De whole breed of 'em that way.'"

Singleton clearly had a deep attachment to the Shelby family. If there was more to the relationship than their memories of what had passed between them during slave times – if there might have been a family connection – it was never disclosed. Pap Singleton lived until 1900. Twenty years earlier he had said, "As soon as we have confidence in the South, I am going to be an instrument in the hands of God to persuade every man to go back."

There is no record that he ever returned to the South for as much as a visit, and during the last two decades of his life, as he observed the hollowed-out world of Jim Crow, the words he had spoken would continue to echo.

22

Nelson Walker

MAXWELL HOUSE
SHAVING SALOON.
THE OLD AND EXPERIENCED BARBER,

NELSON WALKER,

Has again taken charge of the MAXWELL
HOUSE BARBER SHOP, and would be pleased
to see all of his old friends, and as many new
ones as will favor him with their patronage.
feb2-1m

On the last Thursday morning in May, 1875, after he put on his finest clothes, Nelson Walker and his wife, with most or all of their seven children, walked out of their home on North Spruce Street and headed for Fisk University. A half-century earlier Nelson's mother, a young female slave, could not have imagined how her son's life would unfold, or what he would experience later on that May morning.

Nelson Walker was born in Virginia – likely in Lynchburg – in 1824 or 1825. His father was almost certainly William H.L. Tabb, a white man in his mid-twenties. Nelson's mother was probably a young slave woman owned by Tabb. William Tabb had married Calpurnia Featherstone in 1822, and in 1824, close to the time Nelson was born, William and Calpurnia had their first child, Nelson's half-sister Augusta. Of the four slaves Tabb owned in 1830, two were females between ten and twenty-three years old. One was probably Nelson's mother, and if that was the case, she would have been no more than eighteen when her son was born. The other two slaves were boys under ten, one of whom must have been Nelson.

When William Tabb died in 1837, Nelson, along with his mother and her other children, was inherited by Calpurnia and their two children – Augusta, who was around thirteen, and Blucher who was five. Nelson would become the property of his younger half-brother, Blucher, but Calpurnia was effectively the owner of all eight family slaves. Calpurnia Tabb died in March, 1841, and nine months later seventeen-year-old Augusta married J. Knox Walker, a Yale-educated attorney and a nephew of James Knox Polk, who would be elected President of the United States three years later.

Knox Walker and Augusta Walker, with her nine-year-old brother Blucher, her half-brother Nelson, and probably some other half-siblings of color, moved to Tennessee soon after the wedding. They settled in Columbia – some forty-five miles south of Nashville. A family account suggests that Nelson was a well-treated house servant, and he seems to have enjoyed a high degree of independence. It is unclear whether he remained in Columbia throughout the 1840s. Knox Walker took his wife and children to Washington, where they apparently lived in the White House while he served as personal secretary to President Polk, but Nelson may have remained in Columbia.

At some point Nelson took the surname, Walker, and began working as a barber in Columbia, where he kept "the best patronized shop" in town. Sixteen-year-old Blucher Walker, Nelson's half-brother who had become his owner, received an appointment to the Naval Academy in 1849, during the final weeks of the Polk presidency. That same year Nelson married Eliza, a young mulatto woman whose surname was either Frierson or Smart, who had been "reared in the house as a servant of a wealthy family in Maury County."

A year later Blucher, a U. S. Navy midshipman, was serving in the Caribbean when he was killed by street thugs in Mexico while he was on shore leave. Knox Walker subsequently became Nelson's owner, and it was likely in the early 1850s when Nelson was able to save enough money to pay $1800 for his freedom. Around that same time he moved to Nashville, where he opened a barber shop with his partner from Columbia, Thomas Hodge. A newspaper advertisement in 1853 described their business.

The venture became highly successful, and toward the end of the 1850s Nelson was able to buy Eliza, along with the three children they had by then. But for a reason that is unclear, when the 1860 census was taken, Nelson was not listed

THOMAS HODGE.   NELSON WALKER.
HODGE & WALKER.
Barbers, Hair-Dressers, &c., &c.,
No. 13, Cedar street.

HAVE opened their new establishment, and offer to their customers and the public in general inducements never before offered in this city. Having newly fitted up our house, we feel confident that all who give us a call will leave well satisfied. In addition to Barbering, Hair-Dressing, &c., we have large, commodious and neatly furnished Bath-Rooms. These are the finest in the city, and as to convenience and comfort, cannot be surpassed in the country. While passing, gentlemen and patrons, just step in and see with what magic we "make the hair fly," and what a salutary effect our pure water has upon a wearied and *corte* body.   aug 4—tf

Union and American, November 3, 1853

with his family. A fourth child had been born by then, and Eliza was working as a seamstress. She and the children were living in a desirable section of town – next to John Harding, the aging former scion of Belle Meade, the sprawling plantation located a few miles southwest of Nashville.

Colonel J. Knox Walker

When the Civil War broke out, two of the Walker daughters were attending a school for colored children conducted by Daniel Wadkins. Another child was born in 1863, and Nelson and Eliza Walker and all five of their children were still living at the close of the war. But the white Walker family which Nelson once served had been decimated by the time peace finally came. His half-sister, Augusta, died in 1860 in Memphis, where she and her husband had moved after leaving Columbia. And her husband, Nelson's former master Knox Walker, after initially opposing secession, had become a colonel in the Confederacy before dying in 1863 in the wake of a long illness.

Although Eliza was unable to read or write, Nelson was highly literate. That, along with the success of his barber shop, his intelligence, his confidence, and his oratorical ability, made him a highly influential figure in the black community. Walker was one of the speakers at the mass gathering held in 1865 to celebrate the ratification of the proposed amendment ending slavery. His speech was paraphrased in the Nashville Daily Union.

"The Negro has had but a taste of freedom. He wanted more – the elective franchise. They met on that occasion to rejoice over what they had, and to ascertain how to get more as American citizens, for American citizens they claimed to be. Let every one of them die rather than be deprived of his rights. There were different views among colored people, but all must unite to gain their rights as men. They must knock at the door of the Capitol, and if they do not get from the next session what they want, they must knock at another, and so on, until every black man is entitled to vote. Walker stated that throughout the North, associations were formed having the enfranchisement of colored people for their object, and in Tennessee and other parts of the South, the Equal Rights League was uniting for the accomplishment of that object."

The following year Nelson Walker, along with Daniel Wadkins, wrote a letter to Mayor Matt Brown. After acknowledging the crucial role economic engagement would play if blacks were to advance as a race, they asked for protection – a request that suggested the danger being encountered by those pursuing economic advancement. The letter also demonstrated the prominence Walker had in the black community.

"The colored citizens of the state design holding a convention in this city to deliberate on the following subjects: Agriculture, Manufactures, Mining, and Education, and to adopt some plan by which these branches of industry and elevation may be more effectually prosecuted by us as a people. And we also solicit your approbation and protection. Nothing will be tolerated by the convention incompatible with the laws of this country, or with the decorum that should characterize such an assembly."

While the vast majority of southern whites – those who had given their support to the Confederacy – had lost their voting rights after the Civil War, blacks had recently gained the right to vote. As Nelson Walker became more widely known, he sometimes drew criticism in the local press. In 1867, in a response to an inaccurate newspaper article, he explained his position on the issue of voting, and on the confiscation of property owned by those who had opposed the Union.

"My business is not parties. The people of Nashville have been my lifetime friends. I am not their enemy and will not aid in putting my foot on their necks. I am for impartial suffrage, and want above everything else peace between the two races. This cannot be while the white race is disfranchised and colored race is enfranchised. Therefore I have insisted, and now insist, that the right of suffrage should at once be conferred upon all, and I am against any confiscation of the remnant of property left the Southern people."

Being a man of mixed race who owned a business with many loyal customers who had supported the Confederacy, Nelson Walker walked a fine line. Beyond his economic motivations, he had lifelong relationships with those who were no longer allowed to vote.

In August, 1867, just after black men were enfranchised to vote in Tennessee, the local Republican party – made up of blacks, as well as white Union sympathizers and recently-arrived Northerners – split into two factions. The radical wing was led by Augustus E. Alden, a former Union soldier from Maine who was branded by opponents as a corrupt political opportunist. The conservative wing, which included Nelson Walker, was composed of blacks and Unionists with deeper ties to those who had supported the Confederacy. Separate conventions were held and Walker addressed those who had gathered at the courthouse.

"There are not one hundred men in Nashville who ever heard of Major Alden until he was appointed Registration Commissioner. These newcomers should take seats and remain quiet till the old citizens propose to give them office. Major Alden is a stranger, but we know this much of him. While he was at Murfreesboro, the news of

Mr. Lincoln's emancipation reached him and he tore off his shoulder straps and said he would not fight in this abolition war. We are not going to give up our own true Southern people for men who are strangers and have no interest in us, except to get control of offices. I intend to expose this corruption every day till the election. They have endeavored to gag our mouths, but I am a free man and I intend to speak my sentiments."

Despite Walker's political efforts, the Radical candidate, A.E. Alden, won the election, but early in 1868 Walker became a justice of the peace. And the next year he announced that he was a candidate for the Tennessee Legislature.

"I am for free suffrage, free speech, free religion, free labor, and free government. I have been for universal suffrage and universal amnesty as early as anyone among you. The country will never be quiet and happy until all civil debilities, growing out of the late war, are removed."

In July he was one of the speakers at a political event at the State Capitol, and the event was reported in a local newspaper.

"Nelson Walker, a universal suffrage candidate, attempted to address the meeting when a crowd of boisterous Negroes commenced yelling and hooting, crying, 'Take him down. Take him down.' Nelson continued speaking to the few who desired to listen to him."

Many blacks, believing that their rights would be rescinded if whites regained political power, opposed the restoration of voting rights to those who had fought against the Union. Walker, who might have seen his candidacy as hopeless, withdrew a few days later, but his business obligations could have played a role in his withdrawal. When the Maxwell House Hotel opened on the northwest corner of Church Street and Cherry Street in September,

1868, Nelson Walker opened a "tonsorial palace and shaving saloon" there, and received mention in a local newspaper. Four years later Sampson Keeble, his partner in the venture, would be elected to the Tennessee Legislature.

"Nelson Walker, the well-known and experienced barber, has associated with S.W. Keeble, favorably known at the St. Cloud Hotel for years. They have fitted up the mammoth barber shop in the most superb style, and they are prepared to wait on gentlemen at all hours of the day; also to furnish hot

Maxwell House Hotel

and cold baths. They have four of the best and most experienced artists of the age, and their patrons and friends cannot be but pleased if they will call and give them a trial. They have all the modern perfumeries and hair dyes, and their saloon and bath rooms are complete in all their appointments."

Walker was engaged in a number of other pursuits, and he may have had a limited daily role in his establishment at the Maxwell House. He was also studying law. In early 1871 he was sworn in as one of Nashville's first black practicing attorneys, and only a year later he traveled to Cincinnati to serve as counsel in a large lawsuit. In 1873 he sold his barber shop in order to enter the insurance business, and by then, the last of his seven children had been born and Eliza was working as a dress maker.

Despite the political opposition he had faced, he remained influential in the black community, and in 1873 he was given the honor of escorting Frederick Douglass from Gallatin to Nashville. He introduced Douglass to the large crowd that had gathered on Cherry Street to hear Douglass speak from the balcony of the Harding House. By the next year Nelson Walker's health was failing, but he continued with his political activities. In a speech at the State Colored Convention in Nashville, he turned from the need for whites to receive voting rights, to speaking about the racial discrimination in which so many whites continued to indulge. A newspaper article summed up his address.

Virginia Walker Broughton

"Nelson Walker said so long as he lived, he would never give his vote to any man not willing to accord to him equal justice. He would say to those asking for his vote, 'Gentlemen, are you willing, when we have given you our votes, to accord to us, in proportion to our population, an equal share of rights and justice?'"

His health continued to decline over the next few months, but he must have been determined to see his second-oldest daughter, Virginia, graduate from Fisk University. She was one of four members of the school's first graduating class, but one of her classmates, America Robinson, was away on tour with the Jubilee Singers.

Nelson Walker, sitting with his wife and children in the chapel, watched as his daughter, along with James and John Burrus, became the first individuals of color to graduate from a liberal arts college south of the Mason-Dixon Line. And while he listened to J.M.

Langston's commencement address, one part of the speech must have caught his attention. Langston said that if he met the graduates twenty years later, he might congratulate each one on what they had accomplished since that commencement. After that possibility was mentioned, at least a few of those in the Fisk chapel must have spent some time wondering what the young graduates would do with their lives.

Nelson Walker would have known that James and John Burrus were fathered in Rutherford County by a prominent white man, and he would have known that their father had purchased their enslaved, mixed-race mother at an auction in Nashville in the 1840s. It was widely known that their parents lived together as though they were husband and wife, and that they had raised their sons together until the death of the father. Then, along with their mother, they became the property of a female first cousin in Arkansas. After their owner's husband was commissioned as a colonel and then a general in the Confederacy, the brothers were assigned as body servants to Southern officers, and they accompanied the unit as it fought across Arkansas and Missouri.

They were in Texas when the war ended, but by 1866 they had worked their way to Nashville, and gotten jobs as waiters in a local hotel. After being tutored by a pair of ladies who lived in the hotel, and after saving their money, James and John Burrus both enrolled at Fisk in 1867, where they developed into impressive scholars.

As the crowd filed out of Howard Chapel on their way to the commencement dinner, the lives of the graduates were yet to unfold. The event that took place in the chapel at Fisk was described the following day in a pair of articles – one in each of the major local newspapers. But on the same page with each story, there was an article that reflected a separate reality. One article, reprinted from the Springfield Record, was a conservative attack on what it termed Radicals, and on the emigration of blacks from Tennessee.

"The colored man as a rule – and there are some honest exceptions to this rule – are indolent, lazy, and ignorant to perfection. Many are living from hand to mouth. They don't want regular employment. The vagrant law takes hold of this kind. Of course they want to emigrate."

The other article, from the St. Louis Republican, took on a tone of ridicule.

"The Negroes of Nashville, and of a large portion of the state as well, have got it into their heads that they are held in a condition of practical bondage by their white fellow-citizens. Agitators have been stirring them up for some months past, and have succeeded at last in working the African sentiment up to such a pitch of indignation over their fancied wrongs, it is universally agreed that they have submitted to the evils of the situation long enough. It has come to be understood by these oppressed and downtrodden blacks that they must forsake the land of their bondage and seek new homes elsewhere."

When Nelson Walker died less than six weeks later at the age of fifty, his death was noted in both major newspapers.

"Nelson Walker, a prominent colored barber of this city, died at his dwelling yesterday afternoon. He had been ill for some time, and his death was not unexpected. He was much respected by our citizens. He was a self-educated man, served as a magistrate of this county, and studied law and entered into its practice. Walker was a member of the Masonic Order and of the Sons of Relief. He lived to see all of his seven children pretty well educated, and one of his daughters occupies the position of teacher. He and his wife, who has always proved herself to be very industrious, celebrated their silver anniversary last year, and received gifts from several of our oldest and most respectable white citizens."

James Dallas Burrus

After Nelson Walker's death, James Burrus went on to study mathematics at Dartmouth College, where he was the first man of color in America to earn a Master of Arts degree. He became a college professor and later a pharmacist, and when he died in Nashville in 1928, he left Fisk a bequest of $120,000. And his brother, John Burrus, received his Masters degree in mathematics and taught at Fisk. John later became a leader in the Republican Party, studied law and was admitted to the bar, and after serving as president of Alcorn College in Mississippi for ten years, he returned to Nashville where he resumed his law practice. He was a leading advocate for Negro rights until his death in 1917.

At the commencement ceremony, forty days before his death, Nelson Walker must have gazed at his daughter, Virginia, when J.M. Mercer spoke about meeting her two decades into the future. Perhaps her father would not have been surprised to know that she would go on to receive her Masters degree from Fisk, and then become a teacher, a noted Baptist missionary, a lecturer, and an author, or that she would also become the mother of five children.

Eliza Walker remarried a few years before her death in 1886, and her children went on to lead distinguished lives. Their oldest daughter, Selena, was a teacher. Their son, John, attended Meharry Medical School and became a physician, and Rufus, the youngest of their children, followed in the vocational footsteps of his father and became a barber.

John Houston Burrus

When Rufus, the last surviving child of Nelson and Eliza Walker, passed away in 1951, his father had been dead for seventy-five years. By then the right to vote – the right to which Nelson Walker had been so dedicated, and which had been taken away from most blacks in the South decades earlier – was still being limited.

23

Cherry Logue and J. W. Loguen

It was around 1858 when a runaway slave from Davidson County, then living in Syracuse, New York, conveyed the details of his life to an unnamed interviewer. Those details soon appeared in a book – *The Rev. J.W. Loguen, as a Slave and as a Freeman, a Narrative of Real Life* – which was written by an unidentified author and published in 1859. The preface acknowledged that some parts of the book were invented and that, in order to protect certain individuals, real names were not always used, but it went on to explain that the information relating to slavery was factual.

"For obvious reasons, we have not always used real names when writing of real persons. And some few facts, circumstances, and discourse, not connected with Mr. Loguen's experience with slavery, have been supplied to connect the real facts of his life, and furnish variety for the reader. But not a fact is stated relating to his, or his mother's, or brother's, or sister's experience with slavery that is not literally or substantially true. Those facts were history before they were written, and they were written because they were history."

Historical records of the period support details of the account, and help identify some of those who were mentioned in the narrative. The anonymous scribe began with what he had been told about Loguen's background.

"If the mother of Jermain Loguen is now living, she is about seventy years of age. She was a pure African. Her skin was jet black, and her hair short and curled to the head. Her face was fair and her features were marked and regular, and her bodily proportions were large and muscular. A model of health and strength, she was a specimen of the best of her race. She was ignorant of her parents. The extent of her recollection is that she was free during her infancy, and in the guardianship of a man in Ohio named McCoy, with whom she lived until she was about seven.

"She remembered that she was alone and out of sight of McCoy's house, and that a bad man got out of a covered wagon, and with one hand about her body and the other over her mouth, he took her into the wagon and held her in his lap. There were several other little colored children in the wagon, and they were taken over the river in a boat – probably into Kentucky. She did not remember the number of boys and girls who were in the wagon with her, but she remembered their cries and sobs. After they passed the river, the kidnappers sold them one after another. The mother of Mr. Loguen was sold to three brothers – David, Carnes, and Manasseh Logue – who lived in a small log house on Mansker's Creek in Davidson County, about 16 miles from Nashville."

John Logue, a Revolutionary War veteran from Orange County, North Carolina, had brought his family to Davidson County around 1789, and later settled on Manskers Creek, less than twenty miles from Nashville. Logue died in 1793 leaving his wife, Eleanor, their four daughters, and their three sons – Manasseh, Carnes, and David – all of whom were named in his will.

"David, the youngest, was probably not over eighteen years of age. They were large, rough, and uncivilized young men, and owned a miserably cultivated farm and a whiskey distillery. Her purchasers made a lasting impression upon her memory. At first they seemed to be touched with tenderness and concern, and in the hope that they would return her to Ohio, she ventured to tell them how she was stolen.

"Every expression of sympathy vanished, and their kind words changed into threats and curses. One of them took a whip that hung on the cabin and whipped her, and she promised she would never again repeat the fact of her freedom. The name by which she had always been called was Jane, but to cover up the transaction, the name Cherry was given to her. Cherry was put in a cabin with other slaves, a little distance from the cabin where the Logue brothers lived with their widowed mother."

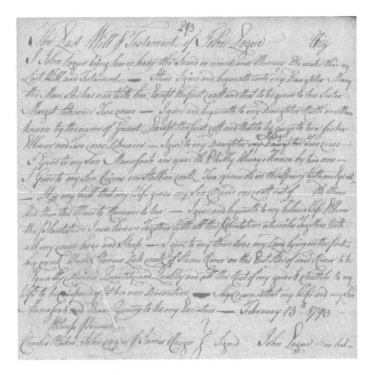

Will of John Logue (1793)

"As Cherry's physical strength developed, she became their main dependence – in the house, the distillery, and in the field. She became an expert in the art of manufacturing whiskey, and was often employed day and night with other slaves in the distillery. And whether it was driving oxen, loading, lifting, plowing, or hoeing, there was nothing she did not do. Her natural disposition was gentle, affectionate, kind, and confiding, but these qualities reposed upon a spirit which was, when roused, as resolute and indomitable as a tigress.

"As ignorant and brutal as her masters were, they respected her.

But what most contributed to her safety was that she was a first class laborer and slave breeder, and that she was the mistress of David Logue, the youngest of the three brothers. Compelled as she was to endure violence from her masters, she never endured it from others. White or black, male or female, if they attempted liberties with her against her consent, she fought.

"Cherry, in the ripeness of youthful development, attracted the casual lust of the vulgar slaveholders who lived along Mansker's Creek, and the distillery was the common resort of that class of lawless men. David, Manasseh, and Carnes Logue were of the same class. They were all hard drinkers, and the distillery was a place for coarse enjoyment and low carousals. Cherry was often at work in the distillery, and was the subject of their brutal remarks."

Cherry was likely born around 1796, and she was probably eighteen or nineteen when her second child, Jermain, was born in or close to 1814. Both children were fathered by David Logue, who was unmarried and in his late twenties when Cherry gave birth to Jermain.

"When she was twenty-four or five and Jermain was about six years of age, a neighboring farmer, finding her alone at the distillery, made insulting advances which she repelled. He pursued her and resorted to violence and threats, and she broke from him and stood in defiance. He attempted to lay hold of her, and she grasped the heavy stick she used to stir the malt, and dealt him a blow which made him reel. He recovered and with threats of vengeance and death, rushed at her with a knife, and she plied a blow upon his temple which laid him at her feet.

"Cherry was shielded from harm, partly by the shame of her violator and partly because her masters prized her as property, but most of all because she was the mistress of David Logue. When she was about twenty-eight, she was the mother of three children. Jermain Logue was called Jarm, and he was the pet of his father. Sometimes he slept in his bed and was caressed by him, and he also received many little kindnesses and favors. Jarm loved and revered him as a father. David Logue was not devoid of noble and generous impulses, but he was an impulsive, drinking rowdy who was unscrupulous in his pleasures.

"At the age of seven or eight Jarm was on the bank of the creek and saw his mother coming. She was in distress, but her sighs and sobs were almost noiseless. When she gave him the cause of her wounds and misery, he fiercely asked, 'Who whipped you?' She said Carnes had struck her on the head and made the wound. She said that Manasseh and Carnes often whipped her, and even David had lately treated her roughly.

"Then she explained how she was stolen and left with the white Logues. She was afraid that Jarm would pursue the subject with the slaves at the house, with David, or even with Carnes. Her intimacy with David was failing, and with Jarm's independence increasing, he was less likely to be indulged. Therefore she determined to satisfy his enquiries and determine him to silence."

Back in 1817, when Jarm was about three years old, David Logue had married Polly Glasgow, a daughter of Jesse Glasgow, who also lived in the neighborhood of Manskers Creek.

"David brought to his home a white woman, by whom he afterwards had children. The distance between Jarm and his father widened as the intimacy between Cherry and David ceased. His father's favors and caresses were less frequent as the months and years came on, and brutal outrages were inflicted upon his mother. David had purchased the interests of Manasseh and Carnes in the estate, and

370

become the sole owner of the slaves. It was not known where Carnes had gone, and Manasseh moved to the southern part of the state.

"Cherry was the mother of three children by David Logue. Granny, as Jarm always called the mother of the Logues, often told him he was not to be a slave like other colored children, and that he should be set free. And David had pledged to Cherry that Jarm should be set free. Since David took the white woman home, his intercourse with Cherry ceased – while she was still in the vigor of young womanhood. A young negress is often her master's mistress until childbearing, as well as years, renders it tasteful or convenient to sell the offspring from his sight, and exchange her for another victim. In respect to Cherry as property, as well as a protection against disturbing domestic influences, her white family thought it best that she have a man who would represent a husband.

"A farmer of unusually high character named Mr. Barry lived in the neighborhood. He was humane and indulgent to his slaves, and they were strongly attached to him. Barry owned a man named Henry – a stout well-built fellow, about thirty years old. Henry was a kind, warm-hearted fellow, but he had seen such misery in the separation of husbands from wives, and of parents from children, that he had resolved to never become a husband or father."

"But Henry's spirit adhered to Cherry. Mr. Barry consented on condition that Henry should be consulted. Henry confessed his willingness that Cherry should be his wife only on condition that neither he or his wife, or any children they might have, should ever be separated by David Logue or Mr. Barry by a distance of more than ten miles. Both David and Barry pledged themselves to the condition, and Cherry was sent for and presented to Henry. For two happy years Cherry enjoyed her hours of refreshment and repose with Henry, and at the end of the first year, their union was blessed by a boy."

The humane neighbor who owned Henry was almost certainly Dr. Redmond D. Barry, an Irish-born physician who lived a few miles to the east in Sumner County, on Station Camp Creek.

"The first ten years of Jarm's life was a period of much freedom. He suffered no treatment from his masters to hint that he was a slave. But he saw little boys and girls brutally handled, and it puzzled him why he was secure and petted, while they were insecure and abused. For a long time there had been quiet at home and in the field, but a small distance from the Logues, on the opposite side of Manskers Creek, lived a savage man by the name of Betts. He was the proprietor of a large farm and had a number of slaves. He was a drunkard and proverbial for his cruelty, and was even despised by the slaveholders of the neighborhood."

Zachariah Betts, the youngest of twelve children in a Quaker family, was born in 1764 and grew up in Bucks County, Pennsylvania. He came to Tennessee in the last years of the Indian wars, and in 1794 he bought a 640 acre tract of land on Manskers Creek, where he oversaw the handful of slaves he owned as they farmed and worked in his tannery – refining animal hides into leather.

"On a spring morning Jarm, who was nearing the age of ten, was beside the creek when a howl of agony arose from the opposite bank. He was covered by the brush which formed a deep fringe on the side of the creek. The distance across the creek was about sixty feet, and Jarm had a clear view of the opposite bank. The sufferer was Sam, a kind-hearted fellow about twenty years old, who a few weeks earlier had saved Jarm from drowning in the creek, when it was swelled with rain.

"Sam was naked, and lashed to a barrel on the steep bank of the creek. His head almost touched the bank on one side, and his feet the other, and his flesh was covered with gore while the blood ran down his back and legs to the ground. His flesh was quivering, and Sam was moaning and pleading for pity. Betts was about forty – stout, square-built, burly, and bushy-headed. His shirt was open at the collar, and showed a broad chest that was sun and whiskey-burnt.

"His sleeves were rolled up like a butcher, and his right hand clenched an instrument which is called a paddle in the slave states. The paddle is a firm board filled with small auger holes. It is the most savage and blood-letting instrument used to torture the slave. With every blow, the sharp wood on the circumference of the holes cuts into the flesh.

"Some half dozen Negroes stood trembling nearby. Betts brandished the bloody paddle and threatened the slaves. He swung the paddle from his shoulder to increase the force of his blow, and the slaves turned their faces to the ground, or covered them with their hands. The blows continued until Betts was weary, and he repeated his threats and curses to the Negroes. He alternated his violence on Sam and his curses on the Negroes until Sam's voice was faint. He continued to utter, 'O Lord. O Lord,' until the only sound was the paddle upon Sam's motionless body.

"Jarm raised his head and he saw Betts place his foot against the bleeding body, and send the barrel and body rolling together down into the creek. Betts stood at the creek washing the sweat from his brow and his arms. One of the Negroes said, 'Sam be dead, massa.' Betts said, 'I'll bring him back to life, and gave the corpse a brutal kick in the ribs, but not a muscle stirred. The last words that Betts muttered were, 'Take the damned dog and bury him,' and he walked away.

"Before the sun went down the same day, the murder was known to every slave and white person on the farm. A slave girl belonging to the Logues was much attached to Sam and had expected to be his wife, and she declared it aloud and sobbed. The Logues were stirred to madness and swore that Betts should be lynched and driven from the neighborhood, but the tempest perished and Betts was as safe, and the Negroes as unsafe, as ever."

Zachariah Betts, who went unpunished for killing his slave, died a few years later – in 1826. Life on the Logue farm was tranquil for a time, but David Logue was struggling to pay his debts. He had borrowed the money to buy his brothers' share of the family homestead, and his creditors were threatening to foreclose on the property. He struggled to find some other solution, but he eventually decided that there was only one way to save his farm.

"Logue dreaded bankruptcy, and he determined to sell all his slaves at the first opportunity and to the best advantage. He was cautious that no suspicion of their fate should be awakened until they were in the power of their purchasers, and he meditated on the possibility of providing Cherry and her children a fate that was as endurable as possible.

"In the fall months, after the crops were harvested – when the slaves were looking forward to the pleasure and leisure of the holidays – his affairs called him to Nashville where he found a slave trader willing to spend a day on the farm, and make an offer for his slaves. The trader was to inform himself of the quality of the chattels without creating suspicion of his intent. On the evening of the same day, Logue and the visitor concluded their contract for the sale of the entire stock of slaves. Logue had learned that the purchaser, on his way to Alabama, would pass the residence of his brother, Manasseh, and it was a condition of the bargain that he would sell Cherry and her children to Manasseh, if he would pay the sum at which they were valued in the bill of sale.

"At the time the contract was closed, Henry had just arrived to indulge in a few moments of comfort with Cherry and their boy, and the slaves were seated around their cabins. Later, in the dead of night, the Negro quarters were surrounded by stout men armed with pistols and shackles. There were about twelve slaves. Cherry waked from her sleep, her infant sleeping at her side. Taken unawares, the victims were in the power of their captors.

"Because of her strength, they put the irons on Cherry, who was placed in a covered wagon with the children. She was told that David had started on a journey that night, and that she no longer belonged to him. But she was told that Henry would meet her on the road, and that she would meet David at Manasseh Logue's and take her and her children.

"The strongest of the Negroes were manacled, and chained together to the wagon. The procession started about the time the sun began to change the color of the eastern horizon. Many of them mourned aloud, and their sighs and sobs mingled with infants screams, the crack of whips, and the curses of the drivers. The captain of this band took his coffle to a sort of slave pen near Nashville, and then made his way again."

Sometime before 1820, after selling his share of the farm on Manskers Creek to his younger brother, David, Manasseh Logue had travelled fifty or sixty miles south of Nashville and settled in Maury

County. And in the Spring of 1827 he paid a little over $1600 for 152 acres of land in the southern part of Maury County. It was probably in the Fall of 1827 when a small group of Logue family slaves, including Cherry, her son Jarm, and her other children – made their way south from Davidson County.

"Day and night the caravan pursued its monotonous course until it arrived at Little Tombigbee Creek. Cherry had been told that she would be met there by her old master and by her husband, and that she and her children would be left with them. Cherry seated herself on the bank of the stream, and waited with her children at her side.

"It was not long before she saw three men approaching on horseback, with a wagon behind them being driven by a colored man. She recognized two of them – the slave trader and Manasseh Logue. Manasseh said, 'Get in the wagon with the children, Cherry, and Jack will show you to the quarters.' Jack told her that David Logue had started back that morning to Manskers Creek, and that no such man as Henry was on the estate. Cherry and the little ones were deposited at the Negro house, which was between the family residence and a small smutty distillery – all of which were log houses.

"After he sold out to his brother, Manasseh Logue kept at his old trade of manufacturing whiskey. He and his wife sank into intemperance, and they were drunken, brutal, and cruel. They had several sons and daughters, most of them older than Jarm, and all of them were idle, ignorant, and gross in their manners and habits. Their habitation, and the habitations of their slaves, were neglected, filthy, and uncomfortable. When their master or mistress were in liquor – if their wrath was attracted to the slaves – the victims were beaten without sense, reason, or limits.

"About the second spring, when Jarm was about fourteen, he was at work in the cornfield with the other hands, and Manasseh was present. Jarm's hoe was a heavy piece of flatted iron, with a large eye on the top for a clumsy handle, and as he raised it, the handle came loose and the iron fell to the ground. Manasseh hurled a stone at him and charged him with negligence in maintaining his tools, and ordered him to go to the yard nearby and wedge the handle back on, and never to expose his carelessness that way again. Knowing if he did not return quickly Manasseh would be after him, he fastened the handle sufficiently for the time his master would be there, planning to finish it after he was gone.

"The instrument answered its purpose for a short time, but Jarm struck the wedge against something and it went off the handle again. Blazing with alcohol, Manasseh picked up the wedge and swore that Jarm should swallow it. He ordered Jarm to open his mouth, and when he hesitated, Manasseh struck him on the side of his head with his fist. Manasseh leaped on him and held him down, pressing the wooden wedge against his lips and teeth.

"Jarm partly opened his teeth and Manasseh crowded in the wedge until it reached the roof of his mouth. Jarm stopped it with his teeth, but Manasseh began to pound it in with his fist. The wedge was driven into the roof of his mouth, and the blood flowed down his throat and from his mouth. Jarm seized the wedge and the hand that held it, and turned his head toward the ground. Manasseh commenced punching him with the sharp end of the wedge, making bloody gashes on his head and mouth.

"Manasseh, tired from his effort, ordered Jarm to get up and learn how to wedge a hoe. Jarm was weak and his lips and mouth were mangled, but he returned to the yard to fasten the handle to his hoe again. For many days it was with difficulty that Jarm swallowed his food or performed his tasks.

"Such was the state of things for a year after the outrage, when the slaves were awakened at the dead of night by a glaring light. The distillery was buried under a pyramid of fire. The Negroes were delighted. It was the whiskey from the distillery that made beasts of their master and mistress, who left to their own natures were endurable.

"Notwithstanding the injustice which, all her life, had been inflicted on Cherry, she was receptive of religious impressions. In the neighborhood of Manasseh's farm was a notable Methodist campground.

"At their annual gatherings, the inhabitants of the surrounding country assembled in great numbers. Slaves were also there, as servants of their masters and mistresses, or to enjoy a holiday or sell what some were allowed to raise on little patches of ground. When the claims of her master and mistress did not require her to stay at home, Cherry attended the meetings.

"Not long after the distillery burned, a religious awakening occurred in the camp. Cherry was one of the first to feel the divine presence, and she fell upon the earth and begged forgiveness. She pleaded for herself and for the divine spirit to fill every soul of the assembly, and she continued her prayer for her master and mistress. In the progress of events Manasseh, first touched by the prayer of Cherry, melted into penitence, and his wife was soon flooded with her sinfulness. Cherry and her owner were soon baptized together in the same church. From that time forward Manasseh assembled his family and slaves in the evening for scripture reading and prayers.

"Such changes had been produced by the loss of the distillery that the spring after Cherry's conversion, Manasseh hired out a few of his slaves, including Cherry and Jarm, to a neighboring farmer. They were transferred in the early spring, and after some two months Jarm was with the hands hoeing corn. The overseer, fancying that Jarm was slighting his work, brought the lash down upon his almost naked body, and raised his arm to repeat the blow. Cherry, hoe in hand, rushed between the overseer and Jarm.

"This increased the rage of the overseer, and he changed ends of the whip to inflict a blow on Cherry with its leaded butt. When she raised her hoe and made toward him, he turned and ran. Cherry would have been the subject of some terrible chastisement, but on that evening Cherry and Jarm were returned to Manasseh Logue.

"After about three days, Manasseh sent the adult Negroes into the field, detaining the children at the house. Some hours later, while the children were playing, two or three men rode up. Manasseh called all of the children into the yard. He commanded them to stand still while the strangers examined them. The Negro traders soon selected Jarm's brother, about thirteen, and his second sister, who was about eight. They were unspeakably dear to Jarm.

"As soon as the ruffian put his hand on the little girl she shrieked, and the children fled into the fields and woods in the direction of their mothers. Jarm remained with his brother and sister. The mothers heard the wail of their children and came running through the fields to relieve them. The trader mounted his horse and held the rope fastened to their hands, and Cherry bounded into the yard and threw her arms around the children.

"He let the lash fall on her shoulders, and the blow produced a gash from which the blood flowed freely. Blow after blow followed, and the blood saturated her garment and flowed down her limbs and upon the ground. Manasseh, fearing that his most valuable chattel would be disabled, told the trader he would separate them. Two of his stoutest men pried her arms apart, and she fell into a frenzy of grief. They held her while the trader led the children to the coffle and fastened their bound wrists to the large rope, and the caravan of children, fastened to a large wagon, were dragged away.

"That she might not follow her children, Cherry was taken to a room used for weaving cloth, and fastened to the loom, where she remained until morning. Cherry refused all food and rest, and raved and mourned for her children. Burdened with sorrows, she laid upon her hard couch for days. A kind-hearted old slave woman washed her wounds and nursed her, and by the soothing attentions of her oldest child, Maria, and the sympathy of Jarm, she was restored to health and sadly took her place among the hands in the field. The separation made a perpetual wound upon her spirit. She was occasionally melancholy, and always nervous and suspicious of danger.

"Jarm was approaching manhood with a strong and active body, and a mind capable of calculating for the future. It was the fall of the year when the fattening of the hogs was given to his charge. The corn was scattered on the ground, and the place where they were last fed was muddy by the nuzzling of the swine. One rainy Sunday morning Jarm proceeded to feed the hogs, and judging that the place where they were last fed was as fit a place to feed them as any, he poured down his corn on that spot.

"It became dirty and muddy, and Manasseh fell into a frenzy. He did not make whiskey, but he and his wife occasionally procured it, and only a small quantity was needed to drive him to uncontrollable excesses. Manasseh seized the hominy pestle – a heavy wooden instrument used to pound corn – and rushed upon Jarm and knocked him down, and he continued striking him with the pestle until Jarm was insensible. Jarm awoke in the loom room, his mother washing the blood from his head and face with cold water. Cherry said that his groans would bring Manasseh on him again, and she feared he would kill Jarm.

"During the succeeding year Manasseh not only refrained from abusing Jarm, as a sort of atonement he allowed him privileges and favors. For the first time he had a hat and shoes and a Sunday suit, which he was allowed to earn by extra labor."

Jarm experienced an extended period of relative peace, and then he was hired out to a kind family that did not own slaves. He was especially well-treated, but after two or three years he was reclaimed by Manasseh Logue. He soon decided that he would run away and try to reach a free state, but many months would pass before he and another young man, a half-white Maury County slave named John, began making detailed plans to escape north.

John was called John Farney, because a Maury County slave-holder of the same name not only owned John's mother, but bore a marked resemblance to the mulatto child. They planned to travel on horses taken from their respective masters, but they would need forged passes as well as money and provisions, and they thought it would be another year before they could make their attempt. John

Farney was to procure the passes, and Jarm looked for a way to make some money.

"Jarm's plan was to steal a barrel of whiskey from a neighborhood distillery, and retail it to make money. One afternoon Manasseh and his wife went to visit their preacher, and Jarm used his master's oxen and cart to bring the barrel of whiskey and place it out of his master's sight. But Manasseh came home and saw Jarm coming back in the cart. The next morning when Jarm came into the yard, Manasseh was there with cords in his hands and a bundle of sticks at his feet.

"Jarm was willing for Manasseh to whip him on the leg, but he resolved not to be tied. A neighboring slave, provoked by jealousy, recently assaulted him, and Jarm had been compelled to disable his assailant. The owner of the slave complained, and a justice of the peace sentenced Jarm to receive thirty-five lashes. His back was still tender, and Jarm folded his arms and looked his master firm in the face. Manasseh was irritated and approached with a rope, but Jarm stood defiantly. Manasseh flew at his slave, and Jarm seized him by the throat with one hand and his breeches with the other, and raised Manasseh off the ground and pitched him onto his head.

"Jarm ran for the woods, and Manasseh concluded not to pursue him. He saw that to punish him would drive his spirit to a desperate extremity, and that he would lose him. He believed that Jarm would wander in the fields until his passions cooled, and then return to his labors. But Jarm thought that Manasseh would rally the slave-catchers to hunt and shoot him, or return him to be scourged and then sold to Georgia."

Jarm and John Farney were not yet prepared to run away. After hiding out in a nearby cave – probably in what came to be called Ingram Cave – Jarm travelled by night to the Farney farm, where John provided him with food, a coat and a blanket, and a few other necessities. A number of days passed without any signs that he was being hunted, and when Jarm began to suspect that Manasseh was not seeking vengeance, he returned to the Logue farm. There was no punishment, and he went back to work.

"From that day forward Manasseh allowed Jarm many privileges, but he was destined to experience another blow upon his heart. His sister Maria was a beautiful young mother with three children, one of whom was a baby at her breast. In the latter part of the summer, Jarm found himself in the midst of a strong-built man with a whip in his right hand, attended by two or three other ruffians. Two of them were attempting to tie the hands of Maria with a rope, and she was resisting and screaming and praying.

"Maria had great strength, but the men finally overcame her. She was forced into a wagon with them, and she was driven away screaming. It was the last time Maria ever saw her children or her mother, or her brothers or sisters. Jarm was obliged to look on – riveted by a sense of impotence and a desire for vengeance."

By the following winter Jarm had sold some of the whiskey, and by selling crops he raised on a single acre of ground he was allowed to tend at night, he managed to save some money. John had approached a white man who lived nearby about providing them with forged passes. The man was known for his kindness to blacks, and around Christmas Jarm and John paid him $10 each for the passes. The same man later provided them with a pair of pistols, and in the dark hours of Christmas morning they prepared to set out.

"Jarm could not leave without a last look at his mother, and he shook his half-brother Henry out of his sleep. He explained his preparation, and Henry regretted he was not a party to it. But one had to stay behind to soothe their mother in the dark days that would come to her. Jarm approached her bedside and took a last look. Then she stirred and he retired, and the brothers embraced and bid each other farewell."

Well before dawn on Christmas morning of 1834 or 1835, Jarm Logue and John Farney made their way north from Little Tombigbee Creek. Later, with Jarm riding Manasseh Logue's finest horse, they took on the appearance of confident free Negroes and managed to pass through Nashville without attracting attention. But when they reached the bridge that led across the Cumberland River, they came to a gate where they would be examined more closely.

"As they advanced upon the bridge, a little boy presented himself to wait on them. Jarm set his high-spirited horse to bounding, and tossing a shilling to the boy, he rushed through the gate and told John to do the same. The keeper of the gate was a lame man instructed to detect fugitive slaves. It was part of his bargain that no colored person could pass without a severe examination, but on that morning he was away."

Continuing to pose as free black travelers, they spent the next several days on the road, and spent their nights in places that would accommodate young men of color. But then, somewhere in Kentucky, their journey was interrupted.

"Their attention was arrested by the appearance of three men on foot, who entered their path by a road through the woods. They resembled negro-catchers – a set of men dreaded by blacks and despised by whites. The footmen seized the horses by the bridles and demanded to see passes. Finding the fugitives obstinate, one of the ruffians took Jarm by the collar, while another was busy with John. The third man struck Jarm in the head with a club. His head flashed and he was near falling before his strength came forth, and he sprang at the throat of the villain who struck him. The wretch tumbled backwards over a log, and Jarm's knees plunged into his bowels and breast, and the assassins who were pressing Farney turned and fled.

"Believing that the men would rouse the whole country in their pursuit, Jarm and John took to their horses and fled. They took obscure roads and travelled with great speed, feeding themselves in fields and lodging at night in hay and corn stacks. They finally met two slaves who informed them of the route to the Ohio River. Then the slaves said that two colored men on horseback had given three notorious negro-catchers a dreadful fight. One had been killed or nearly killed, and couriers had been sent along the road by the slave-catchers."

Two days later, after resting the previous night under a haystack, they were stopped by another band of slave-catchers, but after a sudden blow from John left the leader with a bloody wound, the others ran away. Jarm and John soon came upon a colored man who told them about an obscure route that would take them to the river. The following day they reached the ice-covered Ohio. After trying to haggle with a hostile ferryman, they led their horses out onto the ice and managed to cross safely over into Indiana.

Seeing that they were being closely watched by a group of villagers, they took out their pistols. Then pretending they were merely free blacks coming back from a drunken outing, they fired the pistols into the air. They deceived the men on the shore, and soon encountered a local black man who told them that although they had reached a free state, they were still in danger of being captured and taken back into slavery. He directed them to a village called Corydon, some twenty miles away, and gave them the name of a prominent Negro who lived there and could help them continue their journey.

When they reached Corydon, John Farney and Jarm were fed and given the name of a man in Indianapolis – 100 miles further on.

They left in the middle of the night, and after losing their way in the wilderness they went hungry for a time. Whenever they came to a house they would offer to pay for food, but were repeatedly turned away. It was three days before they finally received help. But while they ate, they learned that they had been moving in the wrong direction, and were only a few miles from the Ohio River. They received directions to Salem, Indiana, and when they arrived, a friendly proprietor provided them with a meal before sending them to a nearby Negro community. They stayed there for a week before they recovered and moved on.

They finally reached Indianapolis and found the educated black man whose name they had been given, and he advised them to head to a Quaker settlement about forty miles away. The Quakers invited Jarm and John to stay until winter had passed, but they declined the invitation. They were given provisions, and along with being informed that they would not be safe from recapture until they reached Canada, they were told that they should journey through Indian territory to avoid slave-catchers.

They moved through remote country for several days before they were overtaken by a blizzard. Soon lost and with no place to take shelter during the night, they travelled through the wind and the driving snow until morning. The storm was still howling when they happened on an Indian dwelling in a clearing. They were taken in, and given shelter and food. The storm subsided and they set out again, and after a number of days they reached the white settlements on the northern side of the wilderness.

Jarm and John made their way to Logansport, a town on the Wabash River. They continued to travel at night, guided by the North Star, but a succession of cloudy nights put them off their course, and instead of making their way toward Detroit, they became lost in the wilderness yet again. The winter ground on and their hunger and hardships continued, but they finally came across a hunter. He told them they were going in the wrong direction, and pointed them toward Detroit, which lay back to the southeast.

They finally reached Detroit, but having been warned repeatedly that local Negro-catchers were continually on the lookout for runaways, they kept a low profile. Three days later there was enough ice on the Detroit River for Jarm to move across into Windsor, Ontario. John Farney followed a little later, but his horse had been stolen and he went back to retrieve it. Jarm never saw him again.

"Not being able to get employment at Windsor, Jarm started on alone. Without money, he managed to get one meal a day, and sufficient feed for his horse until he arrived at Chatham. At Chatham his prospects were no better. Driven to his wits, he swapped the old mare for another horse and two or three shillings, and reached the neighborhood of London. He stayed with a farmer for three or four days, selling the horse for his board and a few shillings, and after availing himself of an opportunity to ride with a stranger, he pushed his way to Hamilton."

Years later Loguen would describe that time in a letter to Frederick Douglass.

"On the western termination of Lake Ontario is the village of Hamilton. On the north is a beautiful lake. Hamilton is a sacred and memorable spot to me. Twenty-one years ago – the very winter I left my chains in Tennessee — I stood on this spot, penniless, ragged, lonely, homeless, helpless, hungry and forlorn – a pitiable wanderer, without a friend, or shelter, or place to lay my head. I had fought a passage through storms and tempests. There I stood, a boy twenty-one years of age, as near as I know my age, the tempest howling over my head, and my toes touching the snow beneath my worn-out shoes – knowing nobody and nobody knowing me or noticing me.

"I could only look to God, and I prayed, 'Pity, my Father – help, or I perish!' Though all was frost and tempest without, within came warmth and trust and love. And an *earthly* father took me to his home, and his angel wife became to me a mother. They thought a body, lusty and stout as mine, could brave cold and cut cord wood and split rails, and they were right. I agreed to earn my bread, and they paid me better than I asked, and taught me many lessons of religion and life. I had a home, and I would have been happy, but for the thought that my mother, sisters, and brothers were in cruel bondage. I gained the favor of the best white people. My story attached them to me. They took me into the Sabbath School at Hamilton, and taught me letters the winter of my arrival, and I graduated as a Bible reader the succeeding summer."

After working for the farmer and his wife for two years – clearing land for $10 a month – Jarm took his new name, Jermain Wesley Loguen. He eventually found work as a servant in the best hotel in Rochester. In 1859 Reverend E.P. Rogers wrote about the next several years of Loguen's life.

"I became acquainted with J.W. Loguen early in the winter of 1838, when I was engaged as a teacher of a public school in the city of Rochester, New York. He made no secret of the fact that he was a fugitive, and he applied and was received as a pupil. Mr. Loguen was under my tuition, and he improved rapidly in the primary branches of education. At the same time he manifested a strong desire to be serviceable in some way to his down-trodden race. A close intimacy sprang up between us, and I observed that he was a man of uncommon energy of mind, and of a truly benevolent spirit.

"His friends saw that he was a man of no ordinary abilities, and counselled him to go forward and prepare for a higher calling. Entering the preparatory department of the Oneida Institute in Whitesboro, New York, he commenced a course of study. The Institute brought him in contact with

Oneida Institute

aspiring students, most of whom were the open and avowed enemies of slavery and the advocates of equal rights. It is not strange that Mr. Loguen dedicated himself to anti-slavery work.

"Such was Mr. Loguen's progress at the Institute, that at the end of the first term he was able to teach school in Utica. After some two seasons at the Institution, where he won the confidence and esteem of both students and professors, he was happily united in marriage to Miss Caroline Storum. He entered the ministry and settled at Syracuse, New York."

J.W. Loguen married in 1840, and the next year the young couple went to Syracuse, where he became the preacher for the local Negro population, conducting services in a small unfinished building. He soon turned his attention to the neglected children of the colored community, and became a teacher as well. After neighborhood opposition came to a head when a school was established, he hired a team of oxen and moved the structure to a new location.

"In the fall of 1844, the anti-slavery tempest had broken into a rage, and the friends of Henry Clay of the Whig Party, James K. Polk of the Democratic Party, and James G. Birney of the Liberty Party – the candidates for the Presidency – had their orators in the field. In the midst of the excitement, Mr. Loguen visited Cortland County, New York, to raise funds to finish building a church."

On a Sunday morning in late September, Rev. Loguen was invited to speak to a local congregation on the subject of slavery. He was so well-received that he was taken to a second church, and that appearance was described fifteen years later in the book, *The Rev. J. W. Loguen, as a slave and as a Freeman, a Narrative of Real Life.* .

Jermaine W. Loguen

"Mr. Loguen did not enter the pulpit, but fell upon his knees before the altar and the people. He poured out the passion of his soul for the redemption of the slave. Then he prayed, 'How long shall my poor brethren suffer? How long shall our little children be torn from their parents, and our innocent sisters and daughters and mothers be given to pollution? Give me my mother! She was robbed of her children, and was flayed and tortured because she grieved for them. My little brother and sister on one occasion, and my beautiful sister Maria on another, were torn from her and driven away by cruel men who lashed her body and covered it with her blood, because she struggled and prayed for her children.'

"No prayer ever made in Cortland melted the people like that. Look which way you might in the great assembly, all were in tears. When he rose from his knees and wiped the water from his brow, he stood confused – as if he had forgotten his audience while he talked with God. Then he commenced his speech in the language of a child. He apologized for his lack of education, and said he had but once before spoken on slavery. He then proceeded to detail the features of slavery as he had felt them and seen them stamped on others. The passions of his hearers burned like fire under his unpretending but harrowing eloquence.

"The Liberty Party men of Cortland were so delighted with Loguen, that they set him on the stump in opposition to Clay and Polk. Appointments were made for him to speak at the principal places in the county, and he filled them with ability and success. His soul became absorbed with his theme, and set him beside the slave in a life-long war for liberty. He has continued a public speaker on behalf of liberty ever since."

It was probably in early 1845 when Rev. Loguen received a generous gesture from some of those who had heard his story.

"The citizens of Cortland County were so overcome by the love Rev. Loguen had for his mother, that they determined to purchase her and give her to him. They opened a correspondence with Manasseh Logue, and concluded a bargain for Cherry at the price of $250. The sum was raised by subscription, and Nathaniel Goodwin went to Tennessee to pay it and bring her north."

Nathaniel Goodwin was in his mid-forties, and he left his wife and his son on their small farm in New York when he made the long journey south to buy Cherry.

"He arrived in Columbia, and found that Manasseh lived about eleven miles off. Goodwin mounted his horse and trotted through a half cultivated country, until he came to a cluster of mean log houses. The center one was Manasseh's dwelling, and the surrounding ones were for his cattle and slaves. Logue, a bloated old man, appeared and invited him in. Manasseh admitted to the contract to sell Cherry, but was inquisitive to know whether it was made for Jarm's benefit. When Goodwin admitted that it was, Manasseh said that he would be glad to take the money and let Cherry go, but he would not let her go until Jarm bought himself.

"When Goodwin told him that Jarm would never buy himself, Manasseh said, 'I shall go and take him. He is my property.' Then Manasseh sent for Cherry. In a short time an aged colored woman entered the room. She was dressed in a single coarse garment, which covered her from her neck to near her ankles, leaving her head and feet bare. She appeared to be about sixty years of age. She was stout and healthy for a woman so old, though her slow and heavy footfall and bent neck told of age and hardship."

When he returned to New York, Goodwin must have given Loguen a full and detailed account of what Cherry had said, and some years later, when he was interviewed for his book, Loguen passed along what Goodwin told him. The exact words that were spoken in the rural home of Manasseh Logue were lost, but the essence of the conversation was probably what appeared in the book about Rev. Loguen.

"Manasseh left her alone with Goodwin. 'Is your name Cherry?' 'Yes, master.' 'Did you have a son you called Jarm?' Her countenance lost its vacancy, and she turned her eyes on Goodwin. 'Yes master, but he died long ago.' By this time her attention was fixed intensely on Mr. Goodwin. 'Jarm is not dead. I came from him a few days since. His friends sent me to buy you and take you to him. He wants to make you free and have you live with him.'

"The dew gathered in her eyes, and her frame was struggling with strong and deep emotions. 'I should like to see Jarm and live with him, but he must come here and live with me. Master will never let me go and live with him.'

"But he can't come here. He will be a slave here. More than that, he has a wife and children, and he would not be willing to bring them here.' Cherry said, 'How does Jarm's wife look? How I should like to see her. Is she a slave?'

"In the midst of this conversation, Cherry's daughter, Ann, came into the room. She was the property of a neighboring farmer, and had been informed that a man had come to purchase her mother and take her to her lost brother. She was permitted to come and see the stranger. Ann was the only child not sold out of the country. 'Mother, go with the man and live with Jarm. One of these days I'll get away and come live with you.'

"Then the sister and mother enquired about Jarm's looks, his age, and the looks and ages of his wife and children. His property and condition, and his intelligence and wisdom and influence, seemed not to interest them. But they sought any personal peculiarity to hang their hearts on. His mother did say once, 'It is just like Jarm to preach.' The interview was a luxury to Goodwin, but he was obliged to close it.

"When he took them by the hand to dismiss them, they wept together, and they sent their separate messages to Jarm. Goodwin started on his return, but Manasseh, still hoping he might get Jarm or get his value, walked a mile or two by the side of Goodwin's horse, all the while urging him to persuade Jarm to buy his freedom. When Goodwin returned and told Loguen he could not have his mother until he owned himself, he was deeply grieved and indignant."

Rev. J.W. Loguen, like escaped slaves who had found refuge across the North, became much more vulnerable after the Fugitive Slave Act was passed by Congress in 1850. The new law, a key part of the compromise meant to prevent a war between the South and the North, not only required authorities to take escaped slaves into custody, anyone aiding a runaway was subject to imprisonment and a substantial fine. A month after the act became law, Rev. Loguen delivered a speech that called on the people of Syracuse to reject the law.

"I don't respect this law. I don't fear it. I won't obey it! It outlaws me, and I outlaw it and the men who attempt to enforce it on me. I place the governmental officials on the ground that they place me. I will not live a slave, and if force is employed to re-enslave me, I shall make preparations to meet the crisis as becomes a man. If you will stand by me – if you will stand with us – in resistance to this measure, you will be the saviors of your country. Your decision

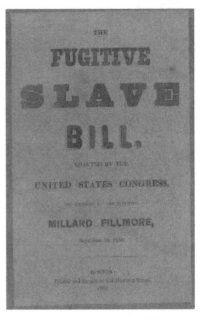

tonight in favor of resistance will give vent to the spirit of liberty. Your example is needed for popular action in Auburn and Rochester and Utica and Buffalo, and in all the West, and eventually in the Atlantic cities. Heaven knows that this act of noble daring will break out somewhere, and may God grant that Syracuse be the honored spot from whence it shall send an earthquake voice through the land!"

Those in the audience voted to disregard the law by an overwhelming margin, influencing Syracuse to become a sanctuary city for runaway slaves. In 1851 the Fugitive Slave Act was tested in Syracuse when the demands of the law collided with public sentiment. William Henry, a fugitive slave from Missouri who was nicknamed Jerry, was arrested in Syracuse, and Rev. Loguen became involved in what became known as "the Jerry Rescue." To avoid losing his freedom in the anticipated backlash from pro-slavery forces, Loguen went to Canada, but after he concluded that the citizens of Syracuse would not allow the Fugitive Slave Law to be enforced, he returned to New York.

Lucius Jared Ormsbee was a white merchant in Syracuse and an active abolitionist. Many years later, when he was interviewed about his activities during the decade leading up to the Civil War, he conveyed some of what Rev. Loguen did to help runaway slaves.

"I was on the executive committee of the Underground Railroad, which was a line of stations between the Mason-Dixon Line and Canada. The refugees were helped from one station to another and enabled to reach Canada. You could always tell a runaway. They had a timid, frightened look, and were always turning around to see if someone was behind them. I used to keep slaves hidden. I'd have them under the sidewalk in front of my store, when the space between their heads and the feet of the Marshals who were after them was only the thickness of a flagstone.

"I'd keep them till after nightfall, and smuggle them out and leave them somewhere under a tree. Then I'd go down to J.W. Loguen's old white house on the corner of East Genesee and Pine Streets. I'd whistle him up, and tell him that under a certain tree there were darkies who needed looking after. It was risky work, but hundreds of runaway slaves passed through our hands to freedom."

Loguen did not keep a low profile. A newspaper article in 1855 conveyed his spirited nature, as well as his subtle sense of humor.

"A man was seated on the train at Albany. He squatted on two seats while others were standing. Rev. Loguen enquired in a very gentlemanly manner, 'Is this seat beside you taken?' He was told, 'Yes it is.' Then Loguen asked, 'Where is the gentleman who claims it?'

When the man said, 'He has stepped out,' Loguen said, 'Then I will take it until he returns.' The gentleman sat in a pout for a time with a touch-me-not sort of stare, before he growled, 'Keep your foot off, will you!' Rev. Loguen said, 'Excuse me.' Bristling up, the man said, 'Let me out of here.' Then with a subdued, respectful air Loguen remarked, 'I'm afraid if you go away, I shan't know, when he comes, the man whose seat I've got.' Greeted with a laugh of derision, the fellow went off, saying something about 'niggers.'"

A few months later, the scale of Loguen's activities was reported in a local newspaper.

"A day or two ago Reverend Loguen was providing for a couple of fellows who fled from Baltimore, and yesterday he had charge of a grandmother and her four grandchildren from Virginia. The stream is constant. The number receiving aid in Syracuse since January is about 140. The agent for the underground railroad, Mr. Loguen, has his hands full."

In 1857 the Fugitive Aid Society published a notice for the benefit of local citizens.

"Since 1850 the labor of sheltering those who flee from slavery, providing for their wants, and helping them to find safe houses in this country or in Canada has been done, for the most part, by Rev. J.W. Loguen. Having been a slave and a fugitive himself, he knows how to provide for and guard them. Mr. Loguen has agreed to devote himself wholly to this humane work. We request that all fugitives from slavery be directed to Rev. Loguen, and that all monies, clothing, or provisions be sent to his house, or to such places as he may designate."

The notice was followed by a card from Rev. Loguen.

"The entire care of the fugitives who may stop in Syracuse for comfort and assistance, having been devolved upon me by the Fugitive Aid Society, I give notice that I shall devote myself assiduously to the duties I have undertaken. For the support of my family, I must depend on the liberality of the friends of freedom. I shall gratefully receive money, clothes, and provisions. I will report the amounts that I have received, and the number of fugitives I have sheltered and found homes for."

In 1859 a group of Syracuse residents signed what amounted to an endorsement of Loguen's work.

"The citizens of Syracuse take pleasure in stating that those in transition from bondage to freedom are promptly entertained and safely conveyed to Canada under the faithful and efficient management of Rev. J.W. Loguen, General Agent of the Underground Railroad for Central New York."

His book, *The Rev. J.W. Loguen, as a Slave and as a Freeman, a Narrative of Real Life*, received national recognition when it was published later in 1859, and its appearance may have been responsible for a letter he received several months later.

"Maury Co., State of Tennessee
February 20th, 1860.

To Jarm –

I now take my pen to write you a few lines, to let you know how well we all are. I am a cripple, but I am still able to get about. The rest of the family are all well. Cherry is as well as Common. I write you these lines to let you know the situation we are in—partly in consequence of your running away and stealing Old Rock, our fine mare. Though we got the mare back, she was never worth much after you took her. As I now stand in need of some funds, I have determined to sell you. I have had an offer for you, but did not see fit to take it. If you will send me one thousand dollars and pay for the old mare, I will give up all claim I have to you. Write to me as soon as you get these lines, and let me know if you will accept my proposition.

In consequence of your running away, we had to sell Abe and Ann and twelve acres of land; and I want you to send me the money that I may be able to redeem the land that you was the cause of our selling. On receipt of the above named sum of money, I will send you your bill of sale. If you do not comply with my request, I will sell you to someone else, and you may rest assured that the time is not far distant when things will be changed with you. Write to me as soon as you get these lines. Direct your letter to Bigbyville, Maury County, Tennessee. You had better comply with my request.

I understand that you are a preacher. As the Southern people are so bad, you had better come and preach to your old acquaintances. I would like to know if you read your Bible? If so, can you tell what will become of the thief if he does not repent? And if the blind lead the blind, what will the consequence be? I deem it unnecessary to say much more at present. A word to the wise is sufficient. You know where the liar has his part. You know that we reared you as we reared our own children. You was never abused, and shortly before you ran away, when your master asked if you would like to be sold, you said you would not leave him to go with anybody.
Sarah Logue"

A few weeks after receiving her letter, Rev. Loguen wrote a response to his former mistress in Tennessee.

"Syracuse, N.Y., March 28, 1860
Mrs. Sarah Logue –
Yours of the 20th of February is duly received, and I thank you for it. It is a long time since I heard from my poor old mother, and I am glad to know she is yet alive, and, as you say, "as well as common." What that means I don't know. I wish you had said more about her.

You are a woman, but had you a woman's heart you could never have insulted a brother by telling him you sold his only remaining brother and sister, because he put himself beyond your power to convert him into money.

You say you sold my brother and sister, Abe and Ann, and 12 acres of land because I ran away. Now you have the unutterable meanness to ask me to return and be your miserable chattel, or send you $1000 to enable you to redeem the *land*, but not to redeem my poor brother and sister! If I were to send you money it would be to get my brother and sister, and not that you should get land. You say you are a *cripple*, and doubtless you say it to stir my pity. You know I was susceptible in that direction. I do pity you from the bottom of my heart.

Nevertheless I am indignant beyond the power of words to express, that you should be so sunken and cruel as to tear the hearts I love so much all in pieces, and that you should be willing to impale and crucify us out of all compassion for your poor *foot* or *leg*. Wretched woman! Be it known to you that I value my freedom, to say nothing of my mother, brothers and sisters, more than your whole body – more, indeed, than my own life; more than all the lives of all the slaveholders and tyrants under Heaven.

You say you have offers to buy me, and that you shall sell me if I do not send you $1000, and in the same breath, and almost in the same sentence, you say, "you know we raised you as we did our own children." Woman, did you raise your *own children* for the market? Did you raise them for the whipping-post? Did you raise them to be driven off in a coffle in chains? Where are my poor bleeding brothers and sisters? Who was it that sent them off into sugar and cotton fields to be kicked and cuffed and whipped, and to groan and die where no kin can hear their groans, or attend and sympathize at their dying bed, or follow in their funeral?

Wretched woman! Do you say *you* did not do it? Then I reply, your husband did, and *you* approved the deed. The very letter you sent me shows that your heart approves it all. Shame on you. But where is your husband? You don't speak of him. I infer, therefore, that he is dead – that he has gone to his great account with all his sins against my poor family upon his head. Poor man! Gone to meet the spirits of my poor, outraged and murdered people, in a world where Liberty and Justice are MASTERS.

You say I am a thief because I took the old mare along with me. Have you got to learn that I had a better right to the old mare, as you call her, than Manasseh Logue had to me? Is it a greater sin for me to steal his horse, than it was for him to rob my mother's cradle and steal me? If he and you infer that I forfeit all my rights to you, shall not I infer that you forfeit all your rights to me? Have you got to learn that human rights are mutual and reciprocal, and if you take my liberty and life, you forfeit your own liberty and life? Before God and High Heaven, is there a law for one man which is not a law for every other man?

Jermaine W. Loguen

If you, or any other speculator on my body and rights, wish to know how I regard my rights, they need but come here and lay their hands on me to enslave me. Did you think to terrify me by presenting the alternative to give my money to you, or give my body to slavery?

Then let me say to you, that I meet the proposition with unutterable scorn and contempt.

The proposition is an outrage and an insult. I will not budge one hair's breadth. I will not breathe a shorter breath, even to save me from your persecutions. I stand among a free people, who, I thank God, sympathize with my rights and the rights of mankind. If your emissaries and vendors come here to re-enslave me, and escape the unshrinking vigor of my own right arm, I trust that my strong and brave friends, in this city and State, will be my rescuers and avengers. Yours, J.W. Loguen"

The Civil War erupted and passed, and in the summer of 1865, less than three months after Appomattox, Rev. Loguen made his way south to Maury County, and finally reached the neighborhood of Little Tombigbee Creek. A newspaper account captured a few details of his visit.

"At the time he ran away, he left a mother, a sister, and a brother on the farm he left. After a period of many years, he

Sarah Loguen Fraser

returned to Tennessee. Reaching the old log hut, Loguen sent a man to see if his mother was there. The man came back saying, 'Yes, old Aunt Cherry is here.' She knew her son as soon as she saw him. 'Here is my son Jermain!' Old Mrs. Logue is still alive, and Mr. Loguen also saw her. Aunt Cherry heard her son preach in Columbia. As soon as

401

he finished his sermon, the old lady made her way to the pulpit and hugged and kissed him. He returns to Tennessee as an educated man – a man of refinement, a minister of the gospel, and a man of great influence."

Reverend Loguen learned that Manasseh Logue had been dead since 1852 and he was likely told that his father, David Logue, had died in 1861. Sarah Logue, Manasseh's widow died the next year – almost a year to the day after the visit. Cherry survived into the 1870s, and may have outlived her son, who died of tuberculosis in Saratoga Springs, New York, in 1872. Rev. Loguen was survived by six children. Among them was his oldest daughter, Amelia, who married the eldest son of Frederick Douglass and served former slaves and their families as both a teacher and a social worker. And his second-born daughter, Sarah, became the first woman graduate of the Syracuse University School of Medicine, and was the first female physician to practice in the Dominican Republic.

Afterword

In order to make *Tell Them We Were Rising* more accessible for the reader, some passages that appear in quotes were edited for clarity, readability, and length. And in a few instances, such as in the autobiographical account by James C. Napier, two or more sources were combined into a single quoted narrative.

Several of those presented in this book were the children or grandchildren of influential whites. It should not be assumed that individuals without ties of kinship to their owners received similar treatment. It should also be noted that the treatment of slaves on the farms of Middle Tennessee tended to be far milder than what took place on the cotton and sugar plantations of the Deep South. And because of the protection and support they often received from leading members of the white community, some of those who appear in this work had far more economic opportunity than the vast majority of people of color during slavery, reconstruction, and the time of Jim Crow.

The individuals who appear in *Tell Them We Were Rising* were not selected because of the nature of their stories. They were chosen because there appeared be enough information for a robust account to be presented – whatever their stories happened to be. Except for Frank Parrish and a couple of others, I knew very little about those

I have written about. I had heard of J.C. Napier and Preston Taylor and R.H. Boyd, but I didn't know the details of their lives, and I was entirely unfamiliar with such people as Randall Vandavell or Minta Allen.

I began with Henry W. and Minta Allen because they were pictured in a beautiful old photograph I had run across. Their story led me to write about Minta's father, John B. Bosley, and from there one account led to the next. I thought that I would eventually come to a person who would have to be abandoned due to a lack of information, but there turned out to be enough to write a reasonably detailed account of every life I researched.

As for the terms I have used, many people have come to feel that the term "enslaved person" should always be used instead of "slave." My preference is to employ the language – including words like Negro and colored and mulatto – that was in use during the time being written about. The individuals whose stories I have presented would have almost certainly referred to themselves as slaves. I wonder if hearing themselves only referred to as "enslaved people" or "the enslaved" would have sounded as synthetic to them as it does to me.

And in my opinion, referring to anyone who ever owned a slave as an enslaver is misleading. It seems that there should be a distinction between those who actively subjected individuals to slavery, and individuals whose involvement was of an entirely different nature. Those who herded African captives onto slave ships – captors who included Africans as well as whites – were nothing like slave-owning individuals such as Peter Lowery or Jefferson Harding or George Trimble, who were all men of color. And although Susannah Parrish and Fanny Harding and Elizabeth Merry all owned slaves, it would be highly inaccurate to equate them with the slave traders and patrollers of the American South, or with Manasseh Logue or Richard

Phillips or James Hoggatt, each of whom personified the more negative connotations of the term, enslaver.

American slavery was, at its core, primitive and inhuman and abhorrent. From my perspective, the experience of slavery should be presented – terminology and all – as it was. Many millions of black Americans had their lives stolen by slavery. Millions more, those who outlived their servitude, had their remaining years crippled by the long period of injustice that followed in the wake of emancipation. It seems to me that the best way to honor them is to present what they experienced with as much authenticity as possible.

I have found myself wondering if individuals such as Cherry Logue and Alonzo Napier – and the others whose lives have been honored in these pages – would have found some consolation had they known that their lives might inspire those of subsequent generations. It has been a privilege to learn about the men and women whose lives are celebrated in *Tell Them We Were Rising*. There are many other such individuals whose lives are yet to be explored – whose stories are yet to be told.

Acknowledgements

Tell Them We Were Rising builds on the work that has been done over the years by local historians such as Dr. Bobby Lovett, Ms. Linda T. Wynn, and the late Dr. Reavis Mitchell. Foremost among those who helped me in the process of putting this book together is Marcia Fraser, head of Special Collections at the Williamson County Public Library. From the hospitality she offered, to the technological information she provided, to the role she played in my selection of the title, Marcia's help was indispensable. I also appreciate the aid I received from Karensa Lee and Amy Shropshire, and from other members of the library staff. I received important help from Robert Spinelli, MLIS, director of Special Collections at the John Hope and Aurelia D. Franklin Library at Fisk University, and from Sandra Parham, MLIS, Library Executive Director, Meharry Medical College Library. In addition, Kelley Sirko and Sarah Arntz of the Metro Archives in Nashville, along with Director Ken Fieth, provided a number of scanned images which added to the appeal of this book. Trent Hanner and Lindsay Hager of the Tennessee State Library and Archives were especially helpful, as were Barbara Nicolson of the Giles County Archives, and Andy Blair and Rick Warwick – both of Williamson County. Lois Bruce, who for years has done excellent research on the family of Henry W. Compton –

an ancestor of her late husband, Bill – shared the image of Annie Compton, as well as the mortuary photograph of Dernice Trimble. My friend Steve Rogers, formerly of the Tennessee Historical Commission was, as always, very generous with his time, helping with several different images, including a photograph taken by Nick Fielder, formerly head of the Tennessee Division of Archaeology. I received encouragement to write on this topic from my friend, Billy Myers, of Hernando, Mississippi, and I found inspiration in a brief conversation I had about race with Bishop T.D. Jakes when he was in Nashville in 2019. And along with my appreciation for the time and expertise given by my oldest son, Paul, who created the cover of *Tell Them We Were Rising*, I am thankful for the support of my other children, Jay, Kate, and John, and of my exceptionally tolerant and loving wife, Ruth.

Selected Bibliography

Bell, L. C., *History of the Dickinson Road*, 28, Robert Cartwright Chapter, DAR, 1936

Bragg, Dr. Emma W., Scrapbook: *Some Family Reminiscences of a Native Nashville Septuagenarian*, 1985, (ISBN 0-9611930-2-6)

Broughton, Virginia Walker, *Twenty Year's Experience of a Missionary*: Chicago, Pony Press, 1907
https://s3.amazonaws.com/nypl-aaww/
SCAAWW_book_4_Twenty_years_experience_of_a_missionary.pdf

Brown, Hallie Q. *Pen Pictures of Pioneers of Wilberforce*, Aldine Publishing Company, Xenia, Ohio, 1937

Caldwell, Joshua W., *Bench and Bar of Tennessee*, Knoxville: Ogden Brothers and Company, 1898

Caldwell, May Winston, *Beautiful and Historic Homes in and Around Nashville*, 1911

Cashin, Sheryll, *The Agitator's Daughter: A Memoir of Four Generations of One Extraordinary African American Family*, 2008

Clayton, W.W., *History of Davidson County, Tennessee*: Philadelphia, J.W. Lewis and Company, 1880

Clements, Paul, *A Past Remembered*, Nashville: Clearview Press, 1987

_____ *Chronicles of the Cumberland Settlements*, Nashville: Clearview Press, 2012

Culp, Dr. D.W., *Twentieth Century Negro Literature, or A Cyclopedia of Thought on the Vital Topics Relating to the American Negro by One Hundred of America's Greatest Negroes*, Toronto, Napierville, Atlanta: J.L. Nichols and Company, 1902

Dresser, Amos, *The Narrative of Amos Dresser*: New York, The American Anti-Slavery Society, 1836

Furman, Jan, *Slavery in the Clover Bottoms*, Knoxville: University of Tennessee Press, 1998

Haley, James T., *Afro-American Encyclopaedia; Or, the Thoughts, Doings, and Sayings of the Race, Embracing Lectures, Biographical Sketches, Sermons, Poems, Names of Universities, Colleges, Seminaries, Newspapers, Books, and a History of the Denominations, Giving the Numerical Strength of Each. In Fact, it Teaches Every Subject of Interest to the Colored People, as Discussed by More Than One Hundred of Their Wisest and Best Men and Women*, Nashville, Tenn.: Haley & Florida, 1895

_____ *Sparkling Gems of Race Knowledge Worth Reading – A Compendium of Valuable Information and Wise Suggestions That Will Inspire Noble Effort at the Hands of Evert Race-Loving Man, Woman, and Child*, Nashville, 1897

Hall, William, *Early History of the South-West*, Nashville: Gallatin Publishing, 1968

Haywood, John, *Civil and Political History of Tennessee*, 1823, reprint, Nashville: Methodist Publishing House, 1891

Hearne, Mary Glenn, editor, *Nashville, A Family Town*, Nashville Public Library, 1978, "The Harding Family" by Ridley Wills, 120-144; "The McGavock Family" by Margaret Lindsley Warden

Loguen, Jermaine Wesley, *The Rev. J. W. Loguen, as a Slave and as a Freeman, a Narrative of Real Life,* Syracuse: J.G.K. Truair and Company, 1859 (https://quod.lib.umich.edu/m/moa/ABT6752.0001.001?rgn=main;view=fulltext)

Lovett, Bobby, PHD, *A Black Man's Dream: The First 100 Years, Richard Henry Boyd and the Baptist Publishing Board,* 1993

Morris, Elias C., *Sermons, Addresses and Reminiscences, With a Picture Gallery of Eminent Ministers and Scholars,* Nashville: National Baptist Publishing Board, 1901

Pike, Gustavus D., *"The Jubilee Singers, and Their Campaign for Twenty Thousand Dollars"* – London, Hodder and Stoughton, 1873 Pike, Gustavus D. https//library. si.edu/digital-library/book/jubileesingersth00pike

Putnam, A. W. *History of Middle Tennessee, or Life and Times of General James Robertson,* 1859, reprint, Knoxville: University of Tennessee Press, 1971

Schweninger, Loren, *From Tennessee Slave to St. Louis Entrepreneur: the Autobiography of James Thomas,* University of Missouri, 1984

Simmons, William J. and Turner, Henry McNeal, *Men of Mark: Eminent, Progressive and Rising:* Cleveland, G.M. Rewell & Company, 1887 (https://docsouth.unc.edu/neh/simmons/simmons.html)

Sistler, Byron, *Davidson County, Tn Marriages, 1838 – 1863,* Sistler and Associates, 1985

Thomas, Miss Jane, *Old Days in Nashville,* Charles Elder Bookseller, 1972

Tomeiko Ashford Carter, *Virginia Broughton: The Life and Writings of a Missionary,* University of Tennessee Press, 2010, p. xxii

Walton, Emily Donelson, *Autobiography of Emily Donelson Walton,* Nashville: Methodist Publishing House, 1949

Ward, Andrew, *Dark Midnight When I Rise – The Story of the Jubilee Singers Who Introduce the World to the Music of Black America,* Farrar, Straus and Giroux, New York, 2000

Washington, Booker T., *The Negro in Business,* Boston, Chicago: Hertel, Jenkins and Company, 1907

Watson, Virginia Gooch, *The Keeble Family Genealogy,* 1986, Tennessee State Library and Archives

Whitely, Edythe Ricker, *Marriages of Davidson County, Tennessee, 1789-1837,* Baltimore: Genealogical Publishing Company, 1981

Williams, Samuel Cole, *Early Travels in the Tennessee Country, 1540-1800,* Johnson City, Tennessee: Watauga Press, 1928

Wills, Ridley, *The History of Belle Meade,* Nashville: Vanderbilt Press, 1991

Woodson, Carter G., *The History of the Negro Church,* Washington DC: The Associated Publishers, 1921

Davidson County, Chancery Court case file ("Priscilla and others vs Edwin H. Ewing, Trustee, and others"), Metropolitan Archives, Nashville

deGregory, Crystal A., *Raising a Nonviolent Army: Four Nashville Black Colleges and the Century-Long Struggle for Civil Rights, 1830s-1930s,* dissertation, Vanderbilt

Encyclopedia of African-American Business, "McKissack & McKissack Architects and Engineers, Inc." (online)
https://bit.ly/3DPk6DV

Hubbard, G.W. "History of the Colored Schools of Nashville, Tennessee," (pamphlet) Nashville, 1874, Daniel Wadkins, "Origin and Progress Before Emancipation," Tennessee State Library and Archives

McDonald, Emma Hicks, untitled reminiscence, copy in possession of Ridley Wills

National Archives at Washington, D.C.; U.S., Southern Claims Commission, Disallowed and Barred Claims, 1871-1880, Records of the U.S. House of Representatives, 1789 – 2015; Record Group Number: 233; Series

Number: M1407[database on-line]. (15272) Ancestry.com

National Archives, Registers of Signatures of
Depositors in Branches of the Freedman's Savings and Trust Company, 1865-1874; Record Group:
Records of the Office of the Comptroller of the Currency; Record Group Number: 101; Series
Number: M816; NARA Roll: 25

Sheppard, Ella, "Before Emancipation," Fisk Library, Special Collections file:///C:/Users/Paul/
Downloads/Ella%20Sheppard_Before%20Emancipation.pdf

Sheppard, Ella, "Negro Womanhood, Its Past," Fisk Library, Special Collections

Singleton, Benjamin "Pap" – Senate testimony https://bit.ly/3oR2Nyn

Mechal Sobel, "They Can Never Prosper Together, Black and White Baptists in Antebellum Nashville,
Tennessee" Tennessee Historical Quarterly, Volume 38 #3 (296-307)

The Journal of Negro History, Vol. 5, No.1, (January, 1920), "Some Negro Members of the Tennessee
Legislature During the Reconstruction Period and After" by J. C. Napier
http://www.gutenberg.org/files/23200/23200-h/23200-h.htm

The Journal of Southern History, Vol. 71, No.2 (May, 2005), Atkins, Jonathan M., "Party Politics and
the Debate over the Tennessee Free Negro Bill, 1859-1860"

Endnotes

While some quoted accounts have been edited for clarity and readability, no details have been added to the information being communicated by the narrator. Images without a clearly identified source, but which are readily available on the internet after a search by the name of a place or an individual, have not been included in these endnotes.

Slaves on the Cumberland Frontier

Image – *Twilight in the Wilderness*, oil painting by Frederic Edwin Church (1860), Cleveland Museum of Art

Jamie, details of – Williams, Samuel Cole, Early Travels in the Tennessee Country, 1540-1800, 104-07, Johnson City, Tennessee (1928)

Cornelius, identified as slave of Robertson – Tennessee State Library and Archives (TSLA), in the Haywood Papers (folder 5, app. 1, doc. 2; fol. 6, doc. 1) is a document with a torn page in which the name of Cornelius is included, but his owner's name is missing. Although Cornelius is not named by Judge John Haywood in his Civil and Political History of Tennessee (95), he refers to the unidentified individual as "A negro fellow… afterward killed at Freeland's Station… when Major Lucas was killed," and in the Draper Papers (TSLA, 6 XX, 50 Sheet 13) there is an account of the attack on Freeland's which includes "…Robertson's negro man was … shot down as he came to the door…" Taken together, these sources indicate that Cornelius was owned by Robertson.

Cornelius, accompanies Robertson in 1779 – Haywood, John, Civil and Political History of Tennessee (95)

Col. Donelson, river journey – Clements, Paul, Chronicles of the Cumberland Settlements, 132-39

("Negro man… being much frosted…") – Col. John Donelson (1780), Donelson Fee Book, TSLA, microfilm # 122

Stewart party, attack on – John Donelson, Jr. and Mary Donelson, Haywood Papers, folder 2 TSLA

("Hagar…") – V. B. McFerrin, South-Western Christian Advocate (1843) TSLA

Aunt Aliph and Aunt Sue, details – L. C. Bell, History of the Dickinson Road, 28, Robert Cartwright Chapter, DAR (1936)

Red River party, attacked – Draper Papers, 12C: 54, 30S: 247, 32S: 317, 32S: 345-46, 6XX63: 10, Haywood Papers, folder 5 TSLA

("fought with distinguished…") – Draper Papers, 30S: 247

("a negro fellow…") – Draper Papers, 8J: 122

Jack Civil ("a bright mulatto…") – Draper Papers, 32S: 308-09

("There was a dead Negro…") – Haywood Papers, folder 4

Somerset, details ("Col. Donelson's servant...") – Putnam, A. W. History of Middle Tennessee, 627-28

Cornelius, death – Haywood, Civil and Political History of Tennessee (95), Haywood Papers (folder 5, app. 1, doc. 2; fol. 6, doc. 1), Draper Papers (TSLA, 6 XX, 50 Sheet 13)

David Goin, death/race – Haywood Papers, folders 5-6, Putnam, 127, South Carolina Magazine of Ancestral Research, Vol. 16, #3 (Summer, 1988)

Peter Barnett, death – Draper Papers 30S, 233-35

Molly Jones ("was scalped in the field...") – Draper Papers 32S: 486, Hall, William Early History of the Southwest, 37, The Mail (Philadelphia), 10/4/1792(2)

Slave killed near Holly Tree Gap – Nashville Banner, 12/10/1884

Robert Renfroe, survivor of massacre – Draper Papers 32S: 345-46

Robert Renfroe, role after Coldwater Campaign – Draper Papers 1S: 91-2

Abraham Bledsoe ("a mulatto fellow...") – Hall, Early History of the Southwest, 21-6

Abraham Bledsoe ("very brave...") – Ibid, 26-8

Abraham Bledsoe, Greenfield Station –Ibid, 21-6

Abraham Bledsoe ("Abraham was passing...") – Hall, William Early History of the Southwest, 26-8

Abraham Bledsoe ("On one occasion...") – Nashville Banner 5/1/1897

The Amos Dresser Affair

The Narrative of Amos Dresser... by Amos Dresser, New York, published by the American Anti-Slavery Society, 1836, p. 3-15. A few errors by Dresser have been corrected. He placed his time in Nashville in the month of July, but both the Union and the National Banner & Nashville Whig ran detailed articles on August 10, 1835 (both on page 3), that clearly establish the events took place in August – not July. Dresser also spells the name of John Broughton, the town constable (see the National Banner & Nashville Whig, 3/7/1836 p. 2), as "Braughton." The individual identified as Stout was S. V. D. Stout, a fifty-eight-year-old carriage maker born in Pennsylvania, and an elder in the First Presbyterian Church. The man identified as "Hunt" was W. Hassell Hunt (also known as W. H. Hunt), a local newspaper editor born in Massachusetts. It should be noted that some members of "the Committee" opposed the whipping. Although they were in the minority, particularly when the mob was calling for Dresser's death, their presence may well have prevented Dresser's hanging (see National Banner & Nashville Whig, 11/16/1835(2). They are named in the National Banner & Nashville Whig, 8/24/1835(3), as well as in the Dresser Narrative (see https://www.loc.gov/resource/rbaapc.08010/?sp=1). This narrative was edited for length and clarity.

Amos Dresser, image of whipping – Ibid

Frank Parrish

"Bathing House" image – Nashville Union 2/28/1837(1)

Frank Parrish, birth – Nashville City Cemetery records, Frank Parrish died 1867 at age 63, http://www.thenashvillecitycemetery.org/aa-I.html

Frank Parrish, son of Clara – 1850 Census, Davidson County, Roll 875, Page 305b; City Cemetery records, "Cleracy Parrish, mother of Frank Parrish, May 10, 1856, age 69," http://www.thenashvillecitycemetery.org/aa-I.html

Frank Parrish, son of Joel Parrish – Loren Schweninger, From Tennessee Slave to St. Louis Entrepreneur: the Autobiography of James Thomas, University of Missouri, 1984, 91

Frank Parrish, raised in Parrish home – Williamson County Archives, Probate Records, "Joel Parrish" see 1840 petition of Susannah Parrish

Frank Parrish, death of father – Schweninger, 91

Frank Parrish, relationship with Susannah Parrish – Ibid

James Thomas, son of John Catron – Schweninger, 2

James Thomas, quote ("Frank's father…") – Schweninger, 91

Frank Parrish, 1829 marriage – Metro Archives Marriages, Francis Parrish/Fanny Dismukes (11/26/1829)

Fanny Dismukes, owned by Shall – Sue Smith, *Davidson County, Tennessee, Deed Books T & W* (1829-1835), 284;

Metro Archives Marriages, Francis Parrish/Fanny Dismukes (11/26/1829 – Shall signed bond)

Frank Parrish, description as pressman – Union & American 6/1/1867(3)

Frank Parrish, height – Schweninger, 91

Frank Parrish, complexion/hair – Tennessee State Library & Archives, Supreme Court Case: "Priscilla Harding vs Edwin H. Ewing, Frank Parrish, et al" (1858)

Frank Parrish, shops in Nashville/New Orleans – G. W. Hubbard, *History of the Colored Schools of Nashville, Tennessee*, (pamphlet) Nashville, 1874, Daniel Wadkins, "Origin and Progress Before Emancipation"

Alonso Sumner, details – Ibid

Frank Parrish, shop on Deaderick St. – Republican Banner 9/11/1837(4)

John Catron, opinion of free blacks – National Banner & Daily Advertiser 4/1/1834(2)

Frank Parrish, 1837 ad – Republican Banner 6/3/1837(1)

Frank Parrish, business details – Tri-Weekly Nashville Union 4/25/1837(1)

Frank Parrish, ("The most conspicuous…") – Schweninger, 91

Frank Parrish, household in 1840 – 1840 Census, Davidson County, Roll 520, Page 276

James Thomas, quote ("When they about got…") – Schweninger, 91

Susannah Parrish, petition/will – Williamson County Archives, Probate Records, "Joel Parrish"

James Thomas quote, ("Mr. Ewing and Frank…") – Schweninger, 92

Frank Parrish, 1838 ad – Republican Banner 8/6/1838(3)

Frank Parrish, barkeeper of the Nashville – Schweninger, 107

Fanny Parrish, death – Republican Banner 1/7/1846(3), Nashville City Cemetery records, "Mrs. Parrish, wife of Frank Parrish" (1/6/1846) http://www.thenashvillecitycemetery.org/aa-I.html

Frank Parrish, household in 1850 – 1850 Census, Davidson County, Roll 875, Page 305b

Frank Parrish, trip with Ewing – Union & American 2/13/1856(3), 6/1/1867(3)

Frank Parrish, ("In 1851…") – Schweninger, 92

Frank Parrish, wounded in Egypt – Union & American 2/13/1856(3)

Frank Parrish, relics from trip – Ibid

Sarah Jane Harding, unstated relationship to David Morris Harding – Schweninger, 97

Frank Parrish/Sarah Jane Harding, petitions – Tennessee State Library & Archives, Supreme Court Case: "Priscilla Harding vs Edwin H. Ewing, Frank Parrish, et al" (1858)

Frank Parrish, marries Sarah Jane Parrish – Metro Archives marriage records, Parrish/Harding (6/18/1853)

Frank Parrish, ("In connection…") – Republican Banner 4/2/1856(2)

Frank Parrish, loss of shop in 1856 fire – Republican Banner 4/15/1856(2)

Frank Parrish, death of mother – City Cemetery records, "Cleracy Parrish, mother of Frank Parrish, May 10, 1856, age 69

Frank Parrish, attacked by dog – Schweninger, 202

Frank Parrish, death of Sarah Jane – Ibid, tombstone inscription (9/30/1832 – 9/23/1856) https://www.findagrave.com/memorial/58069181/sarah-jane-parish (see page 36 of this work)

Frank Parrish, ("Frank Parrish, the most…") – Republican Banner 12/28/1856(3)

Frank Parrish, musician, ("Yesterday was a fine day…") – Memphis Daily Avalanche 5/6/1859(3)

Richard H. Barksdale, details – Jonathan M. Atkins, "Party Politics and the Debate over the Tennessee

Free Negro Bill, 1859-1860," The Journal of Southern History, Vol. 71, No. 2 (May, 2005), pp. 245-278

John Catron, ("The bill before…") – Union & American 12/8/1859(2)

William B. Ewing, ("Mr. Barksdale says…") – Republican Banner 12/21/1859(2), "Free Negroes"

"Harding's servants," court case – "Priscilla Harding vs Edwin H. Ewing, Frank Parrish, et al"

Frank Parrish, property owner – Registers Office/Davidson County book 33/page 369, 35/309

Frank Parrish, slave owner – 1860 Slave schedule, Series # M653, Record Group 29, wards 1-4, (24)

Free Negro bill, details – Atkins, 253-54

Frank Parrish, marriage to Priscilla/1860 household – 1860 Census, Davidson County, District 10, page 170

Frank Parrish, ornithologist – Republican Banner & Nashville Whig, 7/28/1860(3)

Frank Parrish ("Parish"), investigates uprising – Republican Banner 10/17/1866 (3)

Frank Parrish, death ("By his correct…") – Union & American 6/1/1867(3)

1867 streetcar petition/pre-funeral conflict – Union and Dispatch 6/4/1867 (3)

Edwin H. Ewing, death – Schweninger, 77

James Thomas, death – Schweninger, 1

Priscilla and Fanny Harding

Sarah Jane Parrish gravestone photograph – by Nick Fielder, State Archaeologist, taken March, 2003

Cemetery removal, details – The author was present at the removal, which took place March 26 and 27, 2003

Early Harding residence photograph – taken by author, August, 2021

Giles Harding, 1798 land purchase – Davidson County Register of Deed, Book E (57)

Giles Harding, petition signed – Tennessee State Library and Archives, Legislative Petitions, Reel 1, (144-1833-1)

Giles Harding, death – Davidson County Registers Office, Will Book 4 (105) – recorded 8/21/1810

(David) Morris Harding, inherits farm – Ibid Book O (145)

Morris Harding, 1816 marriage – Edythe Ricker Whitely, *Marriages of Davidson County, Tennessee, 1789-1837* (38)

Fanny Davis (Harding), age – according to private family genealogy records, Fanny was born 8/17/1801

Fanny Davis (Harding), family – Ibid

John Davis, biographical details – William Wales, "A Plea for the Men of the Past," South-Western Monthly, Volume 1 (131), Volume 2 (141, 265), Republican Banner 7/18/1853

Priscilla Harding, birthplace/year of birth/description – Xenia (Ohio) Gazette March, 1877 ("Life and Death of Mrs. Priscilla Harding"), Brown, Hallie Q. *Pen Pictures of Pioneers of Wilberforce*, Aldine Publishing Company, Xenia, Ohio, 1937, 35

Priscilla Harding, sister of Mary Ball – 1880 Census, Greene County Ohio, George Harding, son of Priscilla, living with Mary "Harding," who is identified as his aunt.

Morris/Priscilla Harding, no children – Loren Schweninger, *From Tennessee Slave to St. Louis Entrepreneur: the Autobiography of James Thomas*, University of Missouri, 1984, 97

Priscilla Harding, children fathered by Morris – Emma Hicks McDonald reminiscence, ("Among Aunt Fanny's negroes who had been slaves there were several half white children of Morris Harding, to whom Aunt Fanny had made him give half his property.") Mildred Hicks Henegar interview by author, 1986. Given the unusual mortality that would be experienced by the ten children of Priscilla and David Morris Harding – she would outlive all but one, and only two would survive to thirty –

it seems reasonable to consider the possibility that an overly-close kinship could have brought about genetic consequences.

James Thomas, ("One gentleman…") – Schweninger, 97

Fanny/Priscilla Harding, close relationship – Davidson County Registers Office Book 30, p 63 While there is no description of their relationship, this document, along with the wills of Jefferson and Fanny Priscilla, and the reminiscence of Emma Hicks McDonald, strongly suggest that the connection they had was unusually close. And all those indications of trust came in the wake a half-century in which Priscilla, with the full knowledge of Fanny, bore ten children that were fathered by Fanny's husband.

Morris Harding, slave trader – TSLA, unprocessed manuscript collection, Harding bills of sale, slave purchases

Runaway ad image, Morris Harding purchases Sam/John – Nashville Whig 9/4/1822(1)

Harding farm, acreage – Davidson County, Chancery Court case file ("Priscilla and others vs Edwin H. Ewing, Trustee, and others")

1828 runaway ad, image – National Banner & Nashville Whig 4/26/1828(4)

Harding residences, details – Information from author. Both of the early Harding homes continue to stand on what is now the campus of Ensworth High School. The later building is now used for offices, while the older structure is yet to be utilized.

Free Negroes, on place in 1820 – 1820 Census, Davidson County, entry for "David M. Harding"

Jefferson Harding, approximate year of birth – Chancery Court case file ("Priscilla…") Answer of Ewing

Jefferson Harding ("In 1844…") – Chancery Court case file ("Priscilla…") Bill of Complaint (5)

Morris Harding, petitions for Sarah Jane's emancipation – Chancery Court case file ("Priscilla…") "Jane Parrish – Free Papers"

Sarah Jane Harding, age/description – Ibid

Harding estate, value – Ibid, account presented by Ewing to Clerk and Master on 5/17/1859 (5) "The whole fund for distribution among beneficiaries under the trust is $38,340.27"

Frank Parrish, age/description – Ibid "Jane Parrish – Free Papers"

Sarah Jane Harding/Frank Parrish, petition to remain in Tennessee – Ibid "Transcript of Jane Parrish's Emancipation Papers, Exhibit C and D"

Edwin H. Ewing, details – W. W. Clayton, *History of Davidson County, Tennessee*, (121-22)

Fanny Harding, insistence that children be freed – Emma Hicks McDonald reminiscence, ("…there were several half white children of Morris Harding, to whom Aunt Fanny had made him give half his property.")

Morris Harding, will ("I do hereby…") – Davidson County Will Book 16 (427)

Fanny Priscilla Harding, name omitted – Chancery Court case file ("Priscilla…") Answer of Ewing; Bill of Complaint (5)

Free Negroes, political climate in late 1850s – Jonathan M. Atkins, "Party Politics and the Debate over the Tennessee Free Negro Bill, 1859-1860," The Journal of Southern History, Vol. 71, No. 2 (May, 2005), 245-278, Union & American 12/8/1859(2), Republican Banner 12/21/1859(2)

Morris Harding, codicil ("I authorize…") – Davidson County Will Book 16 (427)

Priscilla Harding, deaths of children – Chancery Court case file ("Priscilla…") Answer of Ewing; Bill of Complaint (5)

Harding slaves, division – Ibid "Will, Inventory and Sale – Estate David M. Harding"

Peter, sold after becoming unruly – Ibid Answer of Ewing

Fanny Harding, keeping families together – Davidson County Will Book 16 (517) lists the individuals involved in the division of the Harding slaves, and with adult females followed by children of the appropriate age, it is clear they were grouped as families, and that those families were kept together.

John O. Ewing, buys land – Davidson County Will Book 16 (517-18)

Fanny Harding, repurchase of 715 acres – Registers Office, Book 16 ((517-18)

Morris Harding, legality of will – Chancery Court case file ("Priscilla…") Answer of Ewing (7)

Morris Harding, will/Supreme Court case, involving legality its stipulations – Republican Banner 12/21/1859(2), "Free Negroes"

Harding estate, value – Chancery Court case file ("Priscilla…")

Priscilla Harding, move to Ohio in 1858 – Chancery Court case file ("Priscilla…") Answer of Ewing (6)

Wilberforce University, image – Carter G. Woodson, *The History of the Negro Church*, 202

James C. Napier ("We traveled to Ohio…") – Tennessean 7/4/1937(Magazine – 2) "An Old Colored Man" by Helen Dahnke

Priscilla Harding ("Mrs. Priscilla Harding…bank account") – Brown, Hallie Q. *Pen Pictures of Pioneers of Wilberforce*, Aldine Publishing Company, Xenia, Ohio, 1937, 34-5

Priscilla Harding, gives Fanny Harding power of attorney – Davidson County Registers Office Book 30, p 63

Priscilla Harding, death of children ("Mrs. Priscilla…one child") – Xenia Gazette March, 1877 ("Life and Death of Mrs. Priscilla Harding")

Jefferson Harding, marriage – Greene County Marriage Records 2/15/1859

Jefferson Harding, attends Wilberforce/classmates – Wilberforce University 1860 Catalogue, https://bit.ly/31U38aK

Jefferson Harding, will – Davidson County Will Book 18 (451)

Jefferson Harding, codicil – the codicil reads, "I give to Mrs. Fanny P. Harding my negro woman slave, Emma, who is now in the possession of Mrs. Harding." It seems very likely that his intent was for Emma to be inherited by his former mistress, Mrs. Fanny Harding. At that time his sister, Fanny P., was fifteen or sixteen and unmarried, and she would not have been referred to as "Mrs. Harding."

Jefferson Harding, death – Davidson County Will Book 18 (451)

Spotswood Harding, marriage to Emma Seay – Sistler, Byron/Barbara, *Davidson County Tennessee Marriages, 1838-1863*, 97

Fanny Priscilla Harding, death/attends Wilberforce – Xenia Torchlight 4/23/1862

Fanny Priscilla Harding, will – Greene County, Ohio, Will Book K (306), Probate Court – Estate of George W. Harding, copy of will included in file

Fanny Harding, on farm during Civil War – Henegar interview

Fanny Harding, will – Davidson County Will Book 20, 96 ("F. G. Harding")

Fanny Harding, death – Ibid

Priscilla Harding, in Xenia/household in 1870 – 1870 Census, Greene County, Ohio

Priscilla Harding, death ("Her life…") – Xenia Gazette March, 1877 ("Life and Death of Mrs. Priscilla Harding")

George Harding, children – Greene County, Ohio, Probate Court – Estate of George W. Harding, "Application of Letters Testamentary" lists children

("Among Aunt Fanny's Negroes…") – Emma Hicks McDonald reminiscence

Cemetery removal/exhumation details – On March 26 and 27, 2003, despite considerable lobbying to keep the cemetery where it was, the work of removal took place. The author was present and observed the scattered pieces of blue silk on the site of one of the graves. While they cannot be proven with certainty to be from the burial dress of Mary Ball, they came from where it is assumed she was buried, and Emma Hicks McDonald mentioned her silk dress in her account. The author also observed the opening of Sarah Jane Parrish's iron coffin. Because her grave was marked, there is no question as to the identity of the remains, which were described as they appeared.

John McCline

Note – The length of this account has been substantially shortened to conform to the purposes of this book. The full text is well worth reading. And while no details have been added, this account has been edited for purposes of clarity and readability.

John McCline, photograph with hoe – Collection of New Mexico State University, (referred to at https://www.easttnhistory.org/exhibits/common-people-uncommon-times)

Herbert Hagerman, details ("In 1934…") – Furman, Jan, *Slavery in the Clover Bottoms: John McCline's Narrative of His Life During Slavery and the Civil War*, Knoxville: University of Tennessee Press, 1998, 8-9

("I, John McCline…") – Furman 20

("The four boys…") – Ibid

("Grandmother was doubtless…") – Ibid 47

("My father, John McCline…") – Ibid 20, 34

("Dr. John Hoggatt…") – Ibid 11 While McCline related that Hoggatt's Clover Bottom property consisted of 2000 acres, it was closer to 1700 acres.

Hoggatt family, details – Paul Clements, *A Past Remembered*, Clearview Press (1987), 192-93

John Hoggatt, 1797 land purchase – E 329, 336

Dr. James W. Hoggatt, details – Hoggatt Cemetery (see *Donelson Tennessee: Its History and Landmarks*, by Lenora Aiken, 76; https://www.findagrave.com/memorial/31374421/james-w-hoggatt)

Dr. Hoggatt, household in 1850 – 1850 US Census, Davidson County, District 2, page 224, family 749

("Mrs. Hoggatt…") – Furman 13

("The Doctor's chief hobby…") – Ibid 16

James Anderson, details – Ibid

("There were many superstitions…") – Furman 39

Wyatt, bought from Clopton – Davidson County Registers Office, Book P-243 (1/4/1825)

("The children stood…") – Furman 39

("Wyatt's duties…") – Ibid 18, 39

("500 hogs…") – Ibid 16-17

('During the summer months…") – Ibid 18-19

("The first thing she would do…") – Ibid 18

("There was a large two-story…") – Ibid 17

("In those days the method…") – Ibid 21-22

("In the spring of 1858…") – Ibid 17

("Until the coming of Phillips…") – Ibid 19

("When Phillips came…") – Ibid 22

("Along in August…") – Furman 39

("The entire week…") – Ibid 24

("Fire was discovered…") – Ibid 25-6

("News of John Brown…") – Ibid 26

("Early in May…") – Ibid 21

("The churning was done…") – Ibid 23

("One morning while I was working…") – Ibid

("Late one rainy night…") – Ibid 28

("Many changes were made…") – Ibid 28

Sydnor Zuccarello, details – 1857 Nashville City Directory, 227

("At the time of his death…") – Furman 31-2

("During the time…") – Ibid 30

("Dr. Hoggatt intended…") – Ibid 38

("In January, 1861…") – Ibid 39

("One clear cold day…") – Ibid 51

John McCline, with the 13th Michigan – Ibid 51-105

John McCline, postwar details – Ibid 106-112

John McCline, hotel porter in 1870 – 1870 US Census, Van Buren County, Michigan, Paw Paw Village, 31, entry 23 ("John Kline")

("I felt a desire…") – Ibid 109

Former Hoggatt slaves, 1870 details – 1870 US Census, Davidson County, District 2, pages 29-31

("During the years he had been…") – Ibid 110

John McCline, after leaving Nashville – Ibid 111-12

John McCline, first marriage – Furman 8; Marriage records, St. Joseph Michigan (9/8/1874), "John Kline" to Hattie Moffitt

John McCline, church custodian – Albuquerque Journal 1/20/1948(7)

John McCline, baseball fan/gardener – Furman 8

John McCline, writing manuscript – Ibid xxiv-xxv

Mary Ann Hoggatt, death – Nashville American 4/29/1887(4), 5/1/1887

Richard S. Phillips, death/details of life/photograph – Nashville Banner 7/6/1914(10)

Richard S. Phillips, image – https://bit.ly/31ODvrY

John McCline, photograph in suit – Furman, xxv

John McCline, second marriage – Santa Fe New Mexican 8/31/1990(11)

John McCline, Republican Party involvement – Santa Fe New Mexican 9/25/1944(1)

John McCline, ("A fine human being…") – Ibid, 1/21/1948(4)

Peter and Samuel Lowery

Emancipation Petition of Peter Lowery – Tennessee State Library and Archives, 1837 petition

Peter Lowery, place/year of birth – 1850 – 1880 Censuses, Davidson County, Tn.

Jane Lowery, mother of Peter – 1850 Census, Davidson County, District 2, Roll 875, Page 229a

Peter Lowery, owned by William H. Hamer – Registers Office Davidson County, Deed Book W-569

Hamer/Lowery families in Anson County – Anson Co. Minute Book, 1771-1777, p 51, etc. (Hamer), Petitions, 1770-1789 (Lowery)

Peter Lowery (names of whites), details – Anson Co. Will Book "A" page 47

Jane/Peter Lowery, complexions – 1850 Census, Davidson County, District 2, Roll 875, Page 229a

Hamer family, leaves North Carolina – Williamson County Deed Book C 344 (1811) (James Davis to Daniel Hamer)

Peter Lowery, lived 12 miles from Nashville – Mitchell, p. 144

Peter Lowery, marriage to Ruth Mitchell (Cherokee) – Rev. William J. Simmons, *Men of Mark: Eminent, Progressive and Rising*, Cleveland, 1887, p. 144

Samuel Lowery, birth – 1850 Census, Davidson County, District 2, Roll 875, Page 229a; 1900 Census, Jefferson Co., Alabama, Precinct 25, Page 11, Enumeration District 0110

William H. Hamer, death – https://www.ancestry.com/family-tree/person/tree/165660523/person/212151570052/facts (Martin Family Tree)

Peter Lowery, sold by Hamer children –Davidson County Deed Book W-569

Samuel Seay image – W.W. Clayton, *History of Davidson County*, 208

Samuel Seay, petition – Emancipation petition https://www.ancestry.com/family tree/person/tree/119737886/person/280191551044/facts

Peter Lowery, purchase of mother/siblings – John Mark Hicks, "Three Early African American Leaders Among Nashville Churches of Christ" (https://johnmarkhicks.com/2021/02/28/three-early-african-american-leaders-among-nashville-churches-of-christ/)

Peter Lowery, religious involvement/joining church in 1832 – Union & American 5/28/1870(7), Nashville American 6/19/1880(4), see also Union & American 6/5/1870(3)

Peter/Samuel Lowery, at Franklin College – Mitchell, p. 145, Hicks, "Three Early African American Leaders Among Nashville Churches of Christ"

Ruth Lowery, death – Nashville City Cemetery index, "Jane Lowrey" (4/6/1851)

Peter Lowery/ Lucinda Dotson, marriage – Davidson County marriage records, Book 2, p. 101

Lucinda Lowery, complexion – 1850 Census, Davidson County, District 2, Roll 875, Page 229a

Lucinda Lowery, children – Ibid (Frederick "Lowry" is Frederick Dotson, see 1870 Census), Colored Tennessean 10/14/1865(2) (Caroline)

Peter Lowery, business reputation – Daily Press & Times 4/4/1868

Peter Lowery, real estate purchases – Davidson County Registers Office deeds: 7-201, 9-457, 10-16, 10-210

Peter Lowery, home/household in 1850 – 1850 Census, Davidson County, District 2, Roll 875, Page 229a

Peter Lowery, builder/pastor of church – Daily Press & Times 8/25/1865

Peter Lowery, hack business – 1857 Nashville City Directory, Republican Banner 12/8/1860(3)

Peter Lowery, ice business – Republican Banner 6/12/1856(3)

Peter Lowery, church shut down – Republican Banner 12/5/1856(3)

Peter Lowery, petitions City Council to reopen church – Republican Banner 5/29/1857(3)

Godfrey Fogg, comments – Republican Banner 5/29/1857(3)

Samuel Lowery, early biographical details – Mitchell, p. 144-5

Samuel Lowery image – Ibid 144

Peter Lowery, 1860 real estate value – 1860 Census, Davidson Co. Nashville, Ward 4, Page 388

Peter Lowery, 1860 slave ownership – 1860 Census, Slave Schedule, Davidson Co., Nashville wards 1-4, p. 19

Caroline Dotson, details of sale – Colored Tennessean 10/14/1865(2) ("Information Wanted")

Caroline Dotson, return to Nashville – 1870 Census, Davidson Co., District 13, Roll M593_1521, Page 429A ("Caroline Daniels")

Samuel Lowery, family returns to Nashville – Mitchell, p. 145

Samuel Lowery, 1865 newspaper notice – Daily Press & Times 8/25/1865

Peter/Samuel Lowery, helping to quell rumor – Union & American 10/17/1866(3)

Secretary of State, 1866 letter – Republican Banner 10/16/1866(3)

Newspaper article ("Nashville has for a long time…") – Union & American 10/5/1866(3)

Newspaper article ("About a week ago…") – Memphis Daily Post 10/18/1866(1) – account from Nashville Union & Dispatch, (also see Republican Banner 10/20/1866(2) for a defense of Cheatham and Beach)

Samuel Lowery, resolution – Union & American 10/17/1866(3)

Cheatham/Beach, meet with black leaders – Memphis Daily Post 1/10/1868(1) (report of General Thomas)

Freedmen's Bureau, involvement – Ibid

Minors return to Nashville – Republican Banner 11/21/1866(3)

Number of blacks in Nashville following war – Daily Press & Times 8/12/1865

Article ("In 1866…") – American 9/9/1880(4)

Article ("Reverend Peter Lowery…") – Union & Dispatch 3/28/1867

Tennessee Manual Labor University (TMLU), location – Union & American 3/6/1869(4)

Article ("I see my name…") – Union & Dispatch 4/30/1867

Peter Lowery, list of early donors to TMLU – Republican Banner 4/2/1867(4)

TMLU, officers/appeal – Union & American 11/2/1867(3)

419

TMLU, lack of support from white Christian Church – Dr. Bobby L. Lovett, *The African-American History of Nashville, Tennessee, 1780-1930*, University of Arkansas Press, 1990, p. 145-7

TMLU, students in early 1868 – Union & American 3/11/1868(3)

Peter Lowery, hiring of Daniel Watkins – Union & American 3/6/1869(4), 5/11/1870(3)

Samuel Lowery, raising money for TMLU/contributions – Republican Banner 11/22/1868(4)

TMLU, charges of impropriety – Union & American 5/11/1870(3)

TMLU, political context – Lovett, p. 145-7

Investigation details – Union & American 5/11/1870(3)

TMLU, indebtedness/appeal – American 7/26/1879(4)

Peter Lowery, 1881 fundraising attempt – American 7/12/1881(3)

Samuel Lowery, 1870 household – 1870 Census, Rutherford Co., Tennessee, District 9, Roll M593_1557, Page: 354A

Samuel Lowery, admitted to Nashville Bar – Public Ledger (Memphis) 12/16/1870(2)

Samuel Lowery, admitted to practice in federal court of Tennessee – Republican Banner 4/29/1871(4)

Samuel lowery, admitted to practice before US Supreme Court – Mitchell, p. 145, Times Union (Brooklyn) 2/3/1880(2)

Samuel Lowery, admitted to practice before US Supreme Court, image – Frank Leslie's Illustrated Newspaper 1880

Samuel Lowery, speech on emigration – Republican Banner 5/20/1875(4)

Theobald, exhibition details – Republican Banner 5/23/1875(4)

Theobald, individual details – Selma Times 2/23/1878(4)

Samuel/Ruth Lowery, Huntsville fair premiums – Times-Picayune (New Orleans) 5/31/1878(8) (from NY Herald)

Ruth Lowery (daughter of Samuel), death – Simmons, p. 146

Samuel Lowery, Huntsville speech at courthouse – Huntsville Weekly 7/18/1877(2)

Samuel Lowery, gets help from Reuben Chapman – Times-Picayune (New Orleans) 5/31/1878(8)

Samuel Lowery, NY Times article – Memphis Evening Herald 6/21/1878(2)

Samuel Lowery, at National Conference of Colored Men – The Daily American 5/8/1879(3), The Weekly Louisianan 5/17/1879(3)

Samuel Lowery, fundraising in New York City – The Sun (NYC) 5/27/1880(4)

Samuel Lowery, Brooklyn speech – Brooklyn Daily Eagle 5/19/1880(2)

Samuel Lowery, attends New Orleans Exposition – Huntsville Independent 9/25/1884(3)

Samuel Lowery, wins Exposition grand prize – Simmons, p. 146-7

Samuel Lowery, article ("My plan is…") – Banner 9/9/1885(2)

Samuel Lowery, forms company/circumstances – Simmons, p. 147-8

Peter Lowery, obituary – the Gospel Advocate Feb 15, 1888(10)

Samuel Lowery, household/occupation in 1900 – 1900 Census, Jefferson Co., Alabama, Precinct 25, Page 11, Enumeration District 0110

Samuel Lowery, death – The Journal (Huntsville) 7/24/1902(2)

Thomas Lowery, death – Deaderick Family Tree, https://bit.ly/3pV1Vrv

Daniel Wadkins

Image, "Celebration of Freedom" – Nashville Union 3/21/1865(3)

Daniel Wadkins, reference to arriving in Tennessee in 1835 – Union & American 9/28/1869(1) note – In the American of 4/27/1887(6) there is mention that Wadkins was the uncle of Dr. Isaiah Tuppins, who had been elected mayor of Rendville, Ohio. The 1870 Census (Xenia, Ohio) revealed the parents of Tuppins as James and Zilpha Tuppins. In tracing the siblings of Dr. Tuppins (having hypothesized that Wadkins could have been the brother of Tuppins' mother), the only death certificate that was located was for Don P. Tuppins, who died in Detroit in 1915, and whose mother's name was Zilpha Sarbon, who was born in Tennessee.

Daniel Wadkins, range of birth years – 1850-1880 Census, Davidson County, 1850-1860 ("Watkins"), 1870-1880 ("Watkins")

Daniel Wadkins, anecdote regarding his father – Nashville Union 3/21/1865(3)

Daniel Wadkins, speaker of Greek – Banner 5/10/1883(1)

Daniel Wadkins, speaker of Latin and Hebrew – Republican Banner 4/11/1871(3)

Daniel Wadkins, tutored by Tolbert Fanning – Napier, Journal of Negro History, Volume 5

Alphonso Sumner ("In March 1833…") – *A History of Colored Schools of Nashville, Tennessee*, editor G.W.Hubbard, Nashville, "Origin and Progress Before Emancipation," by Elder Daniel Wadkins, – Wheeler, Marshall & Bruce (1874), At TSLA, What has been taken from this work has been edited for clarity and flow.

Alphonso Sumner, whipping – Ibid, James Thomas, *From Tennessee Slave to St. Louis Entrepreneur: The Autobiography of James Thomas*, University of Missouri Press, 1984, page 32

Mayor Hollingsworth, proposal for black school – Anita Shafer Goodstein, *Nashville 1780 – 1860: Frontier to City*, University of Florida Press, 1989 (151)

Daniel Wadkins, ("There were no more schools…") – Wadkins

J.C. Napier, account of Sallie Player – The Journal of Negro History, Volume 5, number 1, "Some Negro Members of the Tennessee Legislature During Reconstruction Period and After" by J. C. Napier, pages 113-118

James Player, husband of Sallie – 1870 US Census, Davidson County, Nashville Ward 4, Roll M593_1523, Page 254A

Thompson Player, information – 1850 US Census, Davidson County, Roll: 875, Page 299b

Emma Player, daughter of Thomas Yeatman – Miss Jane Thomas, *Old Days in Nashville*, Charles Elder, Bookseller, page 25-6

J.C. Napier, information of Wadkins at Franklin College – Napier, Journal of Negro History, Volume 5

Daniel Wadkins, information re Mrs. A. L. Tate – Wadkins

Daniel Wadkins, marriage to Eliza – 1850 US Census, Davidson County, Roll: 875, Page 145a

Eliza Wadkins, details of – Ibid

Daniel Wadkins, described as "school teacher" – Ibid

Daniel Wadkins ("During 1841…") – Wadkins

J.C. Napier, description of Wadkins' school – Napier, Journal of Negro History, Volume 5

Daniel Wadkins ("In 1855…") – Wadkins

1856 Slave Insurrection, details ("Considerable…") – Republican Banner 11/27/1856(3)

1856 Slave Insurrection, ("A Negro man…") – Republican Banner 12/7/1856(3)

1856 Slave Insurrection, City Council bill – Republican Banner 12/5/1856(3)

1856 Slave Insurrection, ("Yesterday…") – Nashville Gazette 12/4/1856

1856 Slave Insurrection, ("A young man…") – Republican Banner 12/12/1856(2)

1856 Slave Insurrection, ("Thursday evening…") – Gazette 12/5/1856

1856 Slave Insurrection, report from Stewart County – Gazette 12/19/1856

1856 Slave Insurrection, report from Gallatin – Gazette 12/21/1856

Daniel Wadkins, household in 1860 – 1860 US Census, Davidson County, Nashville, Ward 4, page 383

Daniel Wadkins, birth of last child – 1870 US Census, Davidson County, Nashville, Ward 4, Roll M593_1523, Page 257A

Daniel Wadkins ("In the fall of 1862…") – Wadkins

Daniel Wadkins, conflict with Merry and McKee – Crystal A. deGregory, *Raising a Nonviolent Army: Four Nashville Black Colleges and the Century-Long Struggle for Civil Rights, 1830s-1930s*, pages 18-19

Daniel Wadkins, described by Ella Sheppard – "Before Emancipation," Fisk University, John Hope and Aurelia Franklin Library, Special Collections, Fisk Jubilee Singers Archives, Box 6, folder 2, p 7-8

Daniel Wadkins, details of teaching during 1850s – Wadkins

Daniel Wadkins, resumes teaching in 1862 – Ibid

Daniel Wadkins, location of school on High Street – Republican Banner 4/7/1868(4)

Daniel Wadkins (Jr.), work on Fort Negley, enlistment – The National Archives, Washington, D.C., Compiled Service Records of Volunteer Union Soldiers Who Served with the United States Colored Troops, Infantry Organizations, 8th through 13th, Microfilm Serial M1821, Microfilm Roll 107

Daniel Wadkins, account of Emancipation celebration – Nashville Union 3/21/1865(3)

Fisk School, opening – Union & American 7/30/1867(3)

Daniel Wadkins, elected to City Council – Union & American 10/2/1867(3), Daily Press & Times 3/24/1868

Daniel Wadkins, candidate for county register – Union & American 2/21/1868(3), 3/13/1868(3)

Daniel Wadkins, involvement with Manual Labor School – Pittsburgh Weekly Gazette 5/5/1869(3), Union & American 9/28/1869(1), Republican Banner 5/7/1870(4), Union & American 6/5/1870(3)

Daniel Wadkins, opposes emigration of blacks – Union & American 9/28/1869(1)

Daniel Wadkins, defends legislature – Republican Banner 11/12/1869(4)

Tolbert Fanning, remarks about blacks – Union & American 4/2/1871(1) note – Despite his end-of-life opinions, earlier in his life Fanning had been a positive force in the lives of other black men, including Samuel Lowery, Rufus Conrad, and future congressman, James T. Rapier

Daniel Wadkins, response to Fanning – Republican Banner 4/11/1871(3)

Daniel Wadkins, publishes pamphlet – Republican Banner 9/24/1871(4)

Daniel Wadkins, details from pamphlet – Union & American 1/20/1872(4)

Daniel Wadkins, activities in Memphis – Republican Banner 2/8/1873(4)

Daniel Wadkins, theological activities in the 1870s – John Mark Hicks, "Three Early African American Leaders Among Nashville Churches of Christ" https://johnmarkhicks.com/2021/02/28/three-early-african-american-leaders-among-nashville-churches-of-christ/

Daniel Wadkins, publishes Educator and Reformer – Morristown (Tn) Gazette 8/13/1879(2), American 4/7/1880(1)

Daniel Wadkins, appointed prison chaplain – American 3/25/1881(4)

Daniel Wadkins, referred to as deceased – American 4/17/1883(2)

Daniel Wadkins, death – American 5/11/1883(4)

Daniel Wadkins, funeral details – Banner 5/10/1883(4)

Randall Bartholomew Vandavell

The narrative of Rev. Vandavell was changed to a first person treatment from the third person account that appeared in *Men of Mark: Eminent, Progressive and Rising*, by Rev. William J. Simmons, and has been edited for clarity.

Vandavell image – Rev. William J. Simmons, *Men of Mark: Eminent, Progressive and Rising*, Cleveland (1887) 576

Rev. Vandavell, spelling of surname – There are numerous alternate spellings of Reverend Vandavell's last name. He took his name from a former owner, John Vanderville, and the school he founded was called Vandavill School, and his surname is given as "Vandervall" in the book by Rev. Simmons. But the spelling that appears both on his tombstone and in the signature of his daughter, Maggie, in the records (#5517) of the Freedman's Bank is Vandavell.

Rev. Vandavell, funeral account – Daily American 1/4/1899(3)

Rev. Vandavell, autobiographical account – Rev. William J. Simmons, *Men of Mark: Eminent, Progressive and Rising*, Cleveland, 1887, p. 572-578

Rev. Vandavell, possible years of birth – The Simmons book gives Rev. Vandavell's year of birth as 1832, his tombstone inscription says 1823, the 1870 Census lists his age as forty-four, indicating he was born around 1826, the 1880 Census lists him as being fifty, indicating his year of birth as around 1830, and his death record lists him as being seventy at the end of 1898, indicating that he was born in 1828.

Charles Merryman Hall, death – Davidson County Court Minutes, 1824-26, p. 557-8, will of Charles M. Hall Charles Merryman Hall, place of residence – Clarion 9/20/1808(2), Registers Office of Davidson County, Books F 304, F 318, G 126

Charles Merryman Hall, list of slaves – Davidson County Will Book 9, p. 203

Charles Maclin Hall, details – Charles M. Hall (1817-1862) was the son of William Wakefield Hall (1790-1854), and the grandson of Charles Merryman Hall (1748-1826), see https://www.ancestry.com/family-tree/person/tree/156996281/person/332064651902/facts

John Vanderville, owner of Randall – Davidson County Will Book 13, p. 357

John Vanderville, marriage – Edythe Rucker Whitley, *Marriages of Davidson County, Tennessee, 1789-1847* p.67 (John Vanderville to Ann Bryant, 12/22/1821)

John Vanderville, land purchase – RODC R-24, Y-399, 4-87

John Vanderville, livestock/slaves – Davidson County Will Book 13, p. 357

John W. Vanderville, child of John Vanderville – Phillips-Walker Family Tree, Ancestry.com, https://www.ancestry.com/family-tree/person/tree/28047770/person/240068212318/facts?_phsrc=Nsk225&_phstart=successSource

Mrs. Vanderville, sale of Henry – Republican Banner 1/28/1846(2)

Mrs. Vanderville, marriage to Walter O. Carter – Byron and Barbara Sistler, *Davidson County Marriages, 1838-1863*, p. 36 (W. O. Carter to Ann Vanderville, 2//5/1850)

Thomas Jefferson Vanderville, move to Shelby County – Shelby County Marriage Records, 10/19/1858 (to Porter), 1860 Census, Shelby County District 3, Page 266

Rev. Vandavell, probable time of marriage – Later in his narrative Vandavell referred to several deceased children. Eleven-year-old Sarah J. "Vandvil" and eight-year-old Randle "Vandervill" – both of whom were buried in the City Cemetery in 1866 – must have been the children of Randall and Martha. Their ages suggest that they were born around 1855 and 1858. Two other children, Maggie and James M. Vandavell, lived into adulthood. Maggie listed her age as seventeen when she opened an account at the Nashville branch of the Freedmen's Bank in 1873, and according to his marriage record, Dr. James Monroe Vandavell was born in 1859. With four children born before 1860, their marriage probably occurred no later than 1853 or 1854.

Robert L. Bell, identity – Union & American 3/17/1874(4), American 8/11/1877(4)

Nelson Nicholson, details – 1850 Census, Davidson County, Nashville, Roll 875, page 114b; 1860 Census Davidson County, Nashville, Ward 3, Page 363

Rev. Vandavell, establishes church in 1866 – Banner 5/19/1950(36)

Martha Vandavell, birth of last child/residence in 1870 – 1870 Census, Davidson County, District 17, Roll M593_1522, page 46B

Rev. Vandavell, donation of lot – RODC Book 42 -760

"Vandavill" School, involvement of J. C. Napier – Daily American 11/26/1881(4)

"Vandaville" School, description of – Daily American 11/23/1881(4)

Rev. Vandavell, established nine churches/praised by Rev. Whitsett – Banner 1/2/1899(8)

Rev. Vandavell, size of church membership – Simmons, p. 577

Rev. Vandavell, charter of Roger Williams University – Nashville Globe 4/13/1917(1)

Rev. Vandavell, trustee of Roger Williams University – "Catalogue of the officers and students of Roger Williams University, Nashville, Tennessee for the academic year 1884-85, with the courses of study"

Maggie Vandavell, teacher – 1884 Nashville City Directory, p. 582

Dr. James Monroe Vandavell, details – https://www.findagrave.com/memorial/192034778/james-monroe-vandavell

Rev. Vandavell, death – Tennessee State Library and Archives, Tennessee Death Records, 1908-1959, Roll M-4, p. 179 (12/30/1898)

Rev. Vandavell, eulogy – Banner 1/2/1899(8)

Ella Sheppard and the Fisk Jubilee Singers

Ella Sheppard image – G. D. Pike, *The Jubilee Singers, and Their Campaign for Twenty Thousand Dollars*, Boston: Lee and Shepard Publishers (1873), 49

Ella Sheppard, 1865 trip to Nashville – Ibid, 51-2, https://library.si.edu/digital-library/book/storyofjubilees00mars

Ella Sheppard, family owned by Donelsons – Andrew Ward, Dark Midnight When I Rise – *The Story of the Jubilee Singers Who Introduce the World to the Music of Black America*, Farrar, Straus and Giroux, New York (2000), 3-4; Williamson County, Tennessee Archives, Probate Records, Lemuel Donelson, https://www.ancestry.com/imageviewer/collections/1237/images/VDVUSATN1800079000-02235?pId=4973

Ella Sheppard, earlier generations – Ward, 3-4

Ella Sheppard, mother's year of birth – Nashville Globe 8/9/1912(1)

Lemuel Donelson, slave records – Williamson County, Tennessee Archives, Probate Records, Lemuel Donelson, https://www.ancestry.com/imageviewer/collections/1237/images/VDVUSATN1800079000-02235?pId=4973

Emily Donelson Walton, details of Guinea George – Emily Donelson Walton, A*utobiography of Emily Donelson Walton*, Methodist Publishing House, Nashville (1949), 9-10

Ella Sheppard, details of Rosa/Simon – Ward, 3-4

Simon, son of James Glasgow Sheppard – Ibid, 4

Benjamin Harper Sheppard, marriage – District Telegraph and State Sentinel (Jackson, Tn) 8/10/1838(3)

Sheppard family, residence in 1840 – 1840 Census, Tennessee, Williamson County, Roll 537, page 145

Ella Sheppard, combined biographical accounts – The accounts from Ella Sheppard Moore have all been edited for length and clarity. Pike 49-53; "Negro Womanhood: Its Past" and "Before Emancipation," Fisk University, John Hope and Aurelia Franklin Library, Special Collections, Fisk Jubilee Singers Archives, Box 6, folders 1 & 2

Dempsey Weaver, slave woman's murder/suicide – Republican Banner 1/7/1853(3)

Mrs. James K. Polk, suicide/infanticide of slave – "Negro Womanhood" 6, Daily Patriot 11/15/1861(3), Buffalo (NY) Commercial 12/24/1851(2), also see Nashville Gazette 7/23/1857 for murder of three children in Rutherford County, by their mother, a slave of Mrs. Wrather

Phereby Sheppard, birth/death of children – James G. Sheppard Bible, Sheppard Memorial Library, Greenville, NC, https://www.ancestry.com/mediaui-viewer/tree/162806968/person/182118903062/media/b605ec0d-9aa8-4128-9f08-0793ea1fdb5b

Simon Sheppard, partnership with Carroll Napier – Republican Banner 6/13/1854(1), 4/17/1856(4)

Ella Sheppard, ("My father kept a livery stable…") – Pike 50

Ella Sheppard, account of mother in Mississippi – "Before Emancipation," by Ella Sheppard, Fisk University, John Hope and Aurelia Franklin Library, Special Collections, Fisk Jubilee Singers Archives, Box 6, folder 2, pgs 3-5

Ella Sheppard, reunion with mother in 1856/57 – Pike, 51

Ella Sheppard, ("My father had married again…") – Pike, 50

Jacob McGavock, creditor of Simon Sheppard – Nashville Daily Patriot 8/1/1860(1)

Ella Sheppard, ("My father quickly returned…") – Pike, 51

George Leonard White, biographical details – Ward, 13-15

George Leonard Pike, image – Pike 42

Ella Sheppard, ("The first week…") – Pike, 53

George L. White, appointed Fisk treasurer/mentor of Ella – Ward, 77-8/73

Fisk, chartered as university/praised/deteriorating – Ward, 78-9, 82

Ella Sheppard, ("The school was very poor…") – Ward, 79

George White, struggles as treasurer – Ward, 82

George White, has idea for tour – Ward, 116

Ella Sheppard, ("George L. White asked for volunteers…") – Nashville Globe 6/13/1913(1&4), letter of
    Ella Sheppard Moore

Fisk singers, biographical details – Pike, 50-72

Fisk singers, images – Pike, 53-69

Maggie Porter, burning of schoolhouse – Pike, 65; her account is verified by item in Republican Banner
    2/6/1869(4)

Ella Sheppard, recruited by White/quotes from – Pike. 53; Ward, 124

Ella Sheppard, ("Shut out from religious culture…") – "Negro Womanhood," 7

Ella Sheppard, ("Master musicians…") – "Before Emancipation," 6

Ella Sheppard, ("The slave songs were never used…") – Ward, 110

Ella Sheppard, students learning slave songs – Ibid

George White, gathering slave songs – Ibid

Ella Sheppard, learning *Swing Low, Sweet Chariot* from mother – Ibid

Fisk singers, details of departure from Nashville – Ward, 126

Fisk singers, 1904 article ("The trip appeared ill-timed…") – Nashville American, 7/3/1904(17), "Fisk
    Jubilee Hall, How It was Secured" by W. Sheridan Kane

Jubilee Singers, image – photograph (circa 1872) by James Wallace Black, Library of Congress (from
    left, Minnie Tate, Greene Evans, Isaac Dickerson, Jennie Jackson, Maggie Porter, Ella Sheppard,
    Thomas Rutling, Benjamin Holmes, and Eliza Walker)

Ella Sheppard, ("The spiritual life…") – Nashville Globe 6/13/1913(4)

Jubilee Hall, financed by tours – Ward, 165

Ella Sheppard, builds home near Fisk – Ward, 378

Ella Sheppard, details of half-sister – 1880 Census, Tennessee, Davidson Co., Roll 1251, District 13,
Enumeration District 073, Page 204A

Ella Sheppard, 1882 marriage – Ward, 400

George Washington Moore, biographical details – Ward, 400-02

Ella Sheppard, birth of children – Ward, 402-3

Ella Sheppard, promotion of "Negro folk music"/training students – Ward, 403

Ella Sheppard, details of mother's death – Banner 8/6/1912(1)

Ella Sheppard, writings on slavery – "Negro Womanhood: Its Past" and "Before Emancipation," Fisk
    University, John Hope & Aurelia Franklin Library, Special Collections, Fisk Jubilee Singers Archives,
    Box 6, folders 1 & 2

Ella Sheppard, 1914 address – Nashville Tennessean and American 1/19/1914(2)

Ella Sheppard, death – Tennessee State Library and Archives, Tennessee Death Records, 1908-1958,
    Roll 15 (#534), Banner 6/10/1914(11)

Ella Sheppard, funeral at Fisk – Nashville Tennessean and American 6/10/1914(1)

Ella Sheppard, ("If you would know our past…") – "Negro Womanhood: Its Past"

Robert Fulton Boyd

Robert F. Boyd, image – Culp, Dr. D.W., *Twentieth Century Negro Literature, or A Cyclopedia of Thought...* (215)

Robert F. Boyd, birthplace – *Afro-American Encyclopaedia*, Haley, James T., Nashville, 1895 (59)

Boyd, parents – Tn State Library and Archives, Nashville Death Records, 1908-1959, Roll M-16 (#1220)

Edward Boyd, appearance in records – Nashville death certificates of Sallie B. Harwell and Robert F. Boyd, The National Archives, Registers of Signatures of Depositors in Branches of the Freedman's Savings and Trust Company, 1865-1874, Record Group: Records of the Office of the Comptroller of the Currency, Record Group Number 101, Series Number M816, NARA Roll 25, Robert Boyd (#5358)

Edward Boyd, death by 1872 – Ibid

Maria Coffee (Boyd), owned by Rose family – Nashville American 3/2/1897(2)

Maria Coffee (Boyd), details of slave years – Giles County Chancery Court, Box A-1, case file 3 – "Richard B. Allen et al vs William M. Rose et al (1860)

Maria Coffee (Boyd), age at birth of Robert/her birthplace – US Census 1880, Giles County, Pulaski, Roll 1256, Page 125C Enumeration District 105 ("Mariah Crawford")

Coffee/Cockrill, slave ownership, Alabama – US Census, 1850 Slave Schedules, Lauderdale and Franklin Cos.

Maria Coffee (Boyd) (later Maria Crawford), death certificate – Tn State Library and Archives, Nashville Death Records 1908-1958, Roll Number 60, file # 21901

Valeria Cockrill Rose, daughter of John Cockrill (II) – American Historical Magazine Volume 3 (October, 1898), "Cockrill Genealogy" by Graham Goodloe (334)

Maria Coffee (Boyd), identified as mulatto – US Census 1880, Giles County, Pulaski, Roll 1256, Page 125C, Enumeration District 105 ("Mariah Crawford")

John Cockrill (II) sons, ages – "Cockrill Genealogy" (333-334)

John P. Cockrill, in Texas in 1839 – Texas State Library and Archives, U.S. Bonds and Oaths of Office, 1846–1920, Secretary of State Bonds and Oaths of Office (John P. Cockrill)

Cockrill family, traits – National Archives, Confederate Applications for Presidential Pardons, 1865-1867, Case Files –Applications from Former Confederates for Presidential Pardons ("Amnesty Papers") 1865-1867, Records of the Adjutant General's Office, 1780s-1917, for Sterling Cockrill, Record Group 94; Republican Banner 3/30/1856(2) – Sterling Cockrill receives patent; Montgomery (Alabama) Advertiser 6/27/1882(3) "The Cotton Syndicate" re Sterling Cockrill

Robert F. Boyd, in home of Dr. Eve – American 3/2/1897(2)

Sterling Cockrill, neighbor of Dr. Eve – Nashville City Directory 1860

Sterling Cockrill/James Hickman, Mexican War veterans – Banner 3/13/1894(1) article re Hickman death, Index to compiled service records of volunteer soldiers who served during the Mexican War, National Archives microfilm publications, pamphlet accompanying microcopy no. 616 / United States. National Archives and Records Administration (Digital Collection) United States Mexican War index and service records, Collection Record, 1846-1848 (Sterling R. Cockrill, Seibel's Battalion)

Sterling Cockrill, association with Hickman in Nashville – Nashville 1860 City Directory

Sterling Cockrill/Hickman, involvement in slaves/cotton – Cockrill – National Archives, Confederate Applications for Presidential Pardons, 1865-1867, Case Files –Applications from Former Confederates for Presidential Pardons ("Amnesty Papers") 1865-1867, Records of the Adjutant General's Office, 1780s-1917, for Sterling Cockrill, Record Group 94; Hickman – Papers of Andrew Johnson, 1862-64 (346-48), letter of Jere Clemens (9/1863) footnote

Robert F. Boyd, early separation from mother – *Afro-American Encyclopaedia*, (59)

Maria, taking children to Nashville – Ibid

Robert F. Boyd, servant in Eve home – American 3/2/1897(2)

Dr. Paul F. Eve, President of AMA – American Historical Magazine, V 9, October, 1904 (281-342)

Dr. Eve, image – W.W. Clayton, *History of Davidson County,* 280

Dr. Eve, Confederate service – Ibid

Robert F. Boyd, night school at Fisk – Nashville American 3/2/1897(2), Afro-American Encyclopaedia(59)

Boyd, observation of Dr. Eve – American 3/2/1897(2), *Afro-American Encyclopaedia* (56)

Central Tennessee College, image – Ibid 295

Boyd, 1868 return to Giles County – Ibid

Boyd, 1870 return to Nashville – Ibid

Boyd, working for James Hickman – American 3/2/1897(2), *Afro-American Encyclopaedia* (56)

James Hickman, biographical details – Banner 3/13/1894(1)

Boyd, cleaning buildings, etc. – American 3/2/1897(2)

Boyd, teaching in Williamson County – *Afro-American Encyclopaedia* (61)

Boyd, enrolls in Meharry – American 3/2/1897(2)

Boyd, 1882 honors graduate – Ibid

Boyd, teaching/practicing medicine in Mississippi – American 9/23/1886(4)

Boyd, 1883 shooting – Republican Banner 3/3/1883(4)

Boyd, assault case against – 2/12/1889(4)

Boyd, abortion case dismissed – American 6/10/1894(5), Banner 3/29/1895(3)

Boyd, devotion to mother – Nashville American 3/2/1897(2), Globe 7/26/1912(3)

Maria Coffee (Boyd), 1875 marriage – US Census 1880, Giles County, Pulaski, Roll 1256, Page 125C, Enumeration District 105 ("Mariah Crawford")

Maria Coffee (Boyd), unhappy marriage – Tennessean & American 10/10/1912(12)

Robert F. Boyd, Central College graduate – Haley, *Afro-American Encyclopaedia* (61)

Boyd, Meharry Dental Collage graduate – Ibid(61)

Boyd, post-graduate work – Ibid(61)

Laps D. McCord, letter of praise – Nashville American 3/2/1897(2)

Boyd, response to editorial – American 12/6/1888(2)

Boyd, details of medical practice – Globe 7/26/1912(3) account of Dr. G. W. Hubbard

Boyd, Republican Party activity – Banner 9/28/1893(7) – candidate for mayor,

Boyd, size of local practice – *Afro-American Encyclopaedia* (61-2)

Boyd, treatment of indigent – Ibid(61-2)

Boyd, widespread respect – Ibid(62)

Boyd, political activities – *Afro-American Encyclopaedia* (62)

Boyd, involvement in Order of Immaculates – Globe 7/26/1912(1)

Boyd, image (page 152) – Dr. D.W. Culp, editor, 1902, *Twentieth Century Negro Literature* , 215

Boyd, 1895 speech to Negro teachers – *Afro-American Encyclopaedia* (64–70)

Boyd, president of the American Association of Colored Physicians and Surgeons – Tennessean & American 9/11/1910(12)

Boyd, circa 1898 speech re white doctors – Chicago Tribune 9/4/1949(113)

Boyd, 1896 letter re Centennial Parade – American 5/12/1896(5)

Centennial Parade, account – American 6/1/1896(2), Banner 6/1/1896(17)

Boyd, real estate activity – *Afro-American Encyclopaedia* (62), The Colored American (Washington DC) 12/9/1899(1), Nashville American 3/2/1897(2)

Boyd, in 1899 DC newspaper article – The Colored American (Washington DC) 12/9/1899(1)

Boyd, view on Negro-controlled hospitals – New York Age 9/3/1908(10)

Boyd, early operation of clinic – Globe 7/26/1912(3) account of Dr. G. W. Hubbard

Boyd, founding Mercy Hospital – Globe 7/26/1912(3)

Mercy Hospital, image – Globe 9/4/1908(17)

Boyd, 1902 description of Mercy Hospital – Culp, *Twentieth Century Negro Literature* (219–221)

Boyd, appeal for hospital support – American 12/23/1904(8)

Boyd and nurses, image – Meharry Medical College Library and Archives

Mercy Hospital, 1909 newspaper description – Banner 5/22/1909(26)

Mercy Hospital, 1911 fire – Globe 2/17/1911(1)

Mercy Hospital, name changed to Boyd's Clinic – Banner 12/13/1911(7)

Boyd, a founder of the People's Cash Drug Store – Banner 7/13/1903(2)

Boyd, a founder of Peoples Savings Bank and Trust Company – New York Age 2/17/1910(1), Globe 8/26/1910(1)

Boyd, president Peoples Steam Laundry Co. – Globe 5/27/1910(2), Tennessean & American 5/19/1910(4)

Boyd, founding Negro Board of Trade – Globe 7/26/1912(3) address of Rev. Ellington

Negro Board of Trade, account of early Board of Trade meeting – Banner 7/20/1912(2)

Boyd, death/reception of news/account of procession/funeral – Globe 7/26/1912(1, 3-6)

Boyd, church affiliation/Christian principles – Globe 7/26/1912(1)

Maria Coffee (Crawford), death – Tennessee State Library and Archives, Nashville Death Records, 1908–1958, Maria Crawford, Roll Number 60, file # 333

Maria Coffee (Crawford), physician descendants – Pittsburgh Courier 7/31/1937(8)

Henry Harding

Harding House, image – Memphis Evening Post 12/14/1868(2)

Henry Harding (HH), McGavock slave/crime allegations/punishment – Republican Banner 1/11/1860 (3), 1/12 (3)

1860 household comprised of Minta and Catherine – supposition and 1870 Census

Harding and McGavock family details – *Nashville, A Family Town*, "The Harding Family" by Ridley Wills, 120-144; "The McGavock Family" by Margaret Lindsley Warden, p. 70-95

Belle Meade, image – W.W. Clayton, *History of Davidson County*, 422 (A)

Amanda Harding/McGavock marriage – Ibid, 126-7

Clifflawn, image – Clayton, 203 (facing)

HH, birth – burial monument, Greenwood Cemetery, Nashville/1870 and 1880 Census data

HH, description – U.S., Southern Claims Commission, Disallowed and Barred Claims, 1871-1880 [database on-line]. (15272) Ancestry.com

HH, J. C. Napier account – The Journal of Negro History, Vol. 5, #1, page 117. "Some Negro Members of the Tennessee Legislature During the Reconstruction Period and After" by J. C. Napier

John Harding as possible father of Rachel – *The History of Belle Meade* by Ridley Wills, page 39

David Morris Harding siring children by slave woman, Priscilla – *A Past Remembered*, by Paul Clements, Vol. 1, 36-9, Vol. 2, 52, author's 1986 interview with Mrs. Frank (Mildred Hicks) Henegar, Xenia (Ohio) Gazette, March, 1877,"Life and Death of Mrs. Priscilla Harding"

HH, making combs/trinkets while a slave – Nashville Banner 3/9/1888 (4)

HH, a wheelwright/lending money to master/net worth in 1868 – Memphis Daily Post 4/10/1868 (4)

HH, visiting wife and Compton farm – The National Archives at Washington, D.C.; Washington, D.C.; Barred and Disallowed Case Files of the Southern Claims Commission, 1871-1880; Record Group Title: Records of the U.S. House of Representatives, 1789 – 2015; Record Group Number: 233; Series Number: M1407, page 14730

McGavock family going south/mocking article – Daily Nashville Union 10/9/1862 (2)

David H. McGavock, image – portrait by Washington B. Cooper (circa 1850), at Two Rivers Mansion, property of Metro Board of Parks and Recreation

HH, finances at time of emancipation – Nashville Banner 3/9/1888 (4)

Deaths of John and David Morris Harding and Francis McGavock – Wills

HH, marriage to Minta White – Nashville Daily Union 4/1/1866 (3)

HH, buys property in 1866 – Union and Dispatch 5/30/1866 (3)

HH, helps contradict false rumor/resolution – Republican Banner 10/17/1866 (3)

HH, establishes personnel business – Daily Press and Times 1/29/1867

Petition to South Nashville Street Railroad Company/disturbance – Union and Dispatch 6/4/1867 (3)

HH, role in 1867 election – Union and Dispatch 8/2/1867 (3)

HH, providing lot to Mayor Alden – Nashville Union and Dispatch 1/16/1868 (1)

HH, sarcastic article re his building a house after election – Union and Dispatch 9/1/1867 (3)

HH, financial details in 1868 article – Memphis Daily Post 4/10/1868 (4)

HH, altercation with Randall Brown – Republican Banner 7/25/1868 (4)

John B. Bosley connection to Charles Bosley – see Bosley notes within this work X

HH, financial details in 1870 – Union & American 12/11/1870 (3)

Harding House advertisement – Nashville Daily Press & Times 2/7/1868, Memphis Evening Post 11/20/1868 (1)

HH, helps establish Freedman's Bank – [Republican Banner, 11/30/1871 (4)]

HH, praised by Langston – Republican Banner 9/21/1872 (4)

HH, a founder of Tn Agricultural and Mechanical Association – Union and American 4/19/1872 (3)

HH, financing purchase of Colored Fairgrounds – Nashville Banner 3/9/1888 (4)

HH, tired for assault with intent to kill – Union and American 8/17/1872 (4)

HH, death of wife, Minta – Freedman's Bank, Nashville Branch (Catherine Bosley, account # 4519)

Death of Catherine Harding Bosley – Union and American 8/31/1873 (4)

HH, an organizer of Colored Convention/politics – Republican Banner 4/28/1874 (1)

Colored Convention (edited) resolution Republican Banner – 4/30/1874 (4)

HH, losses due to failure of Freedman's Bank – Nashville Banner 3/9/1888 (4)

Minta Bosley as child of John B and Catherine Bosley – Will Book 22/23, p. 552-3 (will of James G. Bosley [signed 9/2/1873 – 3 days after death of Catherine] mentions Minta as child of his brother, John B. Bosley, Nashville Globe 4/29/1910 (3)

Loss of Harding House to creditors – Union and American 5/26/1875 (2)

Maggie Harding description, allegations re attack on Elias Napier – Daily American 7/27/1876 (4)

Maggie Harding railroad altercation – Daily American 10/1/1881 (4)

HH, attends 1884 Republican Convention – Nashville Banner 5/31/1884 (4)

HH, opinion on social equality – Daily American 8/20/1885 (2)

HH, eligible for federal jury duty – Daily American 9/9/1885 (5)

HH, death and biographical details – Nashville Banner 3/9/1888 (4)

HH, members of immediate family – 1880 Census

Maggie Harding 1890 altercation – Nashville Banner 11/19/1890 (5)

Calvin Pickett life details/death – Nashville American 5/1/1898 (5) and Nashville Banner 4/30/1898 (8)

Mabel Harding high school graduation – Nashville Banner 6/5/1896 (2)

Mabel Harding musician/at Fisk – Nashville Banner 5/24/1889 (2)

Mabel Harding teacher – Nashville Banner 3/29/1899 (3)

Minta Bosley biographical details – Nashville Globe 4/29/1910 (3) and various public records

Catherine Allen Latimer, daughter of Minta B. Allen, details – Brooklyn Eagle 9/15/1948 (21)

Minta Bosley Allen Trotman death – Ancestry death records (she died 5/2/1949)

John B. Bosley

"Riding With a Prostitute" image – Republican Banner 1/17/1869(4)

John Beale Bosley Jr. date of birth – Nashville Death Records

John B. Bosley Sr. son of Charles Bosley – Davidson County Will Book 22, p 58 (1870)

Charles Bosley, slave trader – ad of Bosley, National Banner & Nashville Whig, 4/17/1822 (3), W. W. Clayton, History of Davidson County, Tn, p 74 (residents of Harding Pike)

John B. Bosley Jr., parents – 1850 US Census (Roll 875, p 142) & 1860 US Census (Davidson Co. District 23, p 304), Nashville Death Records, 1910 (#640)

Alsey Bosley, possible daughter of William Cloud – 1850 US Census (Roll 875, p 142) & Davidson Co. Will Book 14, p 7 (will of William Cloud, 1845, designates John B. Bosley as executor)

Alsey Bosley, ownership/description of 215 acre tract – Union & American 1/29/1873 (2)

Alsey Bosley, value of land in 1860 – 1860 US Census (Davidson Co. District 23, p 304)

Will of Charles Bosley – Davidson County Will Book 22, p 58 (1870)

Charles Bosley, death – Union & American 10/20/1870 (4)

Laura Ann Bosley, marriage – Tennessee Marriage Records 1838-1864 (page 187, entry # 2041)

Laura Ann Bosley, children – 1860 US Census (Davidson Co., Nashville Ward 4, p 388)

Laura Ann Bosley, death in 1863 – Nashville City Cemetery Records list "Sarah A. Trimble," a free woman of color, age 26, as being buried on 7/14/1863 in the same lot in which Medora and James Trimble, who were siblings of Laura Ann, were buried. But George Trimble, Laura's husband, did have a sister named Sarah. The 1850 Census indicated that she was eighteen years old (born circa 1832) in 1850, while the same census lists Laura Ann as being fourteen (born circa 1836), which made her, at the age of twenty-six of twenty-seven, much closer to the age of the individual who was buried in 1863.

John B. Bosley, Jr., marriage to Catherine Harding – Davidson County Marriage Records (1870), p 85

Henry Harding, McGavock Family slave – Republican Banner 1/11/1860 (3), 1/12 (3)

Minta Gwynn Bosley, born 1873 – Davidson County Will Book 22/23, p. 552-3 (will of James G. Bosley [signed 9/2/1873] mentions Minta as child of his brother, John B. Bosley). Nashville Globe 4/29/1910 (3)

John B. Bosley, Sr., birthplace/year – 1860 US Census (Davidson Co. District 23, p 304)

Charles Bosley, marriage to Eliza Childress – Davidson County Marriage Book 1, p 202

Charles Bosley, children by Eliza Childress – Ancestry family tree of Mehlhoff/Hedington Family

John B. Bosley, family detail (1850) – 1850 US Census (Roll 875, p 142)

John B. Bosley, family deaths – Ancestry, Margery Shute Bosley Family Tree

Alsey Bosley, midwife – Nashville Banner 12/16/1924 (11), "Some Nashville Colored Folk of My Boyhood Days" by S. W. Bransford

Alsey Bosley, recollection of James C. Napier – The Journal of Negro History, Volume 5, # 1 (January, 1920), p 118. "Some Negro Members of the Tennessee Legislature During Reconstruction Period and After" by Honorable J. C. Napier

John B. Bosley household in 1850 – 1850 US Census (Roll 875, p 142), Davidson Co. Will Book 14, p 7 (will of William Cloud, 1845)

Bosley farm/slaves in 1860 – The National Archives in Washington DC; Washington DC, USA; Eighth Census of the United States 1860; Series Number: M653; Record Group: Records of the Bureau of the Census; Record Group Number: 29, Census Place: District 23, Davidson, Tennessee; Archive Collection Number: T1135; Roll: Roll 6; Schedule Type: Agriculture

Laura Ann Bosley, death in 1863 – Nashville City Cemetery Records list "Sarah A. Trimble" (see above note)

Alsey Bosley death – Nashville City Cemetery burial records

John B. Bosley, Jr., student at Wilberforce University – Ancestry.com. U.S., School Catalogs, 1765 to 1935 [database on-line]. Provo, UT, USA: Ancestry.com Operations, Inc., 2012

John B. Bosley Sr. death/inheritance of sons – Davidson County Will Book X (1867)

John B. Bosley, Jr., 1869 incident – Republican Banner, 1/17/1869 (4)

John B. Bosley, Jr., dismissal of case – Union & American, 1/19/1867 (4)

John B. Bosley marriage to Catherine Harding – Davidson County marriage records

Catherine Harding complexion – 1870 US Census

Minta Harding connection to Belle Meade – Republican Banner 1/12/1860 (3)

John B. Bosley home in 1870 – 1870 Census Place: Nashville Ward 4, Davidson, Tennessee, Roll M593_1523 page: 266A, Family History Library Film: 553022

James G. Bosley at Fisk – Ancestry.com U.S., School Catalogs, 1765-1935 [database on-line]

Catherine Harding Bosley, death – Union & American, 8/31/1873 (4)

John B. Bosley, 1871 horse raising details – Union & American 9/15/1871 (4)

John B. Bosley, love of horses – Nashville Globe, 4/28/1910 (3)

John B. Bosley, fight – Union & American, 9/22/1871 (4)

John B. Bosley, chicken fighting – Banner, 5/25/1885 (1)

John B. Bosley, details concerning – Nashville Globe, 4/28/1910 (3)

John B. Bosley, partner of Harding – Nashville American, 9/13/1877 (2)

John B. Bosley, awarded position at Customs House – American, 10/30/1889 (5)

James C. Napier, student at Wilberforce University – Ancestry.com. U.S., School Catalogs, 1765 to 1935 [database on-line]. Provo, UT, USA: Ancestry.com Operations, Inc., 2012

John B. Bosley campaigning with Napier – American, 10/20/1896 (2)

Minta Bosley 1894 marriage – Davidson County Marriages (12/20/1894)

Henry Allen biographical details – Nashville American, 12/27/1903 (7)

John B. Bosley 1898 marriage – Ancestry.com, Tennessee, Marriage Records, 1780-2002 [database on-line]. Lehi, UT, USA: Ancestry.com Operations Inc, 2008. Original data: Tennessee State Marriages, 1780- Nashville, TN, USA: Tennessee State Library and Archives

John B. Bosley, wife attends Peabody Normal College – Buffalo Enquirer, 4/27/1900 (10)

John B. Bosley, director of One-Cent Savings Bank – Banner, 4/23/1910 (3)

Henry Allen death – Nashville American, 12/27/1903 (7)

Bosley home destroyed in 1905 fire – American 4/21/1905 (4)

Minta Bosley Allen residence in Brooklyn/travel to Europe – US passport applications, 1908-1910, Roll 0074 – Certificates: 64339-65243, 20 Nov 1908-15 Dec 1908

Minta Bosley Allen returns for father's funeral – Nashville Globe, 4/29/1910 (3)

John B. Bosley death – Nashville Globe, 4/28/1910 (3)

Minta Bosley Allen (Trotman) biographical details – The New York Age, 5/14/1949 (15) & search.alexanderstreet.com, Nancy Page Fernandez, PHD, "Biography of Minta Bosley Allen Trotman, 1875-1949"

Catherine Allen biographical details – https://nypl-librarians.blogspot.com/2015/10/catherine-bosley-allen-latimer-1896-1948.html

Minta and Henry W. Allen

Photograph – TSLA, Calvert Brothers Studio Collection, "the Henry W. Allen Family" (circa 1899)

Henry W. Allen – Minta Bosley wedding Davidson County Marriages

Allen family residence at time of photograph – Nashville Banner, 12/24/1903 (14)

Racial composition of neighborhood surrounding Allen home – 1900 US Census

Birth of Catherine Allen – Davidson County birth records

Minta Bosley a Fisk graduate – search.alexanderstreet.com, "Biography of Minta Bosley Allen Trotman, 1875-1949"

Minta as speaker/musician – Nashville Banner, 2/21/1891 (3) & 6/12/1893 (2)

James Bosley Revolutionary War service – Union & American 10/20/1870 (4)

Bosley family moves to Davidson County – Union & American 10/20/1870 (4)

Charles Bosley as slave trader – ad of Bosley, National Banner & Nashville Whig, 4/17/1822 (3), W. W. Clayton, History of Davidson County, Tn, p 74 (residents of Harding Pike)

Charles Bosley wealth and death – Union & American 10/20/1870 (4)

Henry W. Allen birth – 1880 (head of household "Charles Robertson" [sic]), 1900 US Census

Charles Allen birth – 1900 US Census

Charles Allen/Sarah Cole marriage – Davidson Co. marriages

Sarah Cole, mother – In Sarah's Dinwiddie County death certificate – #2832 (2/4/1934), Ancestry.com, Virginia, U.S., Death Records, 1912-2014 Virginia Department of Health, Richmond, Virginia – her mother is identified as "Nellie," but her father is not identified. But in 1870 Henry Cole, is named in the Republican Banner of 11/30/1870(4) as the administrator of Nellie Cole, deceased. In the 1850 Census, Henry is listed as a six-year-old mulatto, living in Nashville in the household headed by Margaret Cole. Henry Cole's 1906 Nashville death certificate identifies his mother as "Ellen" Cole and his father as Robert Cole. It seems reasonable to suppose that Nellie was a nickname for Ellen. There appear to have been three men named Cole who lived in Nashville when Robert was sired circa 1844. Of the three possible fathers, the most notable was Robert A. Cole, a white veteran of the Seminole and Mexican Wars, and the far-less-successful older brother of one Nashville's most notable citizens, Edmund W. Cole – a railroad magnate, banker, and philanthropist. Sarah was sired circa 1851 – although her obituary gave her year of birth as 1856. She married in 1866, and she must have been considerably older than ten at that time.

Charles & Sarah Allen parents of 13 children – Tennessean 2/20/1983 (10)

Charles Allen image/employment at Nicholson Hotel – Daily American, 4/22/1888 (3)

Charles Allen begins hotel career in 1868 – Nashville Globe, 12/25/1908 (4)

Charles Allen stabbed – Union & American, 8/21/1873 (4), 8/27/1873 (3), 9/2/1873 (1)

Napier article about Henry Allen – Nashville American, 12/27/1903 (7)

Henry Allen biographical details – Nashville American, 12/27/1903 (7)

Marian Allen birth – 1900 US Census, Davidson County, Tn (Henry Allen household)

Henry Bosley Allen – birth 1910 US Census, Brooklyn, NY (Minta Allen household)

James Julian, appointment as mail clerk – Chattanooga News 11/28/1902(2)

James Julian, achievement of son Percy – Indianapolis Star 5/21/1970(44)

Union Station, image – L.L. Gamble lithograph (1900)

1903 train wreck details – Nashville Banner, 12/24/1903 (14), Nashville American 12/24/1903 (1), Montgomery Advertiser, 12/24/1903 (2)

Bosley home destroyed in 1905 fire – American 4/21/1905 (4)

Dr. James G. Trimble, Harvard Medical School graduate – American, 6/21/1906 (10), 11/9/1906 (8)

Minta Allen residence in Brooklyn/travel to Europe – US passport applications, 1908-1910, Roll 0074 – Certificates: 64339-65243, 20 Nov 1908-15 Dec 1908

Minta Allen returns for father's funeral – Nashville Globe, 4/29/1910 (3)

Minta Allen marriage to William F. Trotman – Certificate # 1709, NY Extracted Marriage Index, 1866-1937

Minta Allen Trotman, political activity – The New York Age, 5/14/1949 (15) & search.alexanderstreet.com, Nancy Page Fernandez, PHD, "Biography of Minta Bosley Allen Trotman, 1875-1949"

Minta Allen Trotman, Baha'i faith activity – baha'i.works search term ("Minta Trotman")

Catherine Allen (Latimer) biographical details – https://nypl librarians.blogspot.com/2015/10/catherine-bosley-allen-latimer-1896-1948.html

Catherine Allen marriage to Benton Latimer – New York Age, 9/3/1921 (8)

Catherine Allen Latimer biographical details – https://nypl-librarians.blogspot.com/2015/10/catherine-bosley-allen-latimer-1896-1948.html

Henry Bosley Allen marriage – New York Age, 6/30/1934 (2)

Henry Bosley Allen, city electrician – Ancestry.com Henry Bosley Allen draft registration card (6/30/1942) & New York Age, 6/30/1934 (2)

Henry Bosley Allen complexion – Ancestry.com Henry Bosley Allen World War 2 draft registration card

Marian Allen marriage – Tampa Bay Times 9/21/1988, (95)

Probyn Thompson biographical details – New York Age 2/27/1954 (15)

Charles A. Allen death – Tennessean, 11/25/1928 (5)

Sarah Cole Allen death – Tennessean, 2/9/1934 (10)

(William D. Allen) hotel proprietor details – Oregon Daily Journal, 10/3/1921 (2)

Catherine Allen Latimer additional biographical details – "Catherine Latimer, The New York Public Library's First Black Librarian" https://www.nypl.org/blog/2020/03/19/new-york-public-library-first-black-librarian-catherine-latimer

Catherine Allen Latimer, image – New York Public Library Digital Collections, image 5186396

Minta Allen Trotman death – New York Age, 5/14/1949 (15)

Marian Allen Thompson death – Tampa Bay Times 4/3/1975 (47)

Lillian Allen Darden quote about father – Tennessean, 2/20/1983 (10)

Nelson Merry

Nelson Merry, mother, Sydney – Republican Banner 6/26/1873(4)

Elizabeth Merry, daughter of Prettyman Merry/nativity – Merry family Bible https://bit.ly/31UB9HN, Virginia Genealogist, April 2006, ""The Will of Pretttyman Merry", Buckingham County, 1817" https://bit.ly/321xVCh

Prettyman Merry, Revolutionary War veteran – W. W. Scott, A History of Orange County, Virginia, from its formation in 1734 to the end of reconstruction in 1870, Chapter 9

Prettyman Merry, Kentucky landowner – The Kentucky Land Grants, Volume 1, Part 1, Chapter II Virginia Grants (1782-1792), The Counties of Kentucky, page 87-88

Prettyman Merry, death of wife – https://www.findagrave.com/memorial/42489578/catherine-merry

Prettyman Merry, death – https://www.findagrave.com/memorial/42489502/prettyman-merry

Elizabeth Merry, household in 1820 – 1820 US Census, Christian County, Kentucky, Hopkinsville, Page: 39, Roll M33_20, Image 49

Catherine Merry, marriage to William Glover – Christian County, Kentucky marriages (9/10/1821)

William Glover, sons – Sumner County Will Book 2, page 124 (William Glover will)

Ann ("Nancy") Merry, marriage – Christian County, Kentucky marriages (6/6/1822)

Jemima Merry, marriage – Christian County, Kentucky marriages (9/13/1823)

Nelson Merry, birth – American 7/15/1884(8)

Sydney Merry, children – (Elizabeth Merry will) Sumner County Loose Records, reel A-5119, item 10069

Liverpool Merry, birth – 1870 US Census, Bedford County, Shelbyville, Ward 2, roll M593_1514, page 240B

Liverpool Merry, lists Abram as his father – Freedman's Bank Records, Roll 24, Memphis, Tn., "L. N. Merry" February 24 (1873) (#5041)

Catherine (Merry) Glover, death – Merry family Bible, Sumner County, Tn. Miscellaneous Records (116)

Elizabeth Merry, living in Sumner County – 1830 US Census, Sumner County, Tennessee, Series M19, Roll 181, Page 154

Elizabeth Merry, in Glover household – Sumner County Will Book 2, page 124 (William Glover will)

Elizabeth Merry, benevolence – Tennessee State Library and Archives, Sumner County Loose Records, reel A-5119, item 10069

Nelson/Sydney Merry, complexion – 1860 US Census, Davidson County, Nashville Ward 4, page 397; 1870 US Census, Davidson County, Nashville Ward 4, Davidson, Tennessee Roll M593_1523 page 237A

Nelson Merry, middle name, Glover – ancestry.com, Merry Family Tree

Nelson Merry, lack of education – Republican Banner 3/25/1868(4), American 7/16/1884(4) (account of T. W. Haley)

Liverpool Merry, pastor – 1870 US Census, Bedford County, Tennessee, Shelbyville, Ward 2, Roll M593_1514, Page 40B

William Glover, will – Sumner County Will Book 2, page 124

Elizabeth Merry, returns to Kentucky – American 7/15/1884(8)

Elizabeth Merry, will – Sumner County Loose Records, reel A-5119, item 10069

Joel Parrish, involvement with slaves – Ibid (Answer of Joel Parrish)

Nelson/Liverpool Merry, details of being hired out – Ibid

Sumner County sawmill – Ibid, TSLA, Supreme Court case file, Middle Tn. "Sidney, et al vs Joel Parrish";

Nashville Union 11/17/1841(1) – ad of C. H. Gray (of Gray & McCall)

Josephus C. Guild, details – https://tennesseeencyclopedia.net/entries/josephus-conn-guild/

Nelson Merry, to Nashville circa 1843 – American 7/16/1884(3) – (see account of Dr. Elliott)

Nelson Merry, buys carriage/hack driver – American 5/19/1890(3), Globe 11/2/1917(8)

Nelson Merry, meets Mary Anna Jones – Globe 11/2/1917(1)

Mary Anna Jones, details – Ibid

First Baptist Church, details – American 6/11/1878(3), 3/15/1886(1), Tennessee Historical Quarterly, Volume 38 #3 (296-307), Mechal Sobel, "They Can Never Prosper Together, Black and White Baptists in Antebellum Nashville, Tennessee"

Nelson Merry, account of relationship with Dr. Howell – Union and American 4/10/1868(3)

Nelson Merry, account of relationship between Dr. Howell and black members – American 6/11/1878(3)

Nelson Merry, baptism/employment at church – Union & American 4/10/1868(3), Sobel (304), Globe 11/2/1917(8), American 7/15/1884(8)

Nelson Merry, details of spirituality – American 7/15/1884(8)

First Baptist Church, number of black members – Sobel (300)

R. B. C. Howell, quote re Negroes – Tennessee Historical Quarterly, Volume 38 #3, Sobel (299)

R. B. C. Howell, opinion regarding Nelson Merry – Ibid (304)

Nelson Merry, instructed by R. B. C. Howell – American 7/15/1884(8)

First Baptist Church, establishes mission church – Sobel (300-305)

Mission church, details – American 3/15/1886(1), Sobel (299-307)

Nelson/Liverpool Merry, neighborhood/household in 1850 – 1850 US Census, Davidson County, Tennessee, Nashville, Roll 875, Page 124b ("Nelson Merritt')

Jackson Merry, detail – Republican Banner 6/19/1850(2)

Nelson Merry, ordination – Tennessee Baptist (Nashville) 12/24/1853(3), Globe 11/2/1917(1)

Nelson Merry, attends M. B. Pilcher's Sunday school class – American 3/15/1886(1), 6/18/1901(7)

Nelson Merry, household in 1860 – 1860 US Census, Davidson County, Nashville, Ward 4, Page 397

Sydney Merry, residence in 1860 – 1860 US Census, Davidson County, Nashville Ward 4, Page 397 ("Gracy" Merry in household of "L. Napoleon Merry")

Liverpool Merry, affiliation with AME Church – 1881 Nashville City Directory, Leaf-Chronicle Weekly (Clarksville) 11/13/1891(1)

Frankey ("Francis") King, residence in 1860 – 1860 US Census, Davidson County, District 13, Page 226, Daily Union 1/13/1864(2) ("Funeral Notice" – Abraham King)

First Baptist Church, during Civil War – Banner 6/27/1874(4)

Nelson Merry, response to rumor of Pilcher death – American 3/15/1886(1), American 6/18/1901(7)

Nelson Merry, stance during Civil War – American 7/16/1884(3) – (account of T. W. Haley)

Nashville population increase during war – Daily Press & Times 8/12/1865

Nashville Provident Association, details – Daily Press & Times 12/15/1865

First Colored Baptist Church, established – American 3/15/1886(1)

Nelson Merry, arrest/trial – Union and American 7/4/1866(3)

Nelson Merry, NYC newspaper account – Republican Banner 7/18/1866(3)

Nelson Merry, quells rumor – Republican Banner 10/17/1866(3)

Nelson Merry, speech at Capitol – Union & Dispatch 4/15/1867

Blacks at debate of franchise bill – Union & Dispatch 1/31/1867

Nelson Merry, 1864-68 baptisms/marriages/ordinations – Republican Banner 3/25/1868(4)

Nelson Merry, autobiographical details –Ibid

Nelson Merry, births of children – 1850 – 1880 US Censuses

Nelson Merry, household in 1870 – 1870 US Census, Davidson County, Tennessee, Nashville Ward 4, Roll M593_1523, Page 237A

Nelson Merry, church finances – The (Tennessee) Baptist 1/25/1873(1)

Sydney Merry, death – Republican Banner 6/26/1873(4)

Nelson Merry, during cholera epidemic – American 7/16/1884(3) – (account of William Stockell)

William Stockell, Confederate sympathizer – Tennessean 6/29/1941(52)

Nelson Merry, baptism of convicts – Republican Banner 4/7/1872(4)

Nelson Merry, involvement with condemned men – Republican Banner 3/3/1874(3)

First Colored Baptist Church, 1874 details – Republican Banner 12/18/1874(4)

Nelson Merry, household in 1880 – 1880 US Census, Davidson County, Roll 1249, Page 128B, Enumeration District 042

First Colored Baptist Church, storm damage – Daily American 2/14/1880(4)

Nelson Merry, details of death – American 7/15/1884(8)

Nelson Merry, tribute from congregation – ibid, Banner 7/16/1884(4), (names "Colored Preachers Association")

Nelson Merry, details of funeral/procession – American 7/17/1884(4) – (Original source account uses term "coaches" instead of carriages)

Nelson Merry, length of funeral procession – American 5/19/1890(3)

Nelson Merry, survivors – American 7/15/1884(8)

Nelson Merry, tribute by McTyeire – Banner 7/15/1884(4)

Mary Anna Merry, details of later life – Globe 11/2/1917(1)

First Colored Baptist Church, subsequent history – https://www.firstbaptistcapitolhill.org/our-history/ First Baptist Church, Capitol Hill, details – Ibid, https://www.blackpast.org/african-american-history/ first- baptist-church-capitol-hill-nashville-tennessee-1835/

The McKissack Family

McKissack family tradition – *Encyclopedia of African-American Business*, "McKissack & McKissack Architects and Engineers, Inc." (https://bit.ly/3GAD8Qc); Family Business Magazine (April, 2018) "From slave labor to thriving business: The storied history of McKissack & McKissack" by April Hall

William McKissack, birth – Tombstone inscription, Spring Hill Cemetery, Spring Hill, Tn. "In Memory of Col. William McKissack who was born in Caswell County N. Carolina Nov. 14 1781. And Died in Maury County Tennessee Feby 23 1855 Age 73 Years 3 Months & 14 Days"

McKissack family, move to Tennessee – 1830 US Census, Maury County, Tennessee, Series M19, roll177, page 398, entry for Spivey McKissack (his brother, William, was still in North Carolina), tombstone of father, Thomas McKissack, in Mt. Moriah Cemetery, Pulaski, Tennessee (died 4/24/1826)

William McKissack, move to Tennessee – 1850 US Census, Spring Hill, Maury County, Tennessee, Roll 890, Page 214b, ("William McKissac") – daughter Lucy (17) born in NC circa 1833, daughter Jesse (14) born Tn circa 1836

William McKissack, number of slaves at time of move – 1830 US Census, Person County, North Carolina, Series M19, Roll 124, Page 38 – 23 slaves; 1840 US Census, Maury County, Tennessee, Roll 532, page 378 ("William McKizzick/McHeggeck") – 42 slaves

Moses McKissack, marriage to Miriam – E*ncyclopedia of African-American Business* (507)

William McKissack, details of slaves in 1840 – 1840 US Census, Maury County, Tennessee, Roll 532, page 378 ("William McKizzick/McHeggeck")

William McKissack, owner of brickyard – "*Hither and Yon*" Volume II, from writings of Jill Garrett, edited by Carese Carter (196)

McKissack slaves, hired out to cotton mill – Giles County Chancery Court, File Box C-19 (Case 1395), "N. F. Cheairs vs Margaret J. Mason, et al (1857)

Theodore, hiring details – Maury County Chancery Court, William McKissack vs Thomas Hodge (1853) – online, Ancestry.com, Maury County, Tennessee, Chancery Court Cases (1807-1890)

William McKissack, being helpful to Moses – Encyclopedia of African-American Business (507), Family Business Magazine (April, 2018) "From slave labor to thriving business: The storied history of McKissack & McKissack" Theodore, hired out at $275 per year – Maury County Archives, Chancery Court, "Susan P. Cheairs vs Nathaniel F. Cheairs et al (1876), in "Rippavilla – Telling the Whole Story of the Civil War Experience" by Laura S. Holder, Annabeth Hayes, and Dr. Carroll Van West (2019) – Appendix A (51) – (https://www.mtsuhistpres.org/wp-content/uploads/2019/09/Rippavilla-Telling-the-Whole-Story-Sept-19.pdf)

Gabriel McKissack, birth – Tennessee State Library and Archives, Tennessee Death Records (1922 – Giles County) Roll Number 139, file # 185

Gabriel McKissack, learning from Moses – *Encyclopedia of African-American Business* (507)

William McKissack, death – Tombstone inscription, Spring Hill Cemetery, Spring Hill, Tn. "In Memory of Col. William McKissack who was born in Caswell County N. Carolina Nov. 14 1781. And Died in Maury County Tennessee Feby 23 1855 Age 73 Years 3 Months & 14 Days"

William McKissack, details of burial – "*They Passed This Way*," Maury County Death Records, II, by Lightfoot and Shackleford (349)

Rippavilla, date of completion – https://www.rippavilla.org/history

James T. McKissack, move to Giles County – 1860 US Census, Northern Subdivision, Giles County, (66)

James T. McKissack, details of farm – Nashville Union & American 6/18/1874(2)

McKissack slave, killed by overseer – Nashville Republican Banner 5/11/1858(3) – (from Pulaski Citizen) Moses/Miriam McKissack, deaths – Ancestry – "Moses McKissack" born 1790, "Bloodlines Family Tree," https://www.ancestry.com/familytree/person/tree/18167102/person/280099820416/facts?_phsrc =rtO56&_phstart=successSource

Gabriel McKissack, marriage – Giles County Marriage Records (2/25/1869)

Gabriel McKissack, details in 1870 – 1870 US Census, Pulaski, Giles County Tennessee, Roll M593_1529, Page 139A

Gabriel/Dolly McKissack, birth of children – 1880 US Census, District 7, Giles County, Roll 1257, Page 138A, Enumeration District 105; 1900 US Census, Civil District 7, Giles County, Page 4, Enumeration District 0020

Moses McKissack II, birth – Tennessee State Library and Archives, Nashville Death Records (1952), Moses McKissack, Sr. (file # 52-29187)

Moses McKissack II, details of early life – *Encyclopedia of African-American Business* (507)

Calvin McKissack, birth – Social Security Death Index (Calvin McKissack, born 2/23/1890)

William McKissack, exhumation – "*They Passed This Way*," Maury County Death Records, II, (349)

Moses McKissack, living with parents in 1900 – 1900 US Census, Civil District 7, Giles County, Page 4, Enumeration District 0020

Moses McKissack, hired by Granbery Jackson – *Encyclopedia of African-American Business* (508)

Granbery Jackson, home on Farrell Avenue – Banner 5/5/1906(7)

Moses McKissack II, Fisk Library project – *Encyclopedia of African-American Business* (508)

Moses McKissack, mentioned in Banner – Banner 4/21/1908(12)

1921 architect licensing requirement – Interior Design Magazine (2/25/2020) "10 Questions With… Cheryl and Deryl McKissack" by Jesse Dorris

Moses/Calvin McKissack, receive licenses – Family Business Magazine (April, 2018) "From slave labor to thriving business: The storied history of McKissack & McKissack"

Morris Memorial Building, image – Nashville Banner 10/18/1925(16)

Gabriel McKissack, death – Tennessee State Library and Archives, Tennessee Death Records (1922 – Giles County) Roll Number 139, file # 185

McKissack & McKissack, project information – *Encyclopedia of African-American Business* (508-9)

McKissack & McKissack, College Hill project – Banner 4/18/1947(1), 4/20/1950(5)

Moses McKissack II, death – Tennessee State Library and Archives, Nashville Death Records (1952), Moses McKissack, Sr. (file # 52-29187)

Calvin/DeBerry McKissack, leadership of company – *Encyclopedia of African-American Business* (508-9)

Leo Sam – quote about business – Leo Sam (VP at McKissack) Tennessean 1/18/1981(2D)

Leatrice McKissack, leadership of company/projects – Family Business Magazine (April, 2018) "From slave labor to thriving business: The storied history of McKissack & McKissack"

Deryl and Cheryl McKissack, details of business success – *Encyclopedia of African-American Business* (507)

Interior Design Magazine (2/25/2020) "10 Questions With… Cheryl and Deryl McKissack"

Sampson W. Keeble

Sampson Keeble, bust – Tennessee State Capitol (on display in legislative area)

Sampson Keeble, birth – Daily American 7/3/1887(4)

Sampson Keeble, location of birthplace – *The Keeble Family Genealogy* by Virginia Gooch Watson, p. 34

Nancy Keeble, birth/birthplace – tombstone inscription/Mount Ararat Cemetery (in "Sampson Wesley Keeble" by Kathy Lauder – included in "This Honorable Body – African-American Legislators in 19th Century Tennessee" https://sharetngov.tnsosfiles.com/tsla/exhibits/blackhistory/keeble.htm

Nancy Keeble, age when she came to Tennessee – Watson, 7

Walter Keeble, owner of Nancy – Lauder

Sampson Keeble – raised in humane conditions – Ibid, the relationship between Keeble and his former master, H. P. Keeble was apparently close, see Union & American 12/6/1872(2)

Walter Keeble, death – Watson, 2

Sampson Keeble, inherited by Horace P. Keeble – Union & American 12/6/1872(2), Lauder

Sampson Keeble, working for newspaper – Ibid

("Sampson used to be…") – Home Journal (Winchester) 11/23/1871(3)

Sampson Keeble, marries Harriet – 1870 Census, Nashville, Ward 5, p. 12, #296 ("Samson Keebles")

Horace P. Keeble, enlists in Confederacy – Rutherford County Historical Society Journal, 2010, https://bit.ly/3oQOee7

Sampson Keeble, accompanies master – Clarksville Chronicle 1/25/1873(1)

Sampson Keeble, opens barber shop – Daily Union 2/28/1865(3), 5/27/1865(4)

Sampson Keeble, Colored Convention delegate – Republican Banner 8/7/1866(1)

Sampson Keeble, helps quell false rumor – Union & American 10/17/1866(3)

("In those days…") – Loren Schweninger, From Tennessee Slave to St. Louis Entrepreneur: the Autobiography of James Thomas, University of Missouri, 1984, 73

("But I have not seen…") – Ibid, 89-90

Sampson Keeble, family tradition re law – Lauder

Sampson Keeble, appointed delegate to Republican convention – Union & American 12/31/1867(1)

Sampson Keeble, seeks nomination in 1869 – Republican Banner 7/11/1869(4)

Sampson Keeble, Colored Fairgrounds leader – Republican Banner 9/27/1870(4)

"Colored Celebration" image, ("The colored people…") – Union & American 5/5/1870(1)

("We greet…") – Republican Banner 5/5/1870 (4)

Harriet Keeble, death – Union & American 6/17/1870(4)

Sampson Keeble, household in 1870 – 1870 Census, Nashville, Ward 5, p. 12, #296 ("Samson Keebles")

Sampson Keeble, buys Harding House – Republican Banner 12/20/1870(4)

("Byron Jackson…") – Union & American 2/7/1871(4), Republican Banner 2/7/1871(4)

("Sampson has made money…") – Home Journal (Winchester) 11/23/1871(3)

Sampson Keeble, receives nomination – Republican Banner 10/24/1872(4)

1872 election details – Republican Banner 11/7/1872(4)

("S. W. Keeble…") – Union & American 12/6/1872(2)

("The present General Assembly…") – Clarksville Chronicle 1/25/1873(1)

("The Tennessee legislature…") – Memphis Daily Appeal 4/1/1873(4)

Sampson Keeble, legislative activity – Lauder

Sampson Keeble, elected magistrate – American 8/6/1876(4), 8/12/1876(4)

Sampson Keeble, accused of extortion – American 5/30/1877(4), 11/15/1878(4)

("We, the journeyman barbers…") – American 8/8/1877(4)

Failure of barbers strike – American 8/14/1877(4)

Sampson Keeble, remarriage – 1880 Census, Nashville, Ward 5, 2nd Div., p. 26, #155, "Sam W Keeble")

Sampson Keeble, family in 1880 – Ibid

Sampson Keeble, survival of only two children into adulthood – Lauder

Sampson Keeble, continues working as barber – Nashville City Directories 1880-1885

Nancy Keeble, death – Davidson County Death Register (1882-84), p. 33 (1/15/1883)

Sampson Keeble, becomes teacher – Nashville City Directory 1886

Sampson Keeble, death – Nashville American 7/3/1887(4)

Jeanette Keeble Cox, details – Lauder

Jeanette Keeble Cox, death/survivors – Tennessean 2/24/1956(48)

The Napier Family

Rebecca Watkins, details of childhood slavery – Nashville American 1/26/1885(4)

William Watkins, Sr., biographical details – Nashville Union 1/11/1841(3), Revolutionary War pension application (1832), filed in Williamson County court papers

Rebecca, becoming the property of William E. Watkins – Tennessean 7/4/1937(26) includes that Rebecca's daughter, Jane, was born in Davidson County. Various records indicate that she was born as early as 1817 (1850 census) or as late as 1826 (1880 census), Revolutionary War application of William Watkins Sr. establishes that he moved to Williamson County circa 1818. While it is possible that she accompanied the elder Watkins instead of remaining with the father of her child (as well as other possible children), it seems unlikely.

Elias Watkins, ownership of iron property/slaves – Daily Nashville Union 4/19/1849(4)

Elias Watkins, charged with bastardy – Dickson Co. Circuit Court Minute Book A (July, 1819)

Watkins and Elias Napier, location of places – American 9/16/1894(5)

Carroll Napier, details of boyhood education – American 12/22/1895(14)

Elias Napier, marriage – Tennessee Genealogical Magazine "Anserchin'" News, Volume 36, Number 4, Winter 1989, p 164

Elias Napier, land purchase – Davidson County deed book N-525

Richard Napier, Revolutionary War officer – *Virginians in the Revolution* (577), Dickson County Herald 10/16/1931

Elias Napier, father of William Carroll Napier – Nashville American 12/22/1895(14) Journal of Negro History, Volume 5, #1 (January, 1920), 117

Elias Napier, 1841 arrival on Richland Creek – Davidson County deed book N-525

Elias Napier, slaves brought to Davidson County – Dickson County, Tennessee Will Book, Volume 2 Will Book A, Page 183

Carroll Napier/Jane Watkins, marriage details – American 9/16/1894(5) "Fifty Years Married"

William E. Watkins residence – May Winston Caldwell, *Beautiful and Historic Homes in and Around Nashville*, 1911, ("The Old Bass Place")

James C. Napier, birth – Tennessean 7/4/1937(Magazine – 2)

Elias Napier, will – Dickson County, Tennessee Will Book, Volume 2 Will Book A, Page 183

Elias Napier, death – www.findagrave.com, Dr. Elias Wills Napier (5 Mar 1783–7 Aug 1848), Find a Grave Memorial no. 139120434, Richard Napier Family Cemetery, Dickson County, Tennessee.

Jane Watkins Napier, leaving Davidson County – Freedmen's Bank Records, E. W. Napier, 23, born Cincinnati, 1860 US Census, Nashville, Ward 4 (399), Jane's son, Elias (age 11), born in Ohio (1849)

Napier entourage, time in Ohio/return to Tennessee/livery stable owner – Journal of Negro History, Volume 5, #1 (January, 1920), 117, Republican Banner 4/17/1856(4) "Hacks" ad of Carroll Napier

Napier family, birth of children – US Census, 1850 & 1860

Napier child, death –William Napier, age 3, listed in 1850 Census, Nashville City Cemetery records list William Thomas Napier, date of death December 29, 1851, buried in lot of W. C. Napier

Jane Napier, learning to read – Crystal A. deGregory, *Raising a Nonviolent Army: Four Nashville Black Colleges and the Century-Long Struggle for Civil Rights, 1830s-1930s* dissertation, Vanderbilt, page 33

Alonzo Napier, birth – www.findagrave.com: Henry Alonzo Napier (17 Jun 1851–16 Dec 1882), Find a Grave Memorial no. 27346822, Greenwood Cemetery, Nashville, Davidson County, Tennessee, USA.

Alonzo Napier, appointment to West Point – Union & American 4/15/1870(1) "The Nashville Cadet"

Alonzo Napier, achievements at Howard University – Chicago Tribune 5/29/1871(1), Ancestry.com US School Catalogs, 1765-1935, Howard University Catalogue, 1870

Alonzo Napier, descendant of Revolutionary War veterans – Revolutionary War pension application

(1832) of William Watkins, filed in Williamson County court papers, Virginians in the Revolution (577), Dickson County Herald 10/16/1931

Alonzo Napier, at Howard University – Republican Banner 5/27/1871(1)

James Webster Smith, persecution at West Point – NY Tribune 6/16/1871(1)

Alonzo Napier, physique/pugilistic capacity – Ashtabula Weekly Telegraph 6/24/1871(1)

Alonzo Napier, taking examination at West Point – Union and American 6/8/1871(1)

Alonzo Napier, at examination/description of classmates – NY Tribune 6/2/1871(1)

Alonzo Napier, description on entering West Point – Fall River Daily Evening News 5/30/1871(2)

West Point cadets, image – United States Military Academy, bicentennial website

Alonzo Napier, nicknamed "Lord Napier" – Chicago Tribune 6/13/1871(2)

Alonzo Napier, last in class – Republican Banner 5/22/1872(4)

Alonzo Napier, departure from West Point/Florida position – St. Louis Globe-Democrat 12/16/1882(5)

Alonzo Napier, West Point persecution account – St. Louis Globe-Democrat 4/25/1880(3) "The Experiences of a Colored Man from St. Louis at West Point" by H. A. Napier, [list of West Point staff and cadets during Alonzo Napier's first year – U. S. Register of Civil, Military, and Naval Service, 1863-1959, pages 251 – 253] James Wesley Smith (12/3/1845 – 12/3/1915) was born and died in Charleston, SC, where he raised a large family and served as a minister

Alonzo Napier, steamship from NY to Charleston – Charleston Daily News 7/10/1872(4)

Alonzo Napier, marriage to Venus Bond – Gadsden County, Florida marriage records, 8/12/1872

Alonzo Napier, 1877 divorce – American 2/11/1877(1)

Alonzo Napier, return to Nashville – American 12/17/1882(6)

Alonzo Napier, principal of school in Nashville – Nashville City Directories, 1876, 1878

Alonzo Napier, Meharry student – American 12/17/1882(6)

Alonzo Napier, City Council candidate – American 8/30/1874(4)

Alonzo Napier, equestrian ability – American 9/25/1874(4)

Emigration of blacks from Middle Tennessee in February, 1875 – Republican Banner 2/21/1875(4)

1875 Civil Rights Act, newspaper description – American 2/28/1875(2)

Nashville, after Civil Rights Act passage – American 3/10/1875(4)

Nashville, after Civil Rights Act passage/Alonzo Napier involvement – American 3/11/1875(4)

Lynching of Joseph Reed – American 5/1/1875(4) A number of subsequent newspaper articles reported that Reed survived his ordeal.

Lynching of David Jones – Republican Banner 3/26/1872(4)

Colored Emigration Manifesto – Republican Banner 5/20/1875(4)

Alonzo Napier, selected to find place to emigrate – Republican Banner 5/20/1875(4)

Alonzo Napier, returning from Kansas – (from Topeka Blade) Leavenworth Times 8/3/1875(2)

Alonzo Napier, reaches Nashville – Republican Banner 8/11/1875(4)

Alonzo Napier, delivery of report – Union and American 8/15/1875(1)

Alonzo Napier, organizes Key Rifles – American 4/3/1877(4)

Alonzo Napier, marriage to Elmira Copeland – Missouri State Archives, Ancestry.com. Missouri Marriage Records, 1805-2002

Alonzo Napier, Meharry graduate – American 12/17/1882(6)

Alonzo Napier, teaching in St. Louis – St. Louis Globe-Democrat 12/16/1882(5), American 12/17/1882(6) "Death of H. A. Napier"

Alonzo Napier, principal of Vandaville School – Daily American 12/6/1882(3)

Alonzo Napier, return to Nashville/accident – American 12/17/1882(6)

Alonzo Napier, Napier School naming – Banner 11/1/1899(2)

Alonzo Napier, newspaper eulogy – American 12/17/1882(6)

Elias Napier (son of Carroll), born in Cincinnati – National Archives, Registers of Signatures of

Depositors in Branches of the Freedman's Savings and Trust Company, 1865-1874; Record Group: Records of the Office of the Comptroller of the Currency; Record Group Number: 101; Series Number: M816; NARA Roll: 25

Elias Napier family, in Davidson County by November, 1850 – 1850 US Census, Davidson County, Tennessee; Roll: 875; Page: 336a

Elias Napier family, in Nashville by 1857 – Nashville, Tennessee, Business Directory, 1857 – listing for W. C. Napier

Jane Napier taking children back to Ohio – Tennessean 7/4/1937(Magazine – 2) "An Old Colored Man" by Helen Dahnke

Elias Napier, student at Fisk – Fisk University catalogues, 1867-68, 1868-69

Elias Napier, working in livery stable – Banner 3/18/1934(10) "Nashville Negroes Have Made Great Progress" by M. B. Morton

Elias Napier, horses awarded premiums at fair – Union & American 9/14/1871 (4)

Elias Napier, incident at fair – Union & American 9/17/1871(4)

Elias Napier, arrested for incident at fair – Union & American 9/22/1871(4)

Elias Napier, fined for assault at fair – Union & American 6/12/1872(4)

Elias Napier, breaking man's nose – Union & American 1/30/1875(4)

Elias Napier, response to Civil Rights Act – Republican Banner 3/11/1875(4)

Elias Napier, marriage – American 4/9/1876

Elias Napier, fight with Mrs. Harding – American 7/27/1876(4) Elias Napier's original words were presented in a second-person account, and have been converted back to a first-person account.

Elias Napier, hunting dogs – American 8/9/1876(4)

Elias Napier, owner of "Red Light Saloon" – 4/12/1885(1)

Elias Napier, knocks down Carter Thompson – Banner 2/6/1888(4)

Elias Napier, arresting carriage thief – American 7/17/1889(10)

Elias Napier, assaults Dugger – American 8/11/1889(5)

Elias Napier, pleads guilty/pays fine – American 8/13/1889(5)

Elias Napier, contract for carrying mail – American 7/8/1896(5)

Elias Napier, provides vehicles to Mrs. Overton – Banner 6/18/1897(1), Banner 6/18/1898(8)

Elias Napier, horses provided for parade – Comet (Johnson City, Tn.) 6/24/1897(2)

Elias Napier, home burns – American 12/4/1897(3)

Elias Napier, death – Nashville Death Records, 1872-1923, page 131 (5/26/1898)

Dr. James Alonzo Napier, biographical details – Banner 4/3/1909(8)

Ida Napier Lawson, biographical details – Hartford Courant 12/22/1965(4), 3/23/1992(169)

R. Augustus Lawson, image – Crisis Magazine, February 1912

Rosalind Lawson (Putnam), biographical details – Hartford Courant 2/1/1976(111)

Warner Lawson, biographical details – Banner 3/12/1933(2), 5/25/1951(6), Hartford Courant 6/8/1971(6A), 2/1/1976(111)

Ida Napier, date of birth – tombstone inscription, Greenwood Cemetery, Nashville

Ida Napier, student at Fisk – Ancestry.com. U.S., School Catalogs, 1765-1935, Fisk University, 1868-70, 1872, 1874-76

Ida Napier, student at Oberlin – Ancestry.com. U.S., School Catalogs, 1765-1935, Oberlin College, 1878

Ida Napier, account of marriage – American 12/27/1878(4)

John Mercer Langston, biographical details – St. Louis Globe-Democrat 6/16/1901(48), New York Sun 11/21/1897(21)

James Carroll Napier, marriage – American 12/27/1878(4)

Arthur Langston, biographical details – St. Louis Globe-Democrat 4/8/1908(13)

Ida Langston, residency in St. Louis – US Census, 1880 – 1930

Ida Napier, death – St. Louis Globe-Democrat 10/31/1937(45)

John Mercer Langston Jr., biographical details – American 2/15/1903(8)

Arthur Langston, death – St. Louis Globe-Democrat 4/8/1908(13)

Carroll Langston Sr., graduates from Oberlin – American 2/15/1903(8)

Carroll Langston Sr., move to Nashville – Nashville City Directory, 1904

J.C. Napier, founding bank – Tennessean 7/4/1937(Magazine – 2)

Carroll Langston, birth of son – Sheryll Cashin, *The Agitator's Daughter: A Memoir of Four Generations of One Extraordinary African American Family* (79-80), WWII Draft Registration Cards for Illinois, 10/16/1940-03/31/1947; Record Group: Records of the Selective Service System, 147, Box: 1018, 1920 US Census 1920, Nashville Ward 9, Davidson County, Tennessee, Roll T625_1734, page 14A Enumeration District: 34

Carroll Langston Sr., move to Chicago – Cashin (80)

Carrol Napier Langston, Jr., images – Hyde Park High School 1934 Yearbook, 51; Tuskegee Flying School cadets (9/30/1943) https://www.ancestrylibrary.com/mediaui viewer/collection/1030/tree/ 158489244/person/222097217632/media/64eb62c2-64bb-4dbd-a158-5afe95715e33?_phsrc=pRi557&usePUBJs=true

Carroll Langston Jr., at Oberlin – Ancestry.com, US School Yearbooks, 1880-2012, Oberlin College, 1938

Carroll Langston Jr., Michigan Law School – Banner 7/14/1944(4), WWII Draft Registration Cards for Illinois, 10/16/1940-03/31/1947, Record Group: Records of the Selective Service System, 147, Box: 1018

Carroll Langston Jr., attorney – Chicago Tribune 5/8/1944(2),

Carroll Langston Jr., military service – Sheryll Cashin, The Agitator's Daughter (79-80), Chicago Tribune 5/8/1944(2)

Carroll Langston Jr., at Tuskegee Air Training School – Ibid, Chicago Tribune 12/19/1943(7)

McKissack and McKissack, construction of Tuskegee Airfield/Facility – Tennessean 10/25/1942(2)

Carroll Langston Jr., service in Italy – Sheryll Cashin, The Agitator's Daughter (79-80), Chicago Tribune 5/8/1944(2)

Carroll Langston Jr., death – Banner 7/14/1944(4)

Carroll/Jane Napier, 50th Anniversary celebration – American 9/16/1894(5)

Carroll Napier, death – American 12/22/1895(14)

Jane Napier, death – St. Louis Globe-Democrat 11/25/1909(13)

Rebecca Watkins, death – American 12/23/1885(4)

J.C. Napier, values taught by parents – From Banner 3/18/1934(10) "Nashville Negroes Have Made Great Progress" by M. B. Morton

J.C. Napier, early life – this first-person account is a compilation taken from four separate sources: The Journal of Negro History, Volume 5, number 1,"Some Negro Members of the Tennessee Legislature During Reconstruction Period and After" by J. C. Napier, pages 113-118; Nashville Banner 9/24/ 1933(25), "J. C. Napier to Head Negro Section of Drive for Fisk;" Nashville Banner 3/18/1934(10), "Nashville Negroes Have Made Much Progress" by M. B. Morton; Tennessean 7/4/1937(Magazine – 2) "An Old Colored Man" by Helen Dahnke. In certain segments, third person accounts were changed to first-person accounts, and passages were edited for readability and clarity.

Rufus Conrad, image – Louisville Courier-Journal 4/13/1893(7)

J.C. Napier, Colored Convention appointment – Republican Banner 2/24/1870(1)

J.C. Napier, meeting with President Grant – Union & American 3/13/1870(2)

J.C. Napier, work at State Department – Cordell Hull Williams, 'The Life of James Carroll Napier from 1845 to 1940," page 9, Thesis, Tennessee A & I (1954)

J.C. Napier, influence of John M. Langston – Banner 3/18/1934(10)

John Mercer Langston, image – Library of Congress (LC-BH83- 30771)

J.C. Napier, oration at Howard – Union & American 3/5/1872(4)

J.C. Napier, admitted to bar – Tennessean 7/4/1937(Magazine – 2)

J.C. Napier, Internal Revenue appointment – Union & American 5/16/1874(4)

J.C. Napier, salary at Revenue Service – Memphis Public Ledger 5/22/1874(2)

J.C. Napier, discrimination incidents – American 6/3/1874(4)

J.C. Napier, murder investigation – Republican Banner 1/24/1875(4)

J.C. Napier, marriage – Burlington (Vermont) Free Press 10/11/1878(3)

J.C. Napier, account of wedding from Cincinnati paper – American 10/16/1878(1)

J.C. Napier, first black to preside over City Council – Banner 3/18/1934(10)

Vandavell School, condition of – Daily American 11/23/1881(4)

J.C. Napier, spearheading establishment of black schools – Globe 3/17/1911(5), Williams thesis, 11 Napier School, named for Alonzo Napier – Banner 11/1/1899(2)

J.C. Napier, pushing for hiring of black teachers – Tennessee Historical Quarterly, Volume 49, #4, "James Carroll Napier: National Negro Leader" by Herbert L. Clark (243), Williams thesis, 12

J.C. Napier, establishment of black fire companies – Clark (243)

J.C. Napier, account of IRS career – Tennessean 7/4/1937(Magazine – 2)

J.C. Napier, speech re baseball – American 8/19/1891(5)

J.C. Napier, Washington DC interview – Colored American 11/2/1901(1)

J.C. Napier, secretary of State Republican Party – American 4/28/1882(2)

J.C. Napier, delegate to national conventions – St. Louis Palladium 7/2/1904(1), Globe 6/19/1908(1-2) Nashville American, editorial re Napier – American 9/14/1898(4)

1898 election returns – American 11/15/1898(3)

J.C. Napier, president Nashville Negro Board of Trade – Tennessean & American 5/28/1914(6)

J.C. Napier, president National Negro Business League/speech – Clark (247)

J.C. Napier, Napier Court/ image – Colored American 11/2/1901(1)

J.C. Napier, account of founding bank – Tennessean 7/4/1937(Magazine – 2)

J.C. Napier, praise from Dr. R. F. Boyd – Globe 3/17/1911(6)

J.C. Napier, appointment to Treasury post – Globe 10/14/1910(4)

J.C. Napier, using office to help blacks – Clark (249-51)

J.C. Napier, restroom segregation/resignation – Clark (251)

J.C. Napier, adoption of Carrie Langston – 1900 US Census, Davidson County, Nashville Ward 6, Page: 2, Enumeration District 84, microfilm # 1241564

J.C. Napier, 1934 newspaper interview – Banner 3/18/1934(10)

J. C. Napier, image as older man – Nashville Public Library, Special Collections

J.C. Napier, 1937 newspaper interview, reading Gone With the Wind – Tennessean 7/4/ 1937(Magazine – 2)

J. C. Napier image, visiting birthplace – Fisk University Library Special Collections, J.C. Napier Collection

J.C. Napier, 1938 birthday interview – Banner 6/10/1938(14)

J.C. Napier, interview re slave markets – Banner 5/6/1934(24)

Nettie Napier, death – Tennessean 9/28/1938(10)

Ida Napier, death – St. Louis Globe-Democrat 10/31/1937(45)

William Napier, burial at City Cemetery – City Cemetery Records (death 12/29/1851)

J.C. Napier, death – Tennessee State Library and Archives, Tennessee Death Records, 1908-1958,Roll 4, 1884 sledding account – American 1/26/1884(5)

Preston Taylor

Preston Taylor, image – James T. Haley *Afro-American Encyclopedia*, 217

Preston Taylor, 1931 article – Banner 4/16/1931(5), Tennessean 4/17/1931(4)

Preston Taylor, 1907 account – Washington, Booker T. *The Negro in Business* (100)

Preston Taylor, 1895 sketch – James T. Haley, A*fro-American Encyclopaedia; Or, the Thoughts, Doings, and Sayings of the Race, Embracing Lectures, Biographical Sketches, Sermons, Poems, Names of Universities, Colleges, Seminaries, Newspapers, Books, and a History of the Denominations, Giving the Numerical Strength of Each. In Fact, it Teaches Every Subject of Interest to the Colored People, as Discussed by More Than One Hundred of Their Wisest and Best Men and Women.* Nashville, Tenn.: Haley & Florida, 1895, (215)

Preston Taylor, early life – Ibid

Preston Taylor, marriage to Ellen Spradling – Ancestry.com. Kentucky Marriage Records, 1783-1965, Madison County, Richmond, Kentucky (4/7/1870)

Preston Taylor, family in 1870 – 1870 Census, Jefferson County, Kentucky, Louisville, Ward 11, Roll M593_476, page 555B

Preston Taylor, post-marriage biographical details – *Afro-American Encyclopedia*, 215-17

Preston Taylor, founding new churches – Public Ledger (Memphis) 4/7/1883(4)

Preston Taylor, establishes Bible College – Washington, Booker T. The Negro in Business (101)

Preston Taylor, railroad contracting details – *Afro-American Encyclopedia*, 216

Preston Taylor, political activity – Louisville Journal 10/9/1884(1)

Preston Taylor, domestic discord – South Kentuckian 7/1/1884(2)

Preston Taylor, move to Nashville – Banner 3/25/1885(4)

Ellen Preston Taylor, choir controversy – *Afro-American Encyclopedia*, page 218

Choir concert, review – American 5/12/1886(5)

Preston Taylor, membership in organizations – *Afro-American Encyclopedia*, 217-18

Preston Taylor, establishes Taylor & Company – Ibid, 220

Preston Taylor, Chancery Court lawsuit – Banner 5/11/1889(5), American 5/12/1889(5), 1/4/1891(13)

Preston Taylor, marriage to Georgia Gordon – Banner 5/7/1890(3)

Preston Taylor, death of son – Tennessee State Library and Archives, Tennessee Death Records, 1908-1959 Roll M-3 (Preston Gordon Taylor, 6/8/1891)

Lea Avenue Church, established – American 6/1/1891(5)

Lea Avenue Church, photo – Haley, *Afro-American Encyclopedia*, 621

Taylor & Company, description – Ibid, 220

Booker T. Washington, address – American 9/23/1897(5)

Preston Taylor, purchases land for cemetery – Banner 3/24/1899(2)

1905 legislative bill, article – American 3/25/1899(6)

Rev. Eugene Harris, letter – Banner 3/25/1899(5)

Taylor and Company, letter – American 4/17/1899(8)

Greenwood Cemetery, dedication – American 6/12/1900(5)

Preston Taylor, provides shelter and coal for poor – American 2/8/1905(5), 3/5/1905(9), 4/17/1905(5)

Booker T. Washington, praises Preston Taylor – Washington, Booker T. *The Negro in Business* (102)

Preston Taylor, buys property on 5th Avenue North – American 9/18/1905(2)

Preston Taylor, plans for property – Banner 9/18/1905(3)

Preston Taylor, transportation company at Taylor & Company – Banner 10/7/1905(6)

Globe, praise for Preston Taylor – Globe 9/4/1908(15)

Preston Taylor, early use of Greenwood Park – Globe 5/31/1907(3)

Globe, criticism of legislative bill – Globe 4/12/1907(1)

Gov. Patterson, veto of bill – Globe 4/19/1907(1,4)

Preston Taylor, explanation of veto – Globe 7/12/1912(4)

Duncan Cooper, details – Summerville, James, *The Carmack-Cooper Shooting, Tennessee Politics Turns Violent*, November 9, 1908, McFarland and Company, Publishers, 1994 (17-18, 52-54, 58, 123-4)

Ben Carr, image – This photograph of Carr has been frequently misidentified as being an image of Dr. Robert F. Boyd. The original photograph is from the Calvert Brothers Studio Collection at the TSLA – glass plate negative #11356. Under the heading 1899, the studio daybook contains the listing, "B.J. Carr colored" followed by the identifying number 11356, and the matching number is on the corresponding glass plate.

Ben Carr, details – American 1/10/1891(1), 2/28/1894(1), 1/4/1899(1), 10/11/1900(4), 2/14/1903(10)

Greenwood Park, description – Banner 7/3/1907(3)

Greenwood Park, opening day details – Globe 7/12/1907(2)

Preston Taylor, plans for Greenwood Park – Globe 8/2/1907(1)

Greenwood Park, grandstand built, fire – American 1/10/1910(5)

Taylor & Company, founding details – Globe 9/4/1908(15)

Georgia Gordon Taylor, image – James T. Haley, *Sparkling Gems of Race Knowledge Worth Reading – A Compendium of Valuable Information and Wise Suggestions That Will Inspire Noble Effort at the Hands of Evert Race-Loving Man, Woman, and Child*, Nashville (1897), 75

Georgia Gordon Taylor, death, funeral – Globe 6/13/1913(1,4)

Preston Taylor, infidelity – Bragg, Dr. Emma W., Scrapbook: Some Family Reminiscences if a Native Nashville Septuagenarian, page 7, (1985, ISBN 0-9611930-2-6)

Preston Taylor, marriage to Ida Mallory – Banner 6/22/1916(13)

Preston Taylor, resignation from church – (Lea Avenue Church History)
   eb.archive.org/web/20150219194345/http://www.newcovenantnashville.org/about.php

Preston Taylor, War Work Campaign activity – Globe 11/15/1918(1)

Preston Taylor, death – Tennessee State Library and Archives, Tennessee Death Records, 1908-1958; Roll Number 4 (4/13/1931 – Certificate # 7757)

Greenwood Cemetery, left to Disciples of Christ – http://greenwoodcemeterytn.com/about.html

Preston Taylor, final quote – Globe 3/1/1907(3)

Richard Henry Boyd

Introductory image – James T. Haley, *Sparkling Gems of Race Knowledge Worth Reading – A Compendium of Valuable Information and Wise Suggestions That Will Inspire Noble Effort at the Hands of Evert Race-Loving Man, Woman, and Child*, Nashville (1897), 193

Richard Henry Boyd (RHB), early life of mother – *A Black Man's Dream: The First 100 Years, Richard Henry Boyd and the Baptist Publishing Board*, Bobby Lovett, PHD, 1993 (13)

RHB, biographical pamphlet – Nashville Banner 3/23/1928 (19) "Born a Slave, He Rose from Obscurity…"

Benoni Gray (BG), birth – 1850 US Census, Lowndes Co. Mississippi

BG, marriage to Martha Speller – Walton Co. Georgia marriage records (12/27/1827)

BG, moves family to Alabama – 1840 US Census, Chambers Co. Alabama (Benin Gray)

BG, moves family to Mississippi – 1850 US Census, Lowndes Co. Mississippi (Benoni Gray)

BG, birthplaces of children – 1860 US Census, Grimes Co. Texas (B. W. Gray)

BG, Bible – Ancestry.com "Bible of Benoni W. Gray" ("posted 9/26/2020 by Diane Bender" – "Ruby Wallace, bible of Benoni Gray, from her brother Kenneth Gray, July, 2008") https://www.ancestry.com/mediaui-viewer/tree/78419960/person/30385116763/media/ 2ae03b09-6170-4c82-8af1-2f3b38d3672e?_phsrc=KEW95&_phstart=successS

BG, 1850 slave ownership – 1850 US Census, Slave Schedule, Lowndes Co. Mississippi (Benoni Gray)

Indiana Gray, birthdates of children – Tennessee State Library and Archives, Nashville, Tennessee, Tennessee Death Records, 1908-1958, Roll Number 1, Davidson Co. death certificate of Samuel L. Dixon (#2880); Texas Department of State Health Services. Texas Death Certificates, 1903–1982. Austin, Texas, Grimes Co. certificate of Martha E. Miller (#18395); Texas Death Certificates, Upshur Co. certificate of Lewis Dixon (#15648), age 72 in 1941, approximate year of birth – 1869 (his mother not listed, but see Nashville Banner 2/4/1936(9) obituary of Rev. S. J. Dixon – lists surviving brother, Louis Dixon of Gilmer, Texas, as well as Boyd family relations)

Martha Gray, death – 1860 US Census, Grimes Co. Texas Mortality Schedule, Martha Gray (died June, 1859, of "flux.")

BG, remarriage – Ancestry.com. Louisiana, U.S., Compiled Marriage Index, 1718-1925, Claiborne Parish, Louisiana, Benoni Gray/Lavina Justiss (12/14/1859)

BG, residence/land holdings in 1860 – 1860 US Census, Agricultural Schedule, Anderson, Grimes, Texas, Archive Collection Number T1134, Roll 4, Page 1, Line 7 (B [or R] W Gray)

BG, family members in 1860, presence of John H. Wilson – 1860 US Census, Anderson, Grimes, Texas, Page 224 (families of B. W. Gray & J. H. P. Gray)

John Hamill Wilson, biographical details – Galveston Daily News 6/14/1887(2) "Navosta"

RHB ("Dick Gray"), pamphlet account of Civil War experience – Nashville Banner 3/23/1928 (19)

Benoni Gray, deaths of sons in CSA – "Bible of Benoni W. Gray" (entries for William Schley Gray and George Hanson Gray); National Archives and Records Administration, Washington, D.C., Compiled Service Records of Confederate Soldiers Who Served in Organizations from the State of Texas, Series Number M323, Roll 357; Ancestry.com, "John Hamilton Posey Gray" – National Park Service. U.S., Civil War Soldiers, 1861-1865, film number M227, Roll 14 (John H. P. Gray, Company A, 12th Texas Infantry)

Richard Henry Gray, CSA service – National Park Service, US, Civil War Soldiers, 1861-1865, film # M227, Roll 14 (Richard H. Gray, 21st Texas Cavalry, Co. H (1st Texas Lancers)

Thomas W. Boyd, CSA service (13th Texas Infantry) – Texas State Library and Archives, Confederate Pension Applications, 1899-1975, Collection # CPA16526, Roll # 472, Pension File # 10816 (Sarah F. Boyd)

RHB, story of taking refuge in Mexico – Elias C. Morris, *Sermons, Addresses and Reminiscences, With a Picture Gallery of Eminent Ministers and Scholars* (278)

RHB, changing name from Dick Gray, postwar work – Banner 3/23/1928 (19)

RHB, 1868 marriage/death of wife – Morris (278)

RHB, 1869 baptism – Ibid

RHB, enters Bishop College, serves as pastor – Early, "Richard Henry Boyd: Shaper of Baptist Identity"

RHB, marries Harriet Moore – Grimes Co. Texas marriage records, 2/15/1872, film # 1006281

RHB, birth of first child – 1880 US Census, Precinct 5, Montgomery, Texas, Roll 1320, Page 103C, Enumeration District 125 (Richard Boyd)

RHB, helps form Texas Negro Baptist Association, forms churches – Early, "Richard Henry Boyd: Shaper of Baptist Identity"

RHB, represents Texas in national organizations – Ibid

RHB, favors black production of Sunday School materials – Early, Joe Jr. Baptist History and Heritage (6/22/2007), "Richard Henry Boyd: Shaper of Baptist Identity" (Early citation: Program, Tenth Annual Session, National Baptist Convention, Richmond, Virginia, September 12-17, 1900, 31)

RHB, family prosperity in 1880 – 1880 US Census, Agricultural Schedule, District 81, Johnson Co. Texas, Number T1134, Roll 30, Page 28, Line 5 (Richard H. Boyd)

National Baptist Convention, formed – *Tennessee History – The Land, the People, and the Culture*, edited by Carroll Vann West, "'The Holy Spirit Come to Us and Forbid the Negro from Taking a Second Place:' Richard H. Boyd and Black Religious Activism in Nashville'" by Paul Harvey (273)

RHB, account of forming National Baptist Publishing Board – American 1/4/1901(2)

National Baptist Publishing Board, image of workers – https://tennesseeencyclopedia.net/entries/national-baptist-publishing-board/

Booker T. Washington, account of RHB's early years in Nashville – Washington, Booker T. *The Negro in Business* (188 -195)

National Baptist Convention, 1899 meeting in Nashville – American 9/15/1899(3)

Attendance of Dr. James M. Frost, speech of RHB – American 9/15/1899(3)

RHB, partnership of Henry Allen Boyd – Harvey "'The Holy Spirit Come to Us…" (282-283)

RHB, 1905 account of NBPB – Banner 12/2/1905(37)

One Cent Savings Bank, founding – Lovett (146-152)

One Cent Savings Bank, renamed in 1920 – Lovett (152)

RHB, letter regarding streetcar segregation – "Negro Automobile Line" Banner 9/27/1905(6)

1905 Streetcar action – Lovett, Bobby L. PHD, A *Black Man's Dream: The First 100 Years, Richard Henry Boyd and the National Baptist Publishing Board* (161), Briggs, Gabriel A. The New Negro in the Old South, Rutgers University Press (2015)

RHB, installation of dynamo – Harvey, Paul "Richard Henry Boyd – Black Business and Religion in the Jim Crow South" in Calhoun, Charles W. The Human Tradition in America (65)

Nashville Globe, founding – Harvey, "The Holy Spirit Come to Us…" (280)

Nashville Globe, role of Henry Allen Boyd – Ibid (282)

National Negro Doll Company, founding – Harvey, "The Holy Spirit Come to Us…" (281)

National Negro Doll Company, quote – Harvey, "Richard Henry Boyd – Black Business…" (65-66)

Nashville Globe, activism in black education – Lovett (172), Harvey, "The Holy Spirit Come to Us…" (283)

NBPB, 1908 article – Globe 9/4/1908(12)

Boyd family photo – *Sermons, Addresses and Reminiscences and Important Correspondence, With a Picture Gallery of Eminent Ministers and Scholars*, E. C. Morris, D. D, Nashville, Tenn. National Baptist Publishing Board 1901, 322

Union Transportation Company, image – https://www.blackpast.org/african-american-history/union-transportation-company-1905-1907/

RHB, opposition to – Harvey, "Richard Henry Boyd – Black Business…" (61-64)

RHB, children working at NBPB – Lovett (96-97)

Indiana (Gray), marriage to Sam Dixon – Tennessee State Library and Archives, Tennessee Death Records, 1908-1958, Roll Number 1, (Samuel J. Dixon, Jr., 2/3/1936, certificate # 353)

Indiana Dixon, number of living children – 1910 US Census, Davidson County, Nashville Ward 5, Roll T624_1495, Page: 5A, Enumeration District 0027, FHL microfilm 1375508

Indiana Dixon, death – Tennessee State Library and Archives, Tennessee Death Records 1908-1958, Roll Number 30 (Indiana Dixon, 4/19/1915, certificate # 120)

Indiana Dixon, description – Lovett (106) (citation National Baptist Union Review 4/24/1915)

RHB, opposition/schism/lawsuit – Lovett (103-111), Harvey, "The Holy Spirit Come to Us…" (277 – 279)

RHB, death – Nashville Tennessean 8/24/1922(5), Tennessee State Library and Archives; Nashville, Tennessee; Tennessee Death Records, 1908-1958 (8/23/1922, certificate #300)

Henry Allen Boyd, biographical details – Lovett (164-178)

T.B. Boyd, Jr./T. B. Boyd III, biographical details – Lovett (179-184)

NBPB, name changed to R. H. Boyd Publishing Company – rhboyd.com/history

LaDonna Boyd, becomes CEO of Boyd Publishing – Tennessean 11/5/2017(D1)

Lula Boyd, birth – Tennessee State Library and Archives, Tennessee Death Records, 1908-1958 (Lula Landers, 4/20/1960, certificate # 60-09621)

Lula Boyd, marriage – Banner 5/15/1905(9) marriage license issued

Lovell Landers (LL), birth – Tennessee State Library and Archives, Birth Records. Nashville, Tennessee, certificate # 771

LL, 1922 article – Banner 9/1/1922(5) "Negro Boy may be Mechanical Genius"

LL, football at Pearl/Fisk – Banner 10/10/1926(16)

LL, move to New York City – 1930 US Census, Manhattan, New York, Page 6A, Enumeration District 1074, microfilm 2341314 (household of Mark Weakley)

LL, details of arrest/conviction – New York Age 8/5/1933(1) "Former Fisk Athlete Faces Chair"

LL, commutation of sentence – Chattanooga Times 8/1/1934(3)

LL, incarceration at Sing Sing/denial of guilt – Lovell Landers Jr, biographical details – New York State Archives; Albany, NY, USA; Sing Sing Prison, 1852-1938; Box: 51; Volume: 102

LL, inventions while in prison/offers technology to government – Dayton (Ohio) Herald 5/23/1942(8)

LL, electrician in Nashville – Nashville City Directories 1965 – 1985

LL, death – Atlanta Constitution 12/11/1999(71) obituary

RHB, 1901 quote on Negro Baptists and the Negro race – Elias C. Morris, *Sermons, Addresses and Reminiscences, With a Picture Gallery of Eminent Ministers and Scholars* (13-14), National Baptist Publishing Board, Nashville, 1901

Annie Compton

Annie Compton, image – this likeness was provided by Lois Bruce of Nashville. Her husband, Bill Bruce, was a descendant of Henry W. Compton and his white wife, Anna Ward. Wanting to know more about the black family that descended from Henry W. Compton, Lois, a gifted and tireless researcher, contacted Annie Lee Brown, who was a great-granddaughter of Compton and his common-law wife, Annie Allen Compton. Lois received a copy of Annie Compton's likeness, as well as a copy of a mortuary photograph of Dernice Trimble, a daughter of Henry W. and Annie Compton.

James Trimble, interview – Nashville Banner 2/9/1907(23)

James Trimble, health issues – Nashville American 7/10/1907(10), New York City Index to Death Certificates, 1862 – 1948, number 13495

1874 petition against colored firemen – Republican Banner 12/22/1874(4)

Petition rejected – Republican Banner 1/19/1875(4)

1892 fire, newspaper article – Nashville Banner 1/3/1892(1)

C. C. Gowdey, image – Nashville American 9/20/1886(3)

Harvey Ewing/Stokely Allen, images -Nashville Banner 1/4/1892(1)

1892 fire, details of body retrieval – American 1/4/1892(1)

Laura Trimble, biographical details – American 4/25/1903(2), Banner 6/16/1903(8), 9/3/1903(5), Nashville Globe 8/9/1907(5)

Dr. James Trimble Jr. practice – American 6/21/1906(10), Nashville Globe 11/22/1907(7), 5/15/1908(3)

Dr. W.C. Councill, image – James T. Haley, *Sparkling Gems of Race Knowledge Worth Reading – A Compendium of Valuable Information and Wise Suggestions That Will Inspire Noble Effort at the Hands of Evert Race-Loving Man, Woman, and Child*, Nashville (1897), 24

Councill remarks, Pearl High School graduation account- American 6/3/1898(5)

Alexander Trimble, grandfather of James – US Census, Nashville, 1850 and 1860

Alexander ("Elac") Trimble, death – Nashville City Cemetery interment records (10/2/1866)

Aleck and James Trimble, ages – City Cemetery interment records, 1860 US Census, Nashville, household of George Trimble

Aleck Trimble, self-employment – Banner 2/9/1907(23)

James Trimble – Joshua W. Caldwell, *Bench and Bar of Tennessee*, 82-3, W. W. Clayton, *History of Davidson County*, 444, Nashville Whig 4/9/1823(1)

Aleck Trimble, buys freedom – Nashville Banner 2/9/1907(23)

Aleck Trimble, buys wife/daughter – Register of Deeds, Book T, 504, 506

George Trimble year of birth – Nashville death register (9/14/1877)

Aleck (Alexander) Trimble, slave ownership – 1840 US Census Davidson Co, Roll 520, Page: 273; Family History Library Film: 0024543

Aleck Trimble, household in 1850 – 1850 US Census Population Schedule ("A Trimble")

Aleck Trimble, slave ownership in 1850 – 1860 US Census Slave Schedule lists one slave for Trimble. His ownership of a slave in 1840, suggests that he owned a slave in 1850 as well

George Trimble marriage to Laura Ann Bosley – Sistler, *Davidson County, Tn Marriages, 1838 – 1863* (218)

Laura Ann Bosley, family – 1850 US Census, Davidson County Population Schedule

George/Laura Ann Trimble, family in 1860 – 1860 US Census, Davidson County Population Schedule

James Trimble, loss of mother in 1863 – Nashville City Cemetery Records list "Sarah A. Trimble," a free woman of color, age 26, as being buried on 7/14/1863 in the same lot in which Medora and James Trimble, who were siblings of Laura Ann, were buried. But George Trimble, Laura's husband, did have a sister named Sarah. The 1850 Census indicated that she was eighteen years old (born circa 1832) in 1850, while the same census lists Laura Ann as being fourteen (born circa 1836), which made her, at the age of twenty-six of twenty-seven, much closer to the age of the individual who was buried in 1863. It may be that the deceased individual is indeed "Sarah A. Trimble," but in addition to the age discrepancy, considering that Laura had the middle initial "A" and that there is no record of Laura's death in the cemetery burial index, it is not an unreasonable hypothesis to propose that Laura was misidentified as "Sarah A." as the individual buried in 1863.

Aleck ("Elac") Trimble, death – Nashville City Cemetery interment records (10/2/1866)

John B. Bosley, death – Davidson County Will Book 21(38) (1867)

James Trimble, inheritance from James G. Bosley – James G. Bosley, Davidson County Will Book 22 (522)

James Trimble, educated at Fisk – Fisk University Catalogue, 1874 (9) Ancestry.com. U.S., School Catalogs, 1765-1935 [database on-line]. Provo, UT, USA: Ancestry.com Operations, Inc., 2012.

James Trimble, marriage to Dernice ("Janice") Compton – Nashville Globe 7/17/1908 (1)

James Trimble, 1880 household – 1880 US Census, Nashville, Davidson County Tennessee, Roll 1250, Page 306D, Enumeration District: 051

Dernice Compton Trimble, death – American 6/1/1904(6), Banner 6/1/1904(5)

Dernice Compton Trimble, mortuary photo – Compton family collection of Annie Lee Brown (see note for "Annie Compton image" – above)

Dernice Compton, parentage – Tennessee State Library and Archives; Nashville, Tennessee; Tennessee Death Records, 1908-1959; Roll #: M-8

Henry Compton, land holdings – The National Archives at Washington, D.C.; Washington, D.C.; Barred and Disallowed Case Files of the Southern Claims Commission, 1871-1880; Record Group Title: Records of the U.S. House of Representatives, 1789 – 2015; Record Group Number: 233; Series Number: M1407, page 14854 (afterward cited as Southern Claims)

Henry Compton, 1860 slave ownership – 1860 US Census Slave Schedule

Henry Compton, childhood health – W. W. Clayton, *History of Davidson County* (444)

Henry Compton, introversion – Southern Claims (15279-15283)

Henry Compton, ownership of Annie Allen – Southern Claims (14850)

Annie Allen Compton, year of birth – 1870 US Census, Nashville, Ward 10

Annie Allen Compton, parents, siblings – National Archives, Registers of Signatures of Depositors in Branches of the Freedman's Savings and Trust Company, 1865-1874, ARC Identifier 566522, Record Group 101, Records of the Office of the Comptroller of the Currency, 1863-2006, Roll 25, Nashville, Tennessee, Dec 23, 1871-Jun 23, 1874, file 5664; Southern Claims (15271), 1870 US Census, Nashville, Ward 10, household of Henry Compton

Fielding Allen, biographical details – 1850 US Census, Population and Agricultural Schedules Fielding Allen, fathering children with slave – Virginia Birth/Christening Records, Fauquier County, Nat and Samuel Allen (7/10 and 7/11/1854)

Fielding Allen, home furnishings – Fauquier County Will Book 24 (424) appraisement of Allen estate

Fielding Allen, death – Virginia Bureau of Vital Statistics, Death Records 1853-1912, Fauquier County (83)

Henry Compton, emotional attachment to Annie Allen – Southern Claims (14848, 14850, 15279-80)

Henry Compton, Democratic Party affiliation – Nashville Union 12/2/1851(2)

Henry Compton, Whig Party affiliation – Southern Claims (15278)

Return J. Meigs, biographical information – "Return Jonathan Meigs 3rd" (http://meigs.org/rjm368.htm)

Henry Compton, role of Annie in bringing about will – Southern Claims (14850, 15279-80)

Henry Compton, will – Southern Claims (14848-50)

William Compton, death/will – Davidson Co. Will Book 13 (324)

William Compton, slave trader – Southern Claims (15276), Nashville Whig 12/19/1825

William Compton, 1825 slave ad – Nashville Whig 12/19/1825

Henry Compton, 1853 runaway slave ad – Union and American 10/27/1853(2)

Henry Compton, slaves in 1850 – 1850 US Census, Slave Schedule

Henry Compton, purchase of Shute place – Davidson County Deed Book 13 (148-9)

H.H. Haynes Co. slaves-wanted ad – Republican Banner 4/25/1858(2)

H.H. Haynes Co slave-sale ad – Daily Patriot 8/25/1858(4)

Charles Allen, to Compton place as a boy – Southern Claims (14810)

Allen and Compton farms, changes in mulatto population – Fielding Allen (Fauquier County, Va) and Henry W. Compton (Davidson County, Tn) 1850 Slave Schedule – The National Archive in Washington DC; Washington, DC; NARA Microform Publication: M432; Title: Seventh Census of United States, 1850; Record Group: Records of the Bureau of the Census; Record Group Number: 29. 1860 Slave Schedule, Eighth Census of the United States 1860; Series Number: M653

Compton homeplace, image – W. W. Clayton, *History of Davidson County,* (following) 442

Joshua Compton, parentage – Tennessee State Library and Archives; Nashville, Tennessee; Tennessee Death Records, 1908-1958; Roll Number: 152, Davidson County Death Certificate, file 274 (5/13/1923)

William Henry Compton, birth/parentage – Tennessee State Library and Archives, Tennessee Death Records, 1908-1958, Roll Number, 5, certificate 9898 (5/21/1948)

Henry Harding, description of Henry/Annie Compton – Southern Claims (14730)

Henry Compton, social impact of relationship with Annie – Southern Claims (15279-80)

Dernice Compton, birth/parentage – Tennessee State Library and Archives, Tennessee Death Records, 1908-1959, Roll # M-8, certificate 847 (5/31/1904)

Annie Compton, possible weaver – Southern Claims (15075). The individual mentioned is merely identified as "Ann," and a slave named Ann was inherited by Henry Compton from his father in the mid-1840s. But Annie was also sometimes called Ann, and the individual identified as Ann who working with Delia was, like Annie, an emancipated Compton slave.

Compton farm, foraging parties – Southern Claims (14720-24)

Maria Compton, birth/parentage – Tennessee State Library and Archives, Tennessee Death Records, 1908-1958, Roll Number 9, certificate 20898 (10/22/1943)

Mary Ann and Thomas Compton, births/parentage – Mary Ann (Stewart): Tennessee Death Records, 1908-1958, Roll Number 8, certificate 18318 (10/22/1943), Thomas: Davidson Co. Will Book 47, p 102

Henry Compton, 1870 household – 1870 US Census, Nashville, Ward 10, Roll M593_1523, Page: 483B, Family History Library Film 553022

Henry Compton, children educated at Fisk – Ancestry.com. U.S., School Catalogs, 1765-1935 [database online]. Provo, UT, USA: Ancestry.com Operations, Inc., 2012. Fisk/Nashville Institute Catalogues 1868 – 1875

Annie Compton, death – Republican Banner, 12/25/1873(4)

Henry Compton, marriage to Anna Ward – Davidson Co. Marriages, Book 6 (383)

Anna Ward, age – although Anna Ward's death certificate gave her year of birth as 1859, the 1870 census listed her age as seventeen, and as twenty-eight in the 1880 census, placing her birth around 1852-3

Henry Compton, emotional connection with Annie Compton – Southern Claims (15279-80)

Henry Compton, birth of white children – (Susan) Knox Co. Tn Death Records, certificate 5841 (3/17/1934), (Mary) Davidson Co. Death Records, certificate 14784 (7/8/1927), (Margaret) Obituary, Tennessean 8/20/1965(33), (Ann E.) Nashville, Calvary Cemetery, tombstone inscription, Section 14/lot 77

Henry Compton, will – Davidson Co Tn Will Book 33, 260

Henry Compton, descendants in neighborhood – 1976 visit to Clarence T. Compton of Tyne Blvd by author

Dernice Compton, marriage to James Trimble – Globe 7/17/1908(1)

Maria Compton, marriage to Dr. Noel – American 6/17/1881

Dr. Noel, biographical details – American 9/23/1886 (4), (Banner 10/14/1899(6)

Mary Ann Compton, marriage to Dr. F.A. Stewart – Tennessee State Library and Archives, Tennessee Death Records, 1908-1958, Roll Number 8, certificate 18090 (8/8/1937)

Dr. Ferdinand A. Stewart, image – James T. Haley, *Sparkling Gems...* 112

Dr. Stewart, biographical details – American 8/28/1888(11), 10/8/1900(5), Tennessean 8/20/1937(6)

Dr. James G. Trimble, biographical details – Tennessean 1/29/1924(2)

James Trimble, death – Nashville Globe 7/17/1908 (1)

Pap Singleton

Benjamin Singleton, in Nashville in May, 1846 – Tri-Weekly Nashville Union 6/13/1846(2)

Nashville, local war news in 1846 – Republican Banner 6/1/1846(3)

Benjamin Singleton, work as cabinet maker – American 4/29/1879(2)

Benjamin Singleton, owned by Robert L. Weakley – Tri-Weekly Nashville Union 6/13/1846(2)

Colonel Robert Weakley, image – W. W. Clayton, *History of Davidson County* 206

Robert L. Weakley, residence – Ibid, 1/25/1845(2)

Robert L. Weakley, officer in 3rd Tennessee – National Archives and Records Administration; Washington D.C., Compiled Service Records of Volunteer Soldiers Who Served During the Mexican War in Organizations from the State of Tennessee, Record Group Title: Records of the Adjutant General's Office, 1762-1984, Record Group Number RG 94, Series # M638, NARA Roll 9

Robert L. Weakley, son of Colonel Robert Weakley – Banner 2/1/1939(13)

Col. Weakley, role in 1834 Constitutional Convention – National Banner & Daily Advertiser 7/17/1834(2)

Benjamin Singleton, family in 1846 – 1870 Census, Davidson County, Nashville, Ward 4, Roll M593_1523, Page 265B

Emily Singleton, age – Ibid

Benjamin Singleton, "blood of a white man…" – Reports of Committees: 30th Congress, 1st Session – 48th Congress, 2nd Session, Volume 8, 381

Benjamin Singleton, "I'se borned…" – Kansas City Star 2/17/1897 (1)

Benjamin Singleton, boyhood jockey – Kansas City Star 2/18/1900(2)

Shelby family, details – Jay Guy Cisco, Historic Sumner County, 104, 108, 112, 123-4

Benjamin Singleton, runaway stories – American 4/29/1879(2)

Benjamin Singleton, never in Louisiana/Mississippi – Reports, Vol. 8, page 390

Robert L. Weakley runaway ad, image – Tri-Weekly Nashville Union 6/13/1846(2)

Benjamin Singleton, fleeing through Indiana – Reports, Vol. 8, page 388

Benjamin Singleton, living in Detroit – 1850 Census, Michigan, Wayne County, Detroit, Roll 365, Page 149b, American 4/29/1879(2)

Benjamin Singleton, return to Nashville – American 4/29/1879(2)

Benjamin Singleton, making coffins – Reports, 382

Benjamin Singleton, at close of decade – 1870 Census, Davidson County, Nashville, Ward 4, Roll M593_1523, Page 265B

Benjamin Singleton, 1878 article – American 4/29/1879(2)

Benjamin Singleton, 1880 account – Reports, 380-4, 390

   https://bit.ly/3m4am2R; The account that is presented was pieced together from various sections of Singleton's testimony, and was lightly edited and presented in a revised order.

Benjamin Singleton, founding Tennessee Real Estate and Homestead Assoc. – Walter L. Fleming, "Pap Singleton, the Moses of the Colored Exodus" American Journal of Sociology, Vol. 15, #1, 64-5

Benjamin Singleton, advice from whites to buy Tennessee land – Reports, 389

Benjamin Singleton, early activities in Kansas – Roy Garvin, "Benjamin or 'Pap' Singleton and his Followers, Journal of Negro History, Vol. 33, #1, 7-23

Benjamin Singleton, description of Singleton Colony – Reports, 380

Benjamin Singleton, association with Johnson and DeFrantz – Fleming, "Pap Singleton, the Moses of the Colored Exodus" 65

Benjamin Singleton, printing/distribution of circulars – Reports, 380-1

Benjamin Singleton, Dunlap and Nicodemus Colonies – Fleming, 68

Benjamin Singleton, conflict with affluent blacks – Bobby L. Lovett, The African-American History of Nashville, Tennessee, 1780-1930, University of Arkansas Press (1999), 82

Nashville emigrants, arrival in Leavenworth – Workingman's Friend (Leavenworth) 4/27/1878(3)

Benjamin Singleton, 1879 response ("Now they say…") – Lawrence (Kansas) Tribune 5/1/1879(4)

Benjamin Singleton, testimony before US Senate Committee – Reports, 379-91

Benjamin Singleton, described in Indianapolis paper – Topeka Daily Capital 9/1/1880(4)

Black population growth in Kansas, 1870-1880 – John G. Van Deusen, "The Exodus of 1879," The Journal of Negro History, Vol. 21, #2, 127

Social relief organizations formed – Fleming, 71, Reports, 371

Benjamin Singleton, other settlement land considered – Fleming, 73, 77-9

Benjamin Singleton, paraphrased in Topeka paper – Topeka Weekly Times 9/28/1883(4)

Dunlap Colony, details – Joseph V. Hickey, "Pap Singleton's Dunlap Colony," Great Plains Quarterly, Volume 11, #1, 23-26,

Benjamin Singleton, at Jo Shelby visitation – Kansas City Star 2/17/1897(1)

Benjamin Singleton, death – Kansas City Star 2/18/1900(2)

Nelson Walker

Nelson Walker barber shop ad, image – Union and American 2/5/1867(3)

Walker family, activity on 5/27/1875 – Union & American 5/28/1875(4), Republican Banner 5/28/1875(3)

Walker home, location – 1830 Virginia Census, Campbell Co., Series M19, Roll 194, Page 338

Nelson Walker, year(s) of birth – Union & American 7/8/1875(4), 1870 Census, Davidson County, Nashville, Ward 5, Roll M593_1523, Page 295B

Nelson Walker, likely son of William H. P. Tabb – Tomeiko Ashford Carter, "*Virginia Broughton: The Life and Writings of a Missionary*," University of Tennessee Press, 2010, p. xxii

William Tabb, age – Tabb family information, https://www.ancestry.com/family tree/person/tree/8783281/person/24440551191/facts

William Tabb, marriage to Calpurnia Featherstone – Ancestry.com. Virginia, U.S., Compiled Marriages, 1740-1850

Augusta Tabb, birth – Tabb family information, https://www.ancestry.com/family-tree/person/tree/8783281/person/24440551191/facts

Tabb family, slaves in 1830 – 1830 Virginia Census, Campbell Co., Series M19, Roll 194, Page 338

William Tabb, death – https://www.ancestry.com/family-tree/person/tree/8783281/person/24440551191/facts

Blucher Tabb, age – Tabb family information, https://www.ancestry.com/family tree/person/tree/8783281/person/24440551191/facts

Nelson Walker, owned by Blucher Tabb – Union & American 7/8/1875(4)

Calpurnia Tabb, death – Tabb family information, https://www.ancestry.com/family-tree/person/tree/8783281/person/24440551191/facts

J. Knox Walker, biographical details – https://bit.ly/3dNvdml

Knox Walker, marriage to Augusta Tabb – Ibid

Knox/Augusta Walker, move to Tennessee – Ibid

Walker family, settles in Columbia – Union & American 7/8/1875(4)

Nelson Walker, treatment as slave – Carter p. xxi-xxii

Knox Walker, family in Washington – 1850 Census, Washington, District of Columbia, Ward 1, Roll 56, Page 44a ("S. Knox Walker")

Knox Walker, family living in White House – Columbia Herald & Mail 9/11/1903(7)

Knox Walker, personal secretary to President Polk – Columbia Herald & Mail 9/11/1903(7), Nashville Banner 10/31/1938(3)

Nelson Walker, barber in Columbia – Union & American 7/8/1875(4)

Blucher Tabb, appointment to Naval Academy – Blucher Tabb, Naval Academy appointment – Navy Department Library – Naval History and Heritage Command; Washington, D.C.; Navy Register: Officers of the U.S. Navy and Marine; Year: 1850 (v.1)

Nelson Walker, marriage to Eliza – Union & American 7/8/1875(4)

Eliza Walker, details as slave – Carter, p. 1 (from "A Brief Sketch of the Life and Labors of Mrs. V. W. Broughton")

Blucher Walker, death – Richmond Enquirer 5/3/1850(2), New Orleans Crescent 4/15/1850(3), Tabb family information, https://www.ancestry.com/familytree/person/tree/8783281/person/24440551191/facts

Nelson Walker, buys freedom – Union & American 7/8/1875(4)

Nelson Walker, moves to Nashville – Ibid

Nelson Walker/Thomas Hodge 1853 advertisement, image – Union & American 11/3/1853(1)

Nelson Walker, buys wife/children – Union & American 5/28/1875(4)

Nelson Walker, family in 1860/ neighbor of Harding – 1870 Census, Davidson County, Nashville, Ward 5, Roll M593_1523, Page 295B

Walker daughter(s), attending Wadkins school – *Virginia W. Broughton, Twenty Years Experience as a Missionary*, Chicago, 1907, p. 7

Augusta Walker, death – Memphis Daily Avalanche 8/1/1860(3)

J. Knox Walker, image – https://www.findagrave.com/memorial/105934710/joseph-knox-walker

J. Knox Walker, political/military details and death – https://bit.ly/31XB9Xz

Nelson/Eliza Walker, literacy – 1870 Census, Davidson County, Nashville, Ward 5, Roll M593_1523, Page 295B

Nelson Walker, 1865 speech – Nashville Daily Union 3/21/1865(3)

Nelson Walker, 1866 letter to Mayor Brown – Republican Banner 8/5/1866(3)

Nelson Walker, 1867 letter – Republican Banner 6/23/1867(4)

Nelson Walker, 1867 courthouse speech – Union & American 8/18/1867(3)

Nelson Walker, becomes justice of the peace – Republican Banner 4/22/1868(4)

Nelson Walker, candidate for State Legislature – Republican Banner 6/12/1869(2)

Nelson Walker, 1868 political platform – Republican Banner 6/12/1869(2)

Nelson Walker, 1868 speech at Capitol – Republican Banner 7/23/1869(4)

Nelson Walker, ends candidacy – Republican Banner 7/30/1869(4)

Nelson Walker, Maxwell House shop details – Union & American 9/23/1869(1)

Nelson Walker, sworn in as attorney – Republican Banner 1/26/1871(1)

Nelson Walker, involvement in Cincinnati case – Republican Banner 5/24/1872(4)

Nelson Walker, sells barber shop/insurance business – Union & American 3/5/1873(2)

Nelson Walker, birth of last child – 1870 Census, Davidson County, Nashville, Ward 5, Roll M593_1523, Page 295B

Eliza Walker, dress maker – Ibid

Nelson Walker, escorts/introduces Frederick Douglass – Union & American 9/18/1873(4), Republican Banner 9/18/1873(4)

Frederick Douglass, image – 1879 photograph by George Kendall Warren, National Archives

Nelson Walker, speech at Colored Convention – Republican Banner 4/30/1874(4)

Virginia Walker, details of graduation – Union & American 5/28/1875(4), Republican Banner 5/28/1875(3)

James D./John H. Burrus, biographical details – Rev. William J. Simmons, *Men of Mark: Eminent, Progressive and Rising*, Cleveland, 1887, p. 281-7

James D./John H. Burrus, war details – https://en.wikipedia.org/wiki/James_Dallas_Burrus#cite_note-Miller-3

Springfield Record, article – Union & American 5/28/1875(4)

St. Louis Republican, article – Republican Banner 5/28/1875(3)

Nelson Walker, death – Union & American 7/8/1874(4), Republican Banner 7/8/1875(3)

John H. Burrus, image – Rev. William J. Simmons, *Men of Mark: Eminent, Progressive and Rising* (1887), 280

John H. Burrus, biographical details – Rev. William J. Simmons, *Men of Mark: Eminent, Progressive and Rising*, Cleveland, 1887, p. 281-7, Globe 3/30/1917(4), *National Cyclopedia of American Biography*, V. 1, p. 278

James D. Burrus, image – https://badahistory.net/view.php?ID=17&sc=all&s=cl

James D. Burrus – biographical details – Simmons, 281-87, Banner 6/22/1930(41), Tennessean 12/7/1928(5), Joe M. Richardson, "A Negro Success Story: James Dallas Burrus" The Journal of Negro History, (October 1965) Volume 50, #4 (October 1965), 274–282

Virginia Walker (Broughton), image – James T. Haley, *Sparkling Gems of Race Knowledge Worth Reading*

– *A Compendium of Valuable Information and Wise Suggestions That Will Inspire Noble Effort at the Hands of Evert Race-Loving Man, Woman, and Child*, Nashville (1897), 99

Virginia Walker, biographical details – Tomeiko Ashford Carter, "*Virginia Broughton: The Life and Writings of a Missionary*," University of Tennessee Press, 2010

Eliza Walker, remarriage – American 2/17/1887(5)

Eliza Walker, death – Atkinson-Walker family tree, https://www.ancestry.com/familytree/person/tree/42194880/person/400075053918/facts

Walker children, biographical details – Carter, p. xxii, Broughton p. 53

Rufus Walker, vocation/death – Nashville Death Records, 1908-1958, Roll 1(certificate # 51-00349)

Cherry Logue and Reverend J. W. Loguen

J.W. Loguen, image – this image may be found at https://www.findagrave.com/memorial/47625370/jermain-wesley-loguen, among many interet sites

Preface selection, ("For obvious reasons…") – *The Rev. J. W. Loguen, as a slave and as a Freeman, a Narrative of Real Life*, iv – v

Jarm Logue, background – Loguen, 12-14

John Logue, Revolutionary War veteran – North Carolina Daughters of the American Revolution, Roster of Soldiers from North Carolina in the American Revolution, (538, 593), Army Accounts Vol. VI, (49), folio 2, roll #S.115.58, Vol VII, (104), folio 2, roll #S.115.59

John Logue, 1789 land ownership in Davidson County – Tennessee State Library and Archives, Early Tennessee/North Carolina Land Records, roll 8, Book E-5 (56)

John Logue, death/will/will image – Davidson County will Book 1 293

Cherry Logue, details ("David, the youngest…") – Loguen 15-22, 24

Cherry Logue, year of birth – Although the 1870 Census lists her age as 80, indicating a birth year of 1790, the Loguen "biography" (20) says that when Cherry was attacked in the distillery, she was "about the age twenty-four or twenty-five" and (22) that Jermain "was then about six years old." In Loguen's letter to Frederick Douglass (339) he indicates that he was born circa 1814 (see next note), placing Cherry's year of birth around 1796.

Jarm Logue, year of birth – Loguen 339. In his 1856 letter to Douglass, Loguen mentions a time "Twenty-one years ago" and being "twenty-one years of age, (as near as I can know my age)," placing his birth in or close to 1814.

David Logue, father of Jarm/age – https://www.ancestry.com/family tree/person/tree/16945472/person/180123143587/facts

Cherry, attacked at distillery ("When she was twenty-four…") – Loguen 20-25

Cherry, beaten ("At the age of seven…") – Ibid 30-32

David Logue, 1817 marriage – Sumner County Loose Records, marriages 1787-1819 (9/10/1817)

Polly Glasgow, daughter of Jesse Glasgow – Tn State Library & Archives, Davidson County Tax list 1811, https://www.ancestry.com/family-tree/person/tree/360490/person/-2090692150/facts

David Logue ("David brought to his home…") – Loguen 22, 36, 40-43

David Logue, purchases the interests of his brothers – This may have taken place around 1821, when he purchased an 80 acre tract from his mother (Davidson County Deed Book Q-507)

Redmond D. Barry, details – *Sumner County Tombstone Inscriptions* (84), Find a Grave, https://www.ancestry.com/discoveryui-content/view/39063437:60525

Jarm Logue, details ("The first ten years…") – Loguen 29-30

Zachariah Betts, details ("At a small distance…") Ibid 44

Zachariah Betts, family information – (family) Genealogy of William Smith of Wrightstown Bucks

County, Pa. (57), https://www.ancestry.com/family-tree/person/tree/360490/person/-2090955514/facts, (1794 arrival in Tennessee) Davidson County Registers Office, Deed Book C-378

Killing of Sam, ("On a spring morning…") – Loguen 44-49

Slave paddle, image – Image published in 1845 by the Anti-Slavery Office in Boston, Massachusetts

Zachariah Betts, death – Ancestry Family Tree (DeMonbreun, Betts, Rains. Glasgow, Meredith) https://www.ancestry.com/family-tree/person/tree/360490/person/-2090956434/facts

David Logue, indebtedness/sale of slaves ("Logue dreaded bankruptcy…") – Loguen 64-70

Manasseh Logue, in Maury County by 1820 –1820 Census, Maury County, p. 50, roll M33_124, Image 40

Manasseh Logue, buys farm in 1827 – Maury County, Tn Deedbook M-372 (5/22/1827)

Trip to Little Tombigbee Creek ("Day and night…") – Loguen 73-77

Manasseh Logue, details ("After he sold out…") – Ibid 93-94

Jarm Logue, hoe incident ("About the second spring…") – Ibid 95-98

Distillery burns ("Such was the state…") – Ibid 99, 102

Camp Meeting, image – Hugh Bridport lithograph, 1829, Library of Congress

Cherry Logue, religious experience ("Notwithstanding…") – Ibid 104-109

Jarm hired out/attacked in field ("Such changes…") – Ibid 109-112

Cherry's children, sold ("After about three days…") – Ibid 112-121

Jarm, attacked with pestle ("Jarm was approaching…") Ibid 123-126

Jarm, privileges ("During the succeeding year…") Ibid 138

Jarm, hired out to kind family- Ibid 149-156

John Farney, details – Ibid 230-35, 243

Jarm, steals whiskey ("Jarm's plan…") – Ibid 236-38

Jarm, fights with Manasseh ("Jarm was willing…") – Ibid 239-41

Jarm, hides out ("Jarm ran for the woods…") – Ibid 241-44

Jarm given privileges/Maria sold ("From that day forward…") – Ibid 256-59

Jarm, selling whiskey/produce – Ibid 257

Jarm, sees Cherry before leaving ("Jarm could not leave…") – Ibid 276-78

Jarm/John Farney, trip to Nashville ("As they advanced…") – Loguen 279-83

Jarm/John, continue north – Ibid 283-92

Stopped by slave-catchers ("Their attention was arrested…") – Ibid 292-96

Sleeping under haystacks/more slave-catchers/crossing river – Ibid 297-303

Deceive villagers, moving from Corydon to Indianapolis – Ibid 304-323

Visit Quakers/through Indian country/lost in storm – Ibid 324-30

Reach white settlements, travel to Detroit – Ibid 332-34

Loss of Farney/Jarm reaches Canada – Ibid 335-37

Jarm in Canada ("Not able to get employment…") – Ibid 338

Letter to Frederick Douglass ("On the western termination…") – Ibid 338-41

Jarm, working for farmer – Ibid 341

Account of Rev. Rogers ("I became acquainted…") – Ibid 445-48

Loguen, 1840 marriage/teacher/pastor – Ibid 342, 352, 371

Loguen, has school building moved – Ibid 373

Loguen, joins abolition movement ("In the fall…") – Ibid 374

J.W. Loguen, engraving – frontispiece of Rev. Jermain Wesley Loguen from his autobiography, *The Rev. J. W. Loguen, as a slave and as a freeman* (1859)

Loguen, speech about slavery (Mr. Loguen did not enter…") – Ibid 377-79

Attempt to buy Cherry ("The citizens of Courtland…") – Ibid 380-87

Loguen, speaks of Fugitive Slave Act ("I don't respect this law…") – Loguen 393-94

The Jerry Rescue – Ibid 398-424

Loguen involvement in rescue/repercussions – Ibid 426-444

Ormsbee account of underground railroad ("I was on the executive…") – St. Louis Globe-Democrat 7/10/1884(5)

Loguen, 1855 train incident ("A man was seated…") – The Liberator (Boston) 3/30/1855(4)

1855 newspaper article ("A day or two ago…") – The Liberator 10/26/1855(3)

1857 Fugitive Aid Society notice ("Since 1850…") – The Liberator 10/16/1857(3)

Card from Loguen – Ibid

1859 endorsement of Loguen's work – The Liberator 1/7/1859(3)

1860 letter from Sarah Logue ("To Jarm…") – The Liberator 4/27/1860(1)

J.W. Loguen, image (older) – Woodson, Carter Godwin, African Methodist Episcopal Zion Church, https://picryl.com/media/j-w-loguen-a-bishop-of-the-zionites-and-an-abolitionist-a22d93

Loguen, response to Sarah Logue – Ibid

Loguen, 1865 visit to Maury County – Nashville Daily Press & Times 7/3/1865, Belvidere Standard (Belvidere, Illinois) 7/18/1865(2)

Manasseh Logue, death – Maury County Will Book 4-219 (page # says 380), will – https://bit.ly/3ylwmLk, inventory – Maury Co. Will Book 4, 244 https://bit.ly/3DRaRDo

David Logue, death – tree/person/tree/16945472/person/180123143587/facts

Sarah Logue, death – Lightfoot, *They Passed this Way*, Volume 2 (J. W. Matthews Diary), p 260 ("old Mrs. Logue died 7/2/1866")

J.W. Loguen, death – The Pioche Record (Pioche, Nevada) 1/8/1873(2) ("Rev. J. W. Loguen, colored minister" died 9/30/1872)

Sarah Loguen Fraser, image – Department of Historical Collections, Health Sciences Library, SUNY Upstate Medical University

Amelia/Sarah Logue, details – (Amelia Douglass) https://en.wikipedia.org/wiki/Lewis_Henry_Douglass, (Sarah Fraser) https://en.wikipedia.org/wiki/Sarah_Loguen_Fraser

Index